Salesforce.com

FOR DUMMIES®

A Wiley Brand

5th Edition

by Liz Kao and Matt Kaufman

FOR DUMMIES
A Wiley Brand

Salesforce.com For Dummies®, 5th Edition

Published by
John Wiley & Sons, Inc.
111 River Street Hoboken,
NJ 07030-5774
www.wiley.com

Copyright © 2014 by John Wiley & Sons, Inc., Hoboken, New Jersey

Published by John Wiley & Sons, Inc., Hoboken, New Jersey

Published simultaneously in Canada

For general information on our other products and services, please contact our Customer Care Department within the U.S. at 877-762-2974, outside the U.S. at 317-572-3993, or fax 317-572-4002.

For technical support, please visit www.wiley.com/techsupport.

Wiley also publishes its books in a variety of electronic formats and by print-on-demand. Not all content that is available in standard print versions of this book may appear or be packaged in all book formats. If you have purchased a version of this book that did not include media that is referenced by or accompanies a standard print version, you may request this media by visiting http://booksupport.wiley.com. For more information about Wiley products, visit us www.wiley.com.

Library of Congress Control Number: 2013948032

ISBN 978-1-118-82214-2 (pbk); ISBN 978-1-118-82583-9 (ebk); ISBN 978-1-118-82584-6 (ebk)

Manufactured in the United States of America

10 9 8 7 6 5 4 3 2 1

Contents at a Glance

Table of Contents

Introduction

Salesforce.com For Dummies, 5th Edition, is for users of Salesforce, including those users who have the Unlimited, Enterprise, Professional, Group, or Contact Manager Edition. It's for Salesforce users who want to quickly know how to use this web-based application for sales, marketing, and customer service, all running "in the cloud," also known as software-as-a-service (SaaS), just so you're up to date on your enterprise application-speak. Don't look in this book to find out how Salesforce works. Use this book to find out how you can manage your customers and your teams and close more business by using Salesforce.

- ✔ **If you're a sales rep,** this book can help you use Salesforce to manage your leads, accounts, contacts, and opportunities. Spend less time doing administrative work and more time focused on making money.

- ✔ **If you're a sales manager,** find out how to use Salesforce to track team activities and pipeline, shorten the ramp-up time on new hires, and pinpoint key deals that require your involvement.

- ✔ **If you're in channel sales,** we show you how to track your relationships with companies that are — or will be — your partners and all the deals they work for you.

- ✔ **If you're a partner,** we show you the world of Salesforce and how you can improve your deal pipeline and win rate with your vendor.

- ✔ **If you're in marketing,** you see how to use Salesforce to make an immediate and measurable impact on your sales organization. We cover how to manage campaigns, track leads, and use social media to interact with your constituents.

- ✔ **If you're in customer service,** we show you how to manage customer issues, from creation to resolution. Support managers will see how to improve agent productivity and customer self-sufficiency.

- ✔ **If you sit on the executive team,** this book shows you how to use Salesforce for internal collaboration and to measure your overall business.

- ✔ **If you're an administrator or involved in your company's customer relationship management (CRM) initiative,** this book gives you practical knowledge for customizing, configuring, maintaining, and successfully implementing your solution. To start, we suggest that you flip through the sales, marketing, and support chapters in Parts III, IV, and V to understand how Salesforce is commonly used by end users. Then use that to guide you in administering Salesforce in Parts VI and VII.

Although this book applies to users of all Salesforce editions, be aware that not all portions of this book necessarily apply to your edition. Different editions have varying degrees of features and functionality. We make sure to point out the differences where relevant.

Updates to the Fifth Edition

This book, its fifth edition, has been revised to reflect the latest salesforce.com product and feature offerings as of the Winter 2014 release. Salesforce is an Internet-based service where new releases occur simultaneously for all customers, about three times a year, without your having to lift a finger (okay, except to just log in). Because of this model, salesforce.com can more quickly release several versions of its product than many traditional software vendors — and us! We did our best to update this book to the current version of the product, but please bear in mind that new versions of Salesforce are always in the works.

References to the product use the word *Salesforce,* and references to the company that makes the family of products, or the family of products as a whole, use the phrase *salesforce.com.* That's a little detail, but we didn't want you to think our eagle eyes had glossed over that.

Here's a bare outline of the parts of this book:

- ✔ **Part I: Salesforce Basics:** Part I gives you the big picture on Salesforce. We show you the best ways to navigate the system, where to go for help, and how to personalize Salesforce. Since the last edition, Salesforce has debuted a new user interface and incorporated more collaborative elements into its standard feature set, among other subtle improvements here and there.

- ✔ **Part II: Keeping Track of Customer Relationships:** Part II shows you how to use Salesforce for the most common facets of your sales, marketing, and support processes. We get into more specifics about Chatter and how it can improve business interactions and internal communications to help sales, marketing, and support departments do their jobs better. We explain how you can use Salesforce for managing your existing business relationships, as well as those with key prospects.

- ✔ **Part III: Driving Sales with Sales Cloud:** Part III shows sales organizations how to use Salesforce to track sales, from lead to close and everything in between. We also discuss how channel managers and partners can use Salesforce Communities to work together to bring in more channel revenue.

✔ **Part IV: Optimizing Demand with Marketing Cloud:** If you're in marketing, Part IV helps you navigate the continuously expanding marketing automation features. Marketing in Salesforce and your business has evolved to much more than just campaign management. You discover how to use Salesforce to manage your social media marketing campaigns, and we also discuss how to organize your sales collateral.

✔ **Part V: Delighting Customers with Service Cloud:** Part V shows customer support agents and managers how to use Service Cloud to more efficiently manage the customer issue life cycle. Agents see how to create, track, and resolve cases in Salesforce. Customer service managers will garner ways to increase their teams' efficiencies by increasing the quality of service while decreasing case resolution time.

✔ **Part VI: Measuring Overall Business Performance:** Part VI shows every rep, manager, and senior executive how to use Salesforce to measure and analyze their business. This book doesn't tell you how to improve your business (that's largely up to you), but Part VI helps you place the data at your fingertips.

✔ **Part VII: Designing the Solution with Force.com:** Salesforce is great out of the box, but you can get more out of it when you customize it to meet your corporate objectives. Part VII is for system administrators and the CRM project team. You get to know the important steps for configuring and maintaining your system, as well as your options if you want to roll up your sleeves and do some more advanced customizations.

✔ **Part VIII: The Part of Tens:** In Part VIII, we give you lists meant for quick wins. Here, we review the best-but-sometimes-overlooked productivity tools and online resources. We also summarize some best practices for successfully implementing Salesforce.

We show you everything you need to know to manage the life cycle of your customer relationships in Salesforce, from qualifying leads to closing opportunities to handling service agent inquiries. Along the way, we share a laugh or two. And this book can expose you to useful features and functionality that you might not have even known existed.

How to Use This Book

This book is divided into parts and then chapters based loosely on three widely accepted pillars of customer relationship management: sales, marketing, and customer service. We organized the sections based on your function in the company and what you might want to know about Salesforce based on your role.

You can choose to read this book from front to back (although you'll find no surprise ending in the last chapter). Or, you can use this book as a reference, similar to other *For Dummies* books. You can go to any topic in this book and know what to do with minimal leafing to other sections.

You can get the most out of this book if you're using it while you're logged in to Salesforce (and sitting in your favorite chair). The best way to know what to do, in our experience, is by doing it, and for that you need the salesforce. com website open, revved, and raring to go.

In this book, we provide you with the easiest or best way to perform a task in Salesforce. Like other easy-to-use applications, the method shown might not be the only way, and sometimes you might find another method that works better for you. That's okay; we promise it won't hurt our feelings.

Foolish Assumptions

Please forgive us, but we make one or two foolish assumptions about you, the reader. We assume these things:

- You have access to a high-speed Internet connection (not dial-up), have used a web browser, and have access to the most up-to-date web browser. If we assumed incorrectly, you have much more pressing problems than understanding the effective use of Salesforce.

- You have a Salesforce account and some interest in knowing how to use it, beyond the mere curiosity of reading our riveting prose.

- You have some business experience — at least enough to understand that winning deals is good, and losing deals is bad.

- You have at least a vague idea of what a database is, including basic concepts such as fields, records, files, and folders. (Imagine an organized filing cabinet and all its contents.)

Icons Used in This Book

To help you get the most out of this book, we place icons here and there that highlight important points. Here's what the icons mean:

Next to the Tip icon, you can find shortcuts, tricks, and best practices to use Salesforce more effectively or productively.

Pay extra attention when you see a Warning icon. It means that you might be about to do something that you'll regret later.

When we explain a juicy little fact that bears remembering, we mark it with a Remember icon. When you see this icon, prick up your ears. You can pick up something that could be of wide or frequent use as you work with Salesforce.

When we're forced to describe something geeky, a Technical Stuff icon appears in the margin. You don't have to read what's beside this icon if you don't want to, although some readers might find the technical detail helpful.

Beyond the Book

This section describes where readers can find book content that exists outside the book itself. A *For Dummies* technical book may include the following, although only rarely does a book include all these items:

- **Cheat Sheet:** There isn't a test at the end of this book, so we don't expect you to memorize it all. Instead we've provided you with a handy Cheat Sheet that tells you how to perform your day-to-day functions in Salesforce. There's even an electronic copy available at

  www.dummies.com/cheatsheet/salesforcedotcom

- **Dummies.com online articles:** If your boss wants you to justify buying this book or if you're just in a rush, check out our online articles about Salesforce. We've provided some key points, useful lists, and more.

  www.dummies.com/extras/salesforcedotcom

- **Updates to this book, if we have any, are at**

  www.dummies.com/extras/salesforcedotcom

Where to Go from Here

If you're just getting started with Salesforce, you may want to turn the page and start reading. If you're an administrator and have a deadline, you may want to jump to Chapters 19 and 20. If you're a manager, try reading about reports and dashboards in Chapters 17 and 18. Sales reps and service reps should start in on Chapters 14 and 15, respectively. Regardless of what you choose, we're sure that you'll find what you're looking for.

Part I
Salesforce Basics

getting started
with
Salesforce

In this part . . .

- ✔ Understand high-level features of Salesforce and how those are applied to typical business challenges

- ✔ Learn basic Salesforce terms so we speak the same language

- ✔ Navigate the standard landscape of Salesforce to know where to go for what

- ✔ Personalize Salesforce as an end-user, to match your productivity needs

Chapter 1

Looking Over Salesforce

*Y*ou might not realize it yet, but every time you log in to Salesforce, you're accessing an extremely powerful lever of change for you, your group, and your company.

Sounds like a tall order, but consider this: What value do you put on your customer relationships? Your partner relationships? If you're a sales rep, it's your livelihood. And if you're in management, you have fewer assets more valuable than your existing partner and customer base. What if you had a tool that could truly help you manage your partners and customers?

Salesforce wasn't the first customer relationship management (CRM) system to hit the market, but it's dramatically different than the other CRM systems you might have used (spreadsheets and sticky notes count as a system, too!). Unlike traditional CRM software, Salesforce is an Internet service. You sign up and log in through a browser, and it's immediately available. We currently call this *cloud computing,* where the customers access "the cloud" (that is, the Internet) for their business needs, and are not required to install any traditional software on, presumably, Earth. As long as you have an Internet connection, you can be anywhere in the world and have access to the clouds. Some of you may already be at companies that use cloud-based applications, as salesforce.com's success has spawned a whole new marketplace full of business applications done "in the cloud." Others may just be entering the workforce but are very familiar with the use of Internet-applications in their personal life (think Facebook). For other readers, this is your first foray into cloud computing, and you might be taking a first step by yourself or with the rest of your company. Don't worry — your company made the right choice by picking Salesforce.

Salesforce customers typically say that it's unique for three major reasons:

- **Fast:** When you sign on the dotted line, you want your CRM system up and running yesterday. Traditional CRM software can take more than a year to deploy; compare that to months or even weeks with Salesforce.

- **Easy:** End user adoption is critical to any application, and Salesforce wins the ease-of-use category hands down. You can spend more time putting it to use and less time figuring it out.

- **Effective:** Because it's easy to use and can be customized quickly to meet business needs, customers have proven that it has improved their bottom lines.

With Salesforce, you now have a full suite of services to manage the customer life cycle, divided into three product families: Sales Cloud, Marketing Cloud, and Service Cloud. These services include tools to pursue leads, manage accounts, track opportunities, resolve cases, and more. Depending on your team's objectives, you might use all the Salesforce families from Day 1, or you might focus on just the functionality to address the priorities at hand.

The more you and your team adopt Salesforce into your work, and you determine how you want your business process to be reflected within the technology, the more information you'll have at your fingertips to deepen customer relationships and improve your overall business.

In this chapter, we reveal the many great things that you can do with Salesforce. Then we describe how you can extend Salesforce to work with many of the common applications that you already use. Finally, we help you decide which Salesforce edition is right for you, just in case you're still evaluating your options.

Using Salesforce to Solve Critical Business Challenges

We could write another book telling you all the great things you can do with Salesforce, but you can get the big picture from this chapter. We focus here on the most common business challenges that we hear from sales, marketing, and support executives — and how Salesforce can overcome them.

Understanding your customer's customer

How can you sell to and retain customers if you don't understand their needs, key contacts, and what account activities and transactions have taken place? Can you serve your customers well if you're not familiar with how your products and services help improve your customer's customer's (no, that's not a typo) experience? With Salesforce, you can track all your important customer data in one place so that you can develop solutions that deliver real value to your customers, which in turn should mean higher customer satisfaction with *their* customers.

Centralizing customer information under one roof

How much time have you ever wasted tracking down a customer contact or an address that you know exists within the walls of your company? What about trying to find out which sales rep owns the relationship with a subsidiary of a global customer? With Salesforce, you can quickly centralize and organize your accounts and contacts so that you can capitalize on that information when you need to.

Expanding the funnel

Inputs and outputs, right? The more leads you generate and pursue, the greater the chance that your revenue will grow. So the big question is, "How do I make the machine work?" With Salesforce, you can plan, manage, measure, and improve lead generation, qualification, and conversion. You can see how much business you or your team generates, the sources of that business, and who in your team is making it happen.

Consolidating your pipeline

Pipeline reports give companies insight into future sales, yet we've worked with companies in which generating the weekly pipeline could take more than a day of cat herding and guesswork. Reps waste time updating spreadsheets. Managers waste time chasing reps and scrubbing data. Bosses waste time tearing their hair out because the information is old by the time they get it. The prevalence of cloud computing makes this traditional method of siloed data collection obsolete (or pretty darn inefficient). With Salesforce, you can shorten or eliminate all that. As long as reps manage all their opportunities in Salesforce, managers can generate updated pipeline reports with the click of a button.

Collaborating effectively with your colleagues

Remember when you were the new guy (or gal) at the company, and you had to find out who knew everything about a particular customer, process, or product? Even at smaller companies, it takes time to discover who possesses that extra bit of historical knowledge that could help you close that important deal or resolve a support issue. Other times, you might be so busy that you're out of the loop on certain key company updates, even when departments try to keep you informed. What if you could harness the insights from others within the company, yet not be overwhelmed by information overload? Chatter (the sales-force.com product, not the noun) increases internal awareness and collaboration on the business issues that matter the most to you, so you're always up to date and never caught unawares.

Working as a team

How many times have you thought that your own coworkers got in the way of selling? Oftentimes, the challenge isn't the people, or even the technology, but standardizing processes and clarifying roles and responsibilities. With Salesforce, you can define teams and processes for sales, marketing, and customer service so that the left hand knows what the right hand is doing. Although Salesforce doesn't solve corporate alignment issues, you now have the tool that can drive and manage better team collaboration.

Collaborating with your partners

In many industries, selling directly is a thing of the past. To gain leverage and cover more territory, many companies work through partners. By using Salesforce Communities, your channel team can track and associate partners' deals and get better insight about who their top partners are. Partners now can strengthen their relationships with their vendors by collaborating more easily on joint sales and marketing efforts.

Beating the competition

How much money have you lost to competitors? How many times did you lose a deal only to discover, after the fact, that it went to your archenemy? If you know whom you're up against, you can probably better position yourself to win the opportunity. With Salesforce, you and your teams can track competition on deals, collect competitive intelligence, and develop action plans to wear down your foes.

Improving customer service

As a salesperson, have you ever walked into a customer's office expecting a bed of roses only to be hit with a landmine because of an unresolved customer issue? And if you work in customer support, how much time do you waste on trying to identify the customers and reviewing the context of previous support interactions? With Service Cloud, you can efficiently capture, manage, and resolve a high volume of customer issues that come in from a variety of communication channels. By managing cases in Service Cloud, sales reps get visibility into the health of their accounts, and service can stay well informed of sales and account activity.

Accessing anytime, anywhere

The mobile revolution that hit your personal life is now a large part of business life, too. People work from home or on the road, oftentimes due to that new universe of cloud-based business programs that has evolved within the last decade. Globalization means that offices are oftentimes spread out. You expect to get access to information from multiple devices, easily and reliably. With Salesforce, you can access and manage your critical customer information, at 3 p.m. or 3 a.m., online or offline, in multiple languages, and from multiple devices.

Measuring the business

How can you improve what you can't measure? Simple, huh? If you use Salesforce correctly and regularly to manage customers, you have data to make informed decisions. That benefits everyone. If you're a rep, you know what you need to do to get the rewards you want. If you're a manager, you can pinpoint where to get involved to drive your numbers. And Salesforce's reporting and dashboards give you easy-to-use tools to measure and analyze your business.

Running your business in the cloud

Salesforce's success has empowered a whole new generation of managers and administrators to become business operations gurus. Cloud computing's generally lower licensing costs, its ability to allow system configuration to happen with no prior programming experience, and its ability to make modifications quickly to the system mean that newer businesses can compete with slower, older, bigger competitors, but at a fraction of the cost.

Extending the Value Chain

Salesforce.com understands that you already rely on existing tools for parts of your business. Such tools might include your e-mail, your word processing and spreadsheet programs, your public website, and your intranet. Salesforce.com isn't naïve enough to think you're going to stop using these tools. In fact, you can readily integrate Salesforce with many of the tools you use today to interact with your customers.

Integrating with your website

For many companies, their public website is a primary way to communicate information to their customers. You might use your website as a channel for visitors to request information or to log customer service issues. When you use Salesforce, you can generate leads and capture cases from your website, route them directly into Salesforce, and automatically assign them to the right reps. No more stacks of e-mails to info@yourcompany.com cluttering up one poor person's inbox before he or she has to reroute them to the right people. And Salesforce's assignment rules can make sure that incoming leads or cases get to the right reps in a timely manner. With minimal effort, you can even offer self-service options in the form of a public knowledge base or a private portal, enabling customers to help themselves.

Connecting to social sites

As part of your job, you might regularly use websites for tasks such as researching potential customers, getting driving directions, and getting the inside scoop on your competition. Your customers, like your own company, probably have a presence on networking sites such as LinkedIn, Facebook, Twitter, or YouTube. Salesforce makes it easy to find a business's or contact's profile on any of these sites, where information is often visible to the public, or only a few degrees of separation apart. Accessing your intranet, populating a web form to provision a demo, creating and propagating a Salesforce record — all these tasks are within reach. And all this means time saved for you.

Integrating with other applications

Your company might have other applications that contain critical customer data — financial and enterprise resource planning (ERP) applications are just a few examples. Many applications provide unique and indispensable value to your organization. Your company isn't going to retire them just because you're using Salesforce. But, based on company objectives, those applications might need to integrate with Salesforce. Because of Salesforce's open architecture, your company can integrate applications if you have the right technical assistance.

Managing other business processes

When you log in to Salesforce, you see several tabs, grouped into tab sets called *apps*. Salesforce.com prioritized the visibility of those tabs based on core CRM functions. However, depending on your business needs, you might require apps that have different functionality for teams that may or may not have anything related to sales, marketing, or support. With salesforce.com's Force.com platform, your company can now easily build or download these custom apps to fit your specific business needs. You can now use Salesforce for more than CRM and ultimately manage a significant portion of your business online.

Deciding Which Edition Is Best for You

If you already use Salesforce, this topic might be a moot point. At the very least, you know which version of Salesforce you have.

If you're not sure which edition you have, look at the top of your browser after you've logged in to Salesforce.

Here we'll review five versions of salesforce.com's service. All versions have the same consistent look and feel, but each varies by feature, functionality, and pricing. If you're considering using Salesforce, consult with an account executive for more details about edition differences, pricing, and upgrade paths:

- ✔ **Contact Manager:** Basic account and contact management for up to five users. No lead or opportunity tracking.

- ✔ **Group:** Basic CRM, which includes the ability to track leads and opportunities, for teams of up to five users. This allows you to view the full sales life cycle, from the initial interaction with a lead to a closed opportunity.

- ✔ **Professional:** Thorough CRM for any size organization that's starting to nail down processes. Again, you can track the full sales life cycle from a new lead to a closed opportunity. Dashboards allow managers to track key metrics at a glance. Some optional features for businesses with more detailed process needs (such as managing marketing campaigns, creating contracts, tracking various products sold, or accessing Salesforce while offline) come at an extra cost.

✔ **Enterprise:** More sales and service functionality for more complex organizations, including the ability to integrate with other systems within your company. This edition provides more value than if you were to pay extra for certain add-on features in more basic editions. If you absolutely need your business processes to look and act a specific way, this edition provides more ways to make that happen for you.

✔ **Performance:** Even more customization capabilities for extending Salesforce to other business uses. You need a dedicated (and usually technical) administrator to take advantage of all the options that this edition delivers.

Salesforce also provides another edition, Developer Edition. This is a free instance of Salesforce with which developers can test and build third-party solutions. It has full functionality but a very limited license count and storage space.

Whichever edition you choose, the good news is that every edition of Salesforce is rich with features that can help companies of every size address their business challenges. You can choose a more basic edition today and upgrade later, as needed. Upgrades happen in the background and are easy, so you can focus on the business processes that drive the need for new functionality. And when salesforce.com rolls out new releases of its service, it provides product enhancements for the different editions wherever relevant.

Professional or Enterprise Edition?

Most companies tend to make a decision between using Professional and Enterprise Editions. Budget might be an issue, but the decision usually boils down to core business needs. Consider these questions: Does your company . . .

✔ Have different groups with distinct sales processes, customers, and products?

✔ Have a lead-generation or service team that relies on a call script when initially speaking with prospects or customers?

✔ Plan to integrate Salesforce with other applications?

✔ Require complex data migration into Salesforce?

✔ Need greater control over users, what they see, and what they can do?

✔ Sell in defined teams with specific roles?

✔ Require consistent, specific workflow or approval steps to further automate processes?

If the answer to any of these questions is a definitive "Yes," your company should probably evaluate at least Enterprise Edition, and possibly Performance Edition.

Chapter 2

Navigating Salesforce

· ·

In This Chapter

▶ Introducing Salesforce terminology

▶ Logging in to the site

▶ Getting to know all the home pages

▶ Working with new records

▶ Detailing the record page

▶ Finding help and setup options

· ·

*I*f an application isn't easy to use, you won't use it. Period. Salesforce succeeds not only because it offers a universe of integrated tools but also because users can pick it up within minutes. You navigate it much the same way you do other websites: by pointing and clicking over text links and buttons.

Still, you have so many ways to navigate Salesforce that it makes sense to lay down the obvious (and not-so-obvious) best practices for getting around the application.

Even if you're familiar with Salesforce, you might want to scan this chapter because we cover terms that we use repeatedly throughout this book.

In this chapter, you can find out how to log in to the Salesforce site and use the home page to manage your activities, create records, and jump to other tabs. We briefly review the major tabs and describe how to use the interior home pages, list pages, detail pages, and related lists. Finally, we cover where you can go for help.

Getting Familiar with Basic Terms

Before we delve into the mechanics of navigating Salesforce, familiarize yourself with these basic terms:

- **Salesforce:** When we use the term *Salesforce,* we mean the secure website that your users log in to that contains your customer information. Salesforce.com, Inc., offers a family of products and has over 100,000 clients who use its service, but each company's secure website is separate from the other websites and might look different to suit that company's unique needs. When we use the terms *Sales Cloud* or *Service Cloud,* those are parts of Salesforce specifically meant for use by sales and marketing, or by a support organization.

- **Home tab:** This is the main page that appears when you log in to Salesforce or click the Home tab.

- **Tabs:** Clickable links appear at the top of any Salesforce page. When selected, a link is highlighted and looks like a tab, and so we continue to call them *tabs*. Each tab represents a major module in which your company needs to know some information. By clicking a tab, you go to a tab-specific home page. For example, if you click the Accounts tab, the Accounts home page appears.

- **Apps:** *Apps* are tabs that have been grouped together and given a name, providing you with the convenience of seeing only those tabs most relevant to you.

- **Tab home pages:** These are the pages where you go to find, organize, and manage specific information related to a particular tab. For example, to access your opportunity records, you could go to the Opportunities home page.

- **Record:** This is made up of a bunch of fields that hold information to describe a specific item. For example, a contact record typically contains fields pertinent to a person, including name, title, phone number, and e-mail address. A record is displayed on a detail page.

- **Detail page:** This web page shows both the saved record and a set of related lists pertinent to the record.

  We often use the terms *record* and *detail page* interchangeably. From a detail page, you can perform and track a variety of tasks related to the specific record. For example, if you have and are looking at an Account detail page for Cisco, you see fields about the company and lists of other records related to Cisco.

- **Related lists:** These lists comprise other records linked to the record that you're looking at. For example, the Account detail page for Acme might display related lists of contacts, opportunities, activities, and so on associated with that company.

> ✔ **Sidebar:** Located on the left margin of a Salesforce page, the sidebar displays messages and alerts, custom links, recent items, and a drop-down list that you can use to create new records.

Accessing Salesforce

You need to log in to your account to access your company's instance of Salesforce because every company's Salesforce website is different, and salesforce.com goes to great lengths to protect your information.

Setting up a password

The first time you log in to the Salesforce service, you receive an e-mail entitled `Salesforce login confirmation`. To set your password, follow these steps:

1. **Open the e-mail and click the link provided.**

   A page appears, prompting you to set a new password and security question.

2. **Complete the fields.**

   Be sure to select a question and provide an answer that can verify your identity if you forget your password. Use this password from now on unless your administrator resets the password.

3. **When you're done, click Save.**

   The home page of Salesforce appears.

Logging in

You log in to Salesforce just as you would any other secure website.

To log in, open a browser and follow these steps:

1. **In your browser's address bar, type** login.salesforce.com **and then press Enter.**

   The salesforce.com login page appears as shown in Figure 2-1.

2. **Enter your username and password and then click the Login button.**

   Your username is typically your corporate e-mail address. Select the Remember User Name check box if you want your computer to remember it. After you click the Login button, your main home page appears.

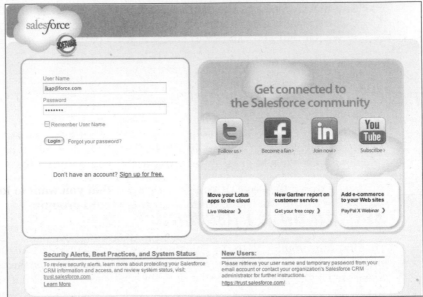

Figure 2-1:
Logging in to
Salesforce.

To save yourself steps when logging in, use your browser tools to bookmark the login page.

For security purposes, Salesforce notices whether you're trying to log in to the website from a different computer or a different browser than the one you first used. If this happens, make sure that you have access to your e-mail inbox or mobile phone because Salesforce e-mails or SMS messages you a confirmation code to confirm that you are who you say you are (and that you're just using a different computer or browser to log in).

Navigating the Home Page

Every time you log in to Salesforce, you begin at your home page. The look and feel of the elements on your home page are similar to other users' home pages, but the tasks and events that appear in the body of the page are specific to you.

Use the home page to manage your calendar and tasks, jump to other areas by clicking tabs, or access recent records by using the sidebar. If your company has customized the home page, you might also see key charts or graphs from your company's dashboards. (*Dashboards* are visual snapshots of key performance metrics based on your custom report data.)

Finding records with Search

At the top of every Salesforce page you will find the Global Search bar. You can find a majority of the information that you want by using Search. To search for information, follow these steps:

1. **At the top of Salesforce, enter keywords into the Search field and then click the Search button.**

   A Search Results page appears, as shown in Figure 2-2. Salesforce organizes the search results in lists according to the major types of records, including accounts, contacts, opportunities, and leads.

2. **Scroll down the page. If you find a record that you want to look at, click a link in the Name column for that record grouping.**

   The detail page appears, allowing you to review the record and its related lists.

3. **If you see too many results, you can limit them to items you own or search for an exact phrase by clicking the Options link on the Search Results page. You can also select a single type of record from the list in the sidebar.**

   If you can't find what you're looking for, try adding the * wildcard before, after, or in the middle of your keywords to expand your search to words that start with, end with, or are similar to your keywords.

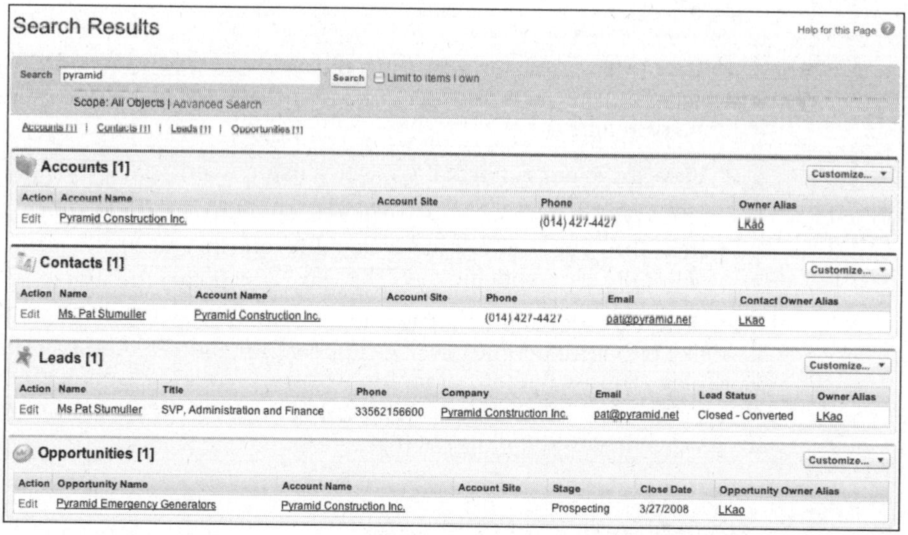

Figure 2-2: Looking at a Search Results page.

TIP

If you're focusing on a page (such as a list of search results or a report) and want to open one of the results in a new window, instead of clicking the link, right-click that link and choose Open Link in New Window from the contextual menu that appears.

Managing your calendar

The calendar section of the home page defaults to a calendar of the current month and your scheduled events for the next seven days. Like other calendar tools, the calendar allows you to drill down. Your scheduled events are based on events that you assigned to yourself or that other users have assigned to you.

From this calendar section (shown in Figure 2-3), you can do the following:

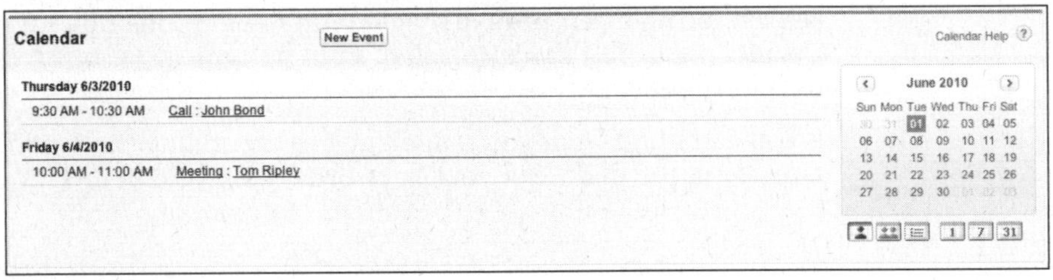

Figure 2-3:
Looking over your calendar options.

Calendar	New Event		Calendar Help
Thursday 6/3/2010			< June 2010 >
9:30 AM - 10:30 AM	Call : John Bond		Sun Mon Tue Wed Thu Fri Sat
Friday 6/4/2010			30 31 **01** 02 03 04 05
10:00 AM - 11:00 AM	Meeting : Tom Ripley		06 07 08 09 10 11 12
			13 14 15 16 17 18 19
			20 21 22 23 24 25 26
			27 28 29 30

✔ **Schedule a new activity:** Click the New Event button, and a New Event page appears in Edit mode. (See Chapter 7 to see how to complete a new event record.)

✔ **View an event record:** If you see a listed event, click the link. A page appears with details on the activity.

✔ **Drill into your schedule:** Click a date on the calendar to drill into your schedule for a specific day. The Day View page appears.

✔ **Schedule a group activity:** Click the Multi User View icon (which looks like two little people). A page appears for the selected day that displays the availability of multiple users. From there, click the New Event button and follow the same instructions for scheduling a new event, as described in detail in Chapter 7.

Tracking your tasks

On the home page, you see a section entitled My Tasks, which displays tasks that you created for yourself or that have been assigned to you.

A *task* is an activity that you need to do, and it can have a due date. Unlike an event, however, a task doesn't have a specific time and duration. For example, if you want to remind yourself to send a proposal, you typically create a task instead of scheduling an event. (See Chapter 7 for additional tips on managing tasks.)

From the My Tasks section (as shown in Figure 2-4), you can do the following:

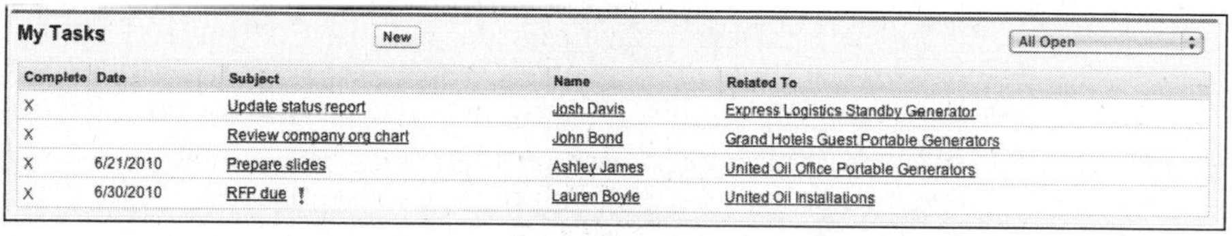

Figure 2-4: Reviewing the My Tasks section from the home page.

My Tasks			New				All Open
Complete	Date		Subject		Name	Related To	
X			Update status report		Josh Davis	Express Logistics Standby Generator	
X			Review company org chart		John Bond	Grand Hotels Guest Portable Generators	
X	6/21/2010		Prepare slides		Ashley James	United Oil Office Portable Generators	
X	6/30/2010		RFP due !		Lauren Boyle	United Oil Installations	

- ✔ **Add a new task:** Click the New button, and a New Task page appears in Edit mode.

- ✔ **Change task view:** Use the drop-down list at the top right of the My Tasks section to select from a list of common task views. For example, select Overdue to see your open tasks that are past their respective due dates.

- ✔ **Review a task:** Click a link in the Subject column to review a task. A task record appears with details.

- ✔ **Go to associated records:** Click links in the Name or the Related To column.

- ✔ **Complete the task and enter any details before saving:** Click the X link in the Complete column. You can also use this link to update a task, but if you haven't completed the task, remember to adjust the Status field before you save it.

- ✔ **See more tasks:** If you have several tasks in your list, the View More link appears at the bottom of the My Tasks section on the home page. Click It to see more tasks on the list. The Day View appears, and the My Tasks section appears in the right column.

Using dashboard snapshots from the home page

If your company has customized your home page, you might also see and select up to three key charts or tables from your dashboards. *Dashboards* display important information from reports in Salesforce that can provide key performance indicators on the health of your business. Each dashboard chart or table is a *component*. (See Chapter 18 for details on building dashboards that can measure and analyze your business.) As of this writing, dashboards are available in the Group, Professional, Enterprise, and Performance Editions.

If you see a chart or table on your home page, you can also perform these actions from the Dashboard section:

- ✔ **Click a chart or table to drill into the detail:** A report page appears with the data that supports the graphic.

- ✔ **Choose a different dashboard:** Click the Customize Page button at the upper right of the section. The Customize Your Home Page page appears, and here you can select from available dashboards if you have the proper administrator permissions. Your home page displays a snapshot of only the three components along the top of any dashboard.

- ✔ **Refresh the dashboard snapshot:** Click the Refresh button at the top of the section. In the left of the section, a date and timestamp appear showing when your dashboard was last refreshed.

Accessing information with the sidebar

The sidebar is the column on the left that appears on just about every page of Salesforce except for dashboards and reports. On the home page, use the sidebar to quickly go back to pages you recently accessed, stay informed about important company messages, click links to useful websites, and create new records.

Creating new records

Use the compact Create New picklist on the sidebar to quickly create any new record.

Revisiting recent items

The Recent Items section displays up to ten records that you most recently clicked. Use the list to quickly get back to records that you've been working on, even if you logged out and logged back in. The recent items show an icon and the name or number of the record. These items include mostly the records that are organized under a tab heading, such as Accounts, Contacts, and so on. To visit the detail record of a recent item, simply click a listed link.

Getting more out of your home page sidebar

With the help of your administrator, you can offer other tools and information from the sidebar on the home page to improve productivity and drive overall adoption. Review the following tips, see Chapter 21 on customizing Salesforce, and consult with your administrator if some of these features could help your organization:

- **Update company messages:** Your administrator can add messages to the home page to keep users informed of important announcements. For example, if you're in sales management, you might want to use the home page to alert reps to end-of-quarter goals or bonus incentives.

- **Emphasize important custom links:** If you rely on other websites to do your jobs, your administrator can help you post them for all your users or just ones that fit certain profiles. For example, if you have a company intranet, your company can add useful links to the home page sidebar so that you can quickly access information outside of Salesforce without ever leaving Salesforce.

If you'd rather not have the sidebar take up some of your browser window's real estate, Salesforce allows you to hide and expand the sidebar when you want. Your administrator can set up this option by choosing Setup➪Build➪Customize➪User Interface and selecting the Enable Collapsible Sidebar check box.

Navigating the Apps

Salesforce allows you to organize tabs into groups. These groups, also known as *apps,* help reduce screen clutter and give you quicker access to the tabs that you use the most. For example, a marketing manager might rarely use the Cases or Opportunities tabs but spend most of her time looking at Campaigns and Leads.

With the salesforce.com Force.com platform, your company can now create custom apps for more specific uses within CRM — or for anything else, for that matter. Sales reps can use an expense reporting app, and product managers can use a product release app to manage their product requirements. The mind-blowing part of all this is that apps can be comprised of standard tabs or *custom ones that you create.* Anyone in your company can benefit from sharing one set of data. And don't worry if you're not the most creative type. Salesforce.com has a bunch of prebuilt apps available (for free or for an additional charge), which we discuss in more detail in Chapter 21.

Discovering the Force.com app menu

In the upper-right corner of any Salesforce page, you can find the Force.com App Menu (see Figure 2-5). The drop-down list allows you to switch between apps. You find some standard tab groupings, such as Sales and Call Center. Administrators can also add or create new apps to address what their specific users need to see. Don't worry if you choose an app and see new tabs. You can always go back to the drop-down list, select your previous app, and have your familiar tabs return.

Figure 2-5:
Choosing apps by using the Force.com app menu.

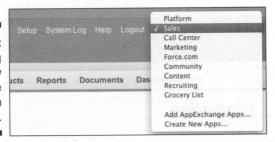

Finding out about the tabs

If the tabs in Salesforce look familiar, they should. When the founders of salesforce.com designed it, they patterned the site after popular websites such as Amazon.com, where you click a tab to jump to an area.

In this section, we describe the major tabs in Salesforce and show you how to use the tab home pages to quickly access, manage, or organize information.

Each tab within Salesforce represents a major module or data element in an interconnected database. That's as technical as we get.

In the following list, we briefly describe each of the standard tabs (as shown in Figure 2-6). We devote a chapter to each of the tabs mentioned here:

Figure 2-6:
Navigating through the tabs.

✔ **Campaigns:** Specific marketing activities that you manage to drive leads, build a brand, or stimulate demand.

✔ **Leads:** *Suspects* (people and companies with whom you want to do business). But don't start grilling your lead about where she was on the morning of June 23 because the only clue you'll gather is the sound of a dial tone.

✔ **Accounts:** Companies with whom you currently do or previously did business. You can track all types of accounts, including customers, prospects, former customers, partners, and competitors.

✔ **Contacts:** Individuals associated with your accounts.

✔ **Opportunities:** The deals that you pursue to track transactions or drive revenue for your company. Your open opportunities constitute your pipeline, and opportunities can contribute to your forecast.

✔ **Cases:** Customer inquiries that your support teams work on to manage and resolve.

✔ **Knowledge:** Answers to cases and other frequently asked questions.

✔ **Products:** Your company's products and services, associated with the prices for which you offer them. You can link products and their prices to your opportunities.

✔ **Reports:** Data analyses for you and your entire organization. Salesforce provides a variety of best practices reports, and you can build custom reports on the fly to better measure your business.

✔ **Content:** The sales and marketing collateral and documents that you use as part of your selling or service processes.

✔ **Dashboards:** Graphs, charts, and tables based on your custom reports. You can use dashboards to visually measure and analyze key elements of your business.

Discovering a tab home page

When you click a tab, the tab's interior home page appears. For example, if you click the Accounts tab, the Accounts home page appears. The tab's home page is where you can view, organize, track, and maintain all the records within that tab.

Do this right now: Click every tab visible to you.

The look and feel of the interior home pages never change, regardless of which tab you click (except for the Home, Reports, and Dashboards tabs). On the left, you have the sidebar with the Create New drop-down list, Recent Items, and (depending on your company and the tab) a Quick Create tool. In the body of the page, you have a View drop-down list, a Recent Items section related to whichever tab you're on (for example, Recent Accounts), and sections for popular Reports and Tools (see Figure 2-7).

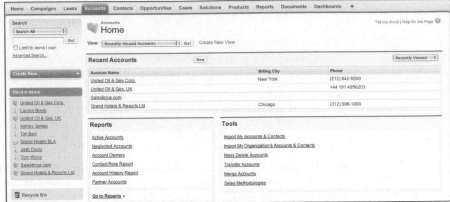

Figure 2-7:
Decon-
structing
the tab
home page.

Using the View drop-down list

Strategy and execution are all about focus. With custom list views, you can see and use lists to better focus on your business. A *list view* is a segment of the tab's records based on defined criteria. When you select a list view, a list of records appears based on your criteria.

On each tab, Salesforce provides a selection of popular default views to get you started. To try a list view (using Accounts as the example), follow these steps (which apply to all tabs):

1. **Click the Accounts tab.**

   The Accounts home page appears (refer to Figure 2-7).

2. **Select My Accounts from the View drop-down list.**

   A list page appears that displays a set of columns representing certain standard account fields and a list of your account records. If no account records appear, you don't own any in Salesforce.

3. **From the list page, you can perform a variety of functions:**

   • *Re-sort the list:* Click a column header. For example, if you click the Account Name header, the list sorts alphabetically, as shown in Figure 2-8.

   • *View records beginning with a certain letter:* Click that letter link above the list to view those records.

   If a user sorts by a column other than name, the letter search looks for values in that column starting with the selected letter. For example, if sorting by State, selecting C filters for accounts with states starting with C rather than account names starting with C.

   • *Display fewer or more records on the page:* Click the up or down button at the bottom of the page or the Next Page link to see the next set of records.

- *View a specific record:* Click the link for that record in the Account Name column. The Account detail page appears, displaying the record and its related lists.

- *Update a specific record:* Click the Edit link at the beginning of its row. The account record appears in Edit mode.

- *Delete a record:* Click the Del link near the beginning of that record's row. A pop-up window appears, prompting you to click OK to accept the deletion. If you click OK, the list page reappears, minus the account that you just wiped out. Don't worry: Later in this chapter, in the section "Resurrecting records from the Recycle Bin," we show you how to bring recently deleted records back to life.

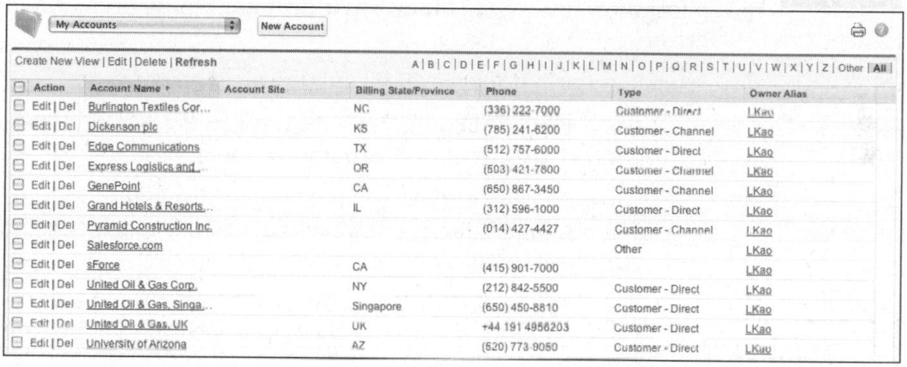

Figure 2-8:
Re-sorting
a list.

Building a custom list view

If you have a particular way that you like to look at records, you can build a custom list view. If you have the right permissions, you can share this view with other groups or your entire organization. (Or maybe you should just keep your views to yourself.)

To create a custom list view (using Contacts as the example), follow these steps (which apply to all tabs):

1. **Click the Contacts tab.**

   The Contacts home page appears.

2. **To the right of the View drop-down list, click the Create New View link.**

   A Create New View page appears.

3. **Name the view by typing a title in the View Name field.**

   For example, if you want to create a list of your contacts that are senior executives, use a title like My Senior Execs.

4. **Select whether you want to search All Contacts or just My Contacts by selecting one of the two radio buttons.**

   In this example, select the My Contacts radio button.

   For this running example, assume that your marketing manager created campaigns. You might want to tie a campaign to filter your List View after identifying which contacts you want the view to search.

5. **Type the campaign name into the Campaign Name field.**

   Tying a campaign to your List View filters your results to those contacts related to a specific marketing campaign. You must have the proper permissions in the Professional, Enterprise, and Performance Editions for this capability.

6. **(Optional) Below the Filter by Additional Fields area, enter search criteria.**

   A basic criteria query is made up of three elements:

   - *Field:* The leftmost box is a drop-down list of all the fields on the contact record. In this example, choose Title.

   - *Operator:* The middle box is a drop-down list of operators for your search. That sounds complicated, but it's easier than you think. For this example, select the Contains option.

   - *Value:* In the rightmost box, type the value that you want in the search. In this example, you might type **vp, vice president, ceo, cio, cto**.

7. **Select the columns that you want to have displayed by selecting a value from the drop-down lists in some of or all the fields provided.**

   Although Salesforce's preset views take common fields, such as Phone and Email, you can select any of up to 15 fields to display on your custom view page.

8. **Decide whether you want others to see your custom view.**

   Administrators and certain users have this permission. Your decision is made simple if the step doesn't appear. Otherwise, select one of the three options. (Basically, the three radio buttons translate to all, none, or selective.) If you choose the third option, use the drop-down list to select a group and then click the arrows to move that group into the Shared To column.

9. **Click Save.**

   A new list view appears based on your custom criteria. If you don't get all the results that you anticipate, double-check and refine the filter criteria. For example, if your list should include directors but doesn't, click the Edit link and update the view.

As long as you save your custom list view, you can use it later from the Views menu.

Reviewing the Recent Items section

On a tab's home page, just below the views, you see a Recent Items section. (The name of the item will match whatever type of record you're on. For example, Recent Accounts is the section name if you're on the Accounts tab.) This section comes with three or four relevant columns that you can modify. You can see as few as 10 items and as many as 25 items at a time by clicking the link at the bottom of the table.

To test the Recent Items section (by using Leads as the example), go to the Leads home page and follow these steps (which you can apply to all tabs):

1. **In the Recent Leads section, select an option from the drop-down list at the upper-right corner of the table.**

   The table reappears with changes based on what you select.

2. **Click a link in the table to go to a record.**

   The detail page appears, displaying the record and related lists.

3. **Click the New button in the upper middle of the table to create a new lead record.**

   A New Lead page appears in Edit mode, ready and waiting. (See Chapter 9 to read more about the fields in the Lead record.)

Reviewing common reports

In the lower-left corner of a tab's home page, Salesforce displays a small selection of commonly used reports associated with that tab. You can click a link to go directly to the report or click the Go to Reports link, which takes you to the Reports home page.

Tooling through the Tools section

In the lower-right corner of a tab's home page, Salesforce provides a set of unique tools associated with a particular tab. Depending on which tab you're viewing, use these tools to help you manage and maintain records within that tab. For example, on the Accounts home page, in the Tools section, you can click the Merge Accounts link to merge duplicate accounts. See the related chapters later in this book for details on using specific tools.

Managing Records

By using the Create New drop-down list on the sidebar of any page in Salesforce, you can easily add new records into Salesforce. You might find yourself in the position of having deleted important files; don't worry, though, because Salesforce gives you a way to put them back in their rightful spots before anyone notices that they're missing.

Creating records

To create a record (by using Contacts as the example), follow these steps (which can be applied to all Create New *Items* on the picklist):

1. **On the home page, select the Contact option on the Create New picklist, as shown in Figure 2-9.**

   A New Contact page appears in Edit mode.

2. **Complete the fields, as necessary.**

   Even while you're in Edit mode, the Create New picklist is available.

3. **When you're done, click Save.**

   The Contact detail page appears, and here you can begin tracking information.

Figure 2-9:
Creating
records by
using the
Create New
drop-down
list.

Resurrecting records from the Recycle Bin

Occasionally, you delete a record and regret it. Don't panic — the Salesforce Recycle Bin gives you 15 days to restore recently deleted records, including any associated records (such as activities deleted in the process) and your credibility.

To restore a deleted record, follow these steps:

1. **On your sidebar, click the Recycle Bin link.**

   The Recycle Bin page appears. If you're an administrator, use the View picklist to view and restore records deleted within the last 15 days by other users.

2. **Navigate the list as you would a normal list page until you find the desired record or records.**

3. **Select the check box(es) in the Action column corresponding to the record(s) that you want to restore.**

   You can click the Select All link to select all the records on the page.

4. **When you're done, click the Undelete button.**

   The Recycle Bin page reappears, and a link to your restored record appears in the sidebar below Recent Items.

Detailing the Record

After you create a record, the record appears on its own detail page (see Figure 2-10). You can use the detail page to update the record fields or manage and track activities and common operations on the related lists displayed below the record. In this section, we show you how to navigate the detail page. The other chapters in this book give you specific details about managing particular related lists.

Many of the features that we describe in the following sections aren't enabled by default. Have your administrator choose Setup➪Build➪Customize➪User Interface to turn on many of these capabilities.

Saving time with hover links

At the top of any record's detail page is a row of several links. Each link corresponds to a list of other records related to the current one. The label for each link consists of the name of that type of record as well as the number that are related. So when you're looking at an Account detail page, instead of scrolling down the page to see whether any contacts exist, you can see how many exist right at the top. But wait, it gets better: You can click the link and immediately jump down to the bottom of the detail page to where that Related List is normally found. And if you want to be even more efficient, instead of clicking the link, just hover your mouse over it. Salesforce will show you a preview of the related list that even includes buttons to create new records and clickable links to existing ones.

Figure 2-10:
Looking
over the
detail page.

Using links and buttons on the detail page

At the top of any record's detail page, you can use several links and buttons to perform different actions. Go to any detail page and try these out:

- **Toggle between list and details.** At the upper left of the page, click the Back to List link. If you've been working from a list, that list page appears. Click the Back button on your browser to return to the detail page.

- **Edit a record.** Click the Edit button to edit the record. The record appears in Edit mode. Click the Cancel button to return to the detail page.

- **Delete the current record.** Click the Delete button to delete the current record that you're viewing. Click the Cancel button in the pop-up window if you change your mind about the deletion.

- **Share the record with other users.** Click the Sharing button. (This button doesn't appear on all records.) Click the Back button within your browser to return to the detail page.

- **Quickly jump to the corresponding related list farther down the page.** Click the related list "hover links" at the top of each detail page, if enabled by your administrator. Alternatively, hover your mouse over the link to open a snapshot of the records displayed in that related list.

- **View a printable version of the page in a new window.** Click the Printable View link in the upper right, and then click the Print This Page link in the upper-right corner of the window to print a copy of the entire page. Many users like to print hard copies that they can review while traveling.

Modifying records with inline editing

To cut down on the number of steps you have to take when you update records in Salesforce, you can edit fields directly in detail pages.

Make sure that your administrator has enabled this feature.

Follow these steps to edit a field directly in that web page, without having to go to another page. Salesforce calls this *inline editing*.

1. **Hover your mouse over any field on a record that you own (or have permission to edit).**

   Figure 2-11 shows the e-mail address of a contact within a company being updated.

An icon appears to the right of a field, telling you whether you can edit that field:

- *Pencil:* This icon appears to the right of editable fields, which become highlighted.

- *Padlock:* This icon appears to the right of fields that you can't edit.

- *None:* You can edit a field that doesn't have an icon, but not with the inline editing feature. You have to edit the record the old-fashioned way, using the Edit button.

2. **Double-click an editable field and update the information in that field.**

3. **Press Enter to complete editing that field.**

4. **After you finish editing all the fields you want for that record, click the Save button for the record.**

If you happen to delete information in a field that requires something in it, don't worry. Salesforce has a couple stop-gap measures to prevent you from messing things up. An Undo arrow icon appears before you save the record, and Salesforce is smart enough to remind you about required fields before letting you save your changes.

Figure 2-11:
Editing a
field inline.

Capitalizing on related lists

Related lists: Say it three times so you don't forget the term. By designing the page with related lists, Salesforce enables you to gain 360-degree customer visibility and ensure that more detailed information is only a click away. For example, if you open an Account detail page for one of your major customers and scroll down below the record fields, you can see multiple contacts, activities, opportunities, cases, notes, attachments, and so on listed as links from organized related lists. And if you don't see these links, you have work to do.

Looking things up with lookup hovers

On any detail page, you can hover your mouse over a lookup field to get a pop-up preview of that other record's contents. Figure 2-12 shows a preview of the account record by hovering over a contact's company name.

The lookup hover feature isn't enabled by default, so if you want it, ask your administrator to set it up for you.

A *lookup field* is any field that actually links to another record. A lookup field's content is underlined to show that it acts as a link to another record. (Just don't confuse lookup fields with the set of related lists that appears below the main body of a record's detail page.)

Figure 2-12:
Hovering
over a
lookup field
provides a
preview of
that record.

Contact	Customize Page	Edit Layout	Printable View	Help for this Page

Ms. Lauren Boyle

« Back to List: Accounts

Opportunities [0] | Cases [2] | Open Activities [1] | Activity History [0] | Campaign History [0] | Notes & Attachments [0] | HTML Email Status [0]

Contact Detail   Save   Cancel

Contact Owner	Liz Kao [Change]	Phone	(212) 842-5500
Name	Ms. Lauren Boyle	Home Phone	
Account Name	United Oil & Gas Corp.	Mobile	(212) 842-5611
Title	SVP, Technolo...		
Department	Technology		(212) 842-5501
Birthdate	9/3/1950		lboyle@uog.com
Reports To	[View Org Chart]		
Lead Source	Public Relations		

Account   View   Edit

Account Name   United Oil & Gas Corp. [View Hierarchy]

Parent Account

Getting Help and Setting Up

In the upper-right corner of any Salesforce page, to the left of the Force.com app menu, you find a set of links that can help you get more out of Salesforce:

- ✔ **Your Name:** This menu will be labeled with your full name. Click the down arrow next to your name to select links to edit your personal information or your personal settings.

- ✔ **Setup:** Click this link to open a page containing the Personal Setup menu. Modify your personal setup, or if you're an administrator, administer and customize Salesforce for your company.

- ✔ **Help & Training:** Click this link to open a window that contains the Salesforce Help & Training home page and additional tabs for help, support, and training.

If the Developer Console link appears in the Your Name menu, ignore it for now. This link is for technical administrators who use it to analyze or troubleshoot automated processes and the use of Apex code.

Chapter 3

Personalizing Your System

In This Chapter

▶ Updating your profile

▶ Finding out about My Settings

▶ Changing your personal settings

▶ Working away from work

▶ Adding your contacts to Salesforce

Salesforce was built by salespeople for salespeople. The tool had to be simple to use, relevant to the business of selling, and customizable so that you could use it to do your job more effectively.

The My Profile page captures information that you want your colleagues to see about yourself, to improve collaboration across your company. Think of it as a light directory listing for everyone who works in Salesforce.

From the My Settings page (formerly known as the Personal Setup page), you can personalize details of your application to better suit the way you look at and manage your daily tasks. And if you capitalize on the tools available to you in Salesforce, you can give yourself an edge against the competition and your peers.

In this chapter, we describe how to update your personal information in My Profile, modify your settings by using My Settings, change your display, and access Salesforce anytime, anywhere.

Completing the My Profile Page

The My Profile page acts like a cross between a corporate intranet page about yourself and a news feed about your collaborations within the company. We talk more later about Chatter, and how the concept of feeds appears in many places in Salesforce. For now, think of feeds as proactive status updates across your company so that people interested in the same things (like an account, contact, or opportunity) can follow each other and stay up to date on the latest news.

To locate and update your My Profile page, follow these steps:

1. **After logging in to Salesforce, click your name in the upper-right corner of the Salesforce page and select the My Profile list option.**

   Your profile page appears. In the left column is room for a photo, some contact details, and some statistics based on various interactions on the feed. The feed is the middle column that shows your most recent activities (similar to a feed on a social network). An overview about yourself, and what Chatter groups you belong to, is accessible from the Overview tab to the right of the Feed tab (see Figure 3-1).

Figure 3-1:
Reviewing the My Profile page.

2. **To upload a photo, click the outline of the head in the left column, and then click Upload.**

   The Upload Profile Photo box appears.

3. **Click the Browse button to upload a small square photo of yourself.**

   A file selection window opens so that you can browse and select your photo from your computer. After you've clicked your photo file, click Open.

4. **Click Save on the Upload Profile Photo screen.**

   Voilà! Your photo appears. A smaller version of your photo will now appear to the left of your name within any Chatter feeds so that you can be quickly identified.

Though you might prefer to submit a photo of your pet or the back of your head, don't forget that this is for work collaboration. Help your fellow employee out (especially the newer ones) by posting a clear photo of yourself.

Now, to update your contact information so that people know a little more about you, follow these steps:

1. **To the right of the Contact heading, click the pencil icon.**

   The Edit Profile page appears. The e-mail associated with your Salesforce account appears, along with other contact information. Complete what you feel is necessary for coworkers who need to reach you.

2. **Click the About tab on the Edit Profile page.**

   Update information here to give your coworkers some more background about yourself.

3. **Click Save All when done.**

   The updates are now reflected on the My Profile page.

This profile page is especially helpful for companies with users who aren't all in the same location.

Using the My Settings Menu

My Settings, which you access by clicking your name after you've logged in to Salesforce, is the enhanced user interface for what used be called the Personal Setup page. In fact, if you don't see My Settings after clicking your name, your organization probably signed up for Salesforce prior to this feature's existence and the administrator hasn't opted to enable this yet (more on that later). You can still follow along and update your settings, because this is largely a visual update to what was the old Personal Setup page.

My Settings is a set of tools and options that you can use to customize Salesforce according to your individual preferences. You can decide to show only certain tabs, synchronize your Salesforce data with your e-mail program, set how often you want to get Chatter updates, and work with Salesforce while you're not connected to the Internet.

Salesforce makes it easy for you to better personalize your system by providing all your setup tools in one area.

To locate and navigate your My Settings area, follow these steps:

1. **Click your name in the upper-right corner of any page, and select the My Settings option from the drop-down list.**

   The My Settings page appears, and you will see a Quick Links and Desktop Add-Ons section (depending on your permissions), as shown in Figure 3-2.

   (If you didn't find a My Settings link below your name, don't worry. This just means that you're on the old user interface. You can still follow along by clicking your name, then the Setup option in the drop-down list, and then the Personal Setup link in the left sidebar.)

   The My Settings page lists each of its main headings in an expandable sidebar. The Quick Links in the body of the page and the sidebar work hand in hand, but we like to use the sidebar so that we don't get lost.

Figure 3-2:
Looking over the My Settings page.

2. **Click each of the section headings to expand them and see the full range of options (see Figure 3-3).**

   Subsections appear. The body of the page doesn't change if you simply expand the section within the sidebar.

3. **Click any subsection.**

   The details for that subsection appear.

4. **Click the Back button in your browser to return to the previous page, or click another section heading to open that heading's page.**

   You've mastered basic navigation on the My Settings menu.

Figure 3-3:
Expanding
the
sections.

Modifying Your Personal Information

By expanding the Personal heading, you can keep your user record current, set preferences, and customize your display to suit your tastes.

Updating your user information

In Salesforce, you have a user record that corresponds to you. You can use that record to keep other users up to date on your contact information.

To find out how to navigate to the My Settings area, see the preceding section.

To modify your user record, follow these steps:

1. **Click the Personal heading on the sidebar (refer to Figure 3-2).**

   A series of options appear below the heading.

2. **Click the Personal Information link.**

   Details of your user record appears in Edit mode. Review the accuracy of your personal information and update it.

   Especially if you travel frequently, make sure that you update your time zone both in Salesforce and on your laptop, reflecting your current location. This is particularly important if you're managing your schedule and synchronizing with offline tools, such as Outlook.

3. **When you're done, click Save.**

   Your user record appears again with the updated information.

Changing your display

If you log in and feel as if you really need only a fraction of the tabs or a select number of related lists, you can customize your display. Your administrator can still override your personal setup, if necessary — for example, after installing an AppExchange application that comes with additional tabs.

Salesforce already provides many standard tabs and groups some of them into apps that you choose from the Force.com app menu. Companies can also create their own tabs. For most users, you just don't need to see all those tabs at the same time.

To customize your tabs, follow these steps:

1. **Click the Display & Layout heading on the My Settings sidebar (refer to Figure 3-3).**

   The Display & Layout heading expands.

2. **Click the Customize My Tabs link if you want to add, remove, or change the order of your tabs within an app.**

   The Customize My Tabs page appears.

3. **Select which app's tab set you want to customize from the Custom App drop-down list.**

   The default Selected Tabs list changes when you change the Custom App selection. Salesforce pregroups its tabs into several standard apps for various common business functions. Depending on your business, having these tabs visible may be perfect, or you may want to see more or fewer tabs.

4. **Use the Add or Remove arrow buttons to highlight a tab and then add it to or remove it from your display, respectively, as shown in Figure 3-4.**

   For example, if you're in marketing and spend most of your time with leads, you might decide to add the Campaigns tab and remove the Customizable Forecasts tab from your Sales custom app.

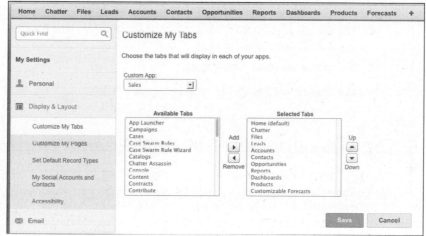

Figure 3-4:
Modifying
your tabs.

5. **Use the up and down arrows to change the order of the tabs.**

   The only exception is that you can't move or remove the Home tab.

6. **When you're done, click Save.**

   The My Settings page reappears, and your tabs reflect your changes.

Customizing pages

You can also personalize your display by changing the layout on a record page. Doing so enables you to see the most relevant sections first. For example, if you work in a call center, you may want to see cases at the top of your related lists on an account page.

To customize the display of a page, follow these steps:

1. **Click the Display & Layout heading on the My Settings sidebar (refer to Figure 3-3).**

   The Display & Layout section expands on the sidebar.

2. **Go to the Customize My Pages subsection and select a specific tab that you want to modify (the Accounts tab, for example). Then click the Customize Page button.**

   The Customize My Page page appears for the tab you selected.

3. **Select a list item from either of the two list boxes, depending on whether you want to add or remove it from your page.**

   For example, if you sell directly to customers, you might want to remove the Partners related list from the Account's Selected List column.

4. **Use the up and down arrows to change the order of how the items will appear on your page layout.**

5. **When you're done, click Save.**

   The Customize My Pages page reappears.

Setting up social accounts and contacts

If researching a person's or company's background is a large part of your job, Salesforce saves you some mouse clicks by letting you quickly see the social profiles associated with accounts, contacts, leads, and person accounts right from that particular record.

To activate viewing of social accounts and contacts, do the following:

1. **From the My Settings page, click the Display & Layout heading.**

   The Display & Layout section expands to show its subsections.

2. **Click the My Social Accounts and Contacts subsection.**

   The My Social Accounts and Contacts detail page appears.

3. **Make sure that the Use Social Accounts and Contacts check box is selected.**

   A list of social networks appears. If you have a LinkedIn, Twitter, or Facebook account, this will allow you to later sign in to those social networks from within Salesforce, to see profiles for the people and companies that you're researching. (You don't generally need a YouTube account.)

4. **Select any check boxes next to the social networks that you'd like to have enabled (see Figure 3-5).**

   Don't worry, the ability to see an account's or contact's social network information is only available to the individual Salesforce user who enables this for himself. Your colleague will need to enable this for herself, and have accounts to those social networks, if she wants to take advantage of this feature.

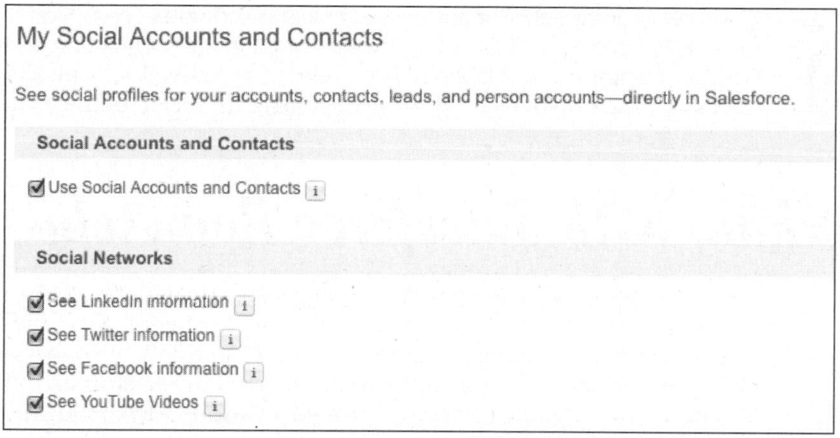

My Social Accounts and Contacts

See social profiles for your accounts, contacts, leads, and person accounts—directly in Salesforce.

Social Accounts and Contacts

☑ Use Social Accounts and Contacts ⓘ

Social Networks

Figure 3-5:
Selecting
your social
networks.

☑ See LinkedIn information ⓘ

☑ See Twitter information ⓘ

☑ See Facebook information ⓘ

☑ See YouTube Videos ⓘ

Also, after Social Accounts and Contacts is enabled, you'll only be able to see as much as your account on that social network allows you to see, and what the person or company that you're looking at wants you to see. If you're in suspense as to how this actually works, Part II delves into this in more detail.

Granting login access

When you need help from your administrator, salesforce.com customer support, or customer support from a third-party AppExchange package that was installed in your organization, you can grant any of these folks temporary login access to your account. By gaining access to your account, the person helping you can provide better assistance from your perspective, because she can view your pages as you.

To grant login access, follow these steps:

1. **Click the Grant Account Login Access subheading from the Personal section of the My Settings page (refer to Figure 3-3).**

   The Grant Account Login Access page appears.

2. **Grant support and/or administrator access for a duration of up to one year by selecting the appropriate time frame from the Access Duration picklist.**

   Your administrator, salesforce.com support, or the AppExchange vendor's support contact will be able to log in as you through the expiration date.

3. **When you're done, click the Save button.**

   The My Settings page appears.

If you're an administrator and a user has granted you access, you can log in to the user's account as follows: Below the Manage Users heading on the Setup sidebar, click the Users link and then select the Active Users picklist view. From the list of users displayed, click the Login link to the left of the user's name.

Working with Salesforce Remotely

For many companies, Microsoft Outlook is a critical piece of your work day: It's how you communicate with customers and schedule your meetings. Salesforce lets you synchronize with Outlook so that key conversations or meetings in Outlook can be reflected and saved in Salesforce. And if you're a road warrior as well, Salesforce provides various ways to log in from your mobile device and close that deal, without having to squint too much looking at that smaller screen.

Synchronizing with Outlook

Salesforce for Outlook is an updated version of what was previously known as Connect for Outlook. The new version (and hence the name evolution) allows you to automatically (or manually — it's your choice) record Microsoft Outlook e-mails, meetings, and tasks into Salesforce. In the following sections, we show you how to install and configure Salesforce for Outlook for your specific synchronization needs.

If you're the administrator responsible for maintaining accurate data in Salesforce, encourage your company to adopt Salesforce as the system of record or "the single source of truth" for customer interactions. For example, tell users to make updates to accounts and contacts in Salesforce rather than in Outlook. Then, have them configure Salesforce for Outlook to allow Salesforce to win if a data conflict occurs between Salesforce and Outlook. By doing this, you can reduce common synchronization issues and influence greater Salesforce adoption.

Installing and configuring Salesforce for Outlook

In most cases, installing Salesforce for Outlook is a simple process. If you connect to the Internet via a proxy server or if your company has a firewall, you might want to consult with your IT department.

To install Salesforce for Outlook, follow these steps:

1. **From the My Settings page, choose Desktop Add-Ons⇨Salesforce for Outlook on the sidebar.**

   The Salesforce for Outlook page appears.

2. **Click the View My Configuration button.**

   The Salesforce for Outlook configuration that is specific to you appears. It shows predetermined settings and objects that will be synchronized. This lets you know what is and isn't going to be syncing with Outlook. And depending on your administrator's configuration, you may be able to modify these settings. In case you disagree with the settings, you get to talk with your administrator first before you actually sync anything.

3. **Click the back arrow on your browser and click the Download button on the Salesforce for Outlook page.**

   Salesforce for Outlook is only available for Microsoft Windows operating system users because Outlook is only available on Windows machines.

   An executable (.exe) file downloads. Before continuing to Step 4, make sure that you have closed Microsoft Outlook on your computer by choosing File➪Exit from the Outlook toolbar.

4. **Double-click the executable file to install Salesforce for Outlook.**

   Select your language, and complete the installation wizard, as shown in Figure 3-6.

Figure 3-6:
Installing
Salesforce
for Outlook.

5. **Open Microsoft Outlook to complete your Salesforce for Outlook settings.**

   The setup wizard appears.

6. **Click Next through the series of setup windows after reading the brief welcome message.**

7. **At the final window, click the Install button.**

8. **When setup is successful, you arrive at the Congratulations screen.**

   Click the Finish button. In the lower-right corner of your screen, you should see a small gray logo of Salesforce for Outlook. This means that it's installed and waiting for Microsoft Outlook to be opened.

9. **Open Outlook.**

   A Salesforce for Outlook login window appears. Enter your Salesforce username and password in the appropriate boxes. Then advance to the next screen.

10. **Review your synchronization settings.**

11. **Click an e-mail to open it.**

    If the e-mail already exists within your Salesforce organization, the contact or lead associated with it will appear in the Salesforce side panel in your Outlook window.

12. **If you want to save that e-mail to Salesforce, associated with that contact or lead, click the small envelope icon to the right of the person's name in the Salesforce side panel.**

    The e-mail is now recorded in Salesforce as an activity.

13. **Click Finish.**

If you discover that you accidentally deleted records in Salesforce while synchronizing, you can go to your Recycle Bin and restore those records within 30 days from the date you deleted the records.

Accessing Salesforce from your mobile device

In today's world of tablets and mobile devices, you can be anywhere and access Salesforce. To best experience Salesforce from your mobile device, find the Salesforce Chatter app in the iTunes store (if you're an iPhone user) or the Google Play marketplace (if you're on the Android operating system). They're free to download and you get instant access to your most-viewed accounts, contacts, opportunities, cases, leads, and any other custom tabs specific to your company.

Importing Your Contacts

One of the keys to making Salesforce productive for you from Day 1 is to get your contacts into the system. If your contacts exist primarily in Microsoft Outlook, you might be better off synchronizing your data. Otherwise, Salesforce provides easy-to-use wizards that help you import contacts and accounts. See Chapter 5 for the details on importing, and see your administrator if your data goes beyond the limits of the import wizard. (For example, if you have historical activity linked to contacts, you can't import those records by using standard wizards.)

Part II
Keeping Track of Customer Relationships

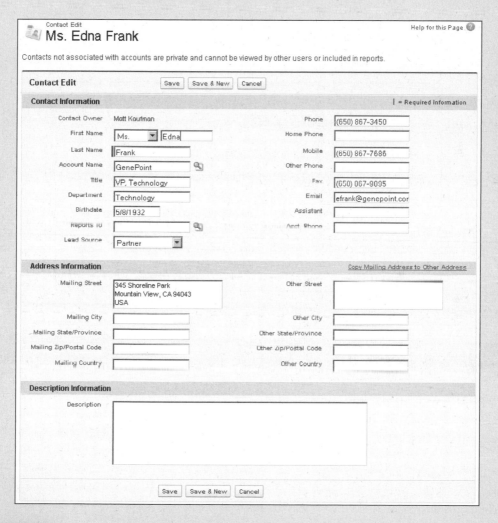

For more on the relationship part of Customer Relationship Management (CRM), go to www.dummies.com/extras/salesforcedotcom.

In this part . . .

- ✔ Find out how to manage your customer data.

- ✔ Learn how to log all activity with customers to ensure a complete perspective.

- ✔ Understand what Chatter is and how your sales, marketing, and customer service organizations can benefit from it.

- ✔ Discover configuration changes you can make to custom-tailor Salesforce to work for your business.

Chapter 4

Managing Accounts

*W*ho are your customers? What do you know about them? What are their top compelling business problems? If you have trouble answering any of these questions, pay close attention to this chapter. In this chapter, we discuss how to use Salesforce to manage your accounts.

In Salesforce, an *account* is a company that you do business with or have done business with previously. Accounts can include all types of companies — customers, prospects, partners, and even competitors. Among the top reasons why companies implement any customer relationship management (CRM) tool is that they need a centralized place where they can store account data, to prevent themselves from searching all over the place for critical customer information. With Salesforce, you can keep all your important account information in one place so that you and your team can apply that knowledge to sell more and keep customers happy. For example, if you work for a pharmaceutical company, you can use the accounts area to manage your territory of hospitals, clinics, and top offices and capture everything from call reports to business plans.

In this chapter, we describe all the ways you can use accounts to manage and track companies. First, you need to get your important company lists into Salesforce and organize them according to the way that you work. Then, you can find out how to make the best use of the account record to profile your companies. Finally, you can discover how to capitalize on the account related lists to gain a 360-degree view of your customers and ensure that no one drops any balls.

Getting Familiar with the Account Record

You use an *account record* to collect all the critical information about the companies with which you interact. That account record is supported by other records (contacts, opportunities, cases, activities, and so on) that collectively give you a complete view of your customer. From this vantage point, you can quickly take in the view from the top, but you can also easily drill down into the details.

Here's a short list of valuable things you can do with accounts:

- Import and consolidate your lists of target accounts in one place.
- Enter new accounts quickly and maintain naming consistency.
- Create parent/child relationships that describe how companies' divisions or subsidiaries relate to each other.
- Realign sales territories.
- Segment your markets with ease.
- Eliminate paper-based business planning.
- Assign account teams to better serve your customers.
- Track your top customers and deemphasize nonstrategic ones.
- Define the movers and shakers within an account.
- Monitor information from your account's social network.
- Manage your channel partners.

Understanding standard fields

An account record comprises fields that make up the information on a company that you're tracking. A record has two modes:

- **Edit:** You can modify fields.
- **Saved:** You can view the fields and the account's related lists, which are located below the record fields.

An account record also comes preconfigured with a set of fields commonly used for account management. Most of the standard fields are self-explanatory, but in the following list, we highlight certain terms that warrant greater definition:

- ✔ **Account Owner:** This required field identifies the person in your organization who owns the account. An account record has only one owner, but many users can still collaborate on an account.

- ✔ **Account Name:** This required field represents the name of the company you want to track.

- ✔ **Account Site:** The Account Site field goes hand in hand with the Account Name field when you're distinguishing different physical locations or divisions of a company. This field, although not required, is very important if your company sells to different locations of a customer with decentralized buying patterns. For example, if you sell mattresses to HappyDaze Hotels but each HappyDaze hotel buys independently, this field is useful for classifying different sites.

- ✔ **Type:** This is one of the fields on an account record that classifies the relationship of an account to your company. The Type field consists of a drop-down list of values, which can prove critical if you want to differentiate types of companies. For example, if you work for a software company that uses value-added resellers (VARs) to sell and service your products, you might want to select Reseller as one of your drop-down list values.

- ✔ **Rating:** Use this drop-down list to define your internal rating system for companies that you're tracking. Salesforce provides default values of Hot, Warm, and Cold, but you can replace these with numbers, letters, or other terms based on how you want to segment companies.

See Chapter 20 for instructions on customizing picklists like the Type and Rating fields.

Customizing account fields

Using standard fields on an account record gives you a simple way to collect basic profiles on companies. To get the most out of your account record, though, think about how you and your company define a target customer. For example, if you're selling corporate healthcare plans, you might want to know certain information about each of your target companies: number of employees, number of people insured, level of satisfaction, and so on.

If the fields on your account record can answer these four questions, that record has a solid foundation:

✔ What attributes describe your target customer?

✔ What are the important components of your account plan?

✔ Is a company's infrastructure important to what you sell?

✔ What information, if you had it, would help you sell to a company?

If you find your account record lacking relevance to your business, write down fields that you want and then seek out your system administrator to add them to customize your account record. (See Chapter 20 for the how-to details on building fields, rearranging your layouts, and other design tricks.) Bottom line: You can have greater success with accounts if you focus on your customer.

Creating and Updating Your Accounts

Before you can begin using Salesforce to manage accounts, you must get the account records into Salesforce. In the following sections, we show you how to get started and then how to update saved records.

Adding new accounts

The best way to enter a new account is to use the Create New drop-down list located on the sidebar of the home page. From the Edit Account page, you get a clear picture of the account fields that are most important to your company. To create accounts by using the Create New drop-down list, follow these simple steps, starting with searching for whether this account already exists.

 Before adding an account (or any other record, for that matter), always search for it first. You might not be the only person to have worked with a particular company. By searching first, you avoid creating duplicate entries, you can potentially profit from prior history on an existing account, and you don't waste time chasing accounts that don't belong to you. (Although we know this *never* happens.)

Follow these steps to add a new account:

1. **Enter the name of the account that you want to create in the Global Search field at the top of any page, and then click the Search button.**

   A Search Results page appears with a list of records that match your query. If you see records that match particular account or lead records, don't throw in the towel yet. Click links listed in the Name columns to drill into the details and see whether the account is being worked.

2. **If you don't get any results, select Account from the Create New drop-down list on the sidebar.**

   The Edit mode of a new account appears, as shown in Figure 4-1.

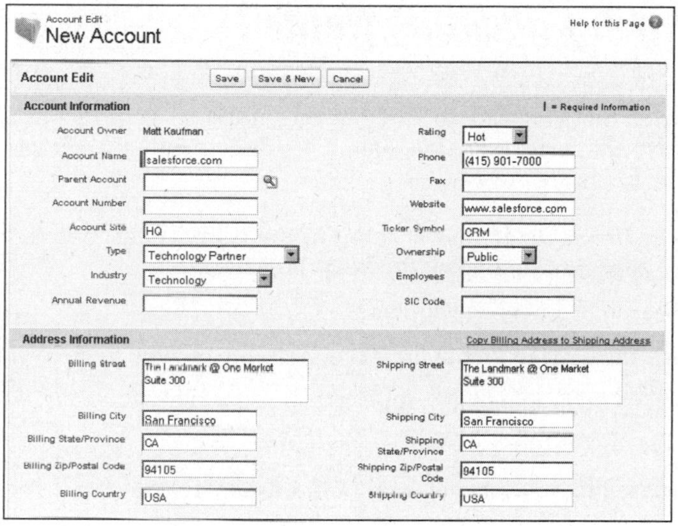

Figure 4-1:
Complete
the account
fields.

3. **Fill in the fields as much as you can or as required.**

   At a minimum, you must complete the Account Name field. Try to provide as much detail as possible to make this new account record valuable for your selling objectives. You can make this data as simple as basic phone and address information, or as detailed as account segmentation data, such as type, industry, annual revenue, and so on.

   When creating account records, strive for accurate and consistent spelling of the corporate name. Your customer database is only as good as the data being entered into the system. As a best practice, look up and use the name of the company from a reliable source (for example, Dun & Bradstreet, Hoover's, or the company name as displayed on its corporate website). For suggested naming conventions, go to the salesforce.com Community website (`http://success.salesforce.com`) and search for "naming convention" to see more ideas and documents from customers.

4. **When you're done, click one of the following buttons:**

   • *Save:* After you click the Save button, the Account detail page appears. On this page, you can click the Edit button whenever you need to modify information on the record.

   • *Save & New:* Clicking this button saves the current account record and automatically opens a new, blank account record in Edit mode.

   A link to the first account appears in your Recent Items list in the left sidebar.

If you have an existing spreadsheet of companies that you want to import into Salesforce, you can use an import wizard tool and avoid the manual entry. See Chapter 3 for how-to details on importing accounts and contacts.

Updating account fields

In the course of working with your accounts, you inevitably collect pertinent information that you want to save directly in the account record. Every time you capture important data on your account, remember to update your record by following these steps:

1. **Enter the name of your account in the Global Search field at the top of any page and then click the Search button.**

    A Search Results page appears.

2. **Click the desired link in the Account Name column to go to your account.**

    The Account detail page appears.

3. **Click the Edit button on the account record.**

4. **Update the fields as necessary, and then click Save.**

    The account reappears in Saved mode, and the fields you edited have been changed.

Organizing Your Accounts

When you have all or a portion of your accounts entered in Salesforce, you can begin to organize them to suit the way that you sell.

In the following sections, we cover how to use views and other tools from the Accounts home page to provide greater focus for you and your sales teams. We also show you an important feature of the account record that allows you to create parent/child relationships between accounts. Then, for even more robust organization of your account information, check out Chapter 17 for specifics on how to use standard and custom account reports.

Using account list views

An *account list view* is a list of accounts that match certain criteria. When you select a list view, you're basically specifying criteria to limit the results that you get back. The advantage of selecting a list view versus searching is that you can use this list view over and over again. On the Accounts home page, Salesforce comes preset with several predefined views including

- ✓ **All Accounts:** All the account records entered into Salesforce. Depending on how your company set up your security model, you might not see this view or its results.

- ✓ **My Accounts:** Just your accounts.

- ✓ **New This Week:** Accounts created this week that you have sharing rights to view.

- ✓ **Recently Viewed Accounts:** Accounts that you recently viewed.

To try out a predefined view, follow these steps:

1. **On the Accounts home page, click the down arrow of the View drop-down list.**

   You see the four options that we mention in the preceding bulleted list as well as other choices that might have been created for you.

   If your screen doesn't change when you select an option from the View drop-down menu, click the Go button to update the page.

2. **Select the My Accounts view.**

   If you've already entered or imported account records, a list page appears, showing accounts that you own. Salesforce lays out the list with six standard columns that correspond to commonly used account fields, plus an Action column from which you can quickly modify a record.

3. **Click a column header to sort the list page.**

   For example, if you click the Billing State column header, the list page sorts by state in alphabetical order. Click the Billing State column header a second time to toggle the sort to reverse alphabetical order.

4. **Access any account by clicking its link in the Account Name column.**

   The Account detail page appears.

5. **(Optional) To edit an account from a list view, click the Edit button on the same row as the account you selected in Step 4.**

   The account record appears in Edit mode, allowing you to make changes to the data.

If you create an account in error, click the Del link on the row of the account to send the Account to the Recycle Bin.

Creating custom account views

If you want special lists for the way that you manage your accounts, build custom list views. For example, if you're a new business sales rep who focuses solely on California telecom companies and always researches the prospect's website before calling, creating a custom view can help you be more effective because you can build your list of target accounts, define columns, and use that view over and over again.

To build a list view from scratch, follow these simple steps:

1. **On the Accounts home page, to the right of the View drop-down list, click the Create New View link.**

   The Create New View page appears.

2. **Name the list view in the View Name field.**

   For our fictitious California telecom example, you might call the view California Telco Prospects.

3. **Select the appropriate radio button, depending on whether you want to search All Accounts or just My Accounts.**

4. **(Optional) Filter by additional fields.**

   A basic criteria query is made up of three elements:

   - *Field:* Select a field on which to search. One example is the Type field.

   - *Operator:* Select an operator for your filter. That sounds complicated, but it's easier than you might think. Taking our example, you'd select Equals from the drop-down list.

   - *Value:* In the third field, type the value that you want in the filter. For our example, you'd type **Prospect** because, for this example, you go after only new business.

5. **Select the columns that you want to be displayed.**

   Although Salesforce's preset views take common fields, such as Phone and Billing State/Province, you can display any of the account fields that you're permitted to see on your custom list page. In our example, you'd add another column for the Website field.

6. **Decide whether you want others to see your custom view.**

   This choice might not be available to you. If it is, select the appropriate option, depending on whether you want to share your view with others. If you choose to make it visible to certain groups of users, you can search for and select groups and roles of users who will see the view.

7. **When you're done, click Save.**

   A new list view appears based on your custom criteria. If you don't get all the results you anticipated, you might want to recheck and refine the search criteria. For example, if your company has a habit of using postal abbreviations (NY) or the full spelling for the State field (New York), this habit impacts results.

By default, each filtering criteria for your list view is joined together with AND parameters. If you want to get fancy with your search criteria, click the Add Filter Logic link to use a combination of AND and OR filters.

Reassigning account ownership

After you set up your accounts in Salesforce, you might need to give them to the right people. Part of organizing your accounts is getting them into the right hands. You might even want to reassign an account to someone else if that account is in another rep's territory.

Reassigning a single account

If you're just reassigning an account on a case-by-case basis, you can transfer ownership directly from an account record. Go to the detail page of an account that you want to reassign and follow these steps:

1. **To the right of the Account Owner field, click the Change link (which appears in square brackets).**

   The Ownership Edit page appears, as shown in Figure 4-2.

Ownership Edit
Help for this Page

MK Partners

This screen allows you to transfer an account from one user to another. When you transfer ownership of an account, the new owner will also gain ownership of the following records related to the transferred account:

- all notes and open activities for this account owned by you
- all contacts within the account owned by you, including all related notes and open activities owned by you
- all opportunities (including closed opportunities if you select the Transfer closed opportunities checkbox below) within the account owned by you, including all related notes and open activities owned by you

Note that completed activities will not be transferred.

The new owner might need to edit sharing.

Select New Owner
I = Required Information

Transfer this account   MK Partners
Owner | Matt Kaufman | 🔍

☐ Transfer open opportunities not owned by the existing account owner
☐ Transfer closed opportunities
☑ Transfer open cases owned by the existing account owner
☐ Transfer closed cases
☑ Send Notification Email

[Save] [Cancel]

Figure 4-2.
Reassign a single account.

2. **Click the Lookup icon to open the Search for a User window and find the user you're assigning the account to.**

3. **Select the appropriate check boxes to determine whether and how associated records change ownership:**

   • *Transfer Open Opportunities Not Owned by the Existing Account Owner:* Changes the owner of any open opportunities on this account.

- *Transfer Closed Opportunities:* Changes the owner of all closed opportunities on this account.

- *Transfer Open Cases Owned by the Existing Account Owner:* Changes the owner of any open cases on this account.

- *Transfer Closed Cases:* Changes the owner of all closed cases on this account.

- *Send Notification Email:* Notifies the new account owner by e-mail.

4. **When you're done, click Save.**

   The account record reappears, and the Account Owner field changes to the assigned user.

Reassigning multiple accounts at the same time

Over the course of managing accounts and salespeople, you'll probably need to quickly and efficiently transfer multiple accounts at the same time. For example, a sales rep leaves the company and accounts need to be moved immediately to someone else.

If you commonly realign account territories, Salesforce transfer tools can make this task a piece of cake. Depending on the method used to carve up territories, plan ahead by customizing and then populating fields that define territories. For example, if you segment by market cap and industry, those account fields should be filled in. Administrators can then mass-transfer accounts to new owners.

To mass-transfer accounts, follow these steps:

1. **Click the Accounts tab on the home page to go to the Accounts home page.**

2. **Click the Transfer Accounts link in the Tools section.**

   The Mass Transfer Accounts Page Wizard appears.

3. **Fill in the Transfer From and Transfer To fields. (Use the Lookup icons as needed.)**

   You can transfer accounts to or from any user.

4. **Select the appropriate check boxes to determine whether and how associated records change ownership.**

5. **Specify the search criteria in the drop-down lists and fields.**

   For example, if you want to transfer all accounts located in California to a new rep, you can use *Billing State contains "California, CA"* (to signify criteria of EITHER "California" OR "CA" in that field) as your search criteria.

6. **Click the Find button.**

   The search results appear at the bottom of the resulting page.

7. **Select check boxes in the leftmost column to select all or a portion of the accounts for transfer, and then click the Transfer button to complete the process.**

   The Mass Transfer Accounts page reappears, minus the records that you transferred.

Building parent/child relationships

If you sell into different locations or divisions of a company and you're currently challenged by how to keep this information organized, use account hierarchies to solve your problem. In Salesforce, you can link multiple offices of a company together by using the Parent Account field on an account record. And you can create multiple tiers to the hierarchy if your customer is organized that way.

To establish parent/child relationships, follow these steps:

1. **Create accounts for the parent and subsidiary companies.**

   See the section "Adding new accounts," earlier in this chapter, if you need help with this step.

   You can skip this step if the accounts are already created. However, you might want to type a term such as **Headquarters** or **HQ** in the Account Site field to signify which account is the parent.

2. **Click the link in your Recent Items list in the left sidebar for the subsidiary account (a *child account*) that you want to link and then click Edit.**

   The record appears in Edit mode.

3. **To the right of the Parent Account field, click the Lookup icon.**

   A pop-up window appears, containing a Search field and a list of recently viewed accounts.

   If you see the parent account in the most-recently viewed results list, skip to Step 5.

4. **Search for the parent account by typing the name of the account in the Search field and then clicking Go.**

5. **From the list of results, click the name of the company to select the parent account (as shown in Figure 4-3).**

   The pop-up window closes, and your selection appears in the Parent Account field.

Figure 4-3:
Select a
sample
parent
account.

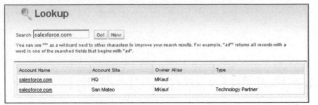

6. **(Optional) To further denote the child account, use the Account Site field.**

   Some companies use city, state, country, division, and so on, depending on how they organize their accounts. For example, if Big Box Office Supplies, Inc., has locations in Dallas and Atlanta, you could type the city into the Account Site field for each child account so that you can tell which is which.

7. **Click Save.**

   The Account detail page appears.

8. **To view the account hierarchy, click the View Hierarchy link to the right of the Account Name field on the record.**

   An Account Hierarchy list page appears, and like other lists, you can click an item to go to a specific account.

Performing Actions with Account Related Lists

Fields on an account record are useful for storing important data specific to a company. But where do you go to capture all the critical interactions and relationships when you're working an account? To keep track of these details, use the related lists located on the Account detail page.

Many of the actions on account related lists are common to other modules. For example, major modules, such as Accounts, Contacts, Opportunities, and Cases, all have related lists for Open Activities, Activity History, and

Notes & Attachments. Instead of being redundant, we point you to Chapter 7 for details on using related lists to track tasks and calendar events. In the following sections, we describe certain related lists that are unique to the account record.

Defining contact roles

Many sales reps do a great job of collecting business cards for contacts within an account, but this action alone doesn't get them closer to a sale. Contacts and their titles often don't tell the whole story about decision makers and the chain of command within an account. To use contact roles in Salesforce, your administrator must proactively reveal this related list on the account record — you can find details on how to do this in Chapter 20.

To better define the buying influences on an account, go to an account record and follow these steps:

1. **Review your records in the Contact related list.**

   If important contacts are missing, add them first, which we describe in Chapter 5.

2. **Click the New button on the Contact Roles related list.**

   The Account Contact Role Edit page appears.

3. **Type the name of a contact in the Contact field and then click the Lookup icon.**

   A pop-up window with your search results appears.

4. **Find the correct contact:**

   - *The contact is part of the search results.* Click the link for that contact's name.

   - *Your search doesn't find the contact.* Refine your search, or click the New button to create the contact record and then select the contact you find or create.

   After you select the contact, the pop-up window disappears, and the Contact field is filled in.

5. **Select the Correct Role from the Role drop-down list.**

   The default roles are strategic, rather than mere job titles. People's strategic roles can change in every deal. If the right role for your contact doesn't appear, advise your system administrator to edit the roles. Many companies match these roles with their particular sales methodology identifiers.

6. **Select the Primary Contact check box if the contact is your primary contact; then click the Save button or the Save & New button:**

   • *Save:* The Account detail page reappears, and your contact appears on the Contact Roles related list for that account's record.

   • *Save & New:* A new Account Contact Role Edit page appears, and you can associate another contact to a role immediately.

Displaying an account's opportunities

Over the course of managing an account, you'll hopefully uncover specific opportunities to sell that company your products or services. You can use the Opportunity related list to quickly perform the following tasks:

✔ Stay aware of all open opportunities that you and your team are pursuing on an account.

✔ Add new opportunities and link them automatically to the account.

✔ Edit and delete opportunity records with a single click.

✔ Gauge the progress of an account by quickly seeing all open and closed opportunities at their various sales stages and amounts.

See Chapter 10 for the scoop on adding, linking, editing, deleting, and managing opportunities.

Viewing cases

Account health is much more than measuring the growth of sales for a customer. After selling, sales reps want to stay informed of customer service issues so that they can continue to keep their customers satisfied, resolve issues early, receive warnings about potential landmines, and track potential upsell opportunities. Use the Cases related list to view all the open and closed customer service cases that relate to an account.

If your company relies on a channel sales team to manage partners, distribute leads, and bring in revenue, consider using Salesforce Communities, which is available in Enterprise and Performance Editions for an extra charge. This partner relationship management (PRM) application gets your partners on board with using Salesforce to manage all the details of their activities with your company and your joint deals. Go to Chapter 12 for a more in-depth discussion.

Tracking your account teams

If you're fortunate enough to work with large companies, you probably know that it takes a team of people to win complex deals and maintain large accounts. The Account Owner field may identify the primary person in charge, but often you need to know who to go to for a specific purpose, or maybe the account owner is just out sick. Account teams lets you list all the individuals at your company who work with an account and detail their specific role.

To give credit to your team and make sure that others know who to call, go to an account record and follow these steps:

1. **Scroll down to the Account Team related list or click the Account Team hover link at the top of the page.**

   If you don't see the Account Team related list, have your administrator activate the feature in Setup.

2. **Click the Add button to add up to five team members.**

   The New Account Team Members page appears, as shown in Figure 4-4.

Figure 4-4:
Add account team members.

3. **Use the Team Member lookups to select fellow users of Salesforce who work on this account.**

   You can always go back and add more later.

4. **Optionally, specify the sharing access you want to give for this account, its opportunities, and its cases.**

   See Chapter 20 for more information on how to setup default sharing.

5. **Select the appropriate role in the Team Role drop-down list.**

6. **Click Save.**

   You will be returned to the account record's detail page with your account team listed.

Maintaining Your Account Database

The more you use Salesforce for account management, the more important it is to maintain it over time.

In the following sections, we show you simple tools for keeping your account database up to date.

Merging duplicate records

Try as you might to avoid it, the best sales reps and teams still create duplicate account records. For example, say that you're a new business rep, and you create and manage an account record for Dependable Electric. Unbeknownst to you, an account manager in the cubicle right next to you has been tracking all his customer activity on an account called DE. Three months later, you both have logged multiple activities, contacts, and other records. Do you throw up your hands in despair and continue working with independent records, delete your coworker's record, or fight it out? The Salesforce merge tool for accounts can help you avoid the loss of friendship and data.

To merge account records, you must be the account owner of the records, the account owner's manager (that is, the account owner must be subordinate to you in the role hierarchy), or a system administrator.

To merge accounts, follow these steps:

1. **Click the Accounts tab to go to the Accounts home page.**

2. **In the Tools section, click the Merge Accounts link.**

   Step 1 of the Merge My Accounts Wizard appears.

3. **Type the name of the accounts that you need to merge and then click the Find Accounts button.**

   A Search Results page appears with a list of records.

   If you don't see one of the accounts you're looking for, rename it with a name similar to its duplicate. For example, you'd rename DE to Dependable Electric Dupe to merge it with the other Dependable Electric account.

4. **Select the check boxes for a maximum of three records that you want to merge, and then click Next.**

   The Step 2 page of the tool appears, containing a side-by-side comparison of the selected account records, as shown in Figure 4-5.

5. **Compare the information and select the appropriate radio buttons to select the values that you want to retain.**

   At the top of each column, you can also choose to keep all the values from one record by clicking the Select All link.

6. **When you finish reviewing, click the Merge button.**

   A pop-up window appears, prompting you to verify that you want to perform the merge.

Figure 4-5: Select values while merging duplicate accounts.

Step 2. Select the values to retain		Step 2 of 2

Previous Merge Cancel

Select the values that you want to retain in the merged record. Highlighted rows indicate fields that contain conflicting data. The Master Record selected will retain read-only and hidden field values. The oldest Created By date and user will be retained in the merged record.

Note: All related records including any notes, attachments, and activities will be associated with the new merged record.

	salesforce.com [Select All]	salesforce.com [Select All]
Master Record	⦿	○
Account Owner	Matt Kaufman	Matt Kaufman
Account Name	salesforce.com	salesforce.com
Account Number		
Account Site		
Type		
Industry		
Annual Revenue		
Rating		
Phone	⦿ (415) 901-7000	○ (877) 776-5727
Fax	⦿ (415) 901-7002	○
Website	⦿ http://www.sforce.com	○
Ticker Symbol		
Ownership		
Employees		
SIC Code		
Billing Address	⦿ The Landmark @ One Market San Francisco, CA 94087 US	○
Shipping Address		
Customer Priority		
Number of Locations		
Active		
SLA		
Description		
Created By	Matt Kaufman, 3/15/2010 2:01 PM	Matt Kaufman, 6/2/2010 10:18 PM
Last Modified By	Matt Kaufman, 6/2/2010 10:17 PM	Matt Kaufman, 6/2/2010 10:18 PM

Previous Merge Cancel

7. **Click OK.**

The Accounts home page reappears. The accounts were merged and any records from related lists are kept. A history of your merge is recorded in the Account History related list on the account record.

Increasing account accuracy with Data.com

Everyone has his or her own way of entering a company name, but when sales reps each use their own method, it leads to duplicate account records. Instead of arguing over whose method is best, you can use Data.com to provide you with the correct name.

Data.com provides top-quality data from Dun & Bradstreet and is available in Salesforce for an added charge. You can use it to automatically clean your account records, providing you with up-to-date information for 83 account fields. Sales reps can also use Data.com to instantly import new accounts and contacts into Salesforce. Whether you are augmenting your existing data or starting from scratch, Data.com can provide the data you need without ever having to leave Salesforce.

Deleting account records

If you (or a subordinate) own accounts that need to be deleted, you can delete them one at a time by using the Delete button on the account records. The one caveat here is that some companies remove your permission to delete accounts altogether. If this is the case or if you want to delete many accounts at one time, consult with your system administrator. System administrators are the only users in your company who have the ability to mass-delete records. (Kind of startling to realize that geeks have all the power, isn't it?)

When deleting records, remember that you're also deleting associated records. So, if you're deleting an account, you can potentially be removing contacts, activities, opportunities, and other records linked to the account. You can rectify a mistakenly deleted record within 15 days of your deletion by retrieving it from your Recycle Bin, but be careful before deleting records.

Chapter 5

Developing Contacts

In This Chapter
- ▶ Customizing the contact record
- ▶ Creating and updating contacts
- ▶ Putting your contacts in order
- ▶ Viewing Contact related lists
- ▶ Building organizational charts
- ▶ Resolving duplicate contacts

If you've been selling for more than a few years, you probably have a big golden list overflowing with business contacts. And if you're just starting out, you probably wish you had one. But how much do you know about those contacts? Where do you keep track of the personal and business information that you've collected throughout the years?

Salesforce enables you to plan, manage, and capture all the important interactions that you normally have with your prospects and customers. Just imagine the value that keeping this shared information in one place can have for you and your teams.

By using the Contacts section in Salesforce, you can effectively keep all your most important contacts together in one place, easily link them with the accounts they work for, gain insight into the relationships between contacts, and capture the critical personal drivers of each contact that are so key to your selling success.

In this chapter, we discuss how to use Salesforce for your contact management needs. You can also find out how to build your contact database by adding information directly or by importing your existing files. Later in the chapter, we describe how to organize your contacts lists so that you can quickly find the people you want to talk to. We also show you how to maintain the integrity of your contact data by editing contact records, merging duplicate records, and deleting old records. These tasks allow you to start putting your contacts to work for you.

Understanding the Contact Record

A *contact record* is the collection of fields that consists of the information about a person you do business with. Unlike a business card or a lead record in Salesforce, however, a contact is linked to an account. Like other records, the contact record has two modes: an *Edit* mode, in which you can modify fields, and a *Saved* mode, in which you can view the fields and the contact's related lists (which are located below the fields).

A contact record comes preconfigured with a standard set of fields commonly used for contact management. The exact number isn't important because your company might add or subtract fields based on the way you want to track your contacts. Most of the standard fields are self-explanatory, but in the following list, we highlight a few fields that are less obvious:

- ✔ **Contact Owner:** This is the person in your organization who owns the contact. A contact has only one owner, although many users can still collaborate on a contact.

- ✔ **Reports To:** This lookup field on the contact record allows you to organize your contacts hierarchically.

- ✔ **Lead Source:** This drop-down list defines where you originated the contact.

- ✔ **Email Opt Out:** This check box reminds you whether a contact should be e-mailed.

- ✔ **Do Not Call:** This check box reminds you whether a contact can be called.

Privacy is a big issue with companies and the selling tactics they employ. Nothing damages a customer relationship more than a contact who's contacted when he or she has asked not to be. To protect your contacts' privacy, be diligent about the Email Opt Out and Do Not Call fields. Users in your company should always check the contact record before calling or marketing to a contact.

Customizing Contact Information

After you complete the standard fields, you never have trouble knowing where to reach your contacts. Whether they take your call is another question, though.

Think about all the personal or professional information that you commonly collect on your best contacts. For example, if Michael Jordan is your client, you might like to know that he loves golf and fine cigars and has five kids. And he's always driven to be number one.

Precision target marketing

A leading telecommunications provider wanted to improve the coordination between sales efforts and marketing programs. Over the course of a year, the provider's marketing department planned numerous campaigns that included direct marketing, trade shows, customer case studies, client outings, and so on. In the past, marketing managers wasted substantial time trying to extract contact information from the sales teams. By customizing the contact record to collect important personal and business information, and then training sales reps to update custom fields on contacts in Salesforce, the company has realized substantial savings in time and better productivity in targeted marketing programs.

Ask yourself these questions while you customize your contact record:

- ✔ What professional information is important in your business (for example, prior employers or associations)?
- ✔ What personal information can help you build a better relationship?
- ✔ How do you evaluate the strength of your relationship with the contact?
- ✔ What probing questions do you commonly ask all contacts? (For example, what are their current initiatives and business pains?)

We always advise keeping it simple, but if any specific fields are missing, write them down and seek out your system administrator. (See Chapter 20 for the how-to details on building fields and other design tricks.) Salesforce can help you remember important details about your contacts, and you can use that information to build better relationships.

Entering and Updating Your Contacts

Your contact database is only as good as the information it contains, so Salesforce has multiple ways for you to get your contacts into the system. You can either start from scratch and manually create new contact records, or if you already have contacts on a spreadsheet or in another tool, you can use Salesforce's simple wizard to import your contacts within minutes. In the following sections, we discuss quick and simple ways to get started and how to update records.

Entering new contacts

Because contacts belong to accounts, the best, most reliable way to create contact records is by starting from the relevant Account detail page. From the Account detail page, you can then add a contact by using either the Create New drop-down list on the sidebar or the New button on the Contacts related list. The result is the same in both situations, and Salesforce automatically pre-fills the Account lookup field. By doing this, you can always find your contact, and your contact's activities also appear in a list on its Account detail page.

To create contacts by using this best practice, follow these steps:

1. **Search for the account, and then click the appropriate Account Name link on the Search Results page.**

   The Account detail page appears.

2. **Click the New button on the Contacts related list.**

   The Edit mode of a new contact appears, as shown in Figure 5-1.

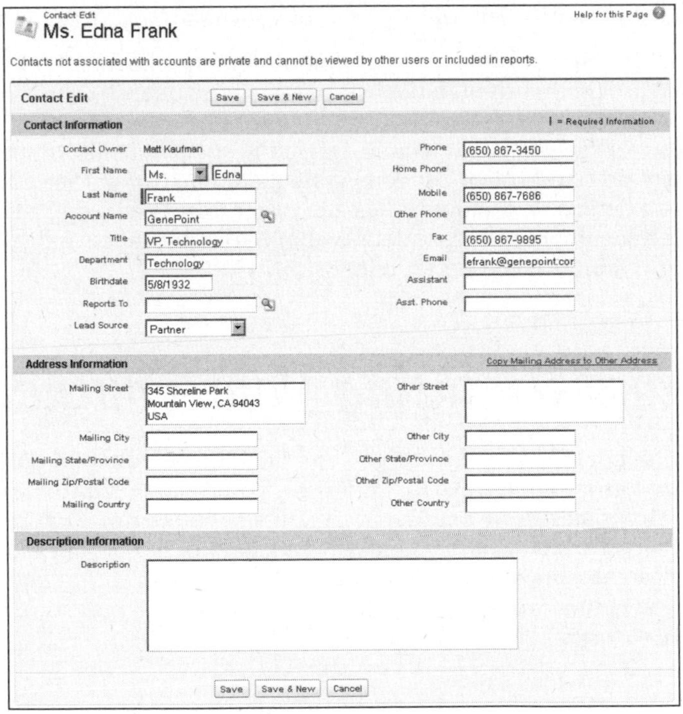

Figure 5-1: Completing fields on a contact record.

3. **Fill in the fields as much as you can or as required.**

   The Account field is prefilled with the account you were working from.

4. **When you're done, click one of the following buttons:**

   - *Save:* After you click the Save button, the Contact detail page appears. On this page, you can click the Edit button whenever you need to modify information on the record.

   - *Save & New:* Clicking this button saves the current contact record and automatically opens a new, blank contact record in Edit mode.

   A link to the first contact appears in your Recent Items list in the left sidebar.

Importing your contacts and accounts

If you already have contact lists from another database (such as Excel), you can use the Import Wizard to create multiple contact records in Salesforce and be done in no time. The Import Wizard is located in the Tools sections of either the Accounts or Contacts home page.

When you import accounts, you can choose to import just companies and their associated information, or you have the option to import companies and their related contacts in one action. Which route you take really depends on your existing data and what you want in Salesforce.

To import your contacts and accounts automatically, follow these steps:

1. **Click the Contacts tab to go to the Contacts home page, and then click Import My Business Accounts & Business Contacts under the Tools section.**

   The Import Business Accounts & Business Contacts Wizard page appears, which includes four steps for importing records, plus helpful hints.

   If you're a system administrator for Salesforce, you can click the Import My Organization's Business Accounts & Business Contacts link, which allows you to import substantially more records at one time with different owners. If you're an administrator, that link also appears under the Tools sections of the Accounts or Contacts home pages. What's the big deal? Most users can import 500 records at a time, but if you're a system administrator, you can import 50,000 at a time and leap over tall buildings in a single bound.

2. **In your existing contact tool or file, compare your current fields with the fields in Salesforce. Add fields to the account or contact records by customizing Salesforce.**

   If you can map all the information you currently have to fields in Salesforce, move on to Step 3. If you have to add fields to Salesforce to match fields, see Chapter 20.

3. **Export your file.**

   You might have contacts and accounts in an existing database, such as Zoho CRM, Microsoft Dynamics, Microsoft Access, or Outlook. Most systems like these have simple tools for exporting data into various formats. Select the records and the fields that you want to export. Then export the file and save it in a comma-separated values (CSV) format. If your accounts are already in spreadsheet format, such as Excel, just resave the file in the CSV format.

4. **Review and prepare your data in Excel.**

   Refine your accounts and contacts before bringing them into Salesforce or clean them up after the import; it's up to you. Some sales reps prefer to make changes on a spreadsheet first because they're more accustomed to spreadsheets.

   When preparing your import file, keep these points in mind:

   - *Enter your column headers in the first row.* We recommend renaming column headers to be consistent with the field names in Salesforce. For example, you could rename the Company field from Outlook as Account Name.

   - *To import data for your entire company* (available as an option only to system administrators), add a column for Record Owner to signify who should own the record in Salesforce. Otherwise, as the person importing, you own all the records from the file.

   - *To differentiate locations of a company* (for example, Sony in Tokyo versus Sony in New York), add a column for Account Site and update the rows in your file to reflect the different sites.

   - *Link accounts in the import file* by adding columns for Parent Account and Parent Site and by filling in fields as necessary to reflect the hierarchy.

   - *Make sure that a Type column exists and that fields are filled to correspond to the types of companies you track* (customers, partners, prospects, competitors, and so on).

   - *For files with more than 500 rows, divide the master file into smaller files to fit the Import Wizard's size limitation.* You have to repeat the Import Wizard for each of the smaller files.

   - *To import contacts and accounts at the same time,* add a column for the billing address fields if those addresses are different from the contacts' mailing addresses.

   For more hints on importing, click the Help and Training link and check out the Training and Support information in Salesforce by searching for the keyword *Importing*.

   When you're figuring out how to import data into Salesforce, we recommend testing an import with five or so records first, just to make sure that you know what you're doing. After importing the test data, review your new records to make sure that they contain all the information you want to have brought in. Delete the test records, refine your import file, if necessary, and then run through the final import.

5. **After preparing the file, click the Start the Import Wizard link.**

   The Select the Source step appears in a new window.

6. **Use the radio buttons to select the source and click Next.**

   You can't go wrong if you select the Other Data Source option, but the other choices are helpful because Salesforce knows how Outlook and ACT! fields map to Salesforce. When you click Next, the Upload the File step appears.

7. **Click the Browse button, shown in Figure 5-2, to locate and select your import file.**

   If you've already prepared your file, you've done the heavy lifting on this page. Salesforce prefills the character coding of your file based on your Company Profile. If you have questions about character coding in general and what your company uses, ask your administrator.

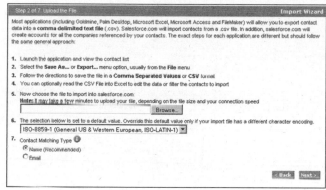

Figure 5-2:
Loading the
contact file.

8. **Select the contact matching type and click Next.**

   If you want Salesforce to avoid importing duplicate records, choose whether you want a duplicate contact to be identified by matching name or e-mail. If a contact record with the matching criteria already exists in Salesforce, Salesforce updates that record with the information in your file.

   When you click Next, the Map Contact Fields step appears.

   If you see an additional request to choose an account record type for import (right after the Contact Matching Type options), check with your system administrator to find out which one you should choose. This advanced option is available only for Enterprise and Performance Edition users. The default type usually is the right answer for most common uses, but better to be safe than sorry.

9. **Map the contact fields between your file and Salesforce, and when you're done, click Next.**

   If you're importing only accounts, skip this step. Otherwise, just go through the fields and use the drop-down lists to select the field from the file that you're importing, which maps to the Salesforce field, as shown in Figure 5-3. (The fields are repeatedly listed in each of the drop-down lists.) When you click Next, the Map Contact Phone and Address Fields step appears.

Mapping fields is simply the process by which you associate a field from one database to a field in another database so that your data appears in the right fields. For example, if you're importing your contacts from MS Outlook, you want data from the field called Company in Outlook to map to the field called Account Name in Salesforce. Take your time when making the mappings. Pay attention to which screens are for account-specific fields and which screens are for contact-specific fields.

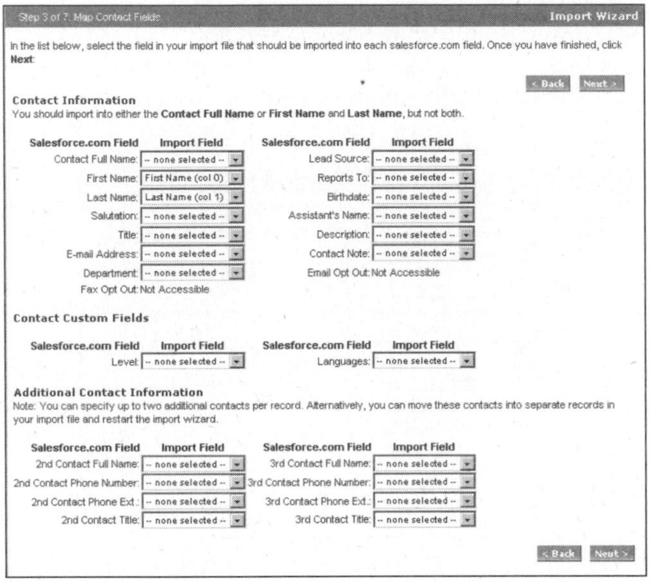

Figure 5-3: Mapping the contact fields.

10. **Map the contact address and phone fields and then click Next.**

    Again, you can skip this step if you're importing just accounts. Map the relevant fields just as you did in Step 9. When you click Next, the Map the Account Fields step appears.

11. **Map the account fields; when you're done, click Next.**

    You map these fields just like you did in Steps 9 and 10. Now you're mapping account data. In addition, you can choose to update existing data. For example, if you already have an account record for Microsoft Corporation in Salesforce, and you entered no other information except the Account Name, you can update that existing account record with the Import Wizard and avoid creating a duplicate account record. So if you want to append existing records, select the Overwrite Existing Account Values check box at the top of this page. When you click Next, the Map Account Phone and Address Fields step appears.

12. **Map account phone and address fields and then click Next.**

    No surprises here; by now, you should be a pro. When you click Next, the Map Extra Import Fields step appears.

13. **Map any extra import fields, and when you're satisfied, click the Import Now button.**

    This step basically warns you about problems with the data or lets you know about fields that haven't been mapped. If you discover an error, you can click the Back button and refine your mapping, or even close the wizard so that you can improve your import file. You might have to start over, but at least you avoid importing bad or incomplete data.

    When you click Import Now, an Importing page appears to confirm that your import is in progress.

14. **Click the Finish button and later check the records that you imported.**

    Salesforce sends you an e-mail after it successfully imports your file. To check your import, click the Accounts tab to go to your Accounts home page. Use the Recent Accounts section drop-down list to select the Recently Created option, and a list of the accounts that were recently created appears. Click the link for an account that you just imported to double-check that the information is accurate.

If you're importing both accounts and contacts, scroll down on an applicable account to its Contacts related list and verify that all the right contacts are linked from your import file. Click into a specific contact record and check to see that the information matches your import file.

Researching contacts on social networks

Visiting a company's website may tell you about its location and phone number, but it won't help you figure out which sports team to mention when calling a customer. For detailed insight on a person's likes and dislikes, you have to turn to social networks. We all do it. Before dialing that prospect's phone number, we look up the person online to see a picture and find out more about him or her. Sure, it's a little creepy, but it definitely helps you avoid saying the wrong thing.

With Social Contacts, Salesforce lets you link to your existing social network accounts and then search and select the right profiles for your contacts from right inside Salesforce. The best part is, from then on, every time you visit that contact, his picture will appear in the upper-left corner of the page with links to his social network profiles.

Updating contact fields

While you work with your contacts, you might need to modify contact information. To update a contact, follow these steps:

1. **Type the name of your contact in the Global Search field at the top of any Salesforce page and click Search.**

    A Search Results page appears.

2. **Click the desired Contact Name link.**

   The Contact detail page appears.

3. **Like with any record, double-click any field that has a pencil icon to its right to edit that field.**

   If a field doesn't have an icon at the right of the field, click the Edit button at the top of the record to make changes. A padlock icon means that you can't edit that field.

4. **Update the fields as necessary and then click Save.**

   The Contact detail page reappears.

Cloning an existing contact

If you want to add a contact that's similar to an existing record, cloning can save you keystrokes and time. To clone a contact, go to the existing contact and follow these steps:

1. **Click the Clone button at the top or bottom of the contact record.**

   A new contact record in Edit mode appears. All the information is identical to the previous record.

2. **Edit the information on the new contact record, where appropriate.**

   Pay attention to what's prefilled because you want to avoid inaccurate information on the new contact record.

3. **When you're done, click Save.**

   You created a new contact without altering your existing contact.

Organizing Your Contacts

When you have all or a portion of your contacts entered in Salesforce, you can begin to organize them to suit the way you sell.

In the following sections, we show you how you can use list views and other tools from the Contacts home page to provide greater focus for you and your sales teams. We also show you an important feature of the contact record that lets you build powerful organizational charts (also called *org charts*) for contacts of an account. (See Chapter 17 to find out how to use standard and custom contact reports.)

Using contact list views

A *contact list view* is a list of contacts that match certain criteria. When you select a list view, you're specifying criteria to limit the results that you get back. The advantage of using a list view versus searching is that you can use the list view over and over again. For example, if you like to send a card on a contact's birthday, you can benefit from a preset list view for this month's birthdays.

The Contacts home page comes with several predefined list views, including

- ✔ **All Contacts:** Provides a list of all the contact records entered into Salesforce. Depending on the way your company has set up your security model, you might not see this view or its results.

- ✔ **Birthdays This Month:** Generates a list of contacts whose birthdays land in the current month (assuming that you collect that information).

- ✔ **New This Week:** Generates a list of contacts that have been created since the beginning of the week.

- ✔ **Recently Viewed Contacts:** Allows you to look at a list of contacts that you've recently viewed.

You use a predefined contact list view in exactly the same way that you use an account list view (as we mention in Chapter 4) or the predefined list view for any other record.

Creating custom contact views

If you want special lists for the way that you track your contacts, we recommend building custom list views, just like you do for any other record. (For an example of how to create a custom view for accounts, see Chapter 4.) For example, if you sell medical equipment, and once per month you like to call your contacts who are dentists, you can create a list view to simplify your work.

Developing Organizational Charts

Having 20 contacts associated with an account is great, but you might not be any further along in understanding the pecking order. In practice, sales reps have been building org charts to strategize on accounts ever since someone thought up org charts, but often, the charts resided on whiteboards and PowerPoint presentations. (And whiteboards are tough to lug around.) By using the org chart feature in Salesforce, you can quickly define the reporting structure for your contacts and use that structure to more easily identify your relationships with your customers.

To build an org chart in Salesforce, follow these steps:

1. **Add all the contacts for an account.**

   See the section "Entering and Updating Your Contacts," earlier in this chapter, for details about adding records.

2. **Go to the contact record for a person who's low on the totem pole and then click the Edit button.**

   The record appears in Edit mode.

3. **Type the name of the contact's boss in the Reports To field and then click the Lookup icon to the right of the field (it looks like a little magnifying glass).**

   A pop-up window that contains search results appears.

4. **Select the correct contact or refine your search until you can select the right contact.**

   The pop-up window disappears, and the Reports To field is prefilled with the selected contact, as shown in Figure 5-4.

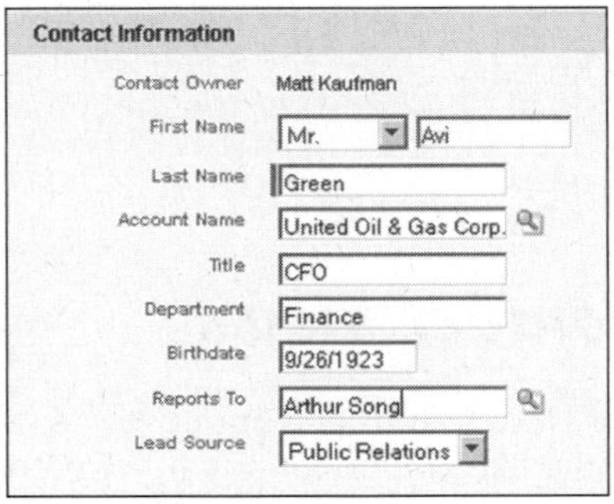

Figure 5-4:
Selecting
the boss.

Contact Information	
Contact Owner	Matt Kaufman
First Name	Mr. ▼ Avi
Last Name	Green
Account Name	United Oil & Gas Corp. 🔍
Title	CFO
Department	Finance
Birthdate	9/26/1923
Reports To	Arthur Song 🔍
Lead Source	Public Relations ▼

5. **Click Save.**

   The Contact detail page appears.

6. **Click the View Org Chart link that appears to the right of the Reports To field on the contact record to display the hierarchy.**

   An Org Chart list page appears, and like other lists, you can click a link to go to a specific contact.

Some sales reps run into certain challenges based on the way they create the org charts in Salesforce. One such challenge is gaps; you just might not know or even care about the entire reporting structure. By getting creative and building placeholder contacts, you can avoid pitfalls. For example, if you sell to both the business and the technology side of a customer, create a contact record called IT Organization and another called Business Organization and then align your contacts accordingly. This technique also works well for *orphans,* where you know one contact in a department and don't want to leave the contact out of the org chart for the entire account.

Performing Actions with Contact Related Lists

Fields on a contact record are useful for capturing the essential contact information for a person. But where do you track and review all the interactions that you've had with a contact? To add, edit, delete, and keep track of this detail, use the related lists located on the Contact detail page.

Turn to Chapter 7 if you want to find out all the wonderful things you can do with related lists to keep track of activities with people and the companies they work for. However, if you're looking for typical ways that salespeople use Contact related lists, go over the following list of features:

- ✔ If you want to track, edit, or close your pending activities for a contact, use the Open Activities related list. In this list, you can click the New Task button to set up a to-do item or click the New Event button to schedule a calendared activity. See Chapter 7 for the how to details on these activities.

- ✔ If you want to view what has happened with a contact to date, review the Activity History related list. Sales reps commonly use Log a Call to capture details for a call taking place or after the fact. Go to Chapter 8 for the ins and outs of sending e-mail.

- ✔ If you send HTML e-mail from Salesforce, you can use the HTML Email Status related list to see how your contact is responding to your e-mail. By using this list, you can send an e-mail, find out whether your contact is viewing your e-mail, and see how quickly he or she views a message after you send it.

- ✔ If you want to store attachments that relate to a contact, use the Notes & Attachments related list. Click the Attach File button to store important documents, such as confidentiality agreements or contact resumes.

Although you can click the New Note button to jot down your comments and even keep them private, we recommend that you track your comments in tasks instead. Using tasks to track your activities allows better timestamping, editing, and reporting on your interactions with your contacts. See section in Chapter 7 for more information on tasks.

✔ If a contact brings you a new deal, you can click the New button on the Opportunities related list and automatically associate your contact with the opportunity record. See Chapter 10 for details on creating opportunities.

✔ To keep track of or edit your contact's participation in campaigns, use the Campaign History related list. And if you want a contact to be part of an active campaign, click the Add Campaign button. For example, if Marketing sends out invitations to a customer event, you can use the Add Campaign feature to efficiently add a contact to the list of recipients. See Chapter 13 for more tips on campaigns.

Merging Duplicate Records

Your once-tiny Rolodex is now a gigantic contact database because you're managing more contacts and covering more territory. However, don't let those large piles of data walk all over you. You have to show that data who's boss. In this section, we show you simple tools that can help you keep your contact database in line and up to date.

Try as you might, sometimes you come across duplicate contact records in the system. Instead of deleting one or several of the duplicate records and potentially losing valuable information in those records, you can use Salesforce to merge contact records easily.

To merge contact records, the contacts must be on the same account and you must be the contact owner of the records, the contact owner's manager (that is, the contact owner must be subordinate to you in the role hierarchy), or a system administrator.

If you accidently merge two contacts, you can always undelete the merged contact from the Recycle Bin.

To merge contacts, go to the account record that has a duplicate contact and follow these steps:

1. **On the Contact related list, click the Merge Contacts button, as shown in Figure 5-5.**

   Step 1 of the Merge My Contacts Wizard appears.

2. **Type the name of the contact that you need to merge in the field to the left of the Find Contacts button and then click the Find Contacts button.**

   A Search Results page appears, displaying a list of records.

3. **Select a maximum of three records to merge and then click Next.**

   In Salesforce, you can merge only three records at a time. The Step 2 page of the tool appears with a side-by-side comparison of the selected contact records.

4. **Compare the information and select the radio buttons for the values that you want to retain.**

   At the top of each column, you can also choose to keep all the values from one record by clicking the Select All link.

5. **Click Merge.**

   A pop-up window appears, prompting you to verify that you want to perform the merge.

6. **Click OK.**

   The contact record reappears, and associated records from related lists are now linked on the contact record

Chapter 6

Collaborating with Chatter

● ●

In This Chapter

▶ Configuring Chatter

▶ Finding Chatter

▶ Updating your profile

▶ Keeping your status up to date

▶ Following people and relevant objects

▶ Joining groups

● ●

*E*very one of us has been the new guy (or gal) at a company at some point in our lives. Even if you received a formal orientation and a review of the organizational chart (a luxury that you shouldn't take for granted), remember still having to meander around finding that person who has the answers? Or maybe you're an old-timer who is extremely busy but always willing to answer a newcomer's questions because you remember how overwhelming it was when you first started.

Organizations possess huge amounts of varying types of knowledge: formal and informal, documented and verbal, current and outdated. Very rarely is knowledge shared in one centralized location. Even when a company is pretty diligent about communicating, the sheer volume of information and the speed with which current information gets outdated can be overwhelming. Chatter bridges the gap between sharing useful information and information overload by allowing you to communicate quickly with colleagues as well as keep track of progress and updates on topics as they happen.

In this chapter, we discuss how Chatter, when used correctly, works to eliminate all that information chaos by providing a central place where Salesforce users can put status updates, post and respond to questions, and see recent activity on records to easily collaborate in a private and secure environment. We walk you through setting up your profile, updating your status, and using groups and feeds so that your sales, marketing, and customer service organizations can work together even more effectively.

At the time of this writing, Chatter has two license types. The free license just lets users see status updates from others, but they can't click into any CRM tabs (like Accounts or Contacts). Chatter Plus is an additional charge for users that may only need to see Accounts and Contacts, and some custom apps, but not Opportunities. Both of these options are for colleagues that don't need to be in Salesforce, but could still benefit from collaborating with people that work in Salesforce often. If you're a daily user of Salesforce, your license comes with Chatter.

Each profile, group, and status update you make is a record in Salesforce, which adds to your data and storage usage numbers. Salesforce has also set some limits on the number of posts and comments that are stored in Salesforce (and for how long). It's usually not an issue, but if you have a bunch of die-hard super-users (who doesn't?), always check with your account executive for more details.

Preparing to Use Chatter

When you get a new car, it's tempting to just drive away as soon as you're handed the keys, but it might serve you better to take a few minutes to read the owner's manual. The same holds true for Salesforce Chatter. By spending a little extra time preparing, you can ensure a successful implementation of this powerful feature and ensure your standing as a Salesforce hero in your company. Here are some key actions that we recommend for every Chatter implementation:

- **Get key executives of your organization to use Chatter.** Engage executives early, help them update their profile (more on that later), and show them how easy it is to follow other employees. They'll love the communication-improvement aspect of Salesforce Chatter and will encourage their employees to post regular updates.

- **Allow the most informational objects to be followed.** If you have a popular product or brand, you might get hundreds of leads a day in Salesforce. Being able to track Chatter on leads is important, especially if you can selectively choose which records to monitor. Other types of records (such as Products) probably won't change that often and thus not warrant tracking via Chatter. As part of your preparation, you have to determine which objects make sense to track for your business.

- **Prepare for the change.** Your organization might not have processes in place to provide routine updates to management. People naturally resist change, especially change that embraces sharing what they're doing. When you put together your communications plan introducing Salesforce Chatter, be sure to focus on the timesaving aspect and reassure people that it's not a surveillance tool used by Big Brother. It's meant to encourage collaboration.

✔ **Lead by example.** Show users how to find and follow your profile. Then be sure to post status updates about the work you're doing so that they can get a feel for how it works. You can even create polls via Chatter to encourage participation.

✔ **Establish basic posting guidelines.** Your colleagues might already be used to an informal posting functionality of social networking sites, but before they post personal information in Chatter, set some basic guidelines. Here are some to get you started:

- Keep Chatter updates related to business matters.

- Don't post anything you wouldn't want to be seen by your CEO, HR department, or peers.

- Never post confidential information that isn't widely available elsewhere in your organization.

- Keep statements constructive and professional. Leave the flame wars and boorishness to anonymous forums.

✔ **Provide training sessions and an FAQ.** Education is the key to success for any Salesforce implementation. Training and documentation not only improve adoption but also ensure that users make fewer mistakes. The same holds true for implementing Chatter. It might seem easy to "just turn it on," but if people aren't all on the same page on when and how to use the tool, information that's posted won't be helpful, which will affect adoption rates.

An FAQ list is a basic question-and-answer document that your users can reference. In addition to the previous guidelines, you can include sample status updates (good and bad ones) and instructions on common tasks. See Chapter 8 to find out how you can create a reusable e-mail template that includes your FAQ and guidelines.

✔ **Continue adoption.** When new employees join your company, be sure to bring them onboard them with training, and review your FAQ and Chatter guidelines with them. This will ensure that they continue the success of your Chatter implementation and prevent any embarrassing mistakes.

Turning On Chatter

Chatter is automatically enabled for all new customers. However, if you subscribed a long time ago or turned it off, then before your company can begin using Chatter, your system administrator has to make some minor changes to your Salesforce configuration.

The first step in using Chatter is activating it in Salesforce Setup. Follow these steps:

1. **Choose Setup⇨Customize⇨Chatter⇨Settings.**

   The Chatter Settings page appears.

2. **Select the Enable check box.**

   Several more sections appear.

3. **Review the fields that have defaulted to having the check box selected.**

   - *Allow Group Archiving:* This allows groups without any activity over 90 days to be archived so that Groups clutter is minimized. Sometimes people create groups for one-time events, and this keeps information without letting people join or add to the conversation. You can search for them if needed.

   - *Allowing Emails and Email Replies:* These two check boxes allow Chatter users to get e-mail notifications of Chatter posts and let them reply via email, too.

   - *Allow Rich Link Previews:* When people post a URL, a preview of a photo or video from that URL is shown.

   - *Allow Approvals:* Allows people to use Chatter to confirm an approval, which is part of a formal workflow process.

   - *Allow Customer Invitations:* This allows Chatter users to invite people outside of your company's e-mail domain into your organization via a private group. They won't have access to anything outside of that group.

If some of your users want external people to be invited into a private Chatter group, pause for a moment and think about that external user's user experience. Is this a great way to collaborate on a project? Will they mind having to log in to a different system on a regular basis to share information? What if they have their own instance of Salesforce — will they get mixed up logging in to two organizations' Chatter conversations each day? Every situation is different, and you can't control 100 percent of it. But make sure that your employees know that adoption by the external person is highly dependent on the context and expectations set.

Understanding Key Chatter Terms

The following are some Chatter-related terms to familiarize yourself with:

- **Profile:** A page about a specific person in your company who is using Salesforce. A profile can include the person's name, a short bio, her contact information, and a photo, for example. The one for yourself is accessed from the top menu, via your name. That page is called My Settings, and we discuss how to update that in Chapter 3.

✔ **Feed:** A Chatter feed shows a chronological list of activities performed by persons or records within your company's Salesforce instance.

✔ **People:** A collection of people within your company who have Chatter profiles.

✔ **@:** Pronounced *at,* type this symbol and then immediately the name of a coworker whom you want to include in your post, in the hopes of giving him a specific heads-up or asking him to join in the conversation. If you have e-mails allowed, the user will get an e-mail notifying him of that specific post.

✔ **Following/Unfollowing:** The act of following (or unfollowing) a person or record to see (or no longer see) her feed updates. These can include comments, posts, and updates to certain fields within a record. Other people in your Salesforce organization can also choose to follow you.

✔ **Post:** A type of update that you make about yourself that's added to your feed for others to see. Because it's called a *post,* you are usually posting an update to some work most likely associated to a record.

✔ **Comment:** A response that you write based on another person's feed activity. For example, if an opportunity that people are following is finally won, your CEO could comment on the feed and say, "Congratulations, team!"

✔ **Like:** A very quick way to cast your vote saying that you also approve of a particular post or comment.

✔ **Share:** A quick way to share a post with your followers or a specific group.

✔ **File:** A document (up to 2GB) that can be attached to a post or comment. It can come from your computer or from within files you own in Salesforce.

✔ **Group:** A way to collaborate with specific people. People can join these freely, or you can make them private so that people have to request entry and its contents are not seen by nonmembers.

Locating Chatter on Your Home Page

After your administrator turns on Chatter, you'll notice it at the top of your home page when you log in to Salesforce.

As shown in Figure 6-1, after you set up your profile, Chatter shows a photo of you, today's date, and a feed of status updates from yourself and others that you're following. All this occurs in the middle section of your home page.

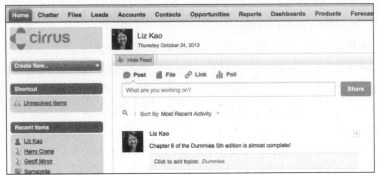

Figure 6-1:
Viewing
your Chatter
feed.

The rest of your home page is still there. Your tasks, dashboard, and calendar have just moved down the screen. You can always click the Hide Feed link right below your top photo to, well, hide the Chatter feed.

Profiling Yourself

The first thing you should do when starting Chatter is to update your profile. When you click your name anywhere in the Chatter feed or click My Profile below your name in the upper-right menu area, you're taken to your My Profile page. Your profile page is your work profile, displaying your profile picture, more information about yourself (your background, contact information, past roles, hobbies, and so on), a history of your status updates, coworkers who follow you, and the coworkers and Salesforce records that you follow.

Your profile is also what others see when they click your name, which means that profiles work like a company directory. Be sure that you don't include any information that you don't want *everyone* in your company to see.

To update your My Profile page, refer to Chapter 3.

Keeping Everyone Informed with Posts

Part of what makes Chatter work is letting your coworkers — even maybe your boss — know what you're up to. In return, you can find out what they're doing. We show you how to post as well as how to comment on others' posts.

Posting a status

Posts are what your followers see, and you can update these to let others know what you're working on, to ask questions, or to share files or website links. The inspiration comes from status updates on websites, such as Facebook and Twitter, that play an increasing role in people's personal lives. If you have a Facebook or Twitter account, you'll pick up Chatter in no time.

To make a post, follow these steps:

1. **Click the Chatter tab or the Home tab.**

   Either option takes you to a page with a Chatter feed in it.

   If you're at the home page, your Chatter feed must be showing. If it's not, click the Show Feed link below your photo at the top of the page.

2. **Make a post in the What Are You Working On field near the top of the page.**

3. **(Optional) Attach a file or a website link, or append a poll to your update by clicking the File, Link, or Poll icon, respectively, directly above the Status box.**

   You might want to link to an interesting article that you read online or upload a file with a presentation you're working on.

4. **Click the Share button to publish your update.**

   Your post is published.

5. **(Optional) From the small drop-down list to the right of your post, select the Delete option to remove it.**

   If you ever make a typo or post something embarrassing, you can always delete that entry and pretend like it never happened.

Commenting on posts

When you're following people, you start seeing their posts in your Chatter feed on the home page. Chatter allows you to add comments to posts, thus creating and managing multiple conversations in an organized fashion.

To add a comment to someone's post, follow these steps:

1. **Locate the post in the Chatter feed.**

2. **Click the Comment link below the status.**

3. **Type your comment in the indented field that appears below the post.**

4. **Click the Comment button when you're done writing.**

   Your comment appears indented below the original update, as shown in Figure 6-2.

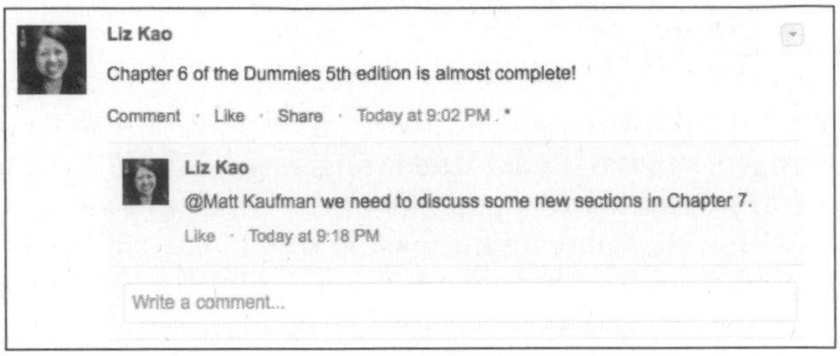

Figure 6-2:
Commenting
on a status.

Choosing What to Follow

Before you can follow anything, your administrator needs to enable Chatter on certain objects. *Objects,* most simply explained, are types of records. They're the nouns that are at the top of your Salesforce page (like Accounts) that you can click and that then look like a highlighted tab. (For a review of how to navigate the default objects in Salesforce, read Chapter 2.)

Your administrator and executive stakeholders should decide which objects to first turn on for following: typically, the one or two objects that your Salesforce users collaborate on the most, such as Opportunities.

Configuring your Chatter feeds

After you determine which objects need to be followed, you can enable Chatter for those objects:

1. **Choose Setup➪Customize➪Chatter➪Feed Tracking.**

   The Feed Tracking page appears, as shown in Figure 6-3.

2. **Click the name of an object in the Object list on the left side.**

   The Fields In page for that object appears.

3. **Select the Enable Feed Tracking check box.**

4. **Select each check box for the fields that you want to track with Chatter.**

   Select fields that others will want to be notified about when a change occurs to that field, for example, Areas of Interest, Next Step, Status, or Stage.

5. **Repeat for other objects and then click Save.**

Feed Tracking

Enable feed tracking for objects so users can follow records of that object type. Select fields to track so users can see feed updates when those fields are changed on records they follow.

		Fields in opportunities		
Entitlement		Save Cancel ☑ Enable Feed Tracking		
Event				
FAQ		You can select up to **20** fields.		
Feed Post Swarm Rule		Account Name ☐		Amount ☐
Google Campaign		Areas of Interest ☑		Close Date ☐
Keyword		DB Days ☐		Description ☐
Lead	0 Fields	Forecast Category ☐		Lead Source ☐
Lead Swarm Rule		Next Step ☑		Number of Users ☐
News		Opportunity Currency ☐		Opportunity Name ☐
Opportunity	0 Fields	Opportunity Owner ☐		Opportunity Record Type ☐
Opportunity Swarm Rule		Primary Campaign Source ☐		Primary Competitor ☐
Product		Private ☐		Probability (%) ☐
Quote		Quantity ☐		Stage ☑
Report		Synced Quote ☐		Tablet Primary Use Case ☐
SFGA Version		Type ☐		
Search Phrase				
Service Contract				
Site	0 Fields			
Solution		Save Cancel ☑ Enable Feed Tracking		
Task				
Text Ad				

Figure 6-3: Selecting fields on objects to follow.

Following people

When you first start Chatter, the feed will be empty because you're not following anyone. In this section, we show you how to follow people in your organization.

Follow the people in your company working on things that interest you or that affect what you're doing so that you can join the conversation. All the people you can follow are listed on the All People subsection of the People heading on the left sidebar of the Chatter app.

To follow people, follow these steps:

1. **Click the Chatter tab from the home page.**

   The Main Chatter feed appears.

2. **From the left sidebar, click the People heading.**

   The People heading expands to show the All People subsection.

3. **Click the All People subheading.**

   The All People list appears.

4. **Find people to follow using one of these methods:**

   • *Find someone specific.* Type that name (such as that of your CEO) into the Quick Find search bar. The list of people automatically updates while you're typing. Look for key executives, peers, and other movers and shakers within your company.

- *Browse for names.* Scroll down the first page and click Next to see the next page of names.

- *Search for people by the first letter of their last name.* Click any of the letters above the list of people.

Be picky about whom you follow first so that you don't get overwhelmed with all the updates you'll be getting in your feed.

Figure 6-4 shows a list of people and whether you're following them.

When you click a person's name, you go to his or her Profile page.

All People

🔍 Type a Name...

Name ↑	Following
Brent, Ludwig	✔ Following ⊗
East, Erik	✔ Following ⊗
Engineer, Erin	⊕ Follow
Kao, Liz Salesforce For Dummies Author	
Kaufman, Matt	✔ Following ⊗

Figure 6-4: Finding people to follow.

5. **After you locate someone you want to follow, click the Follow link that appears in his row.**

   You're now following that person, and the link toggles to Unfollow in case you want to unfollow him in the future. By default, the followed person receives an e-mail notifying him that you're following him so that he can likewise choose to follow you back — or not. His posts now show up in your Chatter feed as long as you have your feed unhidden.

Your secret is safe

Only internal users of your company's Salesforce instance can see your Chatter posts and comments, depending on where you enter that update. (Read through the earlier section for more information on how to update your status.) As far as having outsiders or Google see your updates, you're safe because Chatter uses the built-in privacy and security functionality in the Salesforce native Force.com platform. Internal users can see whatever you post, if they have access to the record you're posting on or about. So if you post from your home page that you're looking for a notary, everyone can see that (what's the point if they can't?). But if you're on the Opportunity record for "Big Secret Government Deal" and make a post there asking about a notary, only people that can see that opportunity will be able to see your post.

Following feeds

One of the key differentiators of Chatter, as compared with other social networking sites — or other services that attempt to bring social networking into the businessplace — is that you can also follow nonhuman things in your Salesforce database. Sounds crazy, right? This feature means that you can follow specific opportunities, accounts, contacts, leads, price lists, cases, and any changes that are made to those records. You can even create or follow groups, focused on a single competitor, region, or vertical. Being able to choose what things you want to stay in the loop about makes Chatter highly relevant to what you need to be successful at work.

To follow a record feed, click the Follow link under the record's name on the record's detail page. Below that link you'll see who else is following that record.

Whenever someone changes a field in an opportunity, for example, you know about it. If you're a sales manager, you can choose to follow a strategic opportunity that one of your reps has been toiling over. The moment she updates that Opportunity Stage field to a Closed-Win, it appears in your feed. If you have key executives following that opportunity, too, they can provide comments that amount to a virtual high-five for all to see.

When you follow a specific record (see Figure 6-5), your profile photo appears as a follower of this object on the record's page so that others will know you're interested in this record.

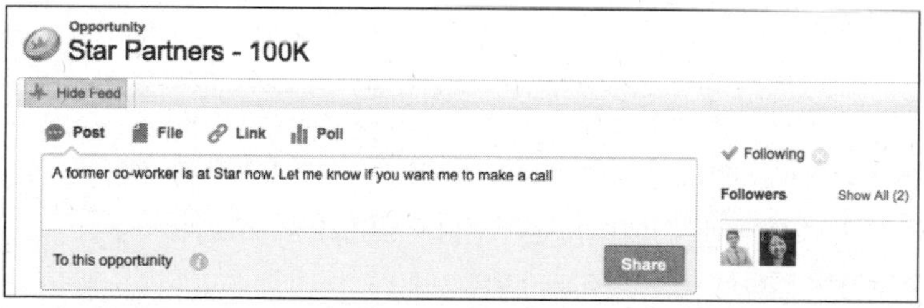

Figure 6-5: Following a record.

You can also add comments to specific records, just like you can with people you follow. (See the previous section.) They appear in your feed on your home page and on the feed on the record's page.

Only users with read access to a record will be able to see any posts that you make on that record. To read more about profiles and permissions, visit Chapter 19.

Being Part of a Group

Similar to finding people to follow, you search for groups to join. By following a group's feed, you can collaborate with a specific subset of people within your company on a regular basis.

Posts made to a private Chatter group can be seen only by members of the group, system administrators, and those with the View All Data permission.

Joining a group

To find a group to join, follow these steps:

1. **Click the Chatter tab.**

   The Chatter feed appears.

2. **Click the Groups heading in the left sidebar.**

   The Groups heading expands to show several subsections.

3. **Select the Active Groups subheading.**

   A list of active groups appears. You can see which groups you're a member of by looking at the Membership column to the right of the group's name.

4. **Use the search bar to look for specific group names.**

   While you type, the list automatically changes to show the results of your search.

   If you don't find a group that you want to join, create a new one yourself. See the next section on how to create a new group.

5. **Click a group's name to view the Group detail page.**

   This provides more details about the group.

6. **Click either of these two links:**

   • *Join:* Join a public group.

   • *Ask Owner:* Ask the owner for permission to join a private group.

Creating a new group

Communication is key when working in teams. With groups, you can set up private feeds where team members can discuss their work outside their normal feed. This is extremely useful for sensitive projects to ensure that online conversations remain secure. You can set up public groups as well for less-confidential discussion.

To set up a new group, follow these steps:

1. **Click the Groups heading on the left sidebar of the Chatter tab.**

   The heading expands. The Recently Viewed Groups home page appears, listing existing groups.

2. **Click the New Group button.**

   The New Group page appears.

3. **Type the name of your group.**

4. **Enter a description to further distinguish it from other groups.**

5. **Select whether you want to have this group automatically archived after 90 days of inactivity.**

6. **Set the Group Access as Public or Private:**

   • *Public:* Anyone can join the group or see its feed.

   • *Private:* Only members, system administrators, and people with the View All Data permission can see and add posts to the feed.

7. **Click Save.**

   Your new group's page appears. You can add members by clicking the Add/Remove link on the right side.

Receiving Chatter Emails

If Chatter Emails was enabled by your system administrator when Salesforce Chatter was activated, you have the option to be notified via e-mail about whenever someone (or something) you're following has made a post.

You can set your preferences as follows:

1. **Choose <*Your Name*>⇨My Settings⇨Chatter⇨Email Notifications.**

2. **Select the Receive Emails check box to ensure that you receive e-mails about updates.**

3. **Select the appropriate check boxes corresponding to the events for which you want to be notified, and how often.**

4. **Click Save.**

Using Chatter Effectively

Here are a few ideas on how your company can benefit from Chatter if some people are reluctant to get onboard:

✔ **Help Sales sell smarter.**

- Follow key accounts and strategic opportunities.

- Ask others for references to help you close a specific deal.

- Create a group to team up to win against a competitor.

✔ **Market more effectively.**

- Get feedback on updated presentations and other marketing materials by attaching them to a status update.

- Share noteworthy press mentions.

- Follow leads to find out more about which types of prospects are converting.

✔ **Improve customer service.**

- Receive and provide help on cases.

- Discuss potential work-arounds and technical solutions in a private group.

- Collaborate on creating the most succinct answer to common customer issues.

✔ **Define a Chatter code of conduct.**

- If you have different generations of employees at your company, they're going to react very differently to this tool. Establish basic norms to ensure that this doesn't turn into yet another medium to post cat photos.

✔ **Install Chatter Desktop or Chatter Mobile.**

- Get proactive alerts on your computer screen whenever someone or a record you're following makes an update so that you're never out of the loop.

✔ **Skim posts from your mobile device.**

Chapter 7

Managing Activities

● ●

In This Chapter

▶ Looking into Salesforce activities

▶ Making new activities

▶ Managing activities

▶ Changing activities

● ●

*A*ctivities in Salesforce are scheduled calendar events and tasks. In many ways, the events and tasks in Salesforce are just like the activities you use in Microsoft Outlook, Google Apps, or any other productivity application. You can schedule events on your calendar, invite people to meetings, book a conference room, and add tasks to your to-do lists so that you don't forget to get things done.

You can synchronize Salesforce with Outlook so that you don't have to input activities twice. (See Chapter 3 to install and configure Salesforce for Outlook.)

However, Salesforce takes activities further: You can easily link events and tasks to other related records, such as accounts, contacts, and so on. You can view activities both in the context of a relevant item (for example, all activities that relate to an account) and as a stand-alone from your calendar and task lists in the comfort and convenience of your home page. And, if you're a manager, Salesforce allows you to stay up to speed on your users and how they're spending their time.

By managing activities in Salesforce, you can better coordinate with your team, quickly assess what's going on in your accounts, and focus on the next steps to close deals or solve issues.

In this chapter, we first show you how to schedule events and create tasks. Then, we cover how to find and view activities, both from your home page and from specific record pages, such as accounts and opportunities.

Reviewing Activities

You can use activities in Salesforce to track all the significant tasks and events involved in acquiring, selling, and servicing customers. Think about all the actions that you and your teams perform to accomplish your job — meetings, calls, e-mails, even the occasional physical letter — and imagine the value of all that information in one place at your fingertips. You can have such a place in Salesforce, and you can easily link your activities together in an organized fashion.

Salesforce features several types of activities that you can access from the Open Activities and Activity History related lists displayed on many of the major records, including accounts, contacts, leads, opportunities, and cases. In this chapter, we focus on events and tasks, but in the following list, we briefly explain all the various activity records you can track in Salesforce:

- **Task:** Essentially a to-do. Use this activity record as your online yellow sticky note. It's an activity that needs to be completed, but it doesn't have a specific time or duration associated with it. For example, if you know that you're supposed to follow up with a contact by sending a written letter, you can create a task such as Send Letter.

- **Event:** A calendared activity. An event has a scheduled time, date, and duration associated with it. Examples of common events are Meetings, Conference Calls, and Tradeshows.

- **Log a Call:** A task record of a completed call. Use Log a Call during or after a call to make sure that you capture important details. For example, use it when a contact calls you and you want to record comments or outcomes from the discussion.

- **Send an Email:** Logs an activity for an e-mail that you send to a contact or a lead. You can send e-mails from Salesforce or a third-party e-mail product like Microsoft Outlook or Gmail for Business, and capture that information directly inside Salesforce.

Salesforce's online suggestion box feature, also known as Salesforce Ideas, allows you and a community of other Salesforce users to post suggestions on any topic for others to vote on and discuss. Ideas can be used just internally within your company and among your peers, or to gather requests from external constituents like your customer base. This sharing of ideas is a valuable way for your company to mine feedback that could result in product or service innovations, or process changes. Ideas are ranked based on popularity over time, and you can group Ideas into multiple subject areas.

To see examples of companies getting feedback from their customers, visit My Starbucks Idea at `http://mystarbucksidea.force.com`, and sale-force.com's own IdeaExchange at `https://success.salesforce.com/ideaSearch`.

Creating Activities

Before you can begin managing your time or activities in Salesforce, you need to know the easiest and most reliable way to add events and tasks.

Creating an event

When you want to schedule activities that have a particular place, time, and duration, use event records. By using event records, you and your sales teams can keep better track of your calendars.

You can create an event from your home page, its calendar views, or the Open Activity related list of a record. The best method to choose often depends on what you're doing. If you're carving out meetings on a specific day, add events from your Home tab calendar's Day View. If you're working on a customer deal, you might create the event from an opportunity record. The end result is the same.

If you're just getting accustomed to filling out records in Salesforce, create events from the record that's most directly associated with the event. By using this method, many of the lookup fields are prefilled for you. So, when you save, you ensure that you can find the activity quickly because it's linked to all the right records.

To create an event from a relevant record (such as a contact or account record), follow these steps:

1. **Enter a name in the search field in the upper left, next to the Salesforce logo. Search for the record to which you want to link the event and click the Go button.**

   For example, if you want to schedule a meeting about an account, you search for the account name.

   When you click Search, a Search Results page appears.

2. **Click the name of the particular record you want.**

   The record's detail page appears.

3. **Scroll down to the Open Activities related list on the page and click the New Event button, as shown in Figure 7-1.**

   A New Event page appears. If you created this event from a relevant record, the name of the person or the related record is prefilled for you.

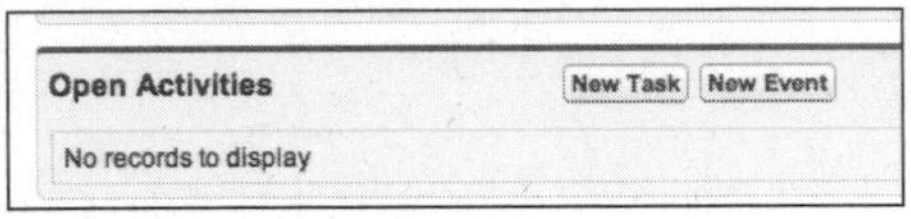

Figure 7-1:
Creating an
event.

Open Activities	New Task New Event
No records to display	

4. **Fill in the relevant fields.**

   Pay close attention to the required fields highlighted with a vertical red bar. Depending on your company's customization, your event record might differ from the standard, but here are tips on some of the standard fields:

   - *Assigned To:* Defaults to you. Use the Lookup icon (the little magnifying glass) to assign the event to another user.

   - *Subject:* The event's subject, which appears on the calendar. Click the combo box icon. A pop-up window appears, displaying a list of your company's event types. When you click a selection, the window closes and your selection appears in the Subject field. To the immediate right of your selection's text, add a brief description. For example, you might click the Meeting link and then type **Define Requirements** to explain the event's purpose.

   - *Related To:* The standard event record shows two drop-down lists that you can use to link the event with relevant records, as highlighted in Figure 7-2. One relates to certain types of records — an account, opportunity, or case. The other relates to a person — a contact or lead. First, select the type of record and then use the associated Lookup icon to select the desired record. For example, if you select Account from the first drop-down list, you can use the Lookup icon to find a specific account.

     If you use the Related To fields on activities, you'll rarely have problems finding an activity later. For example, if you sell through channel partners, you might associate a meeting with a partner contact, but you might relate the meeting to an end-customer account. When you save the event, it appears on the related lists of both records.

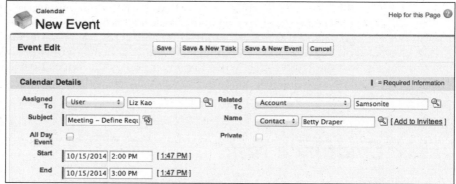

Figure 7-2:
Linking
the event
to related
records.

- *Time:* Allows you to specify the start and end time. You can use basic shorthand and avoid unnecessary key strokes. For example, type **9a** for 9:00 a.m. or **2p** for 2:00 p.m.

- *Recurrence:* Allows you to create a series of events that repeat over a duration of time. This saves you from manually re-creating an event for each occurrence. You can set the frequency of the event, and optionally, when the last occurrence of the recurrence (got that?) happens.

5. **Click Save.**

   The page you started from reappears, and the event appears under the Open Activities related list for the associated records. The event also appears on the home page of the user assigned to the event.

   Alternatively, click the Save & New Event or Save & New Task button if you want to immediately create another activity. A new activity record appears in Edit mode.

Using pop-up reminders

Similar to Microsoft Outlook, Salesforce triggers pop-up reminders about events at a set time before the event is scheduled to start. If you live your life daily in Salesforce and have the application constantly logged in on your machine, this feature will gently remind you via a pop-up window, to make sure that you don't forget an important meeting with a customer.

Make sure that your browser's pop-up blocker protection is set to allow pop-ups that come from the Salesforce domain. Otherwise, if your browser has the pop-up blocker feature turned on, when you create an event, a little warning box appears every time your browser attempts to display a reminder box.

If, on the other hand, you're the type that lets pop-up reminders pile up on your computer screen, or if you log in to Salesforce infrequently (what sacrilege!), you can disable this feature. From your name in the upper-right corner of the Salesforce app, choose My Settings⇨Calendar & Reminders⇨Reminders and deselect the Trigger Alert When Reminder Comes Due check box, along with any of the other boxes that are selected by default. Remember to click Save after you finish.

Creating a task

Some sales reps refer to tasks as *action items;* others call them reminders or to-dos. Whatever your favorite term, use task records when you want to remind yourself or someone else of an activity that needs to get done.

You can create a task from the My Tasks section of your home page or from the Create New drop-down list on any page within Salesforce. We use both methods, depending on whether we're planning out our weeks or strategizing about a particular account, contact, or other record.

To create a task from the relevant record, follow these steps:

1. **Enter a name in the Search bar for the record to which you want to link the task and click the Search button.**

   For example, if you want to set a task to review a proposal that relates to an opportunity, search for the opportunity name. After you click Search, a Search Results page appears.

2. **Click the name of the record you want.**

   The record's detail page appears.

3. **Select Create New Task from the sidebar or click the New Task button on the Open Activities related list of a record, as shown in Figure 7-3.**

   Either way, the result is the same. A New Task page appears.

When creating tasks, go to the record that the task is most directly related to before adding the task. By taking this path, you ensure that your task is easy to find because it's automatically associated with the correct record and its account. For example, if you're creating a task to follow up on an e-mail to a contact, you most likely add the task from the contact record.

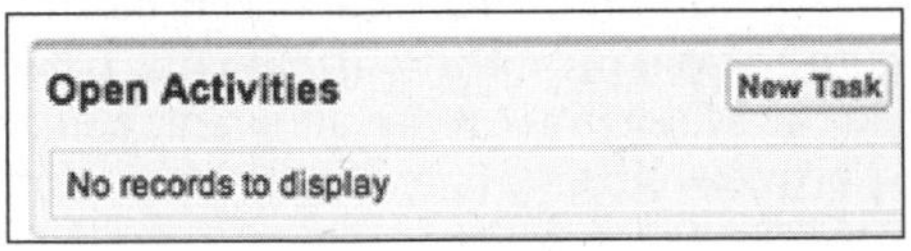

Figure 7-3:
Creating a
new task.

Open Activities	New Task
No records to display	

4. **Fill in the relevant fields.**

   Like the event record, your fields may vary, but here are some tips on adding a task:

   - *Assigned To:* Defaults to you. Use the Lookup icon to assign the task to another user.

   - *Subject:* The task's subject, which appears on the My Tasks section of the Assigned To's home page. Click the combo box icon. A pop-up window appears, displaying a list of your company's activity types. When you click a selection, the window closes and your selection appears in the Subject field. To the immediate right of your selection, add a brief description. For example, you might click the Send Letter link and then type **Introduction** to explain the task's purpose.

   - *Related To:* Shows two drop-down lists that you can use to link the task with relevant records similar to the event fields. First select the type of record and then use the associated Lookup icon to select the desired record.

   - *Priority:* Denotes the task's importance. High-priority tasks display an exclamation mark (!) to the left of the activity on the assigned user's home page.

   - *Status:* Defines the status of the task.

   - *Due Date:* The date by which you expect the task to be completed. This is typically optional. Clicking your cursor in this field makes a calendar window pop up, and you can select a date from this calendar.

5. **(Optional) Select the Send Email Notification check box if you want to notify the user to whom you're assigning this new task.**

   You can't guarantee that every user will log in to Salesforce daily, so e-mail notifications are an effective way to make sure that tasks are delivered to the right people in a timely fashion.

6. **Click Save.**

   The page that you started from reappears, and the task displays under the Open Activities related list for the associated records. The task also appears in the My Tasks section of the home page of the user who's assigned to the task.

   Make sure that you set your My Tasks view on the home page so that your tasks are included in the filter. The view defaults to Overdue, which can confuse some people when they don't see a recently created task in that area.

Always link your tasks with the relevant records in Salesforce. Otherwise, you run the risk of losing valuable customer information that might have been captured in that task.

Logging a call

Sometimes, you perform a task and just want to log the activity after the fact. For example, a contact calls you on the phone, or you get stopped in the coffee room by your boss to talk about a customer issue. In these situations, instead of creating a task and then completing it, use the Log a Call feature.

When you click the Log a Call button, you're simply creating a task record that has a Completed Activity Status. To log a call, go to the record that the call relates to (an account or lead record, for example) and follow these steps:

1. **Scroll down to the Activity History related list and click the Log a Call button.**

   The Log a Call page appears, displaying fields for a completed task at the top of the page and fields for a follow-up activity at the bottom of the page.

2. **Fill out or modify any of the fields to log the call.**

   The Status field is preset to Completed, as shown in Figure 7-4.

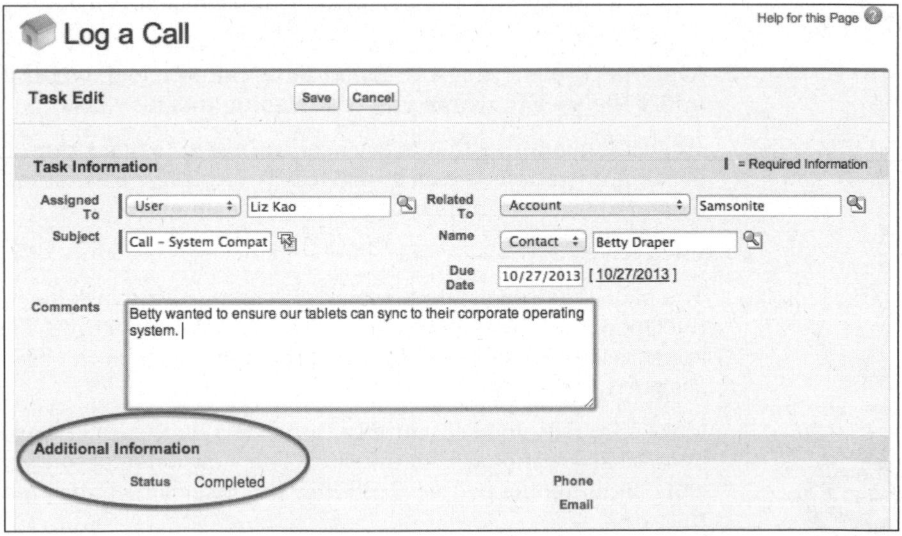

Figure 7-4:
Logging a
call.

3. **If applicable, add another related task by filling out the fields below the Schedule Follow Up Task header.**

   Although certain fields are labeled as required, the follow-up task is optional.

4. **Select the Send Notification Email check box for the logged call (and for the follow-up task if you choose to schedule that) and click Save when you're finished.**

   The detail page that you started from reappears. The call record appears under the Activity History related list. If you set up a new follow-up task, that record appears under the Open Activities related list.

Rather than using the Notes feature in Salesforce to track details of your interactions with customers and prospects, we recommend using Log a Call to record this type of information. Tasks allow for easier reporting, time-stamping, editing, and viewing capabilities. You can even track interactions with multiple people at once using the Shared Activities feature. If you don't see this feature when creating a Task, ask your Salesforce Administrator to turn it on.

If you're an administrator and someone asks you to allow Shared Activity tracking, you could enable that from Settings⇨Customize⇨Activities⇨ Activity Settings⇨Allow Users to Relate Multiple Contacts to Tasks and Events. However, this is an irreversible request, and you should reflect on the majority use case for this. For example, in some financial services businesses, tasks often involve contact in addition to your prospect. However, no one's going to use this (maybe not even the person who asked for it) unless it's properly announced, along with benefits derived from its use.

Organizing and Viewing Activities

You can view your activities from the home page and from a specific record's Open Activities or Activity History related list. If you're planning your calendar, use the home page. If you're working from a particular account, contact, or other item, you can get better context on pertinent activities from the related lists on the record.

After you create (or are assigned to) activities, you probably want to view them so that you can prioritize and complete them.

On the home page, change the default view in the My Tasks section to All Open or to Today, depending on how efficient you are, so that you can see all tasks that you still need to complete. The current default view, Overdue, only shows you tasks after the due date has passed, which we have found to not be many users' first choice.

If you're planning around a specific record, such as a contact or opportunity, you can view linked activities from the Open Activities and Activity History related lists located on a detail page.

The two related lists work hand in hand. An event record automatically moves from the Open Activities related list to the Activity History related list when the scheduled date and time pass. A task record remains on the Open Activities related list until its Status is changed to Completed; then, the record appears on the Activity History related list.

To view activities from a detail page, follow these steps:

1. **Open a saved record.**

   The detail page of the record appears. The saved record appears at the top, and related lists are at the bottom of the page.

2. **Scroll down until you see the Open Activities and Activity History related lists.**

   If you already created related activities, activity links appear in the lists.

3. **Click an item listed under the Subject column.**

   The activity record appears.

Updating Activities

Things happen: Meetings get canceled, and small tasks suddenly become big priorities. With Salesforce, you can perform many of the actions that a normal time-management tool would allow you to do, including delegating activities to other users, rescheduling, editing information, deleting records, and so on.

You can do the following basic functions by clicking buttons at the top of an activity record:

- ✔ **Edit:** Update any of the fields in the record whose fields now appear, and make sure that you save.
- ✔ **Delete:** Delete the record. A pop-up window appears in which you can confirm the deletion.
- ✔ **Create a Follow Up Task:** Generate a related task. A New Task page opens, prefilled with information from the prior record.
- ✔ **Create a Follow Up Event:** Schedule a related meeting. A New Event page appears, prefilled with information from the prior record.

Assigning activities

Sometimes, you may create activities and assign them to others (intentionally, not because you're trying to shirk your duties). Sales Development reps often do this as they set up meetings for their account executives. Salesforce lets you easily reassign tasks and events, and notify users of assignments.

To assign an activity, open the activity record and follow these steps:

1. **Click the Edit button.**

2. **Click the Lookup icon to the right of the Assigned To field.**

   A pop-up window appears, displaying a list of your Salesforce users.

3. **Use the Search field to search for the user or select the user from the list.**

   After you make a selection, the pop-up window disappears, and your selection appears in the Assigned To field.

4. **(Optional) Select the Send Email Notification check box to alert the user by e-mail and then click Save.**

   The activity record reappears, and the Assigned To field has been modified.

Completing a task

When you're done with a task, you want to gladly get it off the list of things to do. You can mark a task as complete from your home page or from the Open Activities related list in which the task link is displayed.

To complete a task, follow these steps:

1. **If you're viewing the task from an Open Activities related list, click the Cls link (Salesforce shorthand for "Close") to the left of the task. If you're looking at the task on the home page, click the X link in the Completed column.**

   Both links create the same result: The task appears in Edit mode, and the Status field changes to Completed. (Your company might have its own terminology for the Completed status.)

2. **Type any changes and click Save.**

   Some reps update the Comments field if they have relevant new information. The detail page reappears, and the completed task now appears under the Activity History related list.

Chapter 8

Sending E-Mail

In This Chapter

▶ Getting to know Salesforce e-mail fields

▶ Setting e-mail options

▶ Sending an e-mail

▶ Delivering mass e-mails

▶ Keeping an eye on e-mails after you send them

E-mail is a fundamental method for communicating with customers, prospects, and friends. By using e-mail correctly, you can manage more sales territory and be responsive to customers. However, by not using e-mail appropriately, you can leave a bad impression or lose a client.

If e-mail is an indispensable part of your business, you and other users can send e-mail from Salesforce and track the communication history from relevant records, such as accounts, contacts, opportunities, and cases. This capability is helpful if you inherit a major customer account because you can potentially view all the e-mail interactions from a single account record.

Sending an e-mail is a cinch, and if that were all this chapter covered, we'd have summarized it in just one section. But Salesforce provides additional e-mail tools to help you better sell to, service, and wow your customers. In this chapter, we show you all the tricks and best practices for sending a basic e-mail, mass e-mailing, using templates, and tracking responses.

Understanding E-Mail Fields in Salesforce

An e-mail in Salesforce is an activity record comprising fields for the message and for the people you want to keep in the loop on the message.

The e-mail record comes with standard fields that people commonly use when sending e-mail. Most fields are self-explanatory, but the following list summarizes some additional fields:

- **Related To:** Use this field to relate the e-mail to an account, opportunity, campaign, case, or other standard or custom object record in Salesforce, depending on your edition. By completing this field, the e-mail is stored under the Activity History related list of that record. See the "Creating and sending e-mail" section, later in this chapter.

- **Additional To:** Use this field to type in additional primary recipients. They don't have to be contacts or leads in Salesforce.

- **Attachment:** Of course, you know what an e-mail attachment is, but we wanted to let you know that the size limit is 10MB per e-mail within Salesforce.

Setting Up Your E-Mail

Before you begin e-mailing people from Salesforce, check out a couple of setup options that can save you time and headaches. In the following sections, we show you how to personalize your outbound e-mail as well as how to build personal e-mail templates for common messages that you send to people.

Personalizing your e-mail settings

When you send an e-mail via Salesforce, the recipient can receive the message just as if you sent the e-mail from your standard e-mail program. The e-mail message appears as if it came from your business e-mail address, and you can use a standard signature to go with your message. And if the recipient replies to your e-mail, that reply e-mail comes right to your standard e-mail inbox. To pull this off, though, you need to personalize your e-mail settings in Salesforce.

To set up your e-mail, follow these steps:

1. **Choose My Settings⇨Email⇨My Email Settings.**

   The My Email Settings page appears in Edit mode.

2. **Modify the first two required fields, as necessary, to specify the outgoing name and the return e-mail address.**

3. **Select the Yes radio button if you want to send a blind carbon copy (Bcc) to your standard e-mail inbox.**

   That way, you can still keep e-mails in customer folders in your e-mail application.

4. **Modify the Email Signature field.**

   If you're personalizing your e-mail settings for the first time, you might notice a default signature from Salesforce. This message appears at the bottom of your e-mail in lieu of your signature. Unless you're using Personal Edition, go ahead and change it.

5. **Click Save.**

   The Email page under Personal Setup appears, and your settings are modified.

Building personal e-mail templates

If you ask your top sales reps about sending e-mail, they'll probably tell you that they don't re-create the wheel every time they send certain messages to customers. It's a waste of their time, and time is money. Instead, they use templates and form letters to send the same message with less work.

In your standard sales process, you probably send a variety of e-mails to customers, including

- ✔ Letters of introduction
- ✔ Thank-you notes
- ✔ Responses to common objections
- ✔ Answers on competition

Although you do need to personalize a message to fit the specific details of a customer, you probably use certain effective phrases and sentences over and over again. Instead of searching for a prior message and cutting and pasting, you can create personal e-mail templates and improve your productivity.

To create a personal template, follow these steps:

1. **Choose My Settings➪Email➪Email Templates.**

   An Email Templates page appears.

2. **Select the My Personal Email Templates folder in the drop-down list, if it's not already set to that.**

3. **Click the New Template button.**

   Step 1 of the template wizard appears.

4. **Select the radio button for Text, HTML, Custom, or Visualforce to set the type of e-mail that you want to create and click Next.**

   • *Text:* Uses a basic text-only template without any formatting.

   • *HTML:* Uses a previously created letterhead and supports HTML formatting.

   • *Visualforce:* Uses a saved Visualforce page.

   • *Custom:* Lets you paste previously created HTML code as your template.

   The next page of the wizard appears, and the content of the page depends on the choice you made. Using HTML is most common and has certain advantages, both from appearance and tracking standpoints, but older e-mail programs cannot receive HTML e-mail.

5. **If you select Text in the previous step, complete the template fields provided (see Figure 8-1) and then click Save.**

   You can use the template only after you select the Available for Use check box.

   After clicking Save, a Text Email Template page for your new template appears in Saved mode with an Attachments related list.

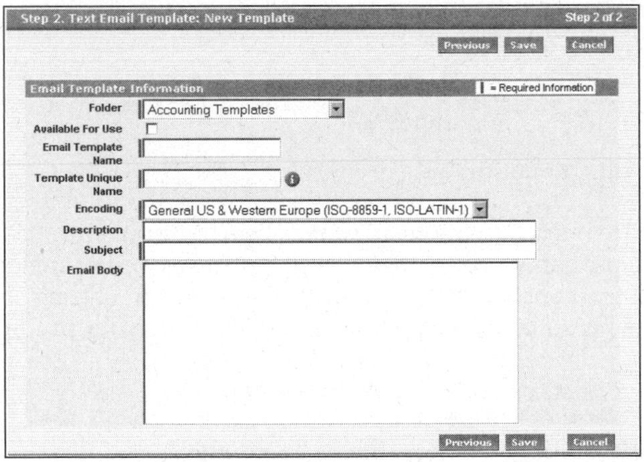

Figure 8-1:
Create
a text
template.

6. **(Optional) Attach a document.**

7. **If you select either HTML option (HTML or Custom) in Step 4, enter the properties for the e-mail template and click the Save & Next button.**

If you choose to build your e-mail template with a letterhead, you have to select a previously created letterhead and then a layout by using the drop-down lists provided. After you click the Save & Next button, the Step 3 page of the wizard appears.

You can create HTML or Custom e-mail templates only if you have the Edit HTML Templates permission. See an admin if you don't have the right permissions.

8. **Create the HTML version by typing and formatting the content and copying and pasting merge fields.**

9. **Click Preview to review your work and, when you're done, click the Save & Next button.**

   The Step 4 page of the wizard appears.

10. **Enter the text version of the e-mail template.**

    For those customers who can't or don't want to receive HTML e-mails, they can receive the text version. If the message is similar or identical to the HTML version, click the Copy Text from HTML Version button and modify the content, as needed.

11. **Click the Save button.**

    An HTML or Custom Email Template page for your new template appears in Saved mode with an Attachments related list, which you can use for attaching standard documents.

We show you how to use your e-mail template in the later section "Using e-mail templates."

Creating letterheads

If you are a system administrator, you can create and save custom branded letterheads to ensure that all your templates have a similar look and feel.

To create a letterhead, follow these steps:

1. **Choose Setup➪Administer➪Communication Templates➪Letterheads.**

   If this is your first time visiting, an Understanding Letterheads page appears. You can bypass it by clicking the Next button.

2. **Click the New Letterhead button.**

   The Letterhead Properties section of the New Letterhead wizard appears.

3. **Select the Available For Use check box. Then fill in the required fields marked in red and optionally enter a description.**

   If you don't want to let anyone use the letterhead just yet, you can leave the Available For Use check box deselected for now.

4. **Click the Save button.**

   The Letterhead Details section of the New Letterhead Wizard appears (see Figure 8-2). This is where you can graphically design your letterhead.

5. **Click the Edit Background Color button.**

   The Background Color window opens with the default color as gray. You can set it to any HTML color code or use the Paint Can button to select from a color chart. When you're done, click the OK button to close the window.

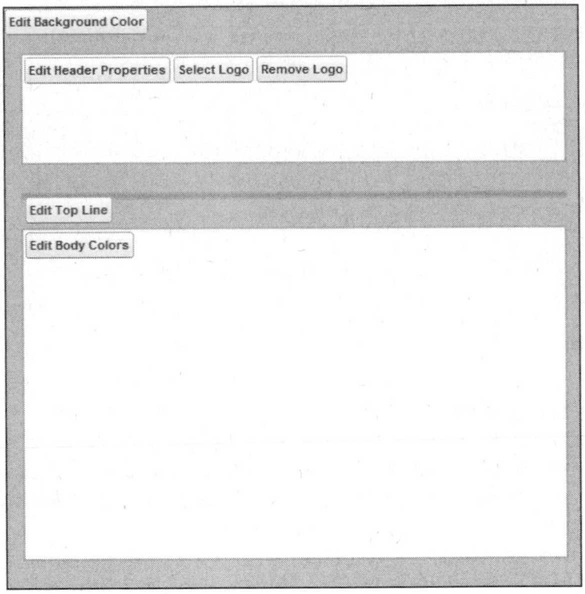

Edit Background Color

Edit Header Properties | Select Logo | Remove Logo

Edit Top Line

Edit Body Colors

Figure 8-2:
Create a
letterhead.

6. **Click the Select Logo button.**

   The Attach File window opens to let you select from any image that has already been uploaded to the Documents tab in Salesforce. When you find the file you want, click its name to select it and close the window.

7. **Click the Edit Header Properties button.**

   The Header Properties window opens. You can specify the background color, the horizontal and vertical alignment, and the height of the Header section to ensure that your logo looks great. When you're done, click the OK button to close the window.

8. **Click the Edit Top Line button.**

   The Top Color and Height window opens. If you don't want a top line, you can set the line color to the same as your background and set the height to 0. When you're done, click the OK button to close the window.

9. **Click the remaining buttons to make additional edits to your letterhead.**

   You can configure the middle and bottom lines, the footer properties and logo, and the body background color, just like you did in the previous steps.

10. **Click the Save button.**

    A preview of your new letterhead is shown. You can always make additional changes by clicking the Edit Letterhead button.

Saving Third-Party E-Mails to Salesforce

Salesforce allows you to send e-mails to leads and contacts; however, the management of the conversations (that is, the back and forth of e-mail dialog that occurs) happens in your company's e-mail management system of choice.

Many companies today are moving their e-mail systems online to reduce the costs of using and maintaining traditional e-mail software systems like Microsoft Exchange and Outlook. Don't get us wrong; Outlook is the big gorilla of the e-mail (officially called "productivity tools") space. At the same time, using web-based e-mail systems like Google Apps or Office 365 has gained a lot of momentum.

Chapter 3 explains how to download the Salesforce for Outlook plug-in to synchronize e-mails in Outlook with Salesforce.

If you're using a web-based e-mail system, you can still save and track your outbound e-mails to Salesforce, too, which allows you to connect an e-mail to a record.

Activating the Email to Salesforce feature

To first activate the Email to Salesforce feature, have your administrator choose Setup⇨Administer⇨Email Administration⇨Email to Salesforce. Click the Edit button in the middle of the Email to Salesforce page to select the Active check box and enable Email to Salesforce.

If you have sophisticated e-mail security policies and know whether your e-mail domains support the SPF, SenderID, or DomainKeys protocols, be sure that the admin also selects the Advanced Email Security Settings check box. Salesforce uses these protocols to verify the legitimacy of the sender's e-mail server. If the e-mail server passes at least one of these protocols, Salesforce processes that e-mail and proceeds to log it as an activity under a lead or contact.

After you make your check box selections and click the Save button in the middle of the page, a pop-up box appears that optionally allows the admin to notify all Salesforce users about the Email to Salesforce feature.

Identifying your Email to Salesforce address

After your administrator activates Email to Salesforce, choose My Settings⇨Email⇨My Email to Salesforce to get to the My Email to Salesforce page. In the middle of the page, a highlighted field notes your Email to Salesforce address. Whenever you're writing an e-mail in your online e-mail system (we use Gmail as the example), paste that address into the BCC field of your e-mail. When you send your e-mail, it's logged as a completed task in Salesforce, under whichever lead or contact record whose e-mail address matches that in the To field.

If you send and receive e-mail from multiple addresses (and possibly from the same inbox), you can list all your e-mail addresses so that Salesforce can associate correspondence from those e-mail addresses to the automatically generated Email to Salesforce address. To edit your e-mail addresses, follow these steps:

1. **In the My Acceptable Email Addresses field, add all the e-mail addresses that apply, separated by commas.**

2. **In the Email Associations section, select the Opportunities, Leads, or Contacts check box, depending on which object(s) you want Salesforce to attach your external e-mails to.**

3. **(Optional) Select the Always Save Email Attachments check box to have Salesforce include any attached files on your external e-mails.**

4. **(Optional) Select the Email Me Confirmation of Association check box to set your preference for whether you want to be sent a link via e-mail of your newly created e-mail record in Salesforce.**

Saving an e-mail to Salesforce

After you set your Email to Salesforce special e-mail address, it's time to use it.

Keeping your web browser open to Salesforce and the My Email to Salesforce page, open a new browser window to access your online e-mail system and compose an e-mail (again, we use Google Gmail as example) to a person whose e-mail you know is in Salesforce, associated with a lead or contact. (Make sure that your relationship with this person allows you to send test e-mails to him or her, or you might have some explaining to do!) Simply copy the special e-mail address and paste it into the BCC field. When you're done writing the body of the e-mail, send it, and *voilà!* Almost instantaneously, it appears as an activity associated with that lead or contact.

Sending E-Mail from Salesforce

You can send an e-mail to any lead or contact stored in Salesforce with a valid e-mail address. By sending from Salesforce, you can ensure that you and your team members can keep track of critical outbound communications to customers and prospects.

Creating and sending e-mail

You can initiate your outbound e-mail from many different records in Salesforce, including opportunity, account, case, campaign, lead, and contact records. To create and send an e-mail, go to the relevant record and follow these steps:

1. **Click the Send an Email button on the Activity History related list.**

   A Send an Email page appears, as shown in Figure 8-3. The Email format is in Text, with a Switch to *Format* link appearing to the right of it. Alternatively, click the Send an Email button in the HTML Email Status related list to default to HTML format. Either way, if you change your mind, you can always switch formats on the Send an Email edit page.

If you have organization-wide e-mail addresses set up in Salesforce, you can select one as your From address. If not, your standard e-mail address will default as the From address.

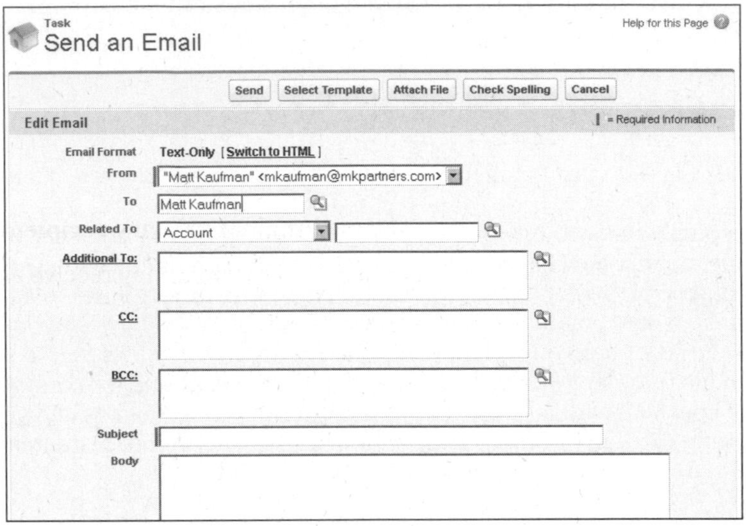

Task

Send an Email

Help for this Page

| Send | Select Template | Attach File | Check Spelling | Cancel |

Edit Email   **I** = Required Information

Email Format   Text-Only [Switch to HTML]
From   "Matt Kaufman" <mkaufman@mkpartners.com> ▾
To   Matt Kaufman
Related To   Account ▾
Additional To:
CC:
BCC:
Subject
Body

Figure 8-3:
Composing
an e-mail.

2. **Decide in what format you want to send your e-mail:**

   • *Switch to Text Only:* You want to send the message using only text — no HTML. A dialog box appears to warn you that any HTML formatting will be removed. When you click OK, the box disappears, and the format is switched.

   • *Switch to HTML:* Send your message in HTML format.

   If you decide to send your e-mail with HTML, you get an added bonus of being able to track your e-mail. See the later section "Tracking HTML e-mails."

3. **Type the recipient's name in the To field and then click the Lookup icon at the right of the field to search for the contact or lead.**

   A pop-up window appears, containing a search tool and a list of search results.

   If you send an e-mail from the relevant lead or contact record, you can eliminate this step because the To field is prefilled. But, remember to use the Related To field to associate the e-mail to other records, such as an opportunity.

4. **Select the correct person by clicking the name, or refine your search by modifying the name or using wildcards; then click Go.**

   When you select the recipient, the pop-up window disappears, and the To field is populated with your selection.

5. **Use the Related To drop-down list to associate the e-mail with the correct type of record, and then click the Lookup icon to the right of the adjacent field to find the exact record — similar to the process in Steps 3 and 4.**

   Depending on which record you started from, the Related To drop down list might already be filled.

6. **In the Additional To field, type additional primary recipient e-mails.**

   These folks get their e-mail on the To list when they receive and open your message. They don't have to be contacts or leads.

7. **Click the CC link or the BCC link to copy other contacts or users to the e-mail.**

   A pop-up window appears, containing a drop-down list for coworkers at your company and for contacts of the account.

8. **Select names in the Contacts list box, use the double arrows to include them as recipients, and then click Save.**

   The pop-up window disappears, and the CC and BCC fields reflect your selections.

9. **Click in the CC or BCC fields and add additional e-mail addresses, as needed.**

   Salesforce allows you to send e-mails to people who aren't contacts, leads, or users. Just type the e-mail address directly into this field.

   If you want to use an e-mail template, stop here and go to the next section.

10. **Complete the Subject and Body fields of the message and then click Send.**

    If your contact or lead in the To field doesn't yet have an e-mail address, this absence is flagged before you send the e-mail. A Click Here to Edit the Email Address link appears that you can click to associate an e-mail with the record without having to leave your Send an Email page.

    The record that you started from reappears, and a link to a copy of your e-mail appears in the Activity History related lists of the records that you linked.

Using e-mail templates

In the section "Building personal e-mail templates," earlier in this chapter, we show you how to create a personalized template. In this section, you find out how to send an e-mail that uses a template you created. First, create an e-mail (as described in the preceding section), and then follow these additional steps before you send it:

1. **Before you modify the Subject and Body fields, click the Select Template button at the top of the page.**

   A pop-up window appears, displaying a list of available templates.

2. **Click the Folder drop-down list and select the folder where you saved your template.**

   The pop-up window refreshes, displaying a list of available templates based on your folder selection, as shown in Figure 8-4.

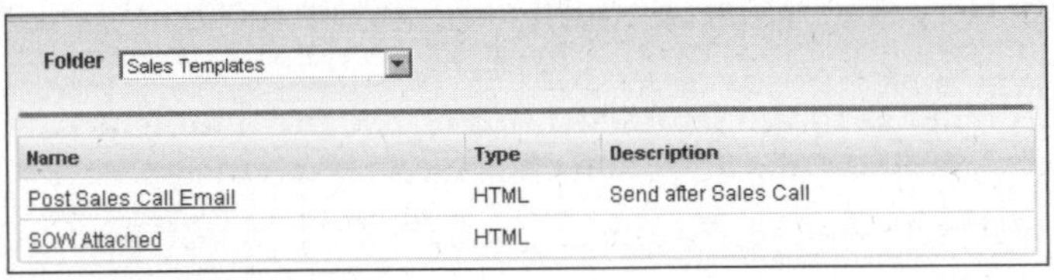

Figure 8-4:
Available
e-mail
templates.

Folder	Sales Templates ▼		
Name		**Type**	**Description**
Post Sales Call Email		HTML	Send after Sales Call
SOW Attached		HTML	

3. **Select the desired template by clicking the relevant link in the Name column.**

   The pop-up window disappears, and the page reappears with content based on the template that you selected.

4. **Modify the message to further personalize the e-mail and then click Send.**

   The record you started from reappears, and a link to a copy of your e-mail appears under the Activity History related lists of the linked records.

Sending Mass E-Mail

If you struggle to stay in touch with prospects or customers on a regular basis, you can use Salesforce to send mass e-mails and shorten your workload. Mass e-mail is particularly helpful for sales reps who send common messages that don't require high levels of personalization. For example, if you're an institutional sales rep selling shares of a hedge fund, you might want to send a monthly e-mail newsletter to sophisticated investors specifically interested in your fund.

When sending mass e-mail, Professional Edition users can send a maximum of 250 e-mails at a time. Enterprise Edition users can send as many as 500 e-mails, and Unlimited and Performance Edition users can send as many as 1,000 e-mails. A company is limited to 1,000 e-mails per day.

You can send a mass e-mail to contacts or leads — the method is similar.

To send out a mass e-mail, go to the Contacts home page or Leads home page, and follow these simple steps:

1. **Click the Mass Email Contacts link or the Mass Email Leads link (depending on which home page you're on) under the Tools section.**

   The Recipient Selection page appears.

2. **Specify the recipients that you want to include in the e-mail from the View drop-down list and click the Go button.**

   If you find the recipients you want, skip to Step 5.

3. **If you can't find the view that you want from the View drop-down list, click the Create New View link.**

   The Create New View page appears. In most circumstances, you need to create a custom view.

4. **To create the new view, fill in the information that you want to use to filter the recipients for your mass e-mail and then click Save.**

   For example, if you want to send an e-mail to all customer contacts located in New York, you can build a view. (See Chapter 4 for general details on how to create custom views.) When you click Save, the Recipient Selection page reappears, displaying a list of contacts that meet your criteria.

   Any of your leads or contacts that have the Email Opt Out check box selected are automatically omitted from these lists.

5. **Review the list and select the check boxes to designate the contacts to whom you want to send the mass e-mail.**

   Contacts or leads that don't have e-mail addresses lack an available check box in the Action column.

6. **When you're satisfied with your selections, click Next.**

   A Template Selection page appears, where you can select an e-mail template from the e-mail template folders and associated lists.

7. **Use the Folder drop-down list to locate the right folder and template.**

   You can skip this step if you already see the desired e-mail template on the list results.

8. **Select the desired e-mail template by selecting the appropriate radio button in the Name column, and then click Next.**

   A Preview Template appears.

9. **Review the content for the mass e-mail and then click Next.**

   A Confirmation page appears, summarizing the number of contacts that will receive the mass e-mail.

10. **Select the appropriate check boxes if you want to receive a blind copy, store an activity, and/or use your signature.**
11. **Give this mass e-mail a name in the Mass Email Name field.**
12. **Use the radio buttons to select whether you want to send the e-mail now or schedule it for delivery (set the time and date in the Schedule for Delivery On and Time Zone fields).**
13. **When you're done, click Send.**

    A Complete page appears, confirming the delivery of your mass e-mail.

Tracking E-Mail

By sending and storing important business-related e-mails in Salesforce, you and your teams can get a more complete picture of what's happening with your accounts, contacts, and so on. In the following sections, we show you the basic ways to view your e-mail records and a special feature in Salesforce that allows you to track HTML e-mails.

Viewing e-mails in Activity History

When you send an e-mail from Salesforce, a copy of your message is logged as a task record on the Activity History related list of related records. For example, if you send an e-mail from an opportunity record in Salesforce, you can view that e-mail from the related Opportunity, Contact, and Account detail pages. See Figure 8-5 for an example.

On an Activity History related list, you can also click the View All button if you want to see the completed activities (including e-mail) on a single page.

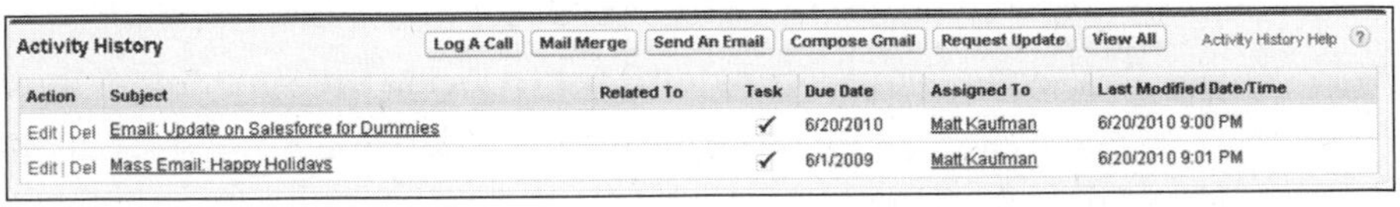

Action	Subject	Related To	Task	Due Date	Assigned To	Last Modified Date/Time
Edit | Del	Email: Update on Salesforce for Dummies		✓	6/20/2010	Matt Kaufman	6/20/2010 9:00 PM
Edit | Del	Mass Email: Happy Holidays		✓	6/1/2009	Matt Kaufman	6/20/2010 9:01 PM

Figure 8-5: Viewing e-mail records on an Activity History related list.

Tracking HTML e-mails

If you often wonder whether customers pay attention to e-mails that you send them, you can use the HTML Email Status related list for confirmation that the e-mail was opened. Sales reps can use this feature to see whether contacts and leads are opening and viewing important e-mails on quotes, proposals, and so on.

When you send an HTML e-mail from Salesforce, the e-mail is embedded with an invisible pixel that can be used for tracking.

You can view that e-mail not only from the Activity History related list but also from the HTML Email Status related list of a lead or contact record.

The HTML Email Status related list (see Figure 8-6) shows data on a number of key elements, including the dates the e-mail was sent, first opened, and last opened, as well as the total number of times it was opened. Although this information isn't a sure-fire way to determine whether your customer wants to buy, some reps use this feature to measure interest on a single e-mail or even mass e-mails.

Figure 8-6:
Viewing
e-mail
records on
an HTML
Email Status
related list.

HTML Email Status		Send An Email	View All			
Action	Subject		Date Sent	Date Opened	# Times Opened	Last Opened
Edit | Del	Email Update on Salesforce for Dummies		6/20/2010 9:00 PM	6/20/2010 9:07 PM	2	6/20/2010 9:40 PM

Integrating with Outlook e-mail

If your company uses Microsoft Outlook for e-mail, you can work from within that application and still track your e-mails in Salesforce. You may be accustomed to receiving and sending your e-mails from Outlook, so this Salesforce feature can help you capture both inbound and outbound e-mail on relevant records in Salesforce. For more information on using Salesforce for Outlook, see Chapter 3.

Part III

Driving Sales with Sales Cloud

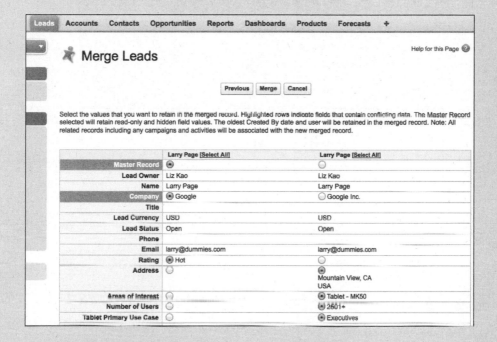

In this part . . .

- ✔ Learn how to track your prospects
- ✔ Organize your sales with Opportunities
- ✔ Manage your product catalog and price books

Chapter 9

Prospecting Leads

*O*ften, we hear frustrated salespeople say, "We could hit our numbers if we just had enough leads to fill our pipeline." Leads are the building blocks by which many companies drive their sales.

Loosely defined, a *lead* is a person or a company that might be interested in your services. Some organizations refer to them as *visitors* because those persons haven't shared any information about themselves yet. Others call them *prospects* because a lead has to be someone who has expressed interest in your service. Whatever your favorite terminology is, you can use leads to efficiently follow up on sales inquiries, aggressively attack new markets, and vastly improve your sales pipeline.

In this chapter, you can discover all the basic tricks you need to convert leads into revenue. You need to get your existing leads into Salesforce, organize them in a logical fashion, and update them when you follow up with them. Also, we discuss how to convert a lead into an actual opportunity that you can link to an account and a contact. If you're an online marketing or e-mail manager or administrator, we devote an entire section to how you can manage and maintain your lead database. Finally, we review how to expand your leads with Data.com.

Introducing the Lead Record

A *lead record* consists of a number of fields that you use to capture information about a potential lead. A lead record has only two modes: an Edit mode, in which you can modify the fields, and a Saved mode, in which you can view the fields and related lists.

The standard record comes predefined with several fields. Most of the terms are immediately clear, but if you want specific definitions, click the Help & Training link in the upper-right corner of Salesforce. In the following list, we describe the most important standard fields:

- **Lead Owner:** The person who owns the lead. If no one owns the lead, Salesforce can automatically place the lead in a queue. You can then assign the lead to a group of users (for example, "Corporate Sales — West Region"), who can take leads in the order in which they arrive in the queue.

- **Lead Status:** One of three required fields on a lead record. Lead Status is a drop-down list of values, and this field is critical if you want to follow a standard lead process. We talk more about lead status in the nearby sidebar "Building an effective lead process."

- **Lead Source:** A standard, but not required, field on a lead record. If you use it, you can define and track the sources of your leads by using this field.

Building an effective lead process

The key to a successful lead program that contributes to sales is a well-constructed lead process built into your Lead Status drop-down list. Salesforce provides a default list of four statuses: Open, Contacted, Qualified, and Unqualified. These statuses may appear straightforward, but they require definition because those four choices might not mirror your process or your terminology. The good news is that after you define the statuses, your administrator can quickly modify the values. The process starts with the Lead Status field, but it doesn't end there. Here are some additional suggestions for how you might construct your lean, mean, lead-generating machine:

- Build fields to capture qualification criteria.

- Make it clear at what point in the process a lead should be converted to an opportunity.

- Decide who'll manage the lead program and what that entails. Usually that's the same person who sends out e-mail campaigns. Make sure that he or she has sufficient permissions to administer the lead database.

- Figure out at what point in the process a lead should be deleted or archived.

- Set up queues, if it makes sense, to manage the workload and drive the competitive spirit.

- When you figure out your process, train your users so that everyone knows what's expected of him or her.

Lead sources are the originators of leads that come knocking at your door. These can be related to broad communication channels (a toll-free number, cold call, or web form, for example), more specific types of marketing venues (trade show, print ad, partner referral, and so on), or a blend of both. It's up to you. Always remember to balance your desire to get really granular data with the tolerance of the users who often have but a few seconds to customize this field (alongside other fields). And if you really want to track granular details of where leads are coming from, seriously consider using campaigns or a third-party marketing automation tool, described further in Chapter 13.

When you first get a lead, you'll likely want to qualify that lead to make sure that a sales opportunity really exists for you. For example, perhaps you want to be certain that the lead has the budget and a real interest and isn't just kicking tires. A marketing-qualified lead is a lead that meets your sales and marketing's teams qualification requirements to hand over the discussion to a salesperson. Teams in the Marketing or Sales department can own this responsibility.

You'll have your own definition of what qualifies as a lead, so jot it down, and then seek out someone to customize your lead record. (See Chapter 20 for the how-to details on building fields, rearranging your layouts, and other design tricks.) You'll have greater success with leads if you collect the right information.

Just like eating vegetables may be a reluctant chore for some of you, writing useful help text and descriptions for each field you create is vital to a healthy CRM system. It may seem laborious at first, and you may write terribly unhelpful descriptions. But fast-forward 6–18 months when new team members are scratching their heads wondering why certain fields were created and you can't remember why . . . do yourself and your teammates a favor. Write down who requested a field, and for what purpose.

Setting Up Your Leads

Before you can begin working your leads, you need to add the lead records into Salesforce. In the following sections, we show you three quick approaches for lead creation, and if needed, how to share your leads with the right people. Then, if you want to capture leads from your website, see Chapter 13 for details on generating Web-to-Lead forms.

Adding new leads

The best way to manually create a lead is to use the Create New drop-down list on the sidebar. To create a lead using this method, follow these simple steps:

1. **Select the Create Lead item from the Create New drop-down list.**

   A New Lead page appears in Edit mode, as shown in Figure 9-1. The only prefilled field is the Lead Status field.

Figure 9-1:
Filling out a
lead record.

2. **Fill in the fields as much as you can.**

   At a minimum, you must complete the Last Name and Company fields.

   You can add a list of target companies as leads, even if you don't yet know the names of the right people. In certain cases, you might have only the name of a company because you know you want to target it, but you don't yet know who to call. You can work with incomplete information. In these cases, we recommend that you type **?** or **unknown** in the Last Name field so that you know this information is missing.

3. **When you're done, click the Save button or the Save & New button.**

   - *Save:* The lead record appears in Saved mode, and your changes are displayed in the fields.

   - *Save & New:* Salesforce knows that salespeople commonly add multiple leads before working them. If you click Save & New, the lead is saved, and a New Lead page appears in Edit mode.

When entering or editing records, click the Save button or the Save & New button when you're done. Otherwise, you don't save the information that you just typed for that record. If you make this mistake and haven't yet logged out of Salesforce, try clicking the Back button on your browser (as opposed to hitting your head in frustration), which hopefully gets you back to the record in Edit mode. Then, click Save and breathe a sigh of relief.

Cloning an existing lead

If you're developing relationships within a particular company and want to enter multiple leads for that company, you can save time by cloning leads. For example, say that you already created a lead record for Sergey Brin at Google. When you talk to his assistant, she courteously refers you to Larry Page. In this case, cloning can save you many extra steps.

To clone a lead record from an existing lead, follow these steps:

1. **Click the Clone button at the top of the lead record.**

   A new lead record appears in Edit mode. All the information is identical to the previous lead record.

2. **Edit the information on the new lead, where appropriate.**

   Pay attention to what's prefilled because you want to avoid inaccurate information on the new lead record.

3. **Click Save when you're done.**

   The newly created lead reappears in Saved mode. To verify this, click the link to the older lead, which you can find in the Recent Items section on the sidebar.

Importing your leads

If you already have a file of leads, you probably want a faster way to get them into Salesforce than entering them manually. You must be an administrator to import leads, so if you're not, find your administrator, tell her what you're trying to do, and have her read this section.

Although you can import up to 50,000 leads at the same time as an administrator, test an import with five or so leads first, just to make sure that you know what you're doing. After the test data is imported, review your new lead records to make sure that they contain all the information that you want to have brought in. Delete the test records, refine your import file, and then run through the final import.

If you're a new salesperson who just came from a competitor and you happened to bring all your leads with you to upload into your new company's CRM system, hold up. It is terrible practice to dump in tens of thousands of unreviewed data into your nice CRM system. You're just moving potentially dirty data from an old home into a new one. Think that's someone else's problem? Just wait until people start going through it and finding quadruplicates, old job titles, and other pollution. Instead, take a more measured approach. Can you name the top 50 companies that you should be targeting? See how many leads are from any of those companies, and start with that as an upload. Broaden your range slowly.

To import lead files, follow these steps:

1. **On the Leads home page, click the Import Leads link at the bottom of the page, below the Tools heading.**

   The Lead Import Wizard page appears, providing you with a four-step process to import your records, plus helpful hints.

2. **In your existing lead file or system, compare your fields against the lead fields in Salesforce. Map all your fields between your current system and Salesforce.**

   If you can map all the necessary fields, move to the next step. If not, add fields to the lead record by customizing Salesforce. (See Chapter 20 for simple instructions on adding fields.)

   While someone is mapping the fields from your current system to Salesforce, you should also be talking with your company about cleaning up that data. Now's a good time to discuss which of your current system's fields are still needed in the new world. Some fields may have been used several years ago, but no one's been filling them in since you can remember, and no one's bothered to remove or hide them from the current system. Even worse, no one can recall what those fields were for, or maybe you have multiple fields with very similar names! Also, you could have lots of duplicate or partial records. Discuss with your company and your Salesforce consultant about best approaches to cleaning up this information.

   Mapping is a technical term for matching one field to another field, typically in different databases, to properly move data. For example, in Microsoft Outlook, you type a corporation's name into the Company field. In Salesforce, you typically use the Account Name field. These two different labels have the same meaning. Mapping is the process by which you decide that data from the Company field in Outlook should correspond to the Account Name field in Salesforce.

3. **Export your file.**

   You might have leads in an existing database or spreadsheet, such as Microsoft Excel, Oracle CRM On Demand, or Microsoft Dynamics. Most systems like these have simple tools for exporting data into various formats. Select the records and the fields that you want. Then, export the file and save it in a `.csv` format. If your leads are already in spreadsheet format (such as Excel), just resave the file in `.csv` format.

4. **Review your lead data.**

   You've probably heard the old adage "garbage in, garbage out." Regardless of whether your company spent some time with initial housecleaning before this step, it's important to review this data again at this point. Clean up your information before you bring it into Salesforce so that you can save yourself the effort later.

5. **When you're done with the preparation, click the Start the Import Wizard link on the Lead Import Wizard.**

   A pop-up window labeled Step 1 of 3: Upload the File appears, as shown in Figure 9-2.

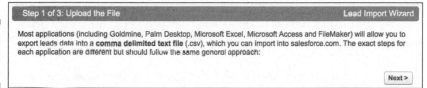

Step 1 of 3: Upload the File   Lead Import Wizard

Most applications (including Goldmine, Palm Desktop, Microsoft Excel, Microsoft Access and FileMaker) will allow you to export leads data into a **comma delimited text file** (.csv), which you can import into salesforce.com. The exact steps for each application are different but should follow the same general approach:

Next >

Figure 9-2:
Uploading
the lead file.

6. **Complete the fields in Step 1 of the wizard.**

   Assuming that you already prepared your file, you probably just need to follow these steps:

   a. *Load the file by clicking the Choose File button and selecting the correct file on your computer.*

   b. *Select a default lead source, if relevant.*

   c. *Apply an assignment rule if you want leads to route directly to assigned reps.*

   If you don't use an assignment rule, all the leads that you import are assigned to you unless you otherwise specify a lead owner in the file. (See the section "Creating assignment rules for automatic routing," later in this chapter.)

   d. *Select the check box if you want to use assignment rule settings to send e-mail notifications to the record owners.*

   e. *Verify the character coding.*

   Salesforce prefills this picklist based on your company profile, and you rarely have to change it.

   f. *Select the matching type.*

   If you want Salesforce to avoid importing duplicate records, choose whether you want to identify a duplicate lead by matching Salesforce ID, name, or e-mail. If a lead record with the matching criteria already exists in Salesforce, that record is updated with the information in your file.

   g. *Select the check box if you want to trigger workflow rules to new and updated records.*

   See Chapter 20 for tips on improving workflow.

7. **When you're done with Step 1 of the wizard, click Next.**

   The Field Mapping page appears.

8. **Map the fields between your file and Salesforce and then click Next.**

   The Field Mapping page displays all the Salesforce lead fields as labels with drop-down lists that correspond to the fields in your file. Simply go through the list of fields and select the field from the corresponding file that you're importing which maps to the Salesforce field, as shown in Figure 9-3.

   After you click Next, the Review and Confirm page appears, displaying a list of warnings, if any, on your impending import.

9. **Review the messages for possible errors.**

   This step basically warns you about problems with the data or lets you know about fields that you haven't mapped. If you discover an error, you can click the Back button and refine your mapping, or even close the wizard so that you can improve your import file. You might have to start over, but at least you avoid importing bad or incomplete data.

10. **When you're satisfied with your mapping, click the Import Now button.**

    An Importing page appears to let you know that the import is in progress, including an estimate of how long it will take.

11. **Click the Finish button.**

    The pop-up window closes.

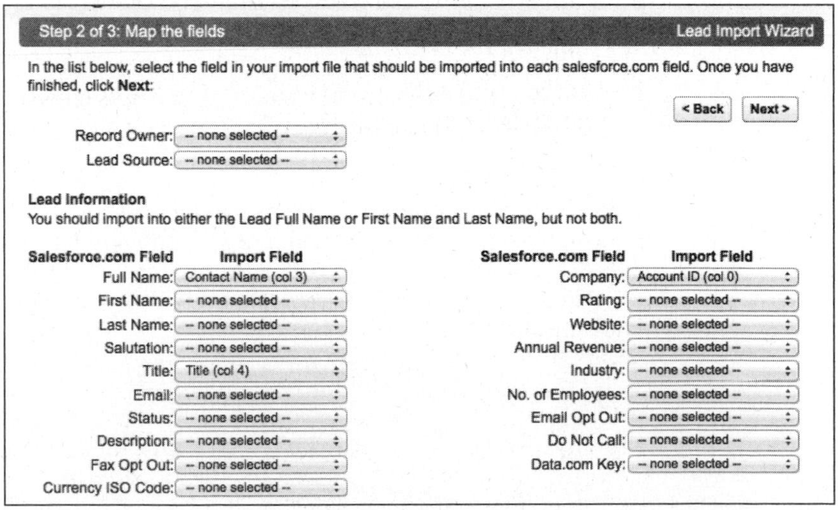

Figure 9-3: Mapping the lead fields.

Breaking into unchartered waters

A leading Internet performance-monitoring company wanted to sell its services to a variety of new, untested markets. This salesforce.com customer had a stronghold in financial services but wanted to extend its client base to other Fortune 500 companies. Because of the specific nature of its business, the actual names of the decision makers that it wanted to target was publicly unavailable.

Marketing simply imported the Fortune 500 list and set the Last Name field as Unknown. Then, the company used Salesforce and a team of sales development reps to generate leads and set up appointments between actual buyers and the company's outside field sales reps. In just a few short months, this use of Salesforce dramatically helped improve qualified lead generation and increased the pipeline and new bookings while breaking ground in new markets.

12. **Check the lead records that you imported.**

   Salesforce sends you an e-mail after your file has been successfully imported. To check your handiwork, click the Leads tab to go to your Leads home page. In the View drop-down list, select Today's Leads to see a list of the leads that were created today. Click the link for a lead that you just imported and review the information for accuracy.

Importing leads is one of the fastest ways for you to set up your leads in Salesforce so that you can begin working them.

Organizing Your Leads

When you have some leads in Salesforce, you want to organize them to make them productive. When we work with companies, we often hear this request from salespeople: "I just want to see my data, and it needs to be the way that I want to look at it." Just like Goldilocks, you want your leads to look just right.

In the following sections, we show you how you can use views on the Leads home page to provide greater focus for you and your sales teams. Then, for even more robust organization of your lead information, see Chapter 17 for specifics on how to build custom lead reports.

Using lead views

When you select a view, you're basically specifying criteria to limit the results that you get back. For example, if you're one of many sales reps, you might not want to waste your time sifting through all your company's leads; you want to see just the ones that you own. With Salesforce, you can do that in one click. On the Leads home page, Salesforce comes with four predefined views:

- **All Open Leads:** Provides a list of all the lead records in which the Lead Status is still Open
- **My Unread Leads:** Gives you a list of your leads that you haven't yet viewed
- **Today's Leads:** Shows you only leads that were created today
- **Recently Viewed Leads:** Allows you to look at a list of recently viewed leads

To try out a preset view, go to the Leads home page and follow these steps (as shown in Figure 9-4):

1. **Click the navigation arrow in the View drop-down list.**

   The four options in the preceding bulleted list appear, maybe along with some other choices that have been created for you.

2. **Select one of the views.**

   For example, if you select the My Unread Leads view, a list page appears, displaying any of your unread leads. From this list page, you can perform a variety of standard operations, including editing, deleting, and viewing a record. See Chapter 2 for details on using list pages.

Figure 9-4: Previewing lead views on the Leads home page.

Creating custom lead views

For many users, the preset views are a good start. If you want special lists for the way that you follow up on your leads, though, build custom views. For example, if you call only on companies in the manufacturing industry located in the state of Florida with revenue over one billion dollars, take a minute and build a custom view. This custom view is always accessible to you, thus saving you time.

To create a view from scratch, follow these simple steps:

1. **On the Leads home page, to the right of the View drop-down list, click the Create New View link.**

   A Create New View page appears, which includes a wizard to help create your view, as shown in Figure 9-5.

2. **Enter a name for the view.**

   For example, you might call the view Big Florida Manufacturers.

3. **Decide whether you want this view to search the entire leads database, your leads, or a queue.**

   If your company's marketing department uses Salesforce's campaign feature, you can further limit your view to leads associated with a specific campaign.

4. **Under the Specify Filter Criteria step, select the criteria for your search.**

   A basic criteria query is made up of three elements:

   - *Field:* The first box is a drop-down list that contains all the fields on the lead record. For example, you could choose the Industry field.

   - *Operator:* The second box is a drop-down list that contains operators for your search. That sounds complicated, but it's easier than you think. Taking the example from the preceding bullet, you'd select Equals from the drop-down list.

   - *Value:* In the third box, you type the value that you want in the search. For this example, you'd type **manufacturing**.

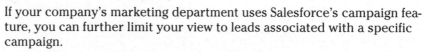

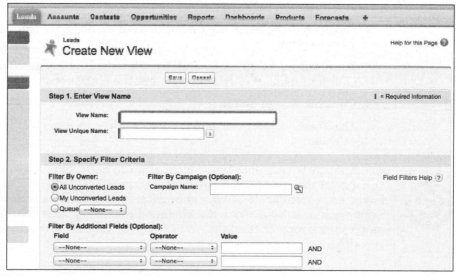

Figure 9-5:
Building a custom lead view.

5. **Select the columns that you want to be displayed on your list page.**

   Although Salesforce's preset views display common fields, such as Email and State, you can select as many as 15 lead fields to display on your list page.

6. **Under the Restrict Visibility step, decide whether you want others to see your custom view and select the appropriate radio button.**

   Your decision is made simple if the Visibility step doesn't appear. Otherwise, think about whether other users can benefit from this view when you complete this step.

7. **When you're done, click Save.**

   You're taken to a new list page, which is completely customized based on the search criteria that you chose in Step 4.

Accepting leads from a queue

If you're a rep assigned to a queue, you can access the queue in the View drop-down list on the Leads home page. The queue list page looks just like a regular list page, but you can use it to grab and claim leads. (See the section "Making use of lead queues," later in this chapter, for details on setting up queues.)

To pull leads from a queue and make them your own, go to the Leads home page and follow these steps:

1. **Select the queue name from the View drop-down list.**

   The queue list page appears.

2. **Select check boxes in the Action column to the left of leads that you want to claim.**

   Your manager might have specific guidelines. This is your chance to click into some records and try to pick the hottest leads.

3. **Click the Accept button.**

   The queue list page reappears, minus the lead or leads that you selected.

 Another way to keep your leads organized is to make sure that multiple versions of the same person don't show up in Salesforce. This can wreak havoc as people update activity information on different records for the same person. Salesforce detects whether duplicate records already exist and merges them for you. Read the next section to see how to de-duplicate lead records.

Following Up on Leads

After you receive a new lead, you want a quick way to follow up and determine what you caught: a big one, a warm one, or just another person kicking tires. Your company might already have a standard lead qualification process, but the following sections talk about some of the ways that you can use Salesforce to pursue leads.

Finding and merging duplicate lead records

Before following up on a new lead, click the Find Duplicates button on the specific lead record to see whether a record already exists. You probably know that duplicates frequently occur with leads. For example, if you capture leads from your website, the same visitor might fill in your web form multiple times, even with the best of intentions. Instead of wasting your time or upsetting the existing lead, check first for duplicates.

By checking for duplicates, you might increase your chances of a qualified lead. When you merge duplicate records, the remaining record inherits not only the information you select but also linked records on related lists.

To merge lead records, you must be the lead owner of the records, the lead owner's manager (that is, the lead owner must be subordinate to you in the role hierarchy), or a system administrator.

To find and merge duplicate leads, follow these steps:

1. **Go to a lead record that you suspect or know has duplicates.**

2. **Click the Find Duplicates button at the top of the lead record.**

   A Search for Duplicates page appears, in five sections. The first section determines how you want to search Salesforce for duplicates. By default, Salesforce looks for a duplicate with a matching name, company, e-mail address, or phone number. The remaining four sections show any matching lead, contact, account, or opportunity records, based on the default matching criteria.

3. **Select or deselect search criteria boxes to narrow or expand your search. Click the Search button to return updated results.**

   Records matching any of the selected search criteria appear in their appropriate sections.

4. **Review the duplicate lead records and select a maximum of three records to merge.**

   In Salesforce, you can merge only three records at a time.

5. **Click the Merge Leads button in the Matching Leads related list.**

   A Merge Leads page appears, displaying, side by side, the selected records and any fields that have been completed, as shown in Figure 9-6.

6. **Compare the information and select the radio buttons to choose the values that you want to retain.**

   At the top of each column, you can also choose to keep all the values from one record by clicking the Select All link.

7. **When you finish reviewing, click the Merge button.**

   A pop-up window appears, prompting you to validate that you want to perform the merge. After you click OK, the merged lead reappears. Any records from related lists are kept.

Tracking leads with related lists

How can you remember all the interactions that took place with a lead? Some of us have a hard enough time remembering what we did yesterday, let alone three weeks ago with 200 leads. Related lists on a lead record can help you capture all that information so that it's at your fingertips the next time you talk to a lead.

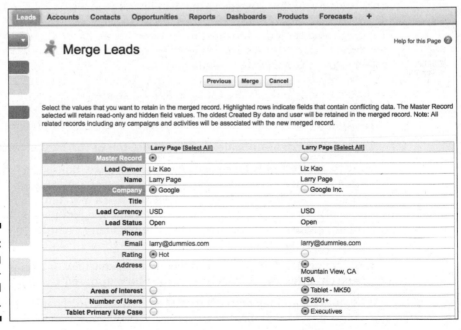

Figure 9-6: Merging duplicate lead records.

If you're looking for typical ways that salespeople use lead-related lists on a lead record, read the following list for an example:

- ✔ **Log a Call:** The next time you respond to a lead and want to record what you said, click the Log a Call button and enter the details.

- ✔ **New Task:** You plan to call the lead back next Friday when you know that the gatekeeper is on vacation. Click New Task and set a tickler for yourself for Friday. (See Chapter 7 for details on how to fill out a new task record.)

- ✔ **Send an Email:** You get through to the lead, and he asks you to send him an introductory e-mail about your company. Click the Send an Email button to send and track the e-mail directly from Salesforce. We talk more about sending e-mail through Salesforce in Chapter 8.

- ✔ **New Event:** The lead agrees to a demo. Click New Event and schedule a meeting so that you don't forget.

Updating lead fields

In the course of your lead qualification, you inevitably collect pertinent information that you want to save directly on the lead record. Every time you capture important data on your lead, update your lead record by doing the following:

1. **Double-click a field on the lead record to modify that field.**

   If you see a padlock icon in that field, you can't modify it. Check with your system administrator to find out whether he specifically locked this field, or whether it's one of those important system fields that Salesforce doesn't allow anyone to change.

2. **Complete the fields, as necessary, to determine whether the lead is qualified.**

3. **Update the Lead Status field when you make progress.**

   Even if you discover that the lead is a waste of your time, that's progress.

4. **Click Save when you're done making changes.**

At some point, you might decide that a lead can't become a qualified opportunity at this time. In that case, you can archive the lead by changing its status. Archiving inactive leads allows you to get a sense of how many leads are still being worked.

Converting qualified leads

When you decide that a lead is actually a qualified opportunity, you can start using Salesforce's full opportunity tracking system. To do so, you must convert the lead to an opportunity. This conversion gives you two benefits:

✓ **Converting a lead to an opportunity allows you to track multiple contacts within an account, which you can do more easily than tracking a single individual lead.**

In other words, if you have ten leads from Microsoft, none of them are linked with each other in Salesforce. But, by converting a lead, you create an account called Microsoft and you link all the Microsoft coworkers as contacts for the same account.

✓ **Your goal is to ABC (always be closing), so the sooner you can start managing opportunities and not just leads, the healthier your pipeline and wallet.**

For a qualified lead, your sales process begins where your lead process ends.

When deciding whether to add names of companies or businesspeople as leads or as accounts with contacts, remember that the leads module of Salesforce is nonrelational from lead to lead. If you're serious about going after a particular company, and the inter-relationships of business contacts will be important, we recommend that you add the target as an account, rather than as a lead.

To convert a lead to an opportunity, follow these steps:

1. **Click the Convert button on a lead record that you want to convert.**

   The Convert button is located at the top and bottom of the lead record. A Convert Lead page appears; see Figure 9-7.

2. **Complete the required fields.**

   Required fields are highlighted in red. Here's a summary:

   - *Record Owner:* If the lead owner remains the record owner, don't change the selection. If the owner changes, click the Lookup icon and choose from the list of users. Select the Send Email to the Owner check box, if needed.

   - *Account Name:* If Salesforce doesn't find an account that closely matches the Company field from your lead, it creates a new account record. In the event that it does find a match, select an option from the drop-down list, depending on whether you want to create a new account or associate the lead to the existing account.

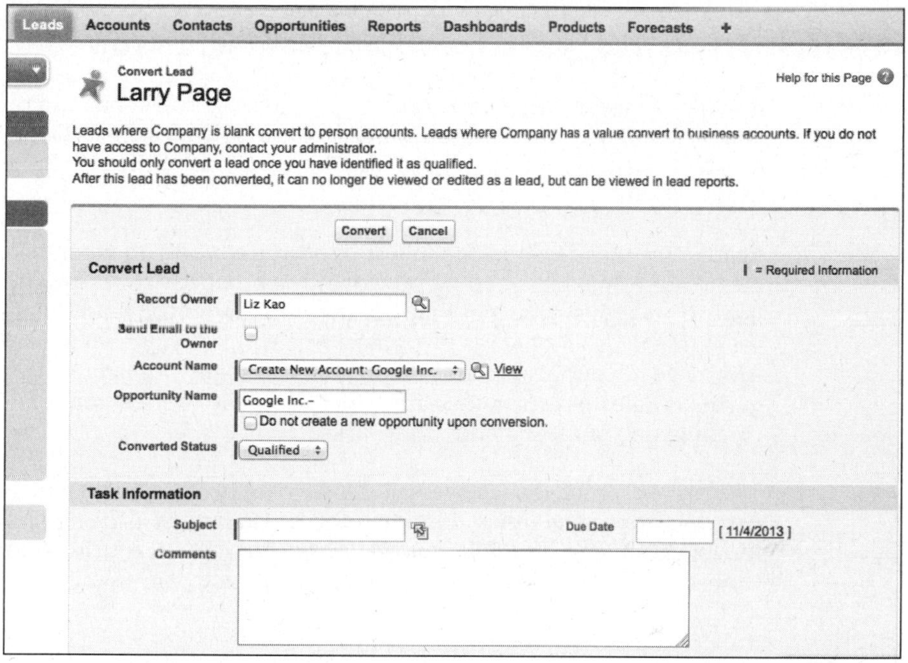

Figure 9-7:
Converting a
lead.

- *Opportunity Name:* If you want to create an opportunity, complete this field by giving the opportunity a name. (We typically recommend that the name of an opportunity be the account name followed by a hyphen and then a summary of the product interest. For example: Amazon – New Hardware.) You don't have to always create an opportunity record when you convert a lead. Sometimes, the lead that you're converting is associated with an existing opportunity. In these situations, select the Do Not Create a New Opportunity upon Conversion check box to avoid creating a new opportunity. Then, see Chapter 10 for details on how to link contacts to existing opportunities.

- *Converted Status:* Salesforce prefills this field with the default value that your company has chosen for a qualified lead. Don't change this field unless your company has multiple selections for a qualified lead.

- *Task Information:* You can create a follow-up task right in these fields, but you don't have to. Complete these fields only if it saves you a step.

3. **When you're done, click the Convert button.**

    If Salesforce finds a contact record that matches your lead, you can then decide to associate it with the existing contact record. Otherwise, a contact record appears for your former lead. That contact is linked to an account corresponding to the lead's Company field, and all associated records from related lists are carried over. If you chose to create an opportunity in Step 2, you can see the opportunity on both the account and contact record's Opportunity related lists.

Maintaining Your Lead Database

If you're a system administrator or a lead manager who has the right permissions (we specify those permissions in the following sections), one of your greatest challenges is managing what hopefully will become a large pool of leads.

Lead databases can become unwieldy over time, so you need to keep them clean. For example, say that you work for a company that regularly collects leads from industry conferences. Someone who hadn't read this book ended up importing a lot of leads into Salesforce without any review beforehand. After a year, your leads database might have many duplicates and plenty of garbage. Salesforce provides a number of simple tools to make short work of cleaning up your leads and other tasks.

The biggest problems we see with leads involve assigning, identifying duplicate records and merging them together (also known as *de-duping*), transferring, archiving, and deleting. We know: You hate to get rid of anything. However, sometimes it's necessary and relatively painless.

Making use of lead queues

If you have a sales team made up of multiple people (often called sales development reps, or SDRs) responsible for harvesting leads collectively, you might want to set up lead queues. For example, some companies hire SDRs to handle leads on a first-come, first-served basis. You might just find that your reps work harder if they all have an equal chance to go after a fresh pool of leads.

If you're an administrator or user who has permission to customize Salesforce, you can set up lead queues. Follow these steps:

1. **Choose Setup⇨Administer⇨Manage Users⇨Queues.**

   A Queues page appears.

2. **Click New to create a new queue.**

   The New Queue page appears in Edit mode, as shown in Figure 9-8.

3. **Name the queue and specify the Lead object to associate with this queue.**

4. **Add members to the queue.**

   Members can be users, groups, or roles in your company who'll be part of the queue. For example, you might label the queue Western Field Sales and then choose users who make up the Western Sales team.

New Queue

Help for this Page ❓

Queue Edit   [Save] [Cancel]

Queue Name and Email Address   ▌ = Required Information

Enter the name of the queue and the email address to use when sending notifications (for example, when a case has been put in the queue). The email address can be for an individual or a distribution list. When an object is assigned to a queue, only the queue members will be notified.

Label [   ]

Queue Name [   ] [i]

Queue Email [   ]

Send Email to   ☐
Members

Supported Objects

Select the objects you want to assign to this queue. Individual records for those objects can then be owned by this queue.

Available Objects | | **Selected Objects**

Available Objects		Selected Objects
Ad Group		Lead
Case		
Case Swarm Rule		
Catalog	Add	
Feed Post Swarm Rule	▶	
Google Campaign	◀	
Keyword		
Knowledge Article Version	Remove	
Lead Swarm Rule		
News		
Opportunity Swarm Rule		
Search Phrase		

Figure 9-8:
Creating a
new lead
queue.

5. **When you're done, click Save.**

   You can now use this queue when you organize and reassign lead records.

REMEMBER

Lead queues can be viewed in the same place on your Leads home page where you view your custom lead views. The name of the lead queue is automatically added to the drop-down list for the lead views. Pretty neat, huh?

Creating assignment rules for automatic routing

If your company generates a lot of leads, assignment rules can help distribute the workload and get leads to the right users. Assignment rules give you a better chance to keep leads from becoming stagnant. A lead *assignment rule* is a feature that lets the administrator define who should receive a lead and under what conditions. For example, if your reps have sales territories defined by ZIP Codes or countries, you can use those ZIP Codes or countries to dictate who gets what leads.

To create a lead assignment rule, follow these steps:

1. **Choose Setup⇨Build⇨Customize⇨Leads⇨Assignment Rules.**

   If you haven't yet set the default lead owner, the Lead Settings page appears, asking you to select the default lead owner. The buck stops with this person or queue, as far as lead routing goes. After you make this selection, Salesforce returns you to the Lead Assignment Rules page.

2. **Click New to create a new assignment rule.**

   The New Lead Assignment Rule page appears in Edit mode.

3. **Enter a title in the Rule Name field, select the check box if you want to make it the active assignment rule, and click the Save button.**

   The Lead Assignment Rule page reappears. You can have only one active rule at any time, but the rule can have multiple entries. Click the rule name to go to the detail page for that rule.

4. **Click New in the Rule Entries related list.**

   A Rule Entry Edit page appears.

5. **Complete the steps as follows:**

   a. *Enter a number in the Order field to set the order.*

   b. *Select criteria to define the rule.*

   See the section "Creating custom lead views," earlier in this chapter, for details on selecting criteria. In this case, you might enter **ZIP Code Equals 02474**.

   c. *Use the drop-down list and Lookup icon to select the user or queue.*

   d. *Use the Lookup icon to choose an Email Notification Template.*

   You can set the assignment rules to send e-mail alerts to recipients of new leads.

6. **When done, click the Save button or the Save & New button.**

   - *Save:* The New Lead Assignment Rule page reappears.

   - *Save & New:* A new Rule Entry Edit page appears, and you can repeat Steps 5 and 6 until you finish.

Transferring leads

You might need to transfer leads for a variety of reasons. For instance, after you set up your lead records in Salesforce, you need to give them to the right people on a different team. Or maybe some reps just weren't following up, so you took their leads away after swatting their noses with a rolled-up newspaper.

To transfer leads, you must be an administrator or a user with Manage Leads and Transfer Leads permissions. If you want to reassign many leads at the same time, take these steps:

1. **From the Leads home page, select a view from which you can see some leads that you want to reassign.**

   The list page appears.

2. **In the Action column of the lead list, select the check boxes to the left of the lead records that you want to assign to someone else.**

3. **Click the Change Owner button at the top of the page.**

   The Change Lead Owner page appears.

4. **Select the user or queue that you intend to reassign leads to, and then click Save.**

   The lead list reappears, and the lead owners have been changed. The new lead owner can be optionally notified via e-mail of this ownership change. Just select the Send Notification Email check box before clicking the Save button.

If you're an administrator, you can use the Mass Transfer Leads tool in Setup to accomplish the same goals of reassigning en masse. See Chapter 22 for details on mass-transferring leads.

If you're reassigning one lead at a time, you can transfer ownership directly from a lead record. Follow these steps:

1. **On the lead record, to the right of the Lead Owner field, click the Change link.**

   The link is in square brackets. The Change Lead Owner page appears.

2. **Select the user or queue that you're assigning the lead to.**

   You use this same page when you're assigning multiple leads, but here, you can choose to notify the recipient with an e-mail.

3. **(Optional) Select the Send Notification check box to notify the new owner of the reassignment.**

4. **When you're done, click Save.**

   The lead record reappears, displaying your ownership change.

Changing the status of multiple records

An administrator or a user who has Manage Leads and Transfer Leads permissions can change the status of multiple records at the same time. This feature comes in handy if, during a process, a lead manager reviews leads prior to assigning them to reps.

To change the status of multiple leads at the same time, follow these steps:

1. **From the Leads home page, select a view.**

   The list page appears.

2. **In the Action column of the lead list, select the check boxes to the left of the lead records that require a status change.**

   To select all the leads in this view, select the check box to the left of the Action column header, which selects all the leads on this page.

   For example, if you're eyeballing a list of leads from a trade show, you might select obviously bogus leads.

3. **Click the Change Status button at the top of the page.**

   The Change Status page appears.

4. **Select a status from the New Status drop-down list and click Save.**

   The lead list reappears.

If you require industrial-strength de-duplication tools, a number of proven technology partners handle de-duplication with Salesforce, plus a variety of other data management tasks. You can check out these offerings on the AppExchange directory by searching for "Data Cleansing" in the search bar.

Mass-deleting lead records

Periodically, be sure to delete records that are unqualified or of no value to your company. You must be an administrator to mass-delete records.

Some companies add a To Be Deleted value to their Lead Status field to denote garbage. Then, periodically, the administrator deletes those records.

If you want to delete multiple records at a time, follow these steps:

1. **On the Leads home page, click the Mass Delete Leads link below the Tools heading.**

   A Mass Delete Leads page appears, including a three-step deletion wizard.

2. **Review the steps and then type the search criteria for the leads that you want to delete.**

   For example, if you want to delete unqualified leads, enter a filter in which Lead Status Equals Unqualified.

3. **Click the Search button.**

   The page reappears, displaying your results at the bottom of the page.

4. **Select all records or just the records that you want to delete by selecting the appropriate check boxes.**

   To select all the search results for deletion, click the Select All link at the top of the list.

5. **Click the Delete button after you complete selecting the records for deletion.**

   The search results are updated to omit the record(s) you deleted.

 When deleting records, always be cautious, but don't overly stress out. When you delete records, that information is placed in your Recycle Bin, and you can access as many as 5,000 records for 30 days. To undelete a record, click the Recycle Bin link on your sidebar, find the record, and undelete it. Then, count your blessings and breathe into a paper bag until the panic attack subsides.

Building Your Lead Database with Data.com

Data.com (www.data.com) is an online source of millions of business professionals and Dun & Bradstreet (D&B) information about companies. It's used to compare, update, and clean lead information in your Salesforce org, against information that exists with D&B. Data.com's partnership with D&B provides the industrial-strength, third-party validation of lead information, because many people who sign up for things online can often use as little real information as possible when they're in the early stages of researching a product. A free, light version (Data.com Connect) is even available if you don't have much of a budget, and it's based on a very simple quid pro quo model. For businesspeople researching others, in particular companies or industries, Data.com Connect lets you view people's phone and e-mail information in exchange for submitting or updating the contact information of someone within your network. I scratch your back, you scratch mine, as the saying goes.

Data.com is a nifty add-on feature that helps both update and expand your leads (and accounts and contacts). Here's a high-level overview on how it works:

1. From within Salesforce, it flags any of your lead data when a discrepancy exists between the information you have and what's in Data.com.

   You get to choose which lead fields Data.com reviews to determine this and which flagged records you want to be updated. Don't worry: You can also lock certain records so that they're not reviewed.

2. You can mine Data.com for new leads based on certain criteria (like Industry = Manufacturing, State = California, Company Revenue = $500 million – $1 billion) that you choose, to build your own custom prospecting list. Data.com searches its database for matches and adds them to your Salesforce database on a regular basis.

Data.com has a few different products to help with each aspect of de-duping or list building. To get more information, visit its website's Products section at www.data.com/products.

Chapter 10

Tracking Opportunities

*Y*our sales pipeline is the lifeblood of your business. It's the list of deals that can help you achieve your sales targets. But try as you might, you can probably never close every deal in your pipeline. Things happen: Budgets get slashed, projects get tabled, you lose to a competitor, decision makers change. So, you need enough deals to give yourself the chance to hit and exceed your revenue goals in a given time frame.

An *opportunity* in Salesforce is a sales deal that you want to track to an ultimate conclusion (ideally, a win). The opportunity record has tools to help you efficiently track and close a sale. By using Salesforce, you can manage more opportunities at the same time and pursue each opportunity with greater precision. For example, if you're a Salesforce sales rep, you can use opportunities to follow a standard process, link distribution partners, associate products, strategize against competition, record your actions and other notes, and more. And you don't have to waste precious time updating a pipeline spreadsheet. Instead, you or your manager can generate the current pipeline with the click of a button.

In this chapter, we show you the techniques and best practices for using opportunities to track sales. First, you find out the most reliable way to create opportunities. Then, we discuss how to view them in the manner that makes sense to you. You can also discover how to update your records so that your information is current.

Getting Familiar with the Opportunity Record

An *opportunity record* is the collection of fields that make up the information on a deal you're tracking. The record has only two modes: In Edit mode, you modify fields; in View mode, you view the fields and the opportunity's related lists.

An opportunity record comes preconfigured with several standard fields. Most of these fields are self-explanatory, but be sure to pay attention to these critical ones:

- ✔ **Amount:** This field displays the intended, best-guess amount of the sale. Depending on the way your company calculates the pipeline report, you might use numbers that include total contract value, the bookings amount, and so on.

- ✔ **Close Date:** Use this required field for your best guess as to when you'll close this deal. Depending on your company's sales process, the close date has different definitions, but this field is commonly used to track the date that you signed all the paperwork required to book the sale.

- ✔ **Expected Revenue:** This read-only field is automatically generated by multiplying the Amount field by the Probability field.

- ✔ **Forecast Category:** This field is typically hidden, but every opportunity automatically includes a value. Each sales stage within the Stage drop-down list corresponds to a default forecast category so that higher-probability opportunities contribute to your overall forecast after they reach certain stages.

- ✔ **Opportunity Owner:** This person in your organization owns the opportunity. Although an opportunity record has only one owner, many users can still collaborate on an opportunity.

- ✔ **Opportunity Name:** This required text field represents the name of the specific deal as you want it to appear on your list of opportunities or on a pipeline report.

When naming opportunities, you and your company should define a standard naming convention for the Opportunity Name field so that you can easily search for and distinguish opportunities from a list. We recommend that the opportunity name start with the account name, then a hyphen, and then the name of the customer's project or the product of primary interest. This naming convention makes for readable reports later.

✔ **Private:** If you want to keep an opportunity private, select this check box to render the record accessible to only you, your bosses, and the system administrator. This field isn't available in Team Edition.

✔ **Probability:** The *probability* is the confidence factor associated with the likelihood that you'll win the opportunity. Each sales stage that your company defines is associated with a default probability to close. Typically, you don't need to edit this field; it gets assigned automatically by the Stage option that you pick. In fact, your administrator might remove write access from this field altogether.

✔ **Stage:** This required field allows you to track your opportunities, following your company's established sales process. Salesforce provides a set of standard drop-down list values common to solution selling, but your system administrator can modify these values.

✔ **Type:** Use this drop-down list to differentiate the types of opportunities that you want to track. Most customers use the Type drop-down list to measure new versus existing business and products versus services, but your system administrator can modify it to measure other important or more specific deal types, such as add-ons, upsells, work orders, and so on.

When customizing your opportunity fields, take into consideration the patience and attention span of your end users. Keep the record as simple as possible to ensure that all your important fields actually get filled in. If you add many fields, you might make the opportunity record harder to use, which then puts user adoption of Salesforce at risk. At the same time, you'll have greater success with opportunities when you can easily capture what you want to track.

Entering Opportunities

Before you can begin using Salesforce to close opportunities, first you must get the records into Salesforce. In the following sections, we discuss the best ways to create opportunities so that they link to the correct accounts, contacts, and other records.

Adding new opportunities

The best method for creating a new opportunity is to start from the relevant account or contact record, which guarantees that the opportunity associates to the correct record, making the opportunity easily trackable. And, if you add the opportunity from a contact, you link both the account and the contact at the same time.

To create an opportunity, go to the relevant Account or Contact detail page and follow these steps:

1. **Select the Create Opportunity option from the Create New drop-down list on the sidebar.**

   Alternatively, scroll down the detail page to the Opportunities related list and click the New button. The result is the same. The Edit mode of a new opportunity appears; see Figure 10-1. The Account Name field is conveniently filled in for you.

2. **Fill in the fields as much as you can or as required.**

   At a minimum, you must complete the required fields. Depending on how you set up your opportunity record, you might have to fill in other required fields, which are highlighted in red. See the section "Getting Familiar with the Opportunity Record," earlier in this chapter, for more details on common required fields.

3. **Click Save when you're done.**

   The Opportunity detail page appears. You can click the Edit button on this page at any time if you need to modify the record.

   If you have the good fortune to need to enter multiple opportunities, one after another, instead of clicking the Save button, click the Save & New button. A new opportunity record appears in Edit mode. You have to fill in the Account Name field, but this technique can save you time.

Figure 10-1:
Completing opportunity fields.

| Accounts | Contacts | Opportunities | Reports | Dashboards | Products | Forecasts | ✦ |

Opportunity Edit
New Opportunity   Help for this Page

Opportunity Edit   Save   Save & New   Cancel

Opportunity Information | = Required Information

Opportunity Owner	Liz Kao	Close Date	[11/5/2013]
Opportunity Name		Stage	--None--
Account Name		Probability (%)	0
Type	--None--	Amount	
		Next Step	

Additional Information

Areas of Interest	--None--	Lead Source	--None--
Tablet Primary Use Case	--None--	Primary Campaign Source	
Number of Users	--None--		
Primary Competitor	--None--		

Description Information

| Description | |

Cloning an opportunity

If you commonly create opportunities that are similar to each other, use the cloning feature to reduce unnecessary retyping. For example, if you're an account manager who creates work order opportunities for additional purchases from the same customer, you might want to clone an existing record and change the details.

To clone an opportunity, go to the opportunity record that you want to clone and follow these steps:

1. **Click the Clone button at the top of the record.**

   A new Opportunity Edit page appears, prefilled with all the data from the previous record.

2. **Modify the fields, as necessary.**

   Pay close attention to content in required fields such as Close Date, Stage, and Opportunity Name because the information prefilled in those fields might be incorrect for the new opportunity. Review data in other fields to ensure that the information is applicable to this new opportunity.

3. **When you're done, click Save.**

   An Opportunity detail page for your cloned opportunity appears.

If your company has legacy databases that contain deal information and you want this data to be in Salesforce as opportunities, you can't use an import wizard to migrate your records like you can with leads, accounts, and contacts. If this is a current challenge, seek out your technical staff, system administrator, Salesforce rep, or a Salesforce consultant. With business guidance, a person with the technical know-how can use the Apex Data Loader to import opportunities and other records into Salesforce, which can help you avoid wasting time manually re-inputting opportunities. See Chapter 22 for additional tips and tricks on migrating data.

Modifying Opportunity Records

After you add opportunities into Salesforce, you can make changes to your records when deals progress, stall, or fade away. In the following sections, we cover three common practices: editing, sharing, and reassigning.

Updating opportunity fields

In the course of working with your opportunities, you inevitably collect information that you want to save directly in the opportunity record. Every time you capture important data on your opportunity, remember to update your record by doing the following:

1. **Click the Edit button on the opportunity.**

    You can also hover your mouse over the specific field that you want to edit. If a pencil icon appears to the right of the field, double-click the field to edit it. (If you see a padlock icon instead, that means the field is not editable, on purpose. Move along and pick another field to update.)

    Alternatively, if you're already in an account or contact record that's linked to the opportunity, scroll down to the Opportunities related list and click the Edit link to the left of the desired opportunity. The result is the same. The Opportunity Edit page appears.

2. **Update the fields, as necessary, paying particular attention to keeping fields such as Amount, Close Date, and Stage up to date.**

    Nine out of ten times, those fields play a key role in your company's sales pipeline reports. By keeping your information up to date, you and other users can get a true measure on the opportunity's progress.

3. **When you're done, click Save.**

    The opportunity reappears in Saved mode. The fields that you edited are changed.

You can keep track of certain critical updates to your opportunity record by using the Stage History related list. Anytime you or one of your team members who has read-write access to your record modifies the Stage, Probability, Close Date, or Amount fields, you can quickly scan this at the bottom of the opportunity record page to see who modified the record and when. See Chapter 17 for further details on using and customizing opportunity reports.

Rolling up opportunity data onto the account record

The opportunity record carries a great deal of quantifiable information about an account, such as how many licenses were sold, the amount of a deal, and so on. By collecting and aggregating key opportunity field information onto an account record, a sales rep can quickly see how valuable a particular customer is by viewing the total number of licenses a customer currently has, how much total revenue a customer has closed with your company, and the highest deal closed with that customer, to name a few examples.

You can aggregate this summary information in two ways:

✔ Run a report that summarizes this information for you. (See Chapter 17 for more details on creating reports.)

✔ Your Salesforce administrator can choose which opportunity fields you want to have summarized automatically on the account record.

To create a custom roll-up of your opportunity data onto the account record, choose Setup⇨Build⇨Customize⇨Accounts⇨Fields and follow these steps:

1. **In the Account Custom Fields and Relationships section, click the New button.**

   The New Custom Field Wizard opens.

2. **Select the Roll-Up Summary radio button and click Next.**

3. **Enter the name of what you're summarizing in the Field Label field and click Next.**

   The Field Name field automatically populates itself based on what you enter in the Field Label. In this example, I type **Total Deals Closed** and click the Next button.

4. **At the Define the Summary Calculation step, by the Summarized Object picklist, select Opportunities.**

   Identifying the summarized object tells Salesforce which records from which objects you want to be combined and summarized onto the account record.

5. **Select the roll-up type from the selection of radio buttons in the Select Roll-Up Type section in the middle of the page. Click Next.**

   This selection tells Salesforce how you want the field of your choice to be summarized. You can choose a count of records, the sum, the minimum value, or the maximum value. If you choose any of the latter three options, you also have to identify which field in the opportunity you want to be summarized by using the Field to Aggregate picklist to make their choice.

   You can filter out certain criteria in your result set.

   If you want to summarize only records that meet certain criteria, select the Only Records Meeting Certain Criteria Should Be Included in the Calculation radio button to reveal a set of filter criteria. For example, you may want a sum of all the Amount fields for opportunities in which the Closed status equals True. (Figure 10-2 shows an example of defining the field calculation.)

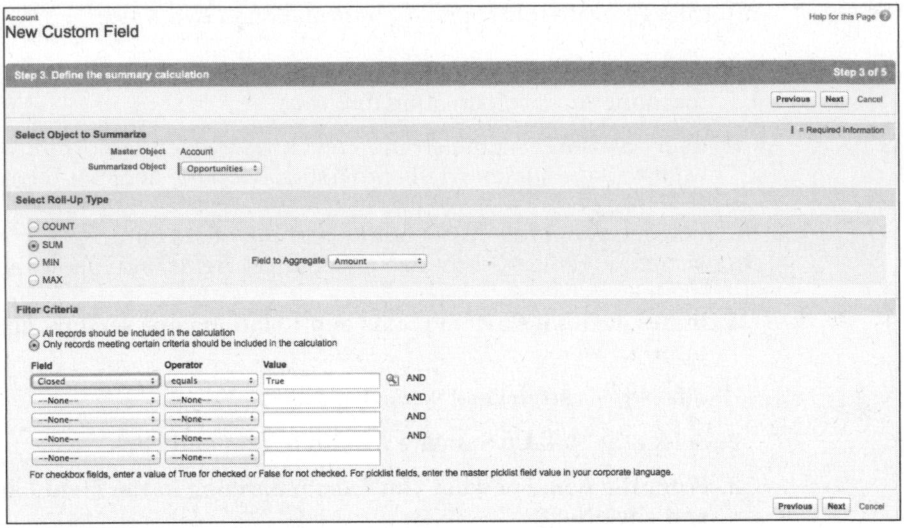

Figure 10-2:
Defining an
opportunity
roll-up field
calculation.

6. **Select which profiles should be able to view the new field and click Next.**

7. **Select on which page layout(s) the field should be displayed and click Save.**

Reassigning opportunity ownership

You might find that after you set up your opportunities in Salesforce, you need to give them to the right people because management has decided to reshuffle sales territories (again). Or your sales teams might be set up in a hunter/farmer configuration, in which you reassign closed opportunities from new business reps to account managers after a certain time has passed.

If you want to reassign an opportunity, open the Opportunity detail page and follow these steps:

1. **To the right of the Opportunity Owner field, click the Change link, which appears in square brackets.**

   The Ownership Edit page appears, as shown in Figure 10-3.

2. **Select the user to whom you're assigning the opportunity.**

3. **(Optional) Select the Send Notification Email check box.**

   The recipient gets notified of the reassignment via e-mail.

4. **When you're done, click Save.**

   The opportunity record reappears. The Opportunity Owner field has changed to the assigned user.

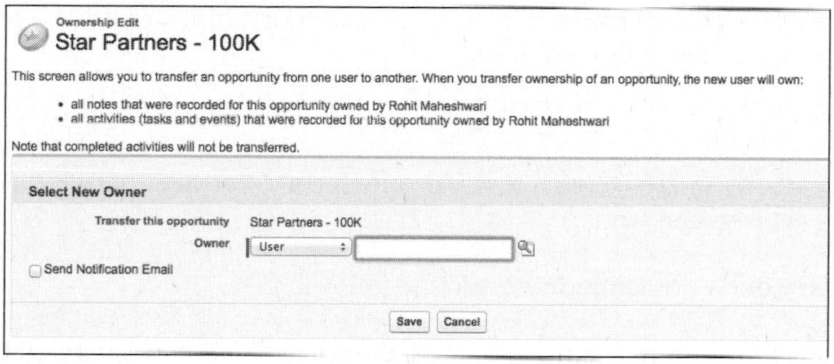

Ownership Edit

Star Partners - 100K

This screen allows you to transfer an opportunity from one user to another. When you transfer ownership of an opportunity, the new user will own:

- all notes that were recorded for this opportunity owned by Rohit Maheshwari
- all activities (tasks and events) that were recorded for this opportunity owned by Rohit Maheshwari

Note that completed activities will not be transferred.

Select New Owner

Transfer this opportunity   Star Partners - 100K

Owner [User ÷] [   ] 🔍

☐ Send Notification Email

[Save] [Cancel]

Figure 10-3:
Reassigning
an oppor-
tunity.

Organizing Your Opportunities

When you have all or a portion of your opportunities entered in Salesforce, you can begin to organize them to suit the way that you sell.

In the following sections, you can find out how you can use views and other tools from the Opportunities home page to provide greater focus for you and your sales teams. Then, for even more robust organization of your opportunity information, check out Chapter 17 for specifics on how to use standard and custom opportunity reports.

Using opportunity views

An *opportunity view* is a list of opportunities that match certain criteria. When you select a view, you're basically specifying criteria to limit the results that you get back. The advantage of a view, versus searching, is that you can use this view over and over again. For example, if you're one of many sales reps, you probably want to see only your opportunities. On the Opportunities home page, Salesforce comes preset with several defined views:

- ✔ **All Opportunities:** Lists all the opportunity records entered into Salesforce

  Depending on the way that your company has set up your security model, you might not see this view or its results.

- ✔ **Closing Next Month:** Displays opportunities in which the close date falls in the following month

- ✔ **Closing This Month:** Displays opportunities in which the close date falls in the current month

- ✔ **My Opportunities:** Gives you a list of just the opportunities that you own

✔ **New This Week:** Generates a list of opportunities that have been created since the beginning of the week

✔ **Recently Viewed Opportunities:** Lets you look at a list of opportunities that you've recently viewed

✔ **Won:** Shows opportunities to which you have access that have been closed and won

To try out a predefined view, do the following:

1. **On the Opportunities home page, click the down arrow in the View drop-down list.**

   Depending on how your company has customized the views, you might see all or none of the options in the preceding bulleted list as well as some other choices that might have been created for you.

2. **Select the My Opportunities view.**

   A list page appears, showing opportunities that you currently own. Salesforce lays out the list with standard columns that correspond to commonly used opportunity fields, plus an Action column so that you can quickly modify a record.

3. **Click a column header to re-sort the list page.**

   For example, if you click the Close Date header, the list page re-sorts by the close dates entered on your opportunity records.

4. **Go to the opportunity record by pointing and clicking an underlined link in the Opportunity Name column.**

   An Opportunity detail page appears.

5. **Click the Back button in your browser and then click the Edit link on the same row as the opportunity you just clicked.**

   The opportunity record appears in Edit mode, and you can make changes to the data.

   Click the Save button on the opportunity before navigating away from it.

Creating custom opportunity views

If you want special lists for the way that you manage your opportunities, you should build custom views. For example, if you want to see only open opportunities closing this month at or above 50 percent, you can create a view that helps you focus on just that part of the pipeline.

To build a view from scratch, follow these simple steps:

1. **On the Opportunities home page, to the right of the View drop-down list, click the Create New View link.**

   The Create New View page appears.

2. **Name the view by entering text in the Name field.**

   In the example used in the preceding section, you might call the view *Closing This Month >= 50%*.

3. **Select the appropriate radio button, depending on whether you want to search All Opportunities or just My Opportunities.**

4. **In the Search Criteria step, select your search criteria.**

   A basic criteria query is made up of three elements:

   - *Field:* In the first drop-down list, you can find all the fields on the opportunity record. An example is the Probability field.

   - *Operator:* The second drop-down list offers operators for your search. That might sound complicated, but it's easier than you think. Taking the example a step further, you'd select the Greater or Equal option from the drop-down list.

   - *Value:* In the third box, you type the value that you want in the search. For this example, you'd type **50** because you want to see only those opportunities that are greater than or equal to 50 percent probability.

5. **Select the columns that you want to have displayed.**

   Although the preset views in Salesforce display common fields, such as Stage and Amount, you can select up to 15 opportunity fields to display on your custom view page.

6. **Decide whether you want others to see your custom view.**

   Your decision is simple if you don't see the Visibility step. Otherwise, select the appropriate option, depending on whether you want to share your view with others. Your options are basically all, none, or limited. If you choose limited accessibility, use the Available for Sharing and Shared To list boxes to select which users can see the view.

7. **When you're done, click Save.**

   A new view appears, based on your custom view criteria. If you don't get all the results you anticipate, you might want to recheck and refine the search criteria.

Defining contact roles

Depending on your sales process, at some early point, you need to identify the decision makers who'll influence the buying decision. Contacts and their titles often don't tell the whole story about decision makers, influencers, and the chain of command within an opportunity.

To better define the buying influences on an opportunity, go to an opportunity record and follow these steps:

1. **Click the New button on the Contact Roles related list.**

   The Contact Roles page appears for that specific opportunity, displaying a list of the available contacts linked to the related account. See Figure 10-4.

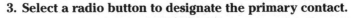

Contact Roles for Global Media - 40K

Contact Roles for Global Media - 40K   Save   Cancel

Primary	Contact	Role
●	No Primary Contact	
○	Jon Amos	--None--
○	Geoff Minor	--None--
○	Carole White	Business User
○		Decision Maker
○		Economic Buyer
○		Economic Decision Maker
○		Evaluator
○		Executive Sponsor
○		Influencer
○		Technical Buyer
○		Other

Save   Cancel

Figure 10-4: Selecting the contact role.

2. **For each relevant contact, use the Role drop-down list to select the appropriate role.**

   Salesforce comes preconfigured with a standard list of contact roles, but your company can customize this drop-down list if you need to modify the list of values. You don't have to classify a role for every contact on the list; you can just leave the Role default value of None.

   If the right role for your contact doesn't appear, advise your system administrator to customize the Opportunity Contract Role Picklist Values.

3. **Select a radio button to designate the primary contact.**

   The primary contact typically refers to the person who's currently your point of contact. One of the benefits of selecting a primary contact is that you can list who the primary contact is on a basic opportunity report.

4. **(Optional) Click the Lookup icon to the right of empty fields in the Contact column to add other contacts who are critical to your opportunity.**

If you work with multitier selling models or if you collaborate with business partners on your deals, use contact roles to add contacts who aren't employees of an account. For example, if your customer's legal gatekeeper works for an outside law firm, you can use the Contact Roles related list to highlight the attorney's role.

5. **When you're done, click Save.**

The Opportunity detail page reappears, and your Contact Roles related list is updated to reflect contacts involved in the opportunity. If you need to add more contact roles, click the New button in the Contact Roles related list again.

Following Opportunities with Chatter

If you work as part of a sales team or just have a lot of deals to keep track of, Salesforce can bring you the news on your opportunities as it happens. You are automatically set to follow updates on any opportunity you create, but sometimes, you don't want to hunt down what's happening on someone else's opportunity.

You can follow an Opportunity record by following these steps:

1. **From the Opportunity home page, click a recently viewed opportunity.**

The Opportunity detail page appears, displaying the Chatter feed front and center, as shown in Figure 10-5.

For more information on how to use Chatter, see Chapter 6.

2. **To follow the discussion on this opportunity, click the Follow link with the green circled plus sign.**

The Opportunity page updates to show a thumbnail photo of your profile picture under the Followers section, alongside photos of other people following this record. The Follow button now appears as a Following status, with a gray "x" next to it that you click if you want to unfollow the record.

Now when there's Chatter activity on this opportunity, it appears in your Chatter feed displayed on your home page too.

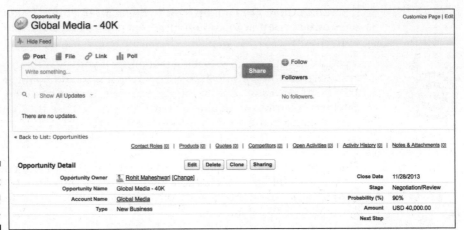

Chapter 11

Tracking Products and Price Books

A product, as its name implies, is a product or service that you sell to customers. Products are the individual line items that make up an *opportunity.* Depending on your goals for Salesforce, you might not need to immediately incorporate Salesforce's product-type features into your opportunities. But if you sell multiple products and services and you struggle with product-level visibility, Salesforce provides powerful and easy tools to implement solutions for Professional, Enterprise, and Performance Edition users.

Using products in Salesforce benefits sales reps and people in product marketing, management, and development throughout your organization. Sales reps can quickly locate the price of a product and select products to calculate an opportunity's amount. Marketing, management, or development professionals can get vital sales information to support strategic business planning, new product development, and product life cycle management.

In this chapter, we show sales teams how to use products and price books with opportunities (if your administrator has already set that up). Before setting up products and price books, though, administrators first need to do some advanced planning. We discuss how to create a product catalog, set up schedules, and build price books. We then show you how to maintain products and price books on an ongoing basis to facilitate your sales goals. We conclude this chapter by showing you how to generate quotes that incorporate items from your product catalog so that you can e-mail them to your contacts.

Discovering Products and Price Books

You need to know two key and interrelated terms before you can begin planning your product strategy in Salesforce:

✔ **Products:** Individual items that you sell through your opportunities. All products belong to one universal product catalog. After you create a product, though, you can associate it to one or multiple price books with identical or different prices. For example, you may use multiple price books if you use one set of prices when selling to qualified nonprofit agencies and a different price list for companies in the private sector.

A product can have an associated *schedule* based on quantity, revenue, or both. If you sell products and break out schedules to forecast revenue recognition or for planning, you can use Salesforce to reflect important schedules for products linked to opportunities.

To access the Products home page, click the Products tab. If you can't see that, confirm that the Force.com drop-down list in the upper-right corner of the screen is set at Sales (versus something like Call Center). If you still don't see it, check with your system administrator.

✔ **Price book:** A collection of products and their associated prices. A product with its associated price is a *price book entry.* You can also create custom price books based on your unique sales model.

You can associate a price book, add products, and build schedules on an opportunity through the Products related list on an Opportunity detail page.

Defining standard product fields

A product record consists of a number of fields that you use to capture information about a product you sell. If you're involved in shaping products for your company, most of the standard fields are obvious. If you want specific definitions, click the Help link in the upper-right corner of Salesforce.

Here are a couple of important pointers on understanding the standard product record fields:

✔ **Product Name:** The name of your product. Make sure to use titles that are clear and familiar to your sales reps and customers.

✔ **Product Code:** An internal code or product ID used to identify your product. If your existing products and product codes reside in a financial database and you want to plan for integration, make sure that the product codes are consistent.

✔ **Product Description:** Text to distinguish products from each other. If you're in product management or marketing, describe your products so that they're obvious and useful for your sales teams.

- ✔ **Product Family:** The category of the product. Use this drop-down list when building reports that reflect sales data by product category. For example, if you work for a technology value-added reseller (VAR), you might want to reflect your pipeline by families that include hardware, software, services, training, and maintenance. You can set up products in Salesforce so that each product automatically maps to a product family.

- ✔ **Active:** This check box must be selected to make the product available to your users.

- ✔ **Quantity Scheduling Enabled:** Select this check box to enable quantity scheduling for a product. If you don't see this check box, your administrator hasn't enabled it.

- ✔ **Revenue Scheduling Enabled:** Select this check box to enable revenue scheduling for a product. If you don't see this check box, your administrator hasn't enabled it.

Understanding the different types of pricing

Salesforce allows you to customize your pricing based on the way you sell. If you use products in Salesforce, your company has three different options for pricing:

- ✔ **Standard Prices:** Default prices that you establish for your products when you set up your standard price book

- ✔ **List Prices:** Prices that you set up for custom price books

- ✔ **Sales Price:** Price of a product determined by the sales rep when he adds a product to an opportunity

  See the following section for details on adding products to opportunities.

Using Products and Price Books

Sales reps can add products with specific prices to their opportunities, and Salesforce automatically calculates the Amount field on an opportunity record. If you're a sales rep selling multiple products and managing multiple opportunities at the same time, you can take the frustration out of remembering what you offered to a customer. If you're a sales manager, you can segment your pipelines and forecasts by product lines. And if you're in product management or marketing, products in Salesforce can give you real insight into product demand from your markets.

Adding products to opportunities

To take advantage of products, your company must first set up a product catalog as well as one or more price books. See the section "Building the Product Catalog," later in this chapter, for the how-to details on setting up your products and price books. After this is done, sales reps can add products to an opportunity by going to a specific opportunity and following these steps:

1. **Scroll down the Opportunity detail page to the Products related list and then click the Choose Price Book button.**

   A Choose Price Book page appears. If your company has made only one price book available to you, you can bypass this step and start with Step 2.

2. **Select the appropriate price book from the Price Book drop-down list and then click Save.**

   The Opportunity detail page appears again. The Products related list now shows the name of the price book in parentheses.

   On an opportunity, you can use only one price book at a time.

3. **Click the Add Product button on the Products related list.**

   A Product Selection page appears, as shown in Figure 11-1. This shows all the products in your selected price book.

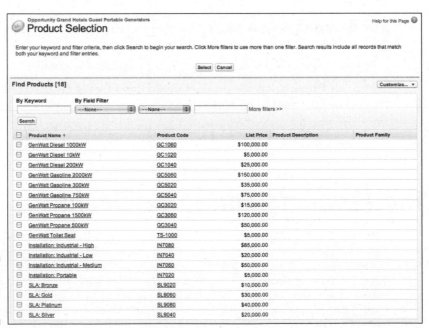

Figure 11-1: Finding your products.

4. **If the resulting list of products is too long for your tastes, you may narrow the results by entering a keyword or filter criteria, and then clicking the Search button to begin your search.**

   The page reappears with your search results in a table at the bottom of the page.

5. **Select the check boxes next to the products that you want, and then click the Select button.**

   An Add Products page appears with your selections and fields for you to provide line item details. The Sales Price field is prefilled with the default sales price from the price book that you selected.

6. **Fill in the line item details.**

   You must, at a minimum, fill in the Quantity and Sales Price fields for each selected product. The Date field is typically used to reflect an expected shipping or delivery date for the product.

7. **When you're done, click the Save button or the Save & More button.**

   Clicking the Save & More button takes you back to the Product Selection page. If you click the Save button, the Opportunity detail page reappears. Notice that the Amount and Quantity fields on the opportunity record have changed based on the total from the products you added.

Updating product details for an opportunity

If you need to change the details on your product selections in the course of the sales cycle, you can do this easily on the Products related list of the opportunity record. For example, if your customer wants to add another product, increase product quantities, or demand a better product discount, you need to know how to modify products.

To modify products on your opportunity, we suggest the following:

- ✔ **Delete a product from the opportunity.** Click the Del link next to the product on the Products related list.

- ✔ **Edit all the products on the opportunity.** Click the Edit All button.

- ✔ **Edit one product at a time.** Click the Edit link next to the product on the related list.

- ✔ **Reorder the products on your Products related list.** Click the Sort button.

If you find yourself unable to modify the sales price on your products, you may want to politely confirm the intent with your sales manager. Some companies lock in the sales price for sales reps so that they must adhere to a predefined discount approval policy.

Adding and updating schedules on opportunities

If you manage opportunities in which your products or services are delivered over time, you can create schedules for your products by quantity, revenue, or both. By using schedules, you and your users can benefit in multiple ways:

- ✔ **If you're on a sales team:** You get a gauge on revenue recognition, which could be significant if that affects compensation.

- ✔ **If you're in product management:** You can better forecast and plan for the amount of units that you'll have to deliver in future quarters.

- ✔ **If you're part of a services organization:** Schedules updated by reps provide a real-time gauge in planning your resources and projects.

Your system administrator must first set up your products with scheduling. (See the section "Setting Up Schedules," later in this chapter, for more specifics on schedules, and see Chapter 20 for the details on customizing Salesforce.)

After scheduling is enabled for a product, set up a schedule by going to the Opportunity detail page and following these steps:

1. **Click the desired product in the Product Name column of the Products related list.**

   An Opportunity Product page appears with a Schedule related list.

2. **Click the Establish button in the Schedule related list.**

   An Establish Schedule page appears.

3. **Complete the fields and click Save.**

   Your fields might vary, depending on whether the product is set up for quantity, revenue, or combined scheduling. When you click Save, a schedule appears based on your choices.

4. **Review and modify the schedule.**

   If the revenues or quantities aren't equal over the periods that you first established, you can type over the values in the schedule.

5. **When you're done, click Save.**

   The Opportunity Product page reappears with the schedule you established.

Over the course of an opportunity, if terms change, you can adjust the schedule on a product by clicking the buttons on the Opportunity Product page. To access an Opportunity Product page, go to the relevant opportunity record, scroll down to the Products related list, and click the desired product link from the Product column. The Opportunity Product page for the selected product appears with a Schedule related list. You can do the following with the schedule:

- ✔ **Modify the schedule.** Click the Edit button.
- ✔ **Delete the schedule.** Click the Delete button.
- ✔ **Establish the schedule all over again.** Click the Re-establish button.

Searching for products

You can search for specific products easily by using the Find Products search tool on the Products home page.

Instead of searching from the Products home page, you can search for products from your main home page. Your administrator must set this up for your company. For details on adding this home page tool, see Chapter 20 for customizing Salesforce and consult with your administrator.

To search for a product, go to the Products home page and follow these steps:

1. **Enter keywords in the Find Products search tool and then click the Find Product button.**

   A Product Search page appears with a list of possible selections, as shown in Figure 11-2.

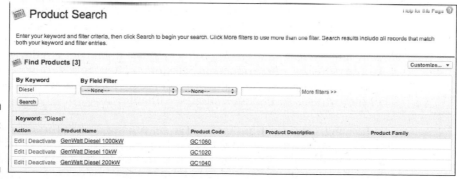

Figure 11-2: Search for a product.

2. **If necessary, use the Find Products search tool to enter more keywords or filters to refine your search and again click the Find Product button.**

   The list results change based on your criteria.

3. **Click a link in the Product Name column to go directly to the product.**

   The Product detail page appears.

Creating custom views for products and price lists

If the existing lists don't provide the views that you want, you can create custom views for products and price lists. You can define your views to see additional standard or custom fields in list form. See Chapter 4 for details on creating custom views.

Building the Product Catalog

If you have a vested interest in your product strategy, be aware and take advantage of all the options that Salesforce provides for customizing products and price books. The more you plan ahead, the better you can implement products and price books for how your sales teams sell. As you make products and price books active, your sales reps can start associating products to their opportunities.

Planning products for success

For products, consider the characteristics of your products outside the standard realm that you want to analyze. In most companies, the product management or marketing teams own and maintain these records in coordination with finance. You should pull together a cross-functional team made up of sales, marketing, finance, and product management users to decide what you want to achieve from products in Salesforce. Then work with your system administrator to customize the product record to meet your specific needs. For more details on customization, see Chapter 20.

For pricing, consider whether to have set pricing on your products or whether you prefer to keep the pricing simple at the beginning. Many customers of Salesforce, for example, set the prices on their products at $0 or $1 and then depend on their sales reps to fill in the sales prices when they prepare an opportunity. Other companies invest time and effort in creating actual standard or list prices on products to provide guidance to their sales reps.

Adding products to the product catalog

Before your sales reps can begin linking products to their opportunities, you need to add the products into Salesforce.

To add a product, log in to Salesforce and follow these steps:

1. **Select the Create Product option from the Create New drop-down list on the sidebar.**

   A New Product page appears, as shown in Figure 11-3.

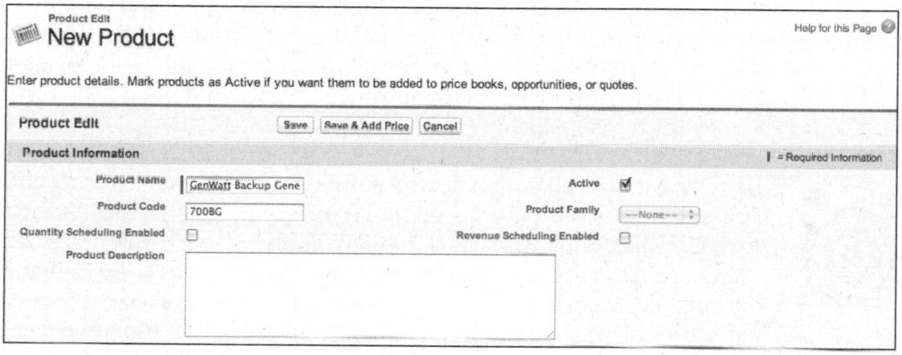

Figure 11-3: Add a product to the product catalog.

2. **Complete the fields.**

   Your exact fields might vary, but see the section "Defining standard product fields," earlier in this chapter, for info on the standard fields.

3. **When you're done, click Save.**

   The Product detail page for your new product appears with related lists for standard prices and price lists.

Changing product details in the product catalog

Over time, marketing or product managers may need to update details about a product. You can make most of your changes to a product from its detail page. Go to a specific product and take a look at this list of actions that you can perform. (You must have "edit" permissions on products to perform these steps. See Chapter 19 for details on granting the right permissions to the right people.)

✔ **Edit the product record.** Click the Edit button. For example, if the name of your product changes, you can change the product name and then save and automatically update all opportunities that include that product with the modified name.

✔ **Delete the product.** Click Delete and then click OK in the dialog box that appears. In circumstances in which you're no longer offering a product but it's linked to opportunities, it's better that you deactivate or archive the product rather than delete it. See the following bullets.

✔ **Deactivate the product.** Click the Edit button, deselect the Active check box, and then click Save. Take this path if you might offer the product in the future.

✔ **Delete and archive the product.** Click Delete and then click OK in the dialog box that appears. In the event that your product is linked to opportunities, a Deletion Problems page appears with suggested options. Click the Archive link if you're still intent on deleting the product but not altering the existing opportunities.

If you want to keep your sales reps informed of any changes to your products (for example, if a product is no longer offered or if its name changed), you can use Salesforce Chatter so that any changes to a product's status or its name are reported in a Chatter feed. Interested users need to just follow the actions of the person who makes those changes (usually someone in Sales Operations), or they can follow the specific product, too. (See Chapter 6 for more information on setting up Chatter and its feeds and following users and records.)

Setting Up Schedules

If your company wants to track annuity streams, stay aware of key shipping dates, or estimate when revenue will be recognized on products, you can also set up schedules on all or some products.

Enabling schedules for your company

Your administrator first needs to enable schedules before you can add them on specific products.

If your company wants to track shipping dates with Salesforce, you need to enable *quantity scheduling*. If your company wants to measure revenue recognition or anticipate upcoming payments, be sure to enable *revenue scheduling*. If your company wants to do both, you'd enable both types of scheduling.

To set up schedules, follow these steps:

1. **Choose Setup⇨Build⇨Customize⇨Products⇨Schedule Setup.**

   The Schedule Setup page appears, as shown in Figure 11-4.

Figure 11-4: Enable schedules for your company.

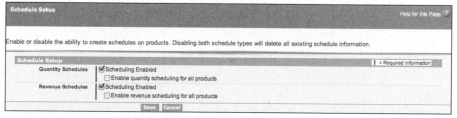

2. **Select the appropriate check boxes.**

   You can choose to enable schedules based on quantities, revenue, or both. You can also choose to enable schedules for all products.

3. **When you're done, click Save.**

   The Products page reappears.

Adding and updating a default schedule

After schedules have been enabled, you can create default schedules on existing products or while you're adding new products.

By creating default schedules, you can simplify repetitive tasks for sales reps. With this setting, a default schedule is created when a sales rep adds a product to an opportunity. A sales rep can still reestablish a product schedule on an opportunity. The product date determines the start date for the installments.

If you sell a basic service with different payment plans, consider creating a unique product for each payment plan and then using default revenue schedules. By doing this, you can simplify the data entry for the rep and reduce the chance of error.

To create a default schedule, follow these steps:

1. **Select the Create Product option on the sidebar or click the Edit button on a product record.**

   A Product page appears in Edit mode. If scheduling is enabled, you see additional fields for quantity and/or revenue scheduling.

2. **Complete the fields, as appropriate.**

   Here are some tips on completing the default schedule:

   - *Schedule Type:* Select Divide if you want to divide the opportunity amount into installments. Select Repeat if you want to repeat the quantity or revenue on each installment.

   - *Installment Period:* Define the frequency.

   - *Number of Installments:* Define the duration.

3. **When you're done, click Save.**

   The Product detail page appears.

If your product has both quantity and revenue default scheduling, quantity scheduling is calculated first and drives the total amount. Then, revenue scheduling divides the amount.

To update a default product schedule, follow these steps:

1. **From the Products home page, search for the product whose schedule you'd like to update, using your preferred method.**

   See the "Searching for products" section, earlier in this chapter, for specifics. A Product Search page appears.

2. **Click the product name of the specific product to edit.**

   The Product page appears.

3. **Click the Edit button to update schedule information.**

4. **When you're done, click Save.**

   The Product page for your product appears with the updated information.

Managing Price Books

Some companies require just one universal price book. Many other companies, however, want custom price books based on their unique selling needs. Examples include price books that are based on the following:

- **Geography:** For a global company, the Japanese sales team might sell a subset of the products sold by their North American counterparts (and at different prices and in different currencies).

- **Partner tiers:** In some companies that sell via partners, strategic partners might get preferential pricing.

- **Sales teams:** If your company is divided into sales teams that sell different products, you can use custom price books to simplify the product selection for groups.

✔ **Volume discounts:** Some companies build price books based on volume purchases.

✔ **Seasonality:** Some companies change their pricing based on seasonal buying patterns. You can use custom price books to communicate pricing changes to your sales reps during these periods.

If the standard price book meets your objectives, keep it simple. Otherwise, in the following sections, we show you how to set up your price books.

Adding to the standard price book

Every time you add a standard price to a product, you automatically associate it to the standard price book. You can do this while you're creating products, or you can add the standard prices after you've built the product records.

Adding standard prices while creating products

The easiest way to add a standard price is while you're creating products. To use this method, start creating a product record as you normally would; see the section "Building the Product Catalog," earlier in this chapter. Instead of clicking Save, though, follow these steps:

1. **Click the Save & Add Price button (refer to Figure 11-3).**

   An Add Standard Price page appears, as shown in Figure 11-5.

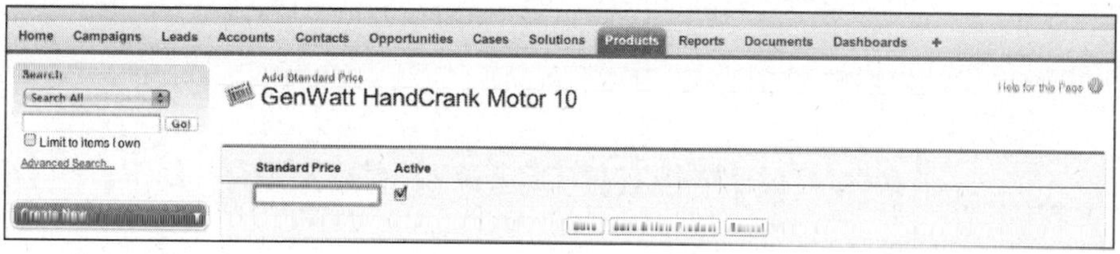

Figure 11-5: Add a standard price.

2. **Complete the field and click Save.**

   The Product detail page appears, and a standard price displays on the Standard Price related list.

Adding or editing standard prices for existing products

You can also create the products first and add prices later. To add or edit a standard price, go to the desired Product detail page and follow these steps:

1. **Click the Add button on the Standard Price related list.**

   If standard prices already exist, you can click Edit or Edit All. The result is the same: An Add or Edit Standard Price page appears.

2. **Complete or modify the Standard Price field, as necessary, and then click Save.**

   The Product detail page reappears with any changes reflected on the Standard Price related list.

Creating a custom price book

To create a price book, you need to be an administrator or have permission to manage price books.

To create a price book from scratch, go to the Products home page and follow these steps:

1. **Click the Manage Price Books link under the Maintenance section, near the bottom of the page.**

   A Price Book page appears with related lists for active and inactive price books.

2. **Click the New button on the Active Price Books related list.**

   A New Price Book page appears in Edit mode.

3. **Complete the fields.**

   Select the Active check box if you want to make the price book available.

4. **When you're done, click Save.**

   The Price Book detail page for your new price book appears with a Products related list.

Adding products to a custom price book

After the price book has been established, you can add products to it. A product listed on a price book is also referred to as a *price book entry.* To add products to an existing price book, go to a price book and follow these steps:

1. **Click the Add button on the Products related list.**

   A Product Selection page appears with a search tool and a list of products.

2. **Enter keywords and filter criteria, and then click the Search button to narrow your search.**

   The Product Selection page reappears with a list of products based on your search criteria.

3. **Use the check boxes on the search results to choose products and then click the Select button.**

   An Add List Price page appears.

4. **Complete the fields.**

   Select the check boxes in the Use Standard Price column if you want to use the standard price for the list price of a product or just enter a list price. You can select the Active check boxes to make products immediately available in the price book.

5. **When you're done, click Save (or Save & More if you want to find more products).**

   After you save the product, the Price Book detail page reappears, and your selected products have been added to the Products related list.

Making global changes to price books

Maintaining accurate and up-to-date product and price lists is challenging, especially if you have an extensive product catalog and/or complex pricing. If you're responsible for such a daunting task, you can use tools that are located on the Products home page to save time.

Changing activation on price books

At times, you'll want to make a price book unavailable to sales reps. Maybe you had to raise prices on a family of products or you stopped selling a product line. You probably need to preserve the current price book because existing customers and some prospects are still being associated to those products and prices, but new customers will need to be tied to the new catalog. Rest assured that you can deactivate one or more price books almost instantly so that sales reps won't be able to tie new opportunities to old information.

To deactivate a price book, go the Products home page and follow these steps:

1. **Click the Manage Price Books link under the Maintenance section.**

   The Price Book detail page appears with related lists for active and inactive price books.

2. **On the Active Price Books related list, click the Deactivate link next to a price book that you want to make unavailable.**

   The Price Book detail page reappears, and the selected price book now appears in the Inactive Price Books related list.

To reactivate price books, you follow a similar process, the difference being that you click the Activate link adjacent to a price book listed in the Inactive Price Books related list.

Cloning price books

On occasion, you might want to create a price book that closely resembles an existing price book. Instead of starting from scratch, you can clone from an existing price book and then make changes, as necessary.

To clone a price book, follow these steps:

1. **Click the Manage Price Books link under the Maintenance section.**

   The Price Book page appears with related lists for active and inactive price books.

2. **Click the New button on the Active Price Books related list.**

   A New Price Book page appears.

3. **Complete the fields and use the Existing Price Book drop-down list to select a price book to clone.**

4. **Rename the clone in the Price Book Name field, and give it a description in the Description field. Select the Active check box when you want the new price book to be available to others for use.**

5. **When you're done, click Save.**

   The new Price Book page appears with a Products related list cloned from the existing price book.

6. **If needed, click Edit or Edit All on the Products related list to change the list prices.**

7. **If needed, click Add or Delete in the Products related list to add or delete price book entries.**

Deleting price books

You can delete price books, but if the price book is associated with existing opportunities, beware. In those circumstances, we recommend the following actions:

- ✔ Deactivate (rather than delete) the price book so that the linkage between opportunities and products stays intact.

- ✔ Delete the associated opportunity records first, and then delete the price book.

- ✔ Archive the price book entries prior to deleting. Then, even if you delete the price book record, the products associated with opportunities are retained.

If you still want to delete a price book, follow these steps:

1. **On the Products home page, click the Manage Price Books link under the Maintenance section.**

   The Price Book detail page appears with related lists for active and inactive price books.

2. **Click the link for the desired price book.**

   The specific Price Book page appears.

3. **Click Delete and then click OK in the dialog box that appears.**

   If you select a price book that isn't associated with opportunities, you return to the Price Book detail page with the lists of price books. If a Deletion Problems page appears, follow the suggestions provided in the preceding bulleted list and on the Deletion Problems page.

Generating Quotes

Salesforce allows the ability to generate quotes from the product and price book information collected in your opportunities. You can make PDFs of quotes to e-mail to customers, and a complete history of what you've created is automatically stored within Salesforce. From the initial creation of a lead, to when you're sending your prospect a quote for new business, Salesforce helps you all the way. You'll still need to use your savvy sales skills to get your prospect to agree to what you're actually quoting, but that's where the art of sales balances the science.

Customizing quotes

Quotes use many standard fields that are prepopulated with information already existing in the Account and Opportunity records. This makes quote creation that much more streamlined in Salesforce because you don't have to spend time retyping a customer's address, contact information, or what they ordered (unless you want to). Check out all the standard Quote fields by choosing Setup➪Build➪Customize➪Quotes➪Fields.

To create a custom field for your quote, follow these steps:

1. **Choose Setup➪Build➪Customize➪Quotes➪Fields.**

   The Quote Fields page appears.

2. **Scroll down to the Quote Custom Fields & Relationship section.**

3. **Click New to create a new field.**

   The New Custom Field Wizard begins, consistent with what we've discussed with other objects. (For example, in Chapter 20, we discuss creating new custom fields.)

4. **Click Save when you're done with the wizard.**

   You return to the Quote Fields page.

Preparing quotes for customers

For those of you working on the front lines with prospects and customers, creating a new quote is a cinch.

To create a new quote, follow these steps:

1. **Select an Opportunity record that matches the potential deal you want to issue a quote for.**

2. **Scroll down and look for the Quotes related list, shown in Figure 11-6.**

   If you don't see it, ask your administrator to enable quotes.

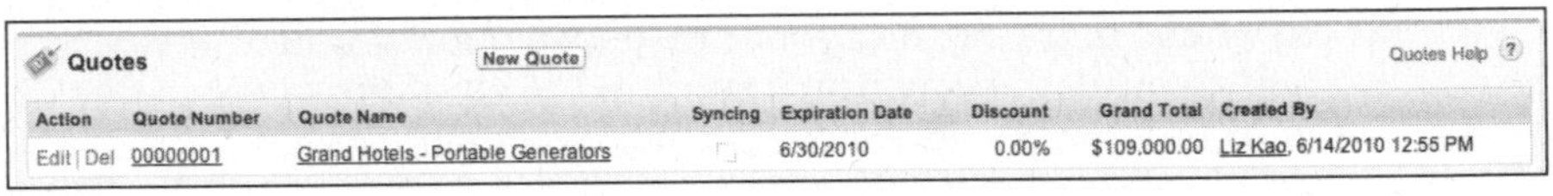

Figure 11-6:
Create a
new quote.

Quotes				New Quote				Quotes Help ?
Action	Quote Number	Quote Name			Syncing	Expiration Date	Discount	Grand Total	Created By
Edit | Del	00000001	Grand Hotels - Portable Generators				6/30/2010	0.00%	$109,000.00	Liz Kao, 6/14/2010 12:55 PM

3. **Click the New Quote button.**

   A New Quote detail page appears, in Edit mode.

4. **Enter the quote name, expiration date of the quote, the quote's status, and other information requested in the fields.**

5. **Click Save when done.**

   The Quote page appears.

Revising quotes

As you progress in your negotiation cycle, you may need to modify the information in your quote. This can include modifying the information captured in the quote fields, or it can mean actually changing the prices of what you originally offered.

To revise your quote, follow these steps:

1. **From the opportunity record, scroll down to the Quotes related list section.**

2. **Locate the quote that you want to revise and click the Edit link to the left of the quote name.**

   The Quote Edit page appears for that quote.

3. **After you make your changes, click Save.**

   The Opportunity page reappears.

To modify the actual line items that you quoted, follow these steps:

1. **Scroll down the page and note the Quote Line Items related list.**

   If you choose to offer an item for below list price, you can edit the information here to record the actual sales price you want to quote.

2. **Click the Edit link to the left of the quote line item description.**

   The Quote Line Item edit page appears.

3. **Modify the applicable fields if you're providing a discount.**

   This spells out the amount of the discount and where it's being applied.

   The Discount field is a percentage (%) discount, and it calculates the equivalent value based on the Subtotal.

4. **Click Save when done.**

   The Quote page reappears.

Sending quotes

After you have your quote just right, it's time to send it to the customer. To e-mail (or fax) your quote to your customer, you first need a PDF copy of the quote.

To create a PDF of your quote, follow these steps:

1. **Go to the Opportunity record's Quote related list.**

2. **Click the quote you want to send.**

   The Quote page appears.

3. **Click the Create PDF button.**

   You're shown a preview of your quote.

4. **When you're ready to save the quote, click Save to Quote or click Save and Email Quote.**

   This allows you to save the PDF to the Quote record as an attachment for later use (or faxing), or to save the quote and also e-mail it to the contact that you prepared the quote for.

If you made modifications to the products listed in your quote, you can sync those with the original Opportunity record associated with the quote. You can only sync one opportunity to one quote at a time, though. This ensures that the prices on the most recent quote you put out there are accurately reflected in the Opportunity record (or vice versa). To sync a quote to an opportunity, click the Start Sync button.

Chapter 12

Managing Your Partners

- -

- -

*B*ecause Salesforce can get sales reps and managers on board to track all their opportunities and sales-related activities, the big pipeline picture should be getting clearer for everyone. *Partners,* which might also be known in your business as third-party companies, value-added resellers (VARs), original equipment manufacturers (OEMs), wholesalers, or distributors, can also be accurately managed in Salesforce almost as if they were full-time dedicated company sales reps. It used to be difficult to create and maintain unique messages and branding for specific groups of partners. Not any longer.

Salesforce Partner Communities extend the existing Salesforce product to partners and the leads and deals they bring in. Additionally, support managers and support reps within a company can more easily resolve issues for your partners.

A detailed discussion of Salesforce Partner Communities could take up a whole book on its own, so in this chapter, we provide a high-level overview of what life is like for partners and channel reps. We then discuss how a channel team manages its partners with Salesforce. For partners asked by their vendors to use this application, we discuss how to access and navigate Salesforce from the Partner Community. Finally, we give channel managers and administrators some pointers on how to set up a Partner Community and begin giving partners access.

Understanding the Partner Life Cycle

Using an indirect sales force of partners to help sell your products allows you to quickly and cost-effectively expand your company's reach into markets that you might otherwise not have the resources to tackle. Some industries that are more partner-intensive include high-tech, insurance, and manufacturing. In this section, we set the stage for two types of business users and describe how Partner Communities can help.

Here are some helpful Partner terms:

- **Vendor:** The company that's using Salesforce and for whom the channel managers work.
- **Channel managers:** The employees within your company that manage a set of partners.
- **Channel conflict:** What happens when your direct sales force and your indirect sales force find the same prospect to woo and start bickering about who's entitled to that lead — a clear sign that your current system is ineffective.
- **Deal registration:** Minimizes channel conflict. These programs get your indirect sales channel registering deals with you (the vendor) to reduce the chances of other partners or the direct sales force competing for a deal.
- **Partner Communities:** Customizable web portals hosted by salesforce.com that allow partner users to access Salesforce. Your company can set up multiple communities for multiple partners, if you need to use different branding.
- **Partner accounts:** Account records that are used by channel managers to manage partner organizations, partner users, and partner activities.
- **Partner users:** Salesforce users with limited capabilities and visibility into your instance of Salesforce. They're associated with a specific partner account and access Salesforce via a Partner Community.

Understanding a day in the life of a channel manager

Channel managers and their direct reports, channel reps, manage relationships with various types of partners and partners-in-waiting. The channel team does whatever it can to empower its indirect sales force with the right selling tools, sticks and carrots, to make sure that the relationship is win-win.

Measuring partner performance

A major communication services company drove its channel sales strategy by partnering with leading wireless equipment manufacturers. Sometimes, the company was introduced to the end customer; other times, the company was involved in opportunities completely managed by the manufacturer. But in all circumstances, the company's channel managers leveraged Partner Communities to track the partner sales performance, to improve mindshare with strategic partners, and to deepen its relationships with end customers.

With Partner Communities, channel managers now have access to Salesforce dashboards, leads, opportunities, accounts, and content records. Dashboards provide a graphical snapshot of the channel's performance so that you can see how much revenue the channel is bringing in. Leads are potential business that either come from a partner or that come to your company and are automatically or manually reassigned to the best partner for the job. Opportunities are the deals sourced or nurtured by your partners. Accounts can be resellers, distributors, agents — any type of partners that your business tracks. Channel managers can also use content to publish copies of sales tools, price lists, or product information for partners.

In addition to these standard tabs, you can also track partner budgets and fund claims if you run joint marketing programs, create and promote rebate programs with your partners, and more. Your administrator needs to set this up, so make sure that she reads the section "Setting Up Salesforce Communities for Your Channel Team," later in this chapter.

Understanding a day in the life of a partner

A partner's perspective is the flip side of the relationship managed by the channel manager. For example, one type of partner could be reselling your company's products. That partner works in a territory that's managed by a channel manager.

With Salesforce Communities, partner users can now access a limited view of your Salesforce information via a Partner Community. The Partner Community provides a centralized view of leads to pursue, opportunities in your pipeline, vendor documents to help with the sales cycle, and optional tabs to help with additional responsibilities, such as making fund requests. Partners get to see leads specifically assigned to them or grabbed from a general "shark tank" in which first come is first served. Additionally, partners can receive other key targeted messages on the website, update their company's information for the vendor to see, and e-mail their channel rep, as needed. Figure 12-1 shows a sample Partner Community that you might set up for your partners.

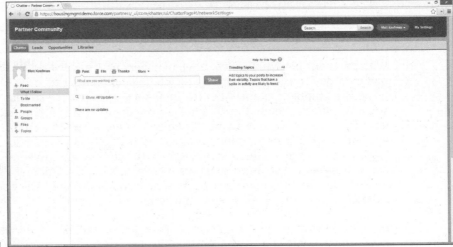

Figure 12-1:
Accessing
the Partner
Community.

Managing Your Channel with Salesforce Communities

After your administrator has set up your organization with Salesforce Communities, the channel team can easily access it from the AppExchange app menu in the upper-right corner of your Salesforce window. This section provides a high-level overview of how the channel team can now use Salesforce Communities to gain better visibility into their partner relationships. We also recommend that you scan Chapters 4 and 9, which talk in more detail about navigating accounts and leads.

Enabling partner relationship management

To allow partners to take part in the benefits of communities while still providing certain privileges specific to partners (such as working leads assigned to them), you have to first turn it on. To enable partner relationship management, follow these steps:

1. **Choose Setup⇨Build⇨Partners⇨Settings.**

   A page appears to enable partner relationship management (PRM). Note that this action is not reversible! We suggest you try out this feature in a Developer Edition instance first.

2. **Click the Edit button and select the only check box on this page to enable PRM.**

   Again, you're reminded that this action is not reversible.

3. **Click the Save button.**

   The Introducing the Convert External User Access Wizard page appears. This wizard helps you adjust sharing settings that might allow certain records or folders to be otherwise shared with external users.

4. **Click the Continue button.**

   The three-step wizard begins.

5. **In Steps 1 to 3 of the wizard, see whether any existing sharing rules need to be updated.**

   Consider whether any records may contain information that you don't want shared with partners.

6. **Click Done when you're finished, or click Cancel if you don't have any rules to modify.**

Creating partner accounts and contacts

First, you should make sure that all your partners are represented as accounts in Salesforce, with the respective channel managers owning the partner account records. This then allows channel managers to monitor and record all activities related to partners in their territory.

To create a new partner account, follow these steps:

1. **Use the Create New drop-down list on the sidebar and select the Account option.**

   See Chapter 4 for more information on managing accounts.

2. **Create the account record.**

3. **Click the Manage External Account button and select the Enable as Partner option from the resulting drop-down list.**

4. **Associate partner users to this partner account record by adding contacts.**

   See Chapter 5 for details on creating new contacts.

5. **Create a new contact, click the Manage External User button on the contact record, and select Enable Partner User for your partner user to receive his or her login and password notification via e-mail.**

   A New User page appears, allowing you to confirm user details before saving the record and generating a password for the user.

Assigning leads to partners

By assigning leads to partners, channel managers ensure an organized way of seeing what potential business their partners are working on.

Leads may be assigned to partners by manually switching the record ownership, by assigning partner leads to a queue (also known lovingly as the "shark tank"), or by adopting a "round robin" method, in which leads are routed evenly to a number of queues. Partners then have access to the queue to grab leads. (You can keep them from getting too greedy by setting a ceiling on how many leads they can accept to work on at one time.) Additionally, lead assignment rules may be set up by your administrator to automatically assign leads to partner users or partner queues based on certain rules.

To reassign a lead to a partner user, follow these steps:

1. **On the lead record, next to the Lead Owner field, click the Change link.**

   The link is in square brackets. The Change Lead Owner page appears.

2. **From the Owner drop-down list, choose the Partner User option.**

3. **Select the partner user to whom you are assigning the lead.**

   This assumes the partner's profile has been added as a member into the community you want him to join. The community has been published and can be viewable by others. And, the partner user is already activated and logged in at least once to the system. If the user is not active, his name will not show up when filtering for partner users.

4. **(Optional) Select the Send Notification Email check box to notify the partner about the lead.**

5. **Click Save.**

   The lead record reappears with your ownership change. The new partner owner instantly receives a customizable e-mail if you selected the Send Notification check box, and the lead appears in his Lead Inbox the next time that he accesses the Partner Community.

You may also reassign leads in bulk. See Chapter 9 for more information.

Salesforce to Salesforce

Salesforce to Salesforce is an amazing alternative feature to Salesforce Communities that allows partners with their own instance of Salesforce to seamlessly share lead and opportunity records with vendors in real time. Traditionally, this sharing occurred through a hairy, expensive, and drawn-out integration process. If a lot of your partners also use Salesforce, think about what partner processes you want to track.

✓ If you have very specific custom processes that are more focused on a high volume of lead and opportunity management, you may lean toward using Salesforce to Salesforce.

✓ At the same time, if you send a lot of customized partner communications, including collateral and content distribution, and you deal with both a Salesforce-owning and non-Salesforce-owning indirect sales force, you may want to lean more toward the Partner Community.

We don't have one correct answer to give you, so make sure that you run things by your Customer Success Manager. Salesforce.com charges extra for an organization that invites others to share information, but the invited organization can accept that invitation for free.

Reducing channel conflict with deal registration

Without a well-thought-out Partner Relationship Management (PRM) process, companies often run into channel conflict when their direct sales and indirect sales forces butt heads over who found which lead first. As the channel manager, you often have to waste time arguing with a direct sales rep and her manager over who has dibs, while the prospect waits for the internal bickering to stop. This isn't an efficient way to close a deal, and it's frustrating for the customer to often hear multiple messages (or even price quotes!) from what's supposed to be a united front. In addition, if the partner loses out on that opportunity, you've just lost some of her trust in how supportive you really are in her efforts — so why should she reveal her pipeline data early or adopt your processes?

By taking the time to design a deal registration process, concisely and consistently communicate the status of deal registrations to partners, efficiently carry out the approval for all submissions, and then be able to measure related conversion and close ratios, you can eliminate channel conflict. The deal registration capabilities of Salesforce Communities help provide clarity on what your deal registration processes are from start to finish, which can increase adoption of your partner program and help increase partner sales because the channel conflict inefficiencies disappear. However, this setup can be successful only if you invest the time to think out your deal registration process. If you have a hard time explaining it or whiteboarding it, how do you think your partners feel?

Here are some key questions to ask before establishing any deal registration program:

- How would you describe your deal registration process, from start to finish?
- What do partners get for registered deals? Exclusivity? A rebate? A different tier or status?
- What do you think would increase deal registrations?
- What information do you need when a deal is registered? Balance your quest for knowledge with the partner's patience in filling out fields.
- What's your process for approving deal registrations?
- What criteria do you evaluate to determine who officially owns a deal?
- Does this approval process work the same for all partners? For which categories would it be different?
- What metrics matter to you?

Accessing Salesforce Communities as a Partner

You can strengthen your vendor relationship by accessing your vendor's instance of Salesforce from a web portal and getting first-hand access to leads, accounts, opportunities, and other tabs to manage your deals. You can get leads assigned to you in real time — no waiting forever after a trade show ends to see which leads to pursue. You can also provide your channel managers with real-time updates on the status of deals that you're trying to bring in. That way, if you need some assistance, your channel manager can view all deal-related activity that occurred up to a certain point and provide you with the appropriate resources to close the deal. In the following sections, we give you a quick overview on accessing and navigating your Partner Community.

As a partner sales rep, you'll receive an e-mail from your vendor's Salesforce administrator after he is ready for you to start accessing the Partner Community. The e-mail welcomes you to the Salesforce Community and provides you with everything you need to log in.

In this e-mail, click the appropriate link to log in directly to your Partner Community and change your temporary password. Remember to bookmark the URL for easy access later. After logging in and changing your password, you're brought to the home page for your Partner Community. Every time you log in to the Partner Community, you begin at your home page. You'll see that the Partner Community is organized into a series of tabs, similar to the navigation of Amazon.com. Refer to Figure 12-1. The look of your portal may resemble your vendor's branding or your own.

Viewing and updating your leads

At the top of the Partner Community is the Leads tab, which contains leads that have been assigned to you directly or a general queue. The queue allows channel managers to make leads available to their partners on a first-come-first-serve basis while also avoiding multiple partners working on the same lead: After you claim a lead from the queue, no other partner may claim it.

Take note to play nicely. The Force.com platform is very customizable, and your vendor could set up rules for how many leads each partner may claim so that a partner with an itchy trigger finger doesn't take away all the goodies.

The leads available to you are viewable from the Lead Views list and are displayed according to columns set by your vendor. Click any column heading to re-sort your list according to that column's criteria. Click the same column header a second time to re-sort your list in reverse order.

If you see a record in your list, that's a lead in a queue that you should claim if you think you're the right partner to pursue it. You'll see that the Action column displays Accept for these types of leads.

To claim a lead from a queue, follow these steps:

1. **Click the Accept link for that record.**

   A link to the lead now appears in the Recent Items section in the sidebar. You can click it to review more information about your lead and update the lead status to begin pursuing this suspect.

2. **Click Edit to update the lead.**

   After all, you want to be able to work on all the leads that you claimed so that your channel manager sees some results.

3. **Click Save after you update the record.**

   The Lead page reappears.

Managing your opportunities

When a lead has progressed far enough in the sales process, you convert it into an opportunity. You can manage your existing opportunities and create new ones from the Opportunities tab. To update the deal information on an existing opportunity, following these steps:

1. **Click the Opportunities tab at the top of your Partner Community.**

2. **Select the My Opportunities option from the List View drop-down menu to see a list of opportunities that you own, as shown in Figure 12-2.**

Figure 12-2:
Viewing
your oppor-
tunities.

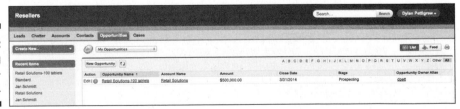

3. **Click the Edit link next to the opportunity that you want to update.**

4. **Update the fields to reflect the latest developments in the sales deal.**

5. **When finished, click Save.**

    You are returned to the List View page.

Setting Up Salesforce Communities for Your Channel Team

Before setting up Salesforce Communities, your Salesforce administrator should meet with a member of the channel sales team to confirm your PRM needs. Discuss the following questions:

✔ What percentage of your sales force is indirect versus direct?

✔ What types of partners do you work with?

✔ Do you message differently to each type of partner?

✔ What are the objectives, challenges, and participation benefits for each type of partner in your program?

✔ How are your channel territories broken out?

✔ How are channel managers tracking partners' sales and marketing activities today?

✔ How do channel managers put together their channel forecasts? How long does it take, and how accurate is the information?

Armed with this information, make sure that you set an appointment with your salesforce.com Customer Success Manager for some free advice or a blessing to go forward with using Salesforce Communities. Chances are that if answers to these questions show that your business relies heavily on an indirect sales force, yet your visibility into the channel pipeline is as clear as mud, you probably need Salesforce Communities. Again, the information we give you is meant to prepare you to successfully implement Salesforce Communities. The details of all the cool features that you can activate are more thoroughly discussed on salesforce.com's success site.

Part IV

Optimizing Demand with Marketing Cloud

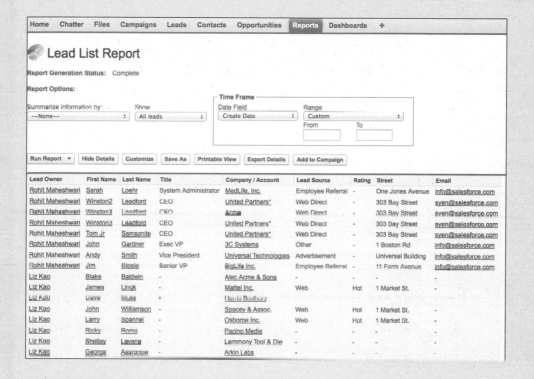

Understand how third-party marketing automation vendors integrate with Salesforce at www.dummies.com/extras/salesforcedotcom.

In this part . . .

- Find out about managing marketing campaigns in Salesforce, using the company's Campaign record.

- Design a campaign from scratch, to track the various life cycle stages that make sense to your business.

- Build a target list based on names already in Salesforce, or even those from purchased lists.

- Design a Web-to-Lead form to drive leads to campaign-related landing pages.

Chapter 13

Driving Demand with Campaigns

In This Chapter

▶ Creating campaigns

▶ Creating a target list

▶ Executing a campaign

▶ Assessing campaign effectiveness

Companies want to increase revenue by spending marketing dollars intelligently. However, because of the disconnect between sales and marketing teams, managers have a harder time executing campaigns, let alone tracking and measuring the results of their marketing programs. Now, more than ever, marketing departments have to prove that they are contributing to the sales funnel versus being regarded as a cost center. Marketing executives have to show that their marketing spending is resulting in new customers. If this sounds familiar to you, campaigns in Salesforce can help you manage and track your marketing programs more effectively, helping you manage your customer acquisition costs, bring in more qualified leads, and contribute more to sales.

A *campaign* is any marketing project that you want to plan, manage, and track in Salesforce. The higher-level goal is to create something (a content piece or an event, for example) that generates demand for your product or service. Depending on your current or planned strategies, types of campaigns include trade shows, search engine marketing, e-mail marketing messages, online promotions, webinars, online events, and print advertising, although this is by no means a complete list.

In this chapter, you find out how to create and manage campaigns, segment target lists, execute campaigns, track responses, and analyze campaign effectiveness.

To administer campaigns, you must be a system administrator or a user with permission to manage campaigns (that is, a marketing manager type). See Chapter 20 for details on configuring your user information and profile to manage campaigns.

Understanding Campaigns

Available for Professional, Enterprise, and Performance Edition users, the *Campaign module* in Salesforce is a set of tools that you use to manage, track, and measure your marketing programs. Its foundation is the campaign record, which can be manually or automatically linked to lead, contact, and/or opportunity records to provide real metrics on campaign effectiveness.

A campaign record comes standard with a set of fields that help you manage and track your campaigns. The following list describes the fields that you use most often to measure campaign effectiveness:

- ✓ **Campaign Name:** This is the name of your marketing project. Choose a name that's readily obvious to sales reps and other users whose leads or contacts might be included in the campaign. For example, if you send monthly e-mail newsletters, you might distinguish each campaign by month, as in "Administrators Newsletter — May 14" and "Support Agent Newsletter — June 15."

- ✓ **Type:** This drop-down list includes the types of campaigns that you run within your marketing mix (Direct Mail, Email, and so on).

- ✓ **Status:** This drop-down list defines the statuses of a campaign. Salesforce provides a simple default drop-down list of statuses to measure a campaign's progress, from the initial planning stages to completion. By using this field, you and others can make sure that the campaign is on track.

- ✓ **Start Date:** This date field tracks when a campaign begins.

- ✓ **End Date:** This date field tracks when a campaign ends.

- ✓ **Expected Revenue:** This currency field estimates how much revenue the campaign will generate.

- ✓ **Budgeted Cost:** This is the amount that you have budgeted for the marketing project.

- ✓ **Actual Cost:** This is the amount that the project actually cost.

- ✓ **Expected Response:** This percentage field is your best guess of the response rate of a campaign. For example, if your e-mail campaigns typically receive a 2 percent response rate, you might use this value to benchmark the effectiveness of the campaign you'll be tracking in Salesforce.

- ✓ **Num Sent:** This is the amount of people targeted in the campaign. For example, if you executed an e-mail campaign to 10,000 e-mail addresses, that would be your Num Sent.

- ✓ **Active:** This check box marks whether a campaign is active. If you don't select it, the particular campaign doesn't appear in reports, or on related lists and other campaign drop-down lists on lead, contact, and opportunity records.

✔ **Description:** This field allows you to describe the campaign so that other users who want more detailed information on the campaign can get a solid snapshot.

Depending on your marketing processes, terminology, and goals, you or your system administrator should modify the drop-down list values and change the fields on the record. (See Chapter 20 for details on customizing Salesforce.)

If you're a marketing manager, you can plan and manage the majority of your campaign preparation inside Salesforce. You can

✔ Lay out your entire marketing plan of projects.

✔ Build the basic framework and business case for a project.

✔ Define statuses and success metrics for campaign responses. *Success metrics* measure how you determine whether the campaign was worth your company's time, money, and effort.

✔ Develop a detailed project plan so that important tasks get accomplished.

In the following sections, we show you where and how to accomplish these tasks.

In mid-2013, salesforce.com acquired ExactTarget, a marketing automation company that itself had previously acquired an e-mail marketing provider called Pardot. We will be following closely to see how ExactTarget technology slowly becomes integrated more into Salesforce's native campaign functionality.

Creating a new campaign

To create a campaign, log in to Salesforce and follow these steps:

1. **Select the Campaign option from the Create New drop-down list on the taskbar.**

   A New Campaign page appears, as shown in Figure 13-1.

2. **Fill in the fields as much as possible or as required.**

   If you manage marketing programs for your company, you should see few surprises in the campaign fields. See the preceding section for a summary of the standard entry fields.

3. **When you're done, click Save.**

   Optionally, you can click Save & New if you have more than one campaign to create and want to immediately start on the next one.

Campaign Edit
New Campaign

| Campaign Edit | Save | Save & New | Cancel |

Campaign Information

		Status	Planned
Campaign Owner	Liz Kao		
Campaign Name	Salesforce For Dummies We		
Active	☑		
Type	Advertisement		
Parent Campaign			
Campaign Currency	USD – U.S. Dollar		
Description			

Planning

Start Date	[12/14/2013]		Expected Revenue	
End Date	[12/14/2013]		Budgeted Cost	
Num Sent	0		Actual Cost	
Expected Response (%)	0.00			

Figure 13-1:
Fill in the campaign record.

After you save your final campaign, the campaign page reappears with the information you entered as well as additional system-generated fields that automatically update as your company makes progress on a campaign.

You can associate campaigns to a parent campaign and see the aggregate performance statistics in one place. For example, our Salesforce.com For Dummies, 5th Edition Launch Event could be a parent campaign to other campaigns such as Email Drop, Banner Ad, and Dreamforce book signing. To group campaigns into a campaign hierarchy, have your Salesforce administrator add the Parent Campaign field to your Campaign page layout. You can then use that field to associate child campaigns with a parent. See Chapter 20 for more information on page layouts.

Modifying the member status

A *campaign member* is a lead or a contact who's part of a specific campaign. Depending on the type of campaign you're running, you can modify the campaign to have a unique set of member statuses. For example, the member statuses that you track for an e-mail campaign (Sent, Responded) are typically different from those of a trade show that you're sponsoring.

To customize member statuses for a specific campaign, follow these steps:

1. **Go to the campaign record and click the Advanced Setup button.**

   The Campaign Member Status page for your campaign appears. When you first begin to create campaigns, Salesforce creates a default set of member status values of Sent and Responded.

2. **In the Member Status Values related list, click the Edit button.**

   The Campaign Member Status page appears in Edit mode, as shown in Figure 13-2.

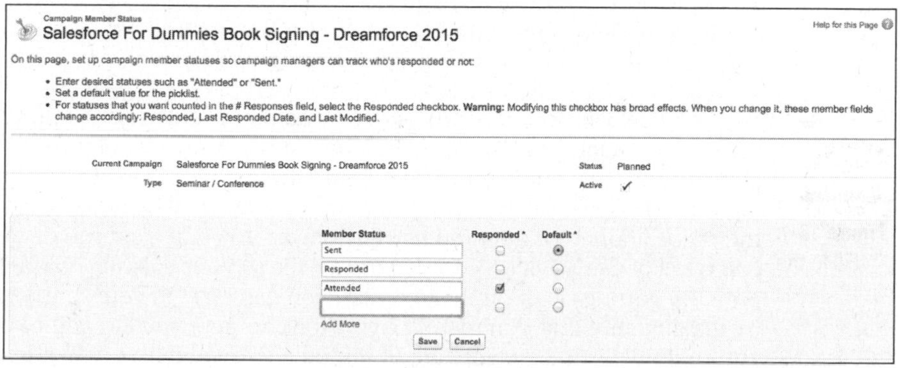

Figure 13-2: Editing the Campaign Member Status.

3. **Modify statuses by entering a new value in the Member Status column.**

   For example, if you're sponsoring a booth at a conference, the preregistrants list is part of the package, and if you want to invite attendees to visit your booth, you might add member statuses of Registered, Invited, Attended, Visited Booth, and Met at Show.

4. **Select the check box in the Responded column to classify a status as responded.**

   This field tracks the Expected Response Rate field against the actual response rate.

5. **Use the Default column to select a default value.**

6. **Click Save.**

   The Campaign Member Status page reappears with your changes.

Building Target Lists

One of the biggest challenges that marketing managers face is developing the right target lists for a campaign. *Target lists* are the lists of people you're targeting in your campaign. Depending on the type of campaign that you're planning, your lists might come from different sources, such as rented or purchased lists from third-party providers or existing lists of leads and contacts already entered in Salesforce. If your target list is comprised of the latter, you can create your target list directly from the Salesforce Reports tab and associate specific campaigns to those leads and contacts, or you may add leads and contacts directly to specific campaigns.

Using rented lists

With a rented list, your options are limited. Depending on the circumstances, sometimes you don't know who's on the list because the list is controlled by the vendor. Other times, you agree to limited use terms, such as one-time usage. In these circumstances, simply use the external list as the target list instead of importing the list into Salesforce.

You can use Salesforce to improve the quality of rented lists. Many third-party vendors look for duplicate names, confirm that they all point to the same person, and then help you merge them into one file. They do this by comparing their database against your customer database when they're generating the record count for a rented list. As long as you can trust the vendor, you can quickly use Salesforce to generate a file of your existing contacts to compare. By getting rid of duplicates first, you can stretch your marketing dollars by making sure that you're not paying for contacts you already have. And if you're doing a mixed campaign of rented and owned lists, you stand a better chance of not upsetting a customer with duplicate mail.

Importing new campaign members

If you own or purchase a list and intend for your teams to follow up on all the records, you can import the list into Salesforce as lead records and automatically link the records to a campaign. Here, we show you how to select a list on your computer to import, mass-associate various characteristics to the list (such as the lead source or campaign), perform the import, and verify that your settings came through.

To import a list and attribute it to a campaign, follow these steps:

1. **On the campaign record, click the Advanced Setup button, verify that the member statuses are accurate, and then return to the campaign record by clicking the Back button in your browser.**

2. **Click the Manage Members button.**

   A drop-down list appears.

3. **Choose the Add Members – Import File option.**

   The Campaign Member Import Wizard starts.

4. **Click the Import Leads button.**

   Step 1 of the Lead Import Wizard appears. Here, you associate various field statuses to the list of leads that you want to import.

5. **Prepare your file, following the instructions that the wizard gives you.**

   Here are the main steps to perform:

   a. *Add and fill in a column for Member Status unless all records will use the default member status.*

   or

   Add and fill in a column for Lead Owner unless you'll be the owner or you're applying lead assignment rules.

   b. *Save the file in a .csv format on your computer.*

6. **In the wizard, click the Browse button to select the file from your computer.**

   A Choose File dialog box appears.

7. **Locate your file and click Open.**

   The dialog box closes, and the filename appears in the field.

8. **Use the drop-down list to select a lead source.**

9. **(Optional) Use the next drop-down list to select an assignment rule.**

10. **(Optional) Select the Use Assignment Rule Settings to Send Notification Emails to Record Owners check box.**

11. **Verify the campaign to which your leads will be assigned.**

12. **Verify the default member status.**

13. **Leave the character encoding unchanged unless necessary.**

    If you're using this within the United States, you most likely won't be changing this. To be sure, check with your system administrator.

14. **(Optional) Select the Trigger Workflow Rules for New Leads check box if you want workflow rules to work on new or updated records.**

15. **When you're done, click Next.**

    Step 2 of the wizard appears, where you confirm the mapping of the Salesforce field to the correct column in your uploaded file.

16. **Map the fields by comparing the Salesforce Field columns against the corresponding drop-down lists in the Import Field columns.**

17. **When you're done, click Next.**

    Step 3 of the wizard appears.

18. **Review and confirm the import, and when you're done, click the Import Now button.**

    Your new campaign members will appear under your campaign record, which you can access from the Campaign tab.

Targeting existing members with the Integrated Campaign Builder

Assuming that your company has already imported users' leads and contacts, you can build your target lists directly in Salesforce in three ways:

- ✔ Associating existing leads and contacts en masse to a campaign
- ✔ Adding members from custom reports
- ✔ Adding members from a List View

After you link your desired leads or contacts with a specific campaign, you can begin to target them.

Adding members from a campaign record

To associate existing leads or contacts to a campaign you're planning, start by making sure that you can see the leads or contacts via a List View. See Chapter 5 (contacts) or Chapter 9 (leads) for information on using List View. You can add as many as 200 leads or contacts per List View page. Then, follow these steps:

1. **From the specific campaign record, click the Manage Members button.**

   A picklist appears.

2. **Select the Add Members – Search option.**

   In this example, we add existing leads. The Manage Members Wizard appears.

3. **In the Manage Members Wizard, do the following:**

   a. *From the Add Members subtab, in the Choose Member Type to Search section, confirm that the Leads radio button is selected.*

   This is the default.

   b. *Specify the Filter Criteria.*

   You may use an existing lead view or create new criteria now to get the leads you want for this campaign.

   If you're not yet sure what subset of leads to use, step back and give this some thought. E-mailing all the leads in your database might not be a wise decision.

4. **Click Go after you select your criteria.**

   The search results appear below the filter criteria.

5. **Select the check box next to the appropriate leads that you want to be added to this campaign, as shown in Figure 13-3.**

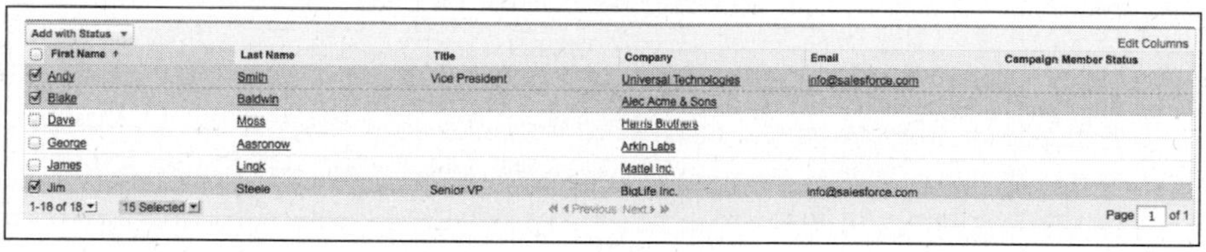

Figure 13-3:
View leads
to associ-
ate with a
campaign.

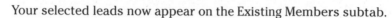

6. **Click the Add with Status drop-down list to immediately select and associate the member status with those selected leads.**

   Your selected leads now appear on the Existing Members subtab.

   Don't worry. If your itchy trigger finger got you to add some members before you were ready, you can use the handy Remove button to disassociate the members from this campaign and start over again.

7. **Repeat Steps 2–5, selecting new views, as needed.**

8. **Click the Back to Campaign: *[Campaign Name]* link below the Manage Members page name when finished.**

   The campaign record reappears.

Adding members from a custom report

As many as 50,000 leads or contacts in a single lead, contact, or campaign report may be associated to a campaign. To add existing members by running a report, follow these steps:

1. **From the Reports home page, click a custom report of the leads or contacts that you'll be targeting. (See Chapter 17 for more information on creating custom reports.)**

   A Reports page appears, as shown in Figure 13-4.

2. **Click the Add to Campaign button.**

   The Add Members Wizard appears.

3. **Select an existing campaign for the Campaign field. Use the Lookup icon to search for your match.**

4. **After a campaign is selected, choose the appropriate status from the Member Status drop-down list, as shown in Figure 13-5.**

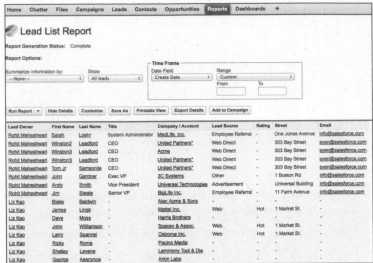

Figure 13-4:
Add report
members to
a campaign.

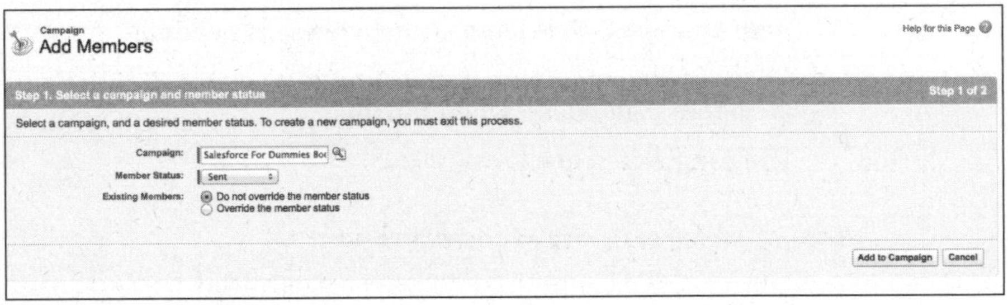

Figure 13-5:
Selecting
the member
status for
report
members.

5. **Use the radio buttons to toggle whether you want the existing member statuses to be overridden by this member status.**

   The default is to not override existing member statuses.

6. **Click Add to Campaign to continue.**

   Step 2 of the wizard appears with a status message of your attempt.

7. **Click Done when information has been verified.**

   You're returned to your custom report page.

Adding members from a view

If you've followed our example to this point, from any lead or contact view page, you can add members to campaigns. Note that the capability to add members to campaigns from any lead or contact view page allows only marketing managers to select and add members one page at a time, so it's best for adding a small amount of members. If your view is more than one page, you have to advance to that page and then add members. To add a member from a List View, make sure that the view has already been created and follow these steps (to see how to make custom List Views, read Chapter 9 or 10):

1. **At the view's results page, select the check box next to the appropriate member names that you want to add to your campaign.**

   In Figure 13-6, we add some contacts to a campaign.

Figure 13-6:
Add list
members to
a campaign.

2. **Click the Add to Campaign button after your members have been selected.**

   The Add Members Wizard appears.

3. **Select an existing campaign for the Campaign field. Use the Lookup icon to search for your match.**

4. **After a campaign is selected, choose the appropriate status from the Member Status drop-down list.**

5. **Click Add to Campaign to continue.**

   Step 2 of the wizard appears with a status message of your attempt.

6. **Click Done when information has been verified.**

   You return to your view page.

Executing Campaigns

Depending on the type of campaigns you're running, you might execute those campaigns online, offline, or in combination. And, based on the complexity of the campaign and your resources, you can use Salesforce to assist with the execution parts of your campaign.

Delivering an online campaign

If you send e-mail campaigns as part of your marketing strategy (and who doesn't nowadays), you can use Salesforce for elements of the execution. Those elements might include

- **Exporting an e-mail list** from Salesforce for delivery to your e-mail execution vendor or internal resource

- **Building a web form** to capture leads as part of your e-mail or webinar campaign

  See the later section "Using Web-to-Lead forms."

- **Using standard e-mail templates with merge fields** so that you can control the look and feel of your messaging

You can use Salesforce to deliver and track mass e-mails, but Salesforce wasn't designed or intended to be used for large-scale, mass e-mail marketing. Some Salesforce customers use the mass e-mailing tool for small campaigns. Depending on which edition of Salesforce you have, you can send 100 (Professional), 500 (Enterprise), or 1,000 (Performance) e-mails per mass mailing. Your company is always limited to 1,000 e-mails per day.

 Several e-mail automation vendors have integrated their campaign execution tools with Salesforce. With this integration, marketing managers can more seamlessly deliver e-mail campaigns from Salesforce. The costs and functionality vary across the e-mail marketing vendors, so check out the options on the Force.com AppExchange directory at www.appexchange.com. Search using the keyword *email*.

Executing an offline campaign

If you execute offline campaigns, you can also use Salesforce in a variety of ways to simplify the process. How you use Salesforce depends on the type of campaign, but here are some suggestions:

> ✔ **If you're sponsoring a conference:** Set up a web registration form for your booth computers to capture information on attendees who visit your booth.
>
> ✔ **If you're sending out direct mail pieces:** Use Salesforce to generate lists for your fulfillment vendor.

Tracking Responses

After you launch a campaign, you can use Salesforce to track responses. In Salesforce, you have three basic types of tracking mechanisms, which we describe in the following sections.

To track responses on a campaign, you need to be able to view the Campaign related list on lead and contact records. If you can't view this list, see Chapter 20 on customizing page layouts or see your system administrator for help.

Using Web-to-Lead forms

Whenever we help clients with using Salesforce, we take a look at their Contact Us web page. If it's filled with a bunch of e-mail addresses (like info@*mycompany*.com), we immediately recommend that they get Web-to-Lead up and running. After all, a company with a website using Salesforce in this day and age should take advantage of capturing information via an online form.

Web-to-Lead is a Salesforce feature that enables your company to easily capture leads from your websites and automatically generate new leads in Salesforce. With Web-to-Lead, you can collect information from your websites and generate as many as 500 new leads daily. Say that you already have a registration or a lead form on your public website. With Salesforce, you can — in minutes — generate HTML code that your webmaster can apply to your existing form. Then, when people fill out the form on your website, the information is routed instantaneously to users in Salesforce. By using Web-to-Lead, your reps can follow up on leads in a timely manner.

Specifically for campaign tracking, you can also create forms for specific landing pages designed for a unique campaign to capture information on a campaign member who responds.

Before you can capture leads from an external web page, though, you need to enable Web-to-Lead, add any additional custom fields to your lead record, generate the HTML code, and add the code into a web page. Of course, involve your web team and web designers to test and review this before it goes live.

Enabling Web-to-Lead

All Salesforce customers can capture leads from web forms. First, check whether you need to turn it on for your company.

Log in to Salesforce and follow these steps:

1. **Choose Setup⇨Customize⇨Leads⇨Web-to-Lead.**

   The Web-to-Lead Setup page appears. Under Web-to-Lead Settings, make sure that Web-to-Lead is enabled. You can tell by looking for the Web-to Lead Enabled check box. If it's selected, you're good to go. If not, go to the next step.

2. **If Web-to-Lead isn't enabled, click the Edit button.**

   The Web-to-Lead Settings edit page appears.

3. **Fill out the fields on the page.**

   Salesforce provides three fields:

   • *Web-to-Lead Enabled:* Select this check box.

   • *Default Lead Creator:* Use the Lookup icon to select the default creator for when a lead is generated from a web form. You usually select the user who manages marketing campaigns for your organization.

   • *Default Response Template:* Select a default e-mail response template. You don't need to have one, but it's a good practice to reply to leads so that they know you got their request.

4. **When you're done, click Save.**

   The Web-to-Lead Setup page reappears.

Generating HTML

You can use a tool in Salesforce that takes the guesswork out of generating HTML code for your web forms.

To generate a general or a campaign-specific Web-to-Lead form, log in to Salesforce and follow these steps. If you just finished the steps in the preceding section, click the Create Web-to-Lead Form button in the Web-to-Lead Setup page, and you'll arrive here.

1. **Choose Setup⇨Customize⇨Leads⇨Web-to-Lead.**

   A Web-to-Lead Setup page appears.

2. **Click the Create Web-to-Lead Form button in the Web-to-Lead Settings section.**

   The Web-to-Lead Setup page appears.

3. **In the Create a Web-to-Lead Form section, customize which fields you want to include on your Web-to-Lead form.**

   Click a field name in the Available Fields column, as shown in Figure 13-7, and then click the Add arrow button to add that field from the Available

Fields column to the Selected Fields column. Conversely, remove fields from the Selected Fields column by similarly clicking a field name in the Selected Fields column and then clicking the Remove arrow.

Balance selecting enough fields so that they help you route the lead to the right person with the patience level of the prospect filling out the form.

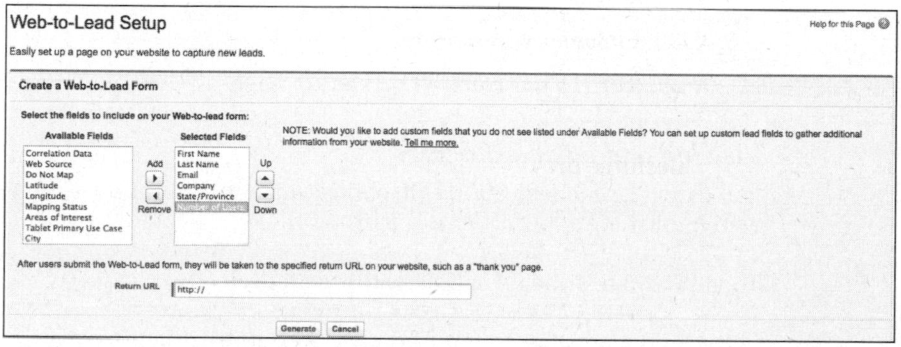

Figure 13-7:
Creating
a Web-to-
Lead form.

4. **In the Return URL field, enter a return URL (if known) and then click the Generate button at the bottom of the page.**

   The return URL corresponds to the landing page that appears after the lead has submitted his information online. If you don't know whether you have one, or which one to use, check with your marketing manager and your web manager. When you click the Generate button, a page appears with HTML code inserted in a box, as shown in Figure 13-8.

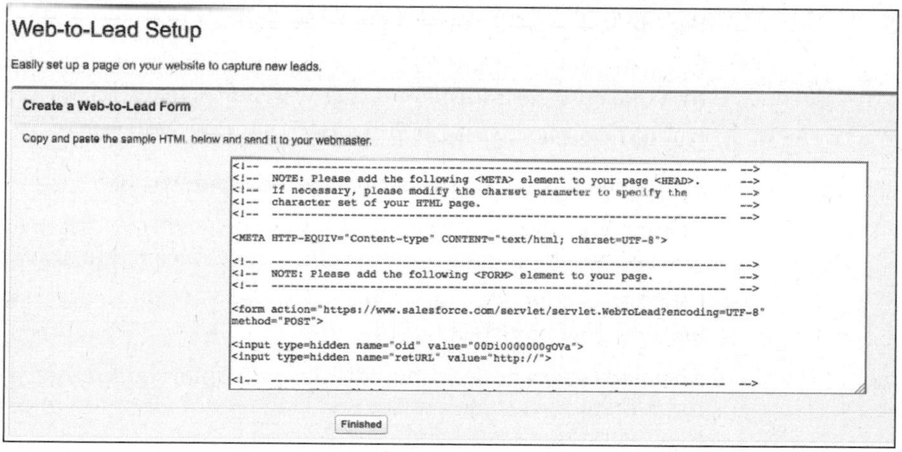

Figure 13-8:
Generating
basic HTML
for your
Web-to-
Lead form.

If you're creating a web form specific to a campaign, create the campaign first, and make sure that you selected the Active check box for that campaign record. By doing this, you can select the fields for Campaign and Campaign Member Status, which enables you to track the specific campaign.

5. **Copy and paste the HTML code into a text file and send it to your webmaster.**

6. **Click Finished when done.**

   You return to the Web-to-Lead Setup page.

Viewing and testing the form

You can view and test the HTML code as an actual form by using your favorite web publishing application and a browser.

To view and test the form, follow these steps:

1. **Open a new file in your favorite web publishing program.**

   Popular programs include FrontPage, Dreamweaver, and HomeSite. You can even use Notepad or TextMate.

2. **Copy and paste the HTML code in the HTML mode.**

3. **Save the web page in HTML format (not `.txt`!) on your computer.**

4. **Open a browser and choose File⇨Open to open the web page.**

   A web form appears with the lead fields that you selected. The form is relatively unformatted, but your webmaster can apply code to make the form fit with your desired look and feel.

5. **Fill out the basic form and click the Submit button.**

   If you inserted a return URL, that page appears. If not, a page appears that displays the information that was sent to Salesforce.

6. **Log in to Salesforce and click the Leads tab.**

7. **Select Today's Leads from the Views drop-down list.**

   The leads list for today appears. If the test lead isn't listed, click the Refresh button in your browser until the test lead appears.

8. **Click the test lead's link under the Name column to validate the information from your test lead.**

   The lead record appears and displays the information that you submitted. Don't forget to delete the test lead record after you're comfortable that everything's working!

9. **Scroll down to the Campaign related list.**

   You should see a link to the campaign and the default member status. If you selected the Campaign Member Status field when generating the HTML code, you can apply a member status to all leads derived from the web form.

Manually updating member statuses

If your campaign is designed to have recipients respond by phone or e-mail, your reps can manually update records as they interact with campaign members. Reps might have to create lead or contact records first if you didn't build your target list from Salesforce. For example, if you rent a third-party list for an e-mail campaign, the respondent might not yet be recorded in Salesforce.

To manually update a lead or contact responding to a campaign, follow these steps:

1. **In the sidebar Search, search for the lead or contact.**

   See Chapter 2 for details on using Search.

2. **If you can't find the lead or contact record, create it.**

   See Chapters 5 and 9 for details on creating contact and lead records, respectively. If you find the record, skip this step.

3. **Go to the specific lead or contact record page.**

4. **Click the Edit button, make any changes to the record, and click Save.**

   For example, you might use the fields to enter additional information supplied by the respondent.

5. **Use the related lists to log any related information or future activities.**

Adding a member to a campaign

In those circumstances when your target list was built externally, reps need to add the member to the campaign.

To manually add a member to a campaign, go to the lead or contact record and follow these steps:

1. **In the Campaign History related list, click the Add to Campaign button.**

   A Lookup box appears.

2. **Select the appropriate campaign view from the Search Within drop-down list to narrow your options, and use the search bar to find a campaign within that view.**

   The Search Results page appears.

3. **Click the campaign name.**

   The New Campaign Member page appears.

4. **Select the appropriate member status from the Status drop-down list and click Save.**

   The Campaign Member detail page appears.

Updating the status of a current member

If the lead or contact is already linked to the campaign in Salesforce, you'll want to update the member status when he or she responds.

To update member status manually, go to the lead or contact record and follow these steps:

1. **Scroll down the page to the Campaign History related list, and click the Edit button next to the relevant Campaign Name.**

   The Campaign Member Edit page appears.

2. **Use the Status drop-down list to change the status and then click Save.**

Mass-updating campaign statuses

If leads or contacts that are part of a campaign respond in a batch, you can do a mass update of campaign members. For example, if you sent an e-mail campaign to existing contacts and received a batch of online registrations as responses, you could perform a mass update. The following sections tell you two ways to update statuses: in a campaign or in a report. Sometimes you'll be working directly out of a campaign. Other times you might be running a specific report that isn't campaign related (for example, an existing "Northern California Active Customers" report), but you might want to update the status of people that turn up in that data set.

Mass updating all member statuses in a campaign

To mass update campaign statuses for all contacts or all leads in a campaign, log in to Salesforce and follow these steps:

1. **Click the Campaigns tab and select the specific campaign whose members' statuses you'd like to update.**

2. **Click the Manage Members button.**

   A picklist appears.

3. **Select the Edit Members – Search option.**

   The Manage Member page appears, with the Existing Members subtab selected.

4. **Use the filter criteria, as needed, to narrow the members that you want to update.**

   You can also manually select which members to update by selecting the check box next to their names in the results.

5. **Select members to be updated for this campaign, as shown in Figure 13-9.**

   You may select up to 200 members to update.

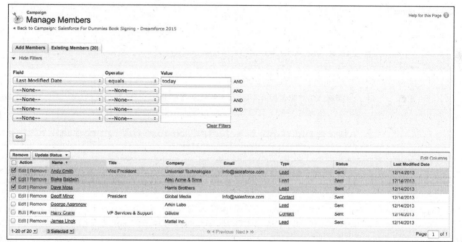

Figure 13-9:
Updating
existing
campaign
member
statuses in
bulk.

6. **Click Update Status to apply the new status to your selected members.**

   A status bar displays the results of the operation. You may continue updating by selecting new views, or click the Back to Campaign: [*Campaign Name*] link when done.

Mass updating all member statuses in a report

To update the status of several members at once, follow these steps:

1. **Click the Reports tab and scroll down to the Campaigns Reports folder from the left sidebar.**

2. **Click the Campaign Call Down Report link.**

   A page appears, allowing you to select a specific campaign.

3. **Use the Lookup icon to choose a campaign and click the Run Report button, as shown in Figure 13-10.**

   A Campaign Call Down Report for your campaign appears.

Figure 13-10:
Selecting a
campaign
from
within the
Campaign
Call Down
report.

Campaign Call Down Report

This report shows all members of a specific campaign.

Select campaign:
Salesforce For Dummies Boo [🔍]   **Run Report**

4. **Click the Add to Campaign button.**

   The Add Members Wizard opens.

5. **Confirm the campaign in the Campaign field. Use the Lookup icon to search for your match.**

6. **After a campaign is selected, choose the appropriate status from the Member Status drop-down list.**

7. **Use the radio buttons to toggle whether you want the existing member statuses to be overridden by this member status.**

   The default is to not override existing member statuses. However, if your goal is to update all statuses of members in this report, choose to override the status.

8. **Click Add to Campaign to continue.**

   Step 2 of the wizard appears with a status message of your attempt.

9. **Verify the information and click Done.**

   You return to your view page.

You may also mass-update campaign statuses for contacts or leads in a campaign by updating the information in a `.csv` file first and then importing it. For example, a trade show exhibitor may give you a file of all show attendees that you can cross-reference with leads that you invited. After you know which of your invitees actually attended, you may import this file into Salesforce. Just make sure to add and edit a column for Member Status (unless all records will use the default status) and have a column for Lead or Contact ID. Then, click the Manage Members button, click the Update Status — Import File link, and follow the guidelines to update the campaign history. See the "Importing new campaign members" section, earlier in this chapter, for more information.

Chapter 14

Driving Sales Effectiveness with Content Management

. . . .

. . . .

*I*f you, as a sales or marketing manager, expect to get the most out of your sales reps, you have to put the best tools at their fingertips. Aside from a desk, chair, phone, and some caffeine, reps need accurate and compelling documentation: sell sheets, white papers, case studies, and so on. All too often, however, sales documents reside in multiple places: network drives, e-mails, laptops, and so on.

If your reps are losing business because they can't access the right documents, take advantage of Salesforce Content, which you can use to store the latest sales collateral in an easy-to-use, searchable library. And as long as your reps have an Internet connection, they can access Content, even if they're sitting in an airport in Omaha, Nebraska.

What does an easily accessible library mean? If you're a sales rep or manager, this means spending more time in front of your customers and less time chasing information. If you're in marketing or product management, you can better control the message to customers with the confidence that sales reps are providing customers with the most up-to-date information available. And regardless of your role, you can individually store documents in your own personal folder.

In this chapter, we show you how to use the Salesforce Content as well as how to search for documents so that your reps can put them to work to sell more effectively.

Understanding Salesforce Content

Salesforce Content is more than just the place where files are stored in Salesforce. With Salesforce Content, you get a full content management system that allows you to collaborate, manage, and share material that's stored anywhere on the web. Because it's part of Salesforce, your Content can take advantage of all the other features of Salesforce, such as custom fields, sharing, validation rules, and even Apex triggers.

For companies that need to organize a large amount of current documents, Salesforce Content allows you to search document contents, notify you when content is updated, and track user feedback. All these features help to further increase your sales and marketing teams' productivity. Best of all, it's built in to Salesforce, so it's waiting for you to use as soon as you're ready.

Identifying content use cases and users

Anyone who has ever managed a document repository for himself or his company can tell you that repositories need to be maintained to remain effective. If you sell a variety of products, for example, your product sheets need to be updated as specs change, deleted if you retire products, and added as you release new products.

And even though Salesforce provides easy-to-use tools to help you manage the workload of document control, keeping a large volume of material up to date can still be a daunting task.

If your company is committed to using Salesforce as the central repository for every department's content, you may want to consider using Salesforce Content for the following reasons: increased collaboration, document tagging, deeper search capabilities, and notification of content changes.

Before users can interact with Salesforce Content, they have to be granted permission to access that feature. Choose Setup➪Administer➪Manage Users➪Users, and then edit the users that you want to have maintaining your content management system. Make sure that the Salesforce CRM Content User check box is selected for those users.

Creating Libraries

If you want Salesforce Content to be a highly effective sales tool for your staff, you have to organize your content so that people can easily find it. By using libraries, you can sort files into logical groupings.

We've seen many different and effective approaches to organizing libraries in Salesforce. Some companies like to separate content by product family; others prefer to take a vertical approach. The only right answer is the one that works for your company, so make sure that you spend some time deciding on a naming convention for your libraries. The My Libraries list on the Libraries home page will grow over time, so a clean and intuitive naming convention will help prevent a cluttered appearance. The following is a list of common libraries that work for many organizations:

- ✔ Hardware
- ✔ Sales presentations
- ✔ Product data sheets
- ✔ Case studies
- ✔ Professional Services
- ✔ Salesforce training

To create a library, you must first have the Create Libraries permission. (If you're not sure, you can quickly find out by seeing whether you get past Step 1 in the following list. If you're not able to get past Step 1, ask your administrator to help.) To continue, click the Libraries tab to go to the Libraries home page and follow these steps:

1. **Click the New button under the My Libraries heading.**

   A New Library Wizard appears.

2. **Type a name and description for the library.**

3. **When you're done, click Save and Close.**

   The Library Name page appears, and you may begin contributing new content to your new library. You can return to your library at any time by clicking the Libraries tab and looking at the My Libraries list.

As you plan your content strategy, keep in mind that not all sales documents need to be in Salesforce Content. Some might be better suited as attachments on an account record; others you might not even want to have in Salesforce. As a general rule, files that might be reusable or have wide applicability are good for Salesforce Content. Documents that relate to a specific account are typically more relevant as attachments to Account detail pages.

Adding Content

Adding content to a library — also known as *contributing content* — is simple. To upload a new document, follow these steps:

1. **Click the Libraries tab in the Content app and then click the Contribute button.**

   The Contribute Content page appears.

2. **Click the Choose File button and browse your hard drive for the file that you want to upload.**

   Salesforce Content automatically uploads the file you select.

   You can add a website link to refer people to an online video or to information stored on your intranet by clicking the Do You Want to Link to a Website Instead link.

   After Salesforce Content uploads your document, it asks you to describe and publish your content, as shown in Figure 14-1.

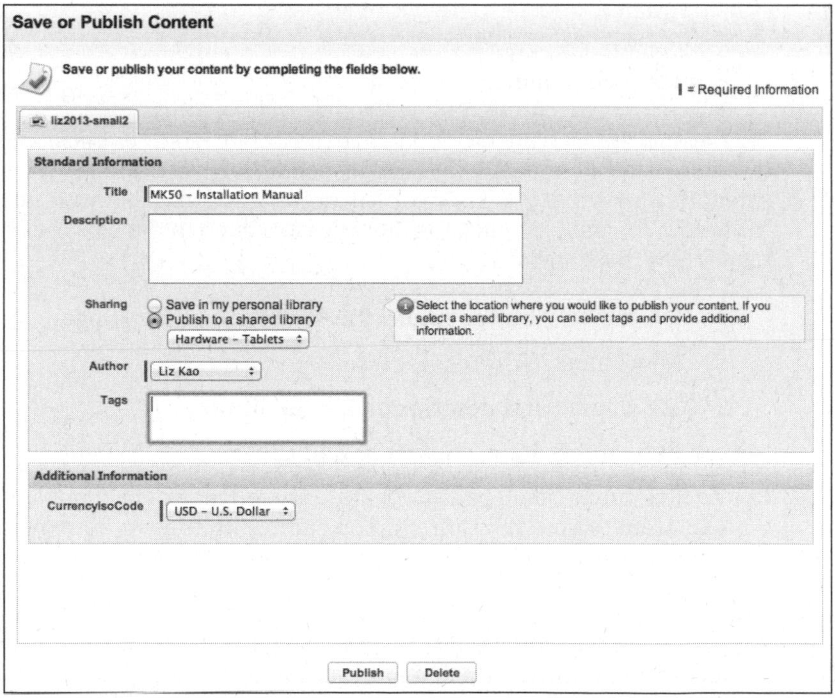

Save or Publish Content

Save or publish your content by completing the fields below.

❙ = Required Information

▣ liz2013-small2

Standard Information

Title	MK50 – Installation Manual
Description	
Sharing	○ Save in my personal library ⦿ Publish to a shared library [Hardware – Tablets ⬥]	ⓘ Select the location where you would like to publish your content. If you select a shared library, you can select tags and provide additional information.
Author	[Liz Kao ⬥]
Tags	

Additional Information

CurrencyIsoCode	[USD – U.S. Dollar ⬥]

[Publish] [Delete]

Figure 14-1:
Contributing new content in Salesforce.

3. **Give your content a descriptive title.**

   Follow standard naming conventions within your company.

4. **Select the Publish to a Shared Library radio button to store this file in a library.**

5. **Select the appropriate library from the drop-down menu.**

6. **If you're not the file's author, select another user from the Author drop-down menu.**

7. **(Optional) Add tags to this document if you want to identify it with words that may not be used in the standard library definitions.**

   Separate tag words with commas. Be sure to use words that people would commonly search for when looking for this document. We recommend that you only allow a subset of content users to determine what tags should be used, if you want to use tags as an alternate way to better filter for content. Otherwise, you risk having redundancy of tag words (like "datasheet" and "data sheets") which reduces their effectiveness.

8. **Click Publish when you're done.**

If you have some content that you want to share with two different groups, like sales and marketing, rather than creating a new library just to house their shared documentation, you can associate content with the two libraries by following these steps:

1. **Return to the Libraries home page.**

2. **Select a document from the Top Content section.**

3. **On the Content details page, click the Edit button.**

4. **Select the Library Actions option and then the Share with Another Library suboption.**

5. **Highlight additional libraries with which to share this document and click the Publish button.**

Editing Content

After you contribute content to Content, you may need to update its details in Salesforce. Search for and go to your Content record from the Content tab and follow these steps:

1. **Click the Edit button.**

   The Edit drop-down list of options appears.

2. **Select the Edit Content Details option.**

   The Edit Content window appears.

3. **Update the title and description.**

   You can also upload new versions of files when changes have been made offline by selecting the Upload New Version option.

4. **(Optional) Add tags to this document if you want to identify it with words that may not be used in the standard library definitions.**

   Separate words with commas. Be mindful of making the tag word too broad or too specific.

5. **Click Save.**

Anyone subscribed to this Content record will be notified of any new versions that are uploaded.

You can subscribe to a Content record by clicking the Subscribe button at the top of the record. You'll get an e-mail anytime someone updates the file, along with an explanation of what changed.

Finding Content

You can search for content from the search box located on the Content home page. Click the Content tab to go to the Content home page and then follow these steps:

1. **In the search box, type search terms, as shown in Figure 14-2.**

   Optionally check the filter check boxes to only search within a subset of all your Content. Filters include standard attributes like the content's file format, or the author. This can also include everyone's tag words, which is why we recommend an organized approach to creating tag words.

   In addition to searching filenames, Salesforce Content searches the actual text contained in files of the following formats: rich text format (RTF), UTF-8 encoded TXT, HTML, XML, Adobe PDF, and Microsoft Office 97–2007 Word, Excel, and PowerPoint files.

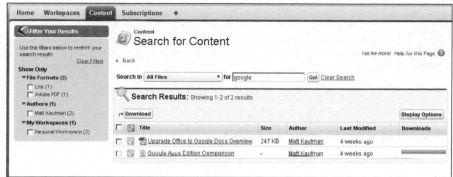

Figure 14-2:
Search for
content in
Content.

2. **Click the Go button.**

   The page reappears with a list of Content results based on your search.

3. **Select the appropriate check boxes for the file(s) you are looking for and then click the Download button to save copies to your computer.**

   Alternatively, click the Title of Content record to see a preview of the file prior to downloading, as shown in Figure 14-3.

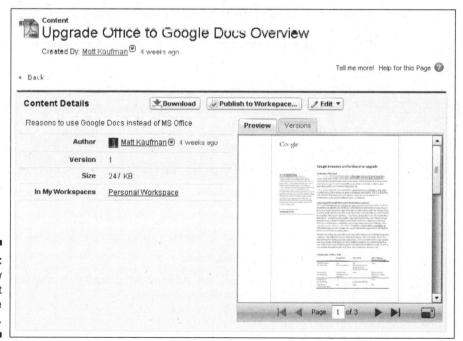

Figure 14-3:
Preview
content
before
downloading.

While your content is a work in progress, you can leverage the Files tab to combine the features of Chatter and Salesforce Content. You'll be able to share with specific coworkers or groups, collaborate and get feedback, and upload revisions. When you're ready to publish, head over to the Libraries tab and show off your work.

Understanding Documents

Prior to the addition of Salesforce Content, you could store files in Salesforce on the Documents tab. Although not as robust as Content, the Documents tab is still available and useful in many ways. For example, you can host images referenced in e-mail templates, custom apps, and even Force.com sites on the Documents tab. These files typically don't change often and definitely don't need to be collaborated on, so you can continue to store them by clicking the Documents tab. Another easy way to regard Documents is as a place where system administrators house files. However, if you need the ability to preview files, collaborate on them with Chatter, or store larger size files, those files belong in Salesforce Content.

Creating folders in the Document Library

To create a document folder, you must first have the Manage Public Documents permission. (If you're not sure, you can quickly find out by seeing whether you get past Step 1 in the following list. If you're not able to get past Step 1, ask your administrator to help.) To continue, go to the Documents home page and follow these steps:

1. **Click the Create New Folder link under the Document Folders heading.**

   A New Document Folder page appears.

2. **Type a name for the folder in the Document Folder field.**

3. **Use the Public Folder Access drop-down list to select the access rights.**

4. **Click the radio buttons to select who should have access to the folder.**

5. **When you're done, click Save.**

   The Folder Name Documents page appears, and you may begin adding new documents to your new folder.

Adding documents

Before reps can begin using documents in Salesforce, you or someone in your company must first add the documents to the Document Library.

When uploading files, the file size limit on any individual file is 5MB. For some companies, this might be the average size of a PowerPoint presentation or a PDF file with graphics, so plan accordingly.

To add a document and upload its file, log in to Salesforce and follow these steps:

1. **Select Document from the Create New drop-down list on the sidebar.**

   An Upload New Document page appears.

2. **Type a name for the file in the Document Name field.**

   If you want the document name to be an exact match of the filename, leave this field blank. After you select the file, the filename automatically populates the empty Document Name field.

3. **Select the For Internal Use Only check box only if you want this document to be confidential.**

   If you select this check box, you don't alter its access, but you flag your end users not to send the file outside the company.

4. **Select the Externally Available Image check box only if you're uploading an image that you'll be sending in HTML e-mail templates to people that should view it without having to log in to Salesforce to see it.**

   For example, logos or letterhead footers should have this box selected.

5. **Use the Folder drop-down list to select a folder.**

   If you haven't yet created the appropriate folder, or you don't have read-write access to the correct folder, you can first store the file in the My Personal Documents folder and refile the document later.

6. **In the Description field, type a brief description of the document.**

7. **In the Keywords field, type keywords that will help your end users find the document.**

   Salesforce provides a Find Documents search tool on the Documents home page, so you should select keywords that you think your users will enter.

   For example, if you're adding a case study, you might enter keywords that include relevant products, customer names, challenges, and so on that sales reps could use for cross-referencing.

8. **Under the Select the File step, the Enter the Path radio button is selected by default, so you just need to click the Browse button to select the desired file.**

   A Choose File dialog box appears.

9. **Select a file from the folders on your computer and click Open.**

   The dialog box closes, and the document path is entered in the File to Upload field.

10. **When you're done, click Save.**

    When the upload is completed, the document record page reappears in Saved mode with information on the document and a link to view the document.

Using documents

After you create documents in Salesforce, you can use them in various ways in the course of your selling. You can search for documents from the Documents home page or browse through your document folders. You can leverage an image that was uploaded from the Documents tab, in Email Templates. If you're an administrator, you can also customize the logo in the upper-left corner of Salesforce with an uploaded image, as long as it is at most 20 kilobytes.

Differentiating between documents, content, and files

If you're a little unsure as to where to store a file, that's okay; here's a simple recap. Use Documents to store images used in Email Templates. Use Files for collaborating on works in progress. Use Content for publishing approved material throughout the business.

Part V
Delighting Customers with Service Cloud

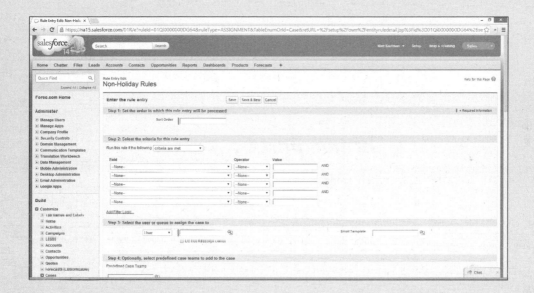

In this part . . .

- ✔ Learn how to manage your customer service case load
- ✔ Build your knowledgebase with Salesforce Knowledge
- ✔ Empower your customers with Communities

Chapter 15

Performing Fast and Accurate Support

Salesforce provides robust customer service functionality in its Service Cloud product. The module is used to track and resolve cases, using a variety of features that allow agents to respond to cases as efficiently as possible. But it's more than that as well.

With Service Cloud, you have all the tools at your fingertips to efficiently deliver excellent customer service while managing the costs of operations. In days and weeks, versus months and years, you can start and manage a fully integrated customer service strategy that supports the many channels that customers use to communicate with you. Service Cloud also provides the ability to handle web chats from customers looking for help on your website, for customers to log in to a private portal where they can submit new cases and check up on existing ones, and a console where agents can minimize the number of clicks and additional pages they have to open to see information about a customer.

In this chapter, we introduce you to basic customer support functionality in Salesforce, starting with its core concept, the case. We first discuss fundamental support agent processes for handling new cases, and then we cover how to manage the growing caseload.

Walking through a Day in the Life of a Service Agent

Salesforce follows a general process when it comes to managing cases. Service agents (you may call them *support reps*) commonly perform these tasks on any given day. The specific tasks may be different in your company, but you probably see some similarities:

- ✔ Responding to inbound e-mails and calls
- ✔ Taking new cases from assigned queues
- ✔ Validating that the inquiry is coming from an authorized contact
- ✔ Creating a case to begin tracking efforts to resolve the issue
- ✔ Working the case backlog, including researching solutions
- ✔ Managing service-level agreements
- ✔ Communicating the resolution to the customer

At its core, customer support is all about accepting questions and answering them in a timely and consistent manner, while providing high levels of customer satisfaction. How you handle your responses — and the scale on which you handle them — are more complicated issues.

High-volume call centers can take advantage of Salesforce's customer management and reporting capabilities by using Salesforce's call center capabilities. Salesforce CRM Call Center integrates Salesforce with third-party computer-telephony integration (CTI) systems, allowing your call center agents to do cool stuff, such as dial and receive calls from softphones on their computers and see what contact records or cases are related to the calls.

If your company's Salesforce users all have full licenses, and just need to capture a fairly manageable influx of basic cases, you can do that without having to purchase full-blown separate Service Cloud licenses.

Understanding the Case Record

A *case* is a record of a customer service inquiry (you may call them *tickets*), as shown in Figure 15-1. Just like other common records, such as accounts and contacts, you can track all interactions on a case from a single detail page. And to manage all your cases, Salesforce comes out of the box with all the tools that you need for routing, queuing, and escalating cases, plus complying with service-level agreements (SLAs), if that applies to your company.

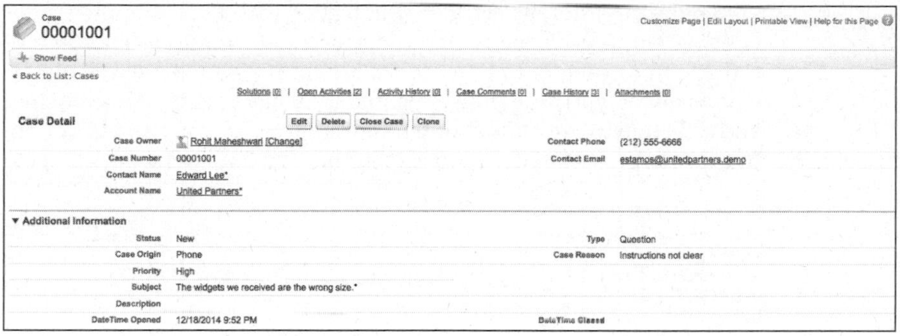

Figure 15-1:
Introducing
the case
record.

A case record comes preconfigured with standard fields and two icons commonly used for case management. Most of the standard fields are self-explanatory, but in the following list, we highlight key fields that are less obvious:

- **Status:** This field defines the important statuses in your case process. It comes preconfigured with a basic process, but you should modify the values to fit your process. If you're an Enterprise or Performance Edition user, you can use this field to distinguish multiple support processes appropriate to the different kinds of cases you want to track.

- **Case Number:** When you create a case, Salesforce automatically assigns a sequential number used for tracking. If you're an administrator, you can change your starting number and numbering format. See Chapter 16 for more information on customizing this.

- **Type:** Use this picklist field to define the type of case. Salesforce presets this list with selections that include Problem and Question, but you can modify the picklist to match your categories.

- **Case Reason:** Use this picklist field to specify the reason the case was opened. Many companies track this field to identify areas of customer service that they can improve. Of course, you can also modify this list to suit your needs.

- **Case Origin:** Use this field to record from which channel the case originated — for example, by phone, e-mail, or web. Many companies report on this field to understand and improve the methods by which customers interact with service and support agents.

- **Internal Comments:** Use this field to jot brief comments on this case to communicate internal messages, as needed. Customers or people outside of your company will not see this field by default. However, internal comments that are marked Public may be viewed by clients in the Customer Portal, if you have it enabled.

You may also hear the term *case feed*. The case feed borrows functionality from Salesforce's Chatter feature so that users can better collaborate around resolving a particular case. Internal discussions about a case appear chronologically above the case details, as shown in Figure 15-2. Each comment can then appear in other employee's feeds, and those with information that could help can reply with a comment of their own. You don't even have to know the coworker who is giving you a response. He just may have seen your comment in his feed, know the answer, or know someone else who knows the answer and can give that other person a heads-up also within the comment.

Figure 15-2:
Posting a comment on a case feed.

Creating a Case

One of the main responsibilities of an agent is handling new inbound inquiries. Writing notes on a little sticky square that you attach to your monitor may not be the best way to track information, especially if you have terrible handwriting. In the following sections, we discuss how to begin the case management process in Salesforce so that the right information is tracked for the right customers.

Validating the contact

The first step in creating a case is validating the company and contact information to see whether any special circumstances or SLAs exist. This is less of a technological innovation then a general business best practice. Can't have just any random person taking up your precious time, can we? This information should reside in custom fields on the account record. For example, to do this in response to an inbound call, log in to Salesforce and follow these steps:

1. **Type the company name (or account number — whatever your company uses to identify its customers) into the Search field on the sidebar on your Home page and then click the Go button.**

   The Search Results page appears. Hopefully, you see the account name listed. If it's not listed, you should have some business processes in place to determine how to verify that the person or business calling in is indeed a customer.

2. **Click the Account Name field.**

   The Account record appears. Verify the business's information on this record that helps you identify that you're allowed to support this company. You might verify an address or an account number. You should confirm those processes first before using cases.

3. **Look at the Contact detail list to locate the person with the problem.**

   Again, depending on your company's policies, you may or may not have specific customer contacts authorized to call you for support.

4. **Click the Contact Name field.**

   The Contact record appears. Verify information on this record that helps you identify that this person is permitted to call for support. If the contact record doesn't already exist, create a new contact record. For more information, read Chapter 5.

Entering new cases

After you qualify the customer, you have to associate a case to each new issue you receive. Because cases are associated with contacts, the best, most reliable way to create case records is by starting from the relevant Contact detail page. From the Contact detail page, you can add a case by using either the Create New drop-down list on the sidebar or the New button on the Cases related list. The result is the same in both situations, and you automatically prefill the Contact lookup field. By doing this, you can always find your case, and your case activities will be listed on the overall Contact detail page.

To create cases by using the best practice, follow these steps:

1. **From the Contact detail page, click the New button on the Cases related list.**

   The Edit mode of a new case appears.

2. **Fill in the fields as much as you can or as required.**

   Notice that the Contact field is prefilled with the contact you were working from.

3. **When you're done, click one of the following buttons:**

  - *Save:* Brings up the Case detail page.

  - *Save & Close:* Saves the current case info and automatically takes you to the Close Case detail page, as shown in Figure 15-3, where you select the appropriate closed case status and add additional details. Use this to quickly resolve an issue.

  - *Save & New:* Saves the current contact info and automatically opens a new, blank contact record.

  - *Check Spelling:* Checks the spelling of the contents of the Description field.

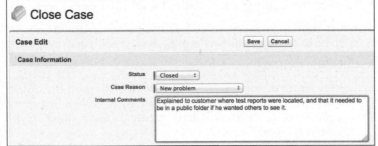

Figure 15-3:
Closing a case.

To clone a case, click the Clone button at the top or bottom of the case record. If it's the day of a new product or feature release, and many customers are reporting the same problem, the Clone button will come in handy for you. This is similar behavior across other records in the Salesforce family.

You can also set up Salesforce to generate a new case from an e-mail sent to specific addresses (like `support@yourcompany.com`), also known as the Email-to-Case feature. You have a few options, depending on your company's e-mail requirements. For example, if you need to have all e-mail traffic behind your firewall and will be receiving attachments larger than 10MB, check out Email-to-Case at

```
http://wiki.developerforce.com/index.php/Members:Email_To_Case
```

Check with your account executive to discuss other options. Of course, you could always have a Web-to-Case form set up (similar to the Web-to-Leads that we discuss in Chapter 13), too.

Managing Cases

As a service or support agent, one of your key goals as a case owner is to address and resolve many customer issues as quickly as possible. Ideally, the need for speed is balanced with some defined processes to ensure a sense of order. Over time, your caseload will build up as different cases take different lengths of time to resolve. You'll work off the Cases home page, which you access by clicking the Cases tab at the top of the page. There you'll be able to see the most recent cases and adjust your views so that you can see the cases that are most relevant to you (for example, maybe you handle all the Platinum requests for the West Coast and just want to see those). In the following sections, we describe how to efficiently update a case as you work it, and then we discuss how to manage your growing caseload.

Updating case fields

As you work your cases, you may need to modify case information. To update a case, follow these steps:

1. **Type the case number in the Search tool and then click Go.**

   If you don't have this information (usually from your customer), don't worry; you can still enter whatever information you have about the customer into the search tool. It may take a few extra hops to get to the case as you return a contact or account record, but the beauty of Salesforce is that these records are all related, via the account record. A Search Results page appears.

2. **Click the desired Case Number link.**

   The Case detail page appears.

3. **Click the Edit button at the top of the case record.**

   The case record appears in Edit mode.

4. **Update the fields, as necessary, and then click Save.**

   The Case detail page reappears. Notice that the fields you edited have been changed.

Case comments can't have their own related list on the case detail record and are meant to record any short internal conversations that agents may review at a glance. If you have a Customer Community set up (see Chapter 16 for more information), agents may optionally share certain comments with contacts on a case.

Reassigning case ownership

After you create cases in Salesforce, you might need to transfer them — reassign them — to the right people: folks who become responsible for case resolution after it's been escalated, for example.

To reassign a case, go to the case record and follow these steps:

1. **Next to the Case Owner field, click the Change link.**

   The link is in square brackets. The Change Case Owner page appears.

2. **Select the user to whom you're assigning the case.**

   (Optional) Select the check box to choose to notify the recipient with an e-mail.

3. **When you're done, click Save.**

   The case record reappears. Notice that the Case Owner field has changed to the assigned user.

Getting a clue on views and queues

Case views and case queues are accessed from the same location — the Case View drop-down list on the Cases home page.

A *case view* is a list of cases that match certain criteria. When you select a view, you're basically specifying criteria to filter the results that you get back. The advantage of using a view, versus searching, is that you can use the view over and over again.

If your company has several agents resolving cases for a variety of products and services, your administrator may set up *case queues* to automatically funnel cases to the right pairs of eyeballs. For example, you may use your website to collect both product and billing inquiries. Case queues would allow support agents to grab new cases from the product queue, while accounting operations staff can monitor the billing queue.

To try out a predefined view, do the following:

1. **On the Cases home page, open the Cases Views drop-down list.**

   The four default options appear and maybe some other choices that have already been created for you.

2. **Select the All Open Cases option.**

   The All Open Cases list opens, as shown in Figure 15-4.

   Notice that Salesforce lays the list out with standard columns that correspond to commonly used case fields, plus an Action column so that you can quickly modify a record.

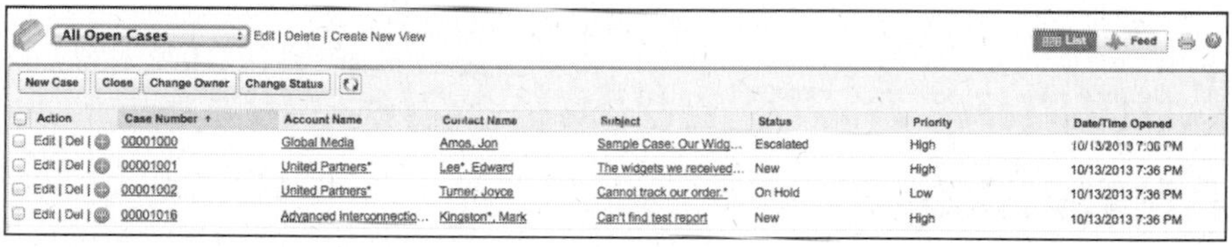

Figure 15-4: Viewing a preset case list.

3. **Click a column header to re-sort the list page.**

4. **Open the record for any case by clicking a link in the Case Number column.**

   A Case detail page appears.

5. **Click the Back button in your browser, and then click the Edit button on the same row as the case you just clicked.**

   The case record appears in Edit mode, and you can make changes to the data.

6. **Select the check boxes on certain rows if you'd like to close, change ownership, or change the case status *en masse*. Then, click the corresponding button to perform the group action.**

   The case record appears in Edit mode for that action, and you can make changes, as appropriate.

Queues ensure that everyone has an equal chance at the latest cases.

To choose a case from a queue, follow these steps:

1. **From the Cases home page, select the view that corresponds to a queue that you're supposed to monitor.**

   The list page appears.

2. **In the Action column of the case list, select the check boxes for the case records that you want to accept and begin working on.**

3. **Click the Accept button to take ownership of these cases.**

   You've now claimed these cases from the general pool of new cases.

Creating custom case views

If you want special lists for the way that you track your cases, we recommend building custom views. For most objects with tabs in Salesforce, you can create a custom view. See Chapter 4 to find out how to generally create a custom view.

Knowing More about Salesforce Knowledge

Salesforce Knowledge introduces a more robust knowledge base option for support departments and call centers. It's smart enough to return relevant answer options to internal support agents or customers, based on its evaluation of your problem description. Multiple filtering options also let you find information based on multiple attributes, for example, based on the type of product and the topic of the issue (GenWatt Engine products and Broken Circuit topics). It's available for Enterprise and Performance Edition users, and possibly for an additional price, depending on your edition. (Talk to your account executive for more information.)

We discuss Salesforce Knowledge in depth in Chapter 16.

Researching and Resolving Cases

When you have your set of assigned cases, the next milestone is to resolve the customer's issue. In general, case resolution means responding to the issue and doing it efficiently so that you minimize time spent on repetitive tasks. For example, typing out the same explanation to "Where's the Any key?" (you know, when the manual says to "press any key") can tend to get stale after a while.

Understanding solutions

A *solution* is a basic text boilerplate response to a commonly asked question. As you resolve cases, service reps can both apply existing solutions and create new ones that your teams can use in the future. Using solutions helps

new agents ramp up more quickly and makes any agent on your team profi-
cient on a wider range of topics. The following list describes additional terms
used when discussing solutions:

- A solution has a related list that indicates all the cases that use the solution. This association is the key to a feature called *Suggested Solutions,*
  which substantially reduces the amount of time it takes to get answers
  to cases. In essence, it finds similar cases and suggests solutions that
  have answered those cases.

- *Solution Categories* group similar solutions together. One solution may
  belong to one or more categories.

- Your collection of solutions is often referred to as the *knowledge base*
  and can populate both a Customer Portal and a searchable FAQ for a
  public website. See the earlier section "Knowing More about Salesforce
  Knowledge" for more information about the Salesforce knowledge base.
  (Yes, it can be a bit confusing when the brand name of a salesforce.
  com feature is also a commonly used noun. In this book, we refer to the
  add-on product as Salesforce Knowledge.)

So what is the difference between Salesforce Knowledge and solutions? Solutions
were an original part of the product and are no longer being enhanced. They
are sufficient when working with a manageable volume of cases, and a more
basic, straightforward set of products or services to support. If your company
is new to the world of customer support, this is a good introduction as you
get your feet wet with what support processes work or don't work for your
particular company. This is why we go into a little bit more depth in this chapter
about this option. For companies with an extremely varied set of products
to support, or for those that need to have very precisely reviewed templates
of public-facing information, Salesforce Knowledge may be a better option.
Its native functionality lets information get captured in multiple formats. For
example, a Salesforce Knowledge article could include an attachment that is an
installation manual. When an agent tries to search for an answer to a particular
problem, deep searching capabilities allow Salesforce to search for keywords
even within that attachment. Also, salesforce.com will continue to enhance
Salesforce Knowledge. Discuss your needs with your success manager to
better understand which option is the better fit for your company's needs.

Finding solutions

From the case record, look for solutions by using the method described in
this section.

You'll see a Find Solution button on the Solutions related list, as shown in
Figure 15-5. Click the Find Solution button to view relevant solutions. We
generally recommend that you associate only reviewed solutions with cases.

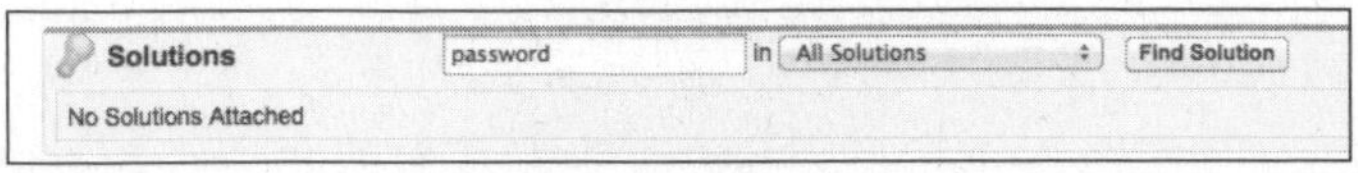

Figure 15-5:
Viewing
suggested
solutions.

Solutions	password	in All Solutions ▾	Find Solution
No Solutions Attached			

To look for solutions by using the Search box in the Solutions related list, follow these steps:

1. **In the Search box of the Solutions related list, enter keywords related to a possible solution.**

   After you get more familiar with solutions and their unique IDs, you may even look up a solution by part of its solution number.

2. **If your company uses solution categories, select a category in which to search.**

3. **Click Find Solution.**

   The Find Solution for Case *Number* page appears. If Solutions Categories are enabled, search results are first shown by category and subcategory groupings.

Attaching solutions to a case

When you're viewing the relevant solutions, you want to find the appropriate solution(s) and associate it (or them) to your case. You may do this in two ways:

✔ From the reviewed list of relevant solutions, click the Select link next to a reviewed solution.

✔ If you need to confirm the details of the solution first, click the Solution Title link, and then click the Select button on the Solution detail page when you're sure of the right solution.

After either method, you're returned to the Case Record page. In the Solutions related list, you see the solution that you just attached. If you add more than one solution to a case, simply repeat the steps for finding solutions and associate them to your case, as appropriate.

Attaching a solution to a case counts as a solution being "used" in Salesforce. This tally can later be analyzed in reports so that support executives and product managers can see which problems or questions are being reported the most (which, in turn, warrant the use of certain solutions). By getting measurable feedback on issues, the support and product teams can work more closely to address the actual issue before cases need to be logged.

Communicating the Outcome

After you research your case and find the right solutions for it, you now must communicate this resolution to your customer before you officially mark the case closed. Make sure that your administrator has created appropriate case resolution e-mails for your support team.

Responding with standard e-mail templates

Standard e-mail templates allow you to merge your attached solutions into the body of an e-mail template, which you then send to your customer. This increases the efficiency with which the support team can answer questions. To provide a response to a customer using an e-mail template, read through Chapter 8 for details.

Closing a case

After you resolve your case and successfully notify your customer, it's time to close the case and move on to the next one. One of the key advantages of Salesforce is its easy-to-use reporting system (more about that in Chapter 17). Additional information is collected after you close a case, so support executives can use the collective feedback to continuously improve the customer experience.

To close a case, follow these steps:

1. **From the case record, click the Close Case button.**

   Alternatively, if you're on the Edit page for the case record, click Save & Close. The Close Case page appears in Edit mode.

2. **Select the appropriate closed case status and add any internal comments, if needed.**

   Other fields are shown based on your company's customizations. If you're a Professional, Enterprise, or Performance Edition user, you'll also see an additional section allowing you to create a solution from this case.

3. **Edit the solution title as needed so that the solution may be applicable for all customers.**

4. **Select the Submit to Public Solutions check box to submit the solution for review by your team's designated solution managers.**

   This will also link the case to your new solution.

5. **Click Save when finished.**

If you want to display common solutions to the public so that customers can look for their own solutions, you have a few options. Both Salesforce Knowledge and the default solutions can be set up for this. Check with your account executive or customer success manager for details.

Chapter 16

Managing Your Contact Center with Service Cloud

*T*he heart of any successful customer service application is case management, and Salesforce Service Cloud provides a fully integrated solution to track, resolve, and manage all customer interactions, regardless of the point of entry.

Your support team can log in and begin using cases immediately, but they'll be much more successful if you invest some time up front to customize the program to the team's exact needs.

In this chapter, we guide the support executive or administrator on setting up case processes and customizing cases. Next, we review how to configure a scalable knowledge base. Then, we cover the different methods for automating customer service processes to improve agent efficiency.

Preparing Your Salesforce Service Cloud Strategy

As a support executive, if you want to get Salesforce Service Cloud working for you, you need to do some careful up-front planning. After you think through your processes, you can customize cases either by yourself or with your

Salesforce Service Cloud administrator. Here are some tips to think about before you get started:

- ✔ **Define and prioritize your service and support objectives.**

- ✔ **Identify and acknowledge your key challenges.** Try to identify the biggest ones first.

- ✔ **Start with the end in mind.** The best way to customize your application is to decide what you want to measure first.

- ✔ **Map out your key processes.** If you're a Visio whiz, use that tool. If not, grab a marker and diagram your key processes on a whiteboard or flip chart. For different types of support issues, think about the similar and different types of information that you want your reps to capture.

- ✔ **Figure out the best approach for your business.** You have many different ways to tackle a business issue with Salesforce Service Cloud — some of these approaches work better than others.

- ✔ **Assess how much of your support efforts you and your team can share with your customers.** If your users would welcome this sort of change, you may want to set up the Community.

- ✔ **Keep it simple.** Don't sacrifice your objectives just to keep things simple. The more complexity you build, the greater the risk that people won't use the application.

For cases, as with other objects, Salesforce Service Cloud provides some common design elements that let you customize the record. As you consider customizing cases, keep in mind that you should strive for ease of use, relevance, and data that can help you manage your support executive job while allowing your agents to efficiently manage theirs. (See Chapter 20 for the how-to details on adding new fields, customizing page layouts, adding record types, and other design tricks.)

Automating Case Management

As a support executive or system administrator with the right permissions, one of your biggest challenges will be managing and administering a growing collection of cases. And because support centers need to maintain customer satisfaction, efficiently opening and resolving cases and keeping customers happy are paramount to your bottom line.

The Salesforce Service Cloud provides built-in tools to help efficiently queue, route, and escalate cases according to your support needs. By distributing and managing case workload more effectively, you ensure that the right agents address the right cases to comply with internal or external service-level agreements (SLAs).

Adding case queues

To set up a case queue, choose Setup⇨Administer⇨Manage Users⇨Queues, and then follow these steps:

1. **From the Queues page, click the New button.**

2. **Complete the required fields for Label and Queue Name Email and the optional field for Queue Email.**

   The e-mail address will be used for notifications, such as when a new case has been added to the queue. The e-mail can be for an individual or point to a distribution list (on your e-mail server).

3. **In the Supported Objects section, move the Case option from the Available Objects into the Selected Objects column.**

4. **In the Queue Members section, move Available Members into the Selected Members column to add them to the queue.**

5. **When you're finished, click Save.**

   The Queues page reappears with your new queue displayed.

Using assignment rules for routing

Assignment rules are key to efficient and timely routing of new cases. Your team can apply these assignment rules when adding or editing cases, or when customers submit cases themselves through your website, e-mail, or a Community. (See later sections for more on supporting multiple channels.) These rules allow cases to route directly to users or queues.

For assignments, escalations, and other support automation tools, don't forget to set up e-mail templates for notifications — both internal and external. See Chapter 8 for tips on customizing e-mail templates.

To set up assignment rules, choose Setup⇨Build⇨Customize⇨Cases⇨ Assignment Rules, and then follow these steps:

1. **From the Case Assignment Rule page, click the New button.**

   A New Case Assignment Rule page appears.

2. **Select a Default Case Owner or Automated Case User if prompted.**

   - A *default case owner* is the person where the buck stops — the person to whom the case routes when the assignment rules can't seem to find anyone else.

   - *Automated case users* are the owners of cases that are created by Salesforce Service Cloud, as opposed to being manually created by a human being.

3. **Type a rule name and select the Set This as the Active Case Assignment Rule check box if you want this to be the active rule; then click Save.**

   Typically, you have one case assignment rule to serve all your case assignment purposes. So, for example, you may have an active assignment rule called US Standard Support and another called US Holiday Support that you activate only when your holiday schedule is running.

   The Case Assignment Rules page appears with your rule listed.

4. **Select the rule name for the assignment rule you just created.**

   The Case Assignment Rule page for your rule appears.

5. **Click New under the Rule Entries related list.**

   A Rule Entry Edit page appears, as shown in Figure 16-1.

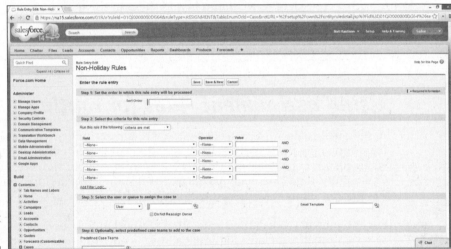

Figure 16-1: Creating a new case assignment rule.

6. **In Step 1 of the Rule Entry Edit page, enter a number for the order of the entry you're about to make.**

   The Salesforce Service Cloud evaluates these rule entries until it finds a match and then stops. The first successful match satisfies the rule, and an assignment is made accordingly.

7. **In Step 2 of the Rule Entry Edit page, enter criteria for the rule entry.**

   For example, if your company provides a different support team for partner inquiries, you might enter a criterion of **Account: Type Equals Partner** to denote cases that relate to partners.

8. **In Step 3 of the Rule Entry Edit page, select the user or queue to assign the case to and the notification template that goes to the new owner.**

9. **When you're finished, click Save, or click Save & New to set up another rule entry.**

   When completed, the Case Assignment Rule page for your assignment rule appears with the related list of rule entries.

Automating case escalation

To make sure that no case is ever overlooked and proper attention is paid to priority cases, you can apply *escalation rules*. Escalation rules prevent Chicken Little–type overreactions — so that you don't unnecessarily run around telling your team that the sky is falling . . . unless it really is. Instead, these rules allow you to create automated actions when cases with certain criteria are still open or untouched after a set duration. When escalating, you set up rule entries (similar to assignment rule entries) to notify users, reassign the case, or both.

To establish escalation rules, choose Setup➪Build➪Customize➪Cases➪ Escalation Rules, and then follow these steps:

1. **From the Case Escalation Rules page, click the New button.**

2. **Type a name, select the check box if you want this to be the active rule, and click Save.**

   As with case assignment rules mentioned in the preceding section, only one case escalation rule may be in effect at one time.

   A Case Escalation Rules page appears with your rule listed.

3. **Click the rule name for the escalation rule you just created.**

   The Case Escalation Rule page for your rule appears.

4. **Click New under the Rule Entries related list.**

   The Rule Entry Edit page appears.

5. **Complete the rule entry fields, following these guidelines:**

   - For tips on completing Step 2 of the rule entry fields, see Steps 5–7 in the preceding section.

   - In Step 3, select the Ignore Business Hours check box only if you want the escalation rules to be in effect at all times (this means weekends and holidays, folks).

   - In Step 4, select a radio button to determine how you want escalation times to be set.

6. **Click Save, or click Save & New to repeat the process for additional rule entries.**

   The Rule Entry Edit page reappears with a related list for Escalation Actions.

7. **Click the New button on the Escalation Actions related list.**

   An Escalation Action Edit page appears, as shown in Figure 16-2.

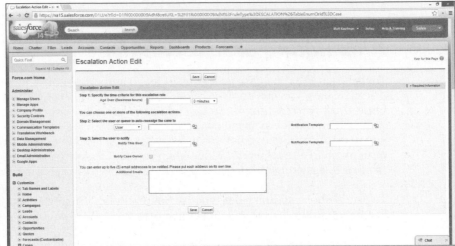

Figure 16-2:
Specify
actions
related to an
escalation
rule entry.

8. **In Step 1, specify the time criteria in the Age Over (Business Hours) field to trigger the escalation rule.**

   You can set escalations to occur after 30-minute intervals.

9. **In Step 2, select the user or queue that will be reassigned ownership of the escalated case.**

   You may also select a notification template for the recipient.

10. **In Step 3, select a user to notify after an escalation occurs.**

    You must also select a notification template for the recipient.

11. **Select the Notify Case Owner check box to ensure that the case owner is notified when one of his cases escalates.**

12. **In the Additional Emails field, enter as many as five e-mail addresses that you want to be notified of this escalation.**

    These addresses don't have to belong to Salesforce Service Cloud users.

13. **Click Save.**

    The Rule Entry Edit page reappears.

    Repeat Steps 8–13 as often as needed to add your escalation rule entries, plus corresponding actions.

Another way to automate assigning tasks and sending e-mail alerts within your organization is through workflow rules. Workflow is available to Enterprise and Performance Edition customers only; for details, see Chapter 20.

Capturing and Associating Cases Efficiently

In addition to using the phone, customers want to access support in two other common ways: directly from the web and via e-mail. You can have your customers use a web-based form or let them send an e-mail to your support organization. For either method, the Salesforce Service Cloud can enable these additional channels and make it easy for your agents to follow up. In this section, we describe the various options that you can use to begin collecting this information from your website.

Where do customers go when they have problems? Many customers would be happy if they could simply log the problem and be assured of a prompt response. With Web-to-Case, you can quickly generate an HTML form that captures cases submitted from your website. Then, by using case assignment rules, new cases can route directly to the agents or queues responsible for handling these inquiries. (See the section "Using assignment rules for routing," earlier in this chapter, for information on automating assignments.)

To automate Web-to-Case, choose Setup➪Customize➪Self-Service➪Web-to-Case and follow these steps:

1. **From the Capturing Cases from Your Website page, review the general outline, and then click the Generate the HTML link.**

   The Capture Cases page appears, as shown in Figure 16-3.

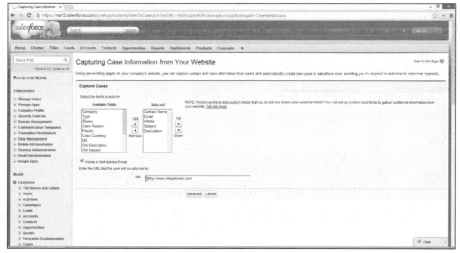

Figure 16-3: Generating the HTML to capture cases from your website.

2. **At this page**

   a. *Type a return URL where the users will end up after submitting their cases.*

   b. *Choose whether you want the form to be visible in the Self-Service Portal so that customers can submit new cases while monitoring existing ones (more on that later).*

   c. *Select the case fields to include on the form.*

   d. *Click Generate.*

   The return URL that you specify usually leads to a thank-you page or your support home page. After you click Generate, a new page appears with the HTML code in a box.

3. **Copy and paste the HTML code into a page hosted on your web server. Click Finished when done.**

   You'll want to review the notes at the top of the HTML, but this step is pretty simple. If such a review seems foreign to you, simply copy and paste the HTML into an e-mail and send it to your webmaster for help with this step. She knows what to do.

   You return to the Capturing Cases from Your Website page.

When the web page with your case-capturing form is live, fill out the form, like the unformatted sample in Figure 16-4, and test it to make sure that the case routes to the right resource.

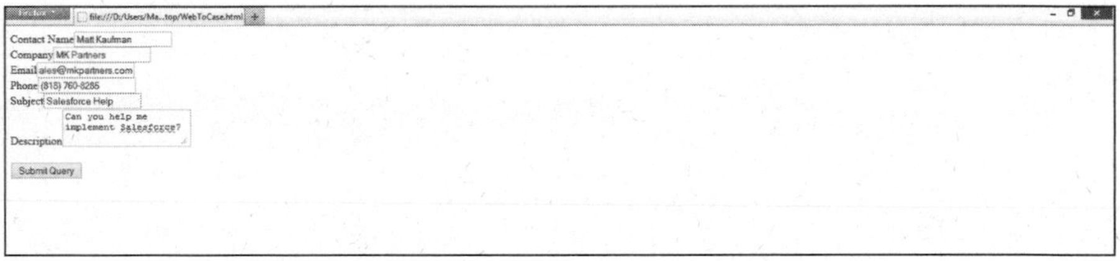

Figure 16-4:
Test an unformatted sample Web-to-Case form.

Contact Name Matt Kaufman
Company MK Partners
Email alex@mkpartners.com
Phone (815) 760-6286
Subject Salesforce Help

Description | Can you help me implement Salesforce?

Submit Query

When customers have issues, they often want to send an e-mail to your support team, expecting a timely response. With Email-to-Case, customers can send e-mail messages to aliases you create, which route new cases directly to the assigned resources and populate relevant case fields. Even attachments stay attached to the original e-mail message. Setting this up is simple and can be done by choosing Setup⇨Build⇨Customize⇨Cases⇨Email-to-Case. Follow the onscreen instructions and coordinate with your mail server administrator.

The Salesforce Service Cloud can also route responses to your customers after they submit a case by using the web or e-mail. This response informs the customer that your company has gotten the submission, and it can explain support policies, too. As long as you have those e-mail templates defined (see Chapter 8), you can assign them to use when responding to cases from Web-to-Case, Email-to-Case, or even the Customer Portal. Choose Setup⇨Build⇨Customize⇨Cases⇨Auto-Response Rules to configure this.

Harvesting Knowledge

Service Cloud from salesforce.com enables you to join the conversations happening on the web about your products and services. Instead of creating an additional channel for your agents to monitor, salesforce.com has already thought about how to capture these conversations and respond efficiently to the topics discussed.

Understanding Salesforce Knowledge

Salesforce Knowledge provides a knowledge base solution for support departments and call centers. It's available for Enterprise, Performance, and Developer Edition users for an additional price (talk to your account executive for more information).

If you're using an existing knowledge base solution, you can import those solutions into Salesforce Knowledge. The details are available in the Help & Training section, accessible from the upper-right of your Salesforce page.

Articulating articles

Salesforce Knowledge has its own vocabulary:

- ✔ **Articles** are the pieces of content and knowledge contributed by internal and external experts. Figure 16-5 shows an article that could solve a customer's problem.

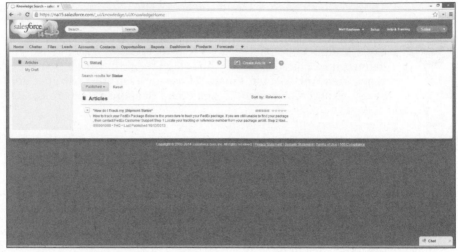

Figure 16-5:
Searching
for
Salesforce
Knowledge
articles.

✔ **Article Types** identify each article and determine which template the article will follow. For example, an article type of FAQ could have the mandatory fields of Question and Answer. When you create a new article, you must define what article type it's associated with, which then determines the layout of the fields you'll need to fill out.

✔ **Data categories** organize articles in Salesforce Knowledge. They can be nested if you need it — for example, if you organize your products by product line and then part number.

Data categories can be mapped to users' roles to decide what articles users can and can't see.

✔ **Category groups** are containers for data categories with hierarchies. If you have a Nimbus line of flying broomsticks, that category could be nested below a Products category group.

✔ **Channel** describes one of various methods in which an article is available for viewing: the Internal app (where only Service Cloud users can see the article), the Customer Portal (where customers with the right permissions may see it on the portal page), and the Public Knowledge Base for Salesforce Knowledge (available on the AppExchange).

✔ **Synonyms** are words or phrases that you associate together so that article searches matching one of those words or phrases will return additional related results associated with the other words. For example, you could associate the words *headset* and *head set* so any relevant articles with either keyword would appear in the search results.

✔ A **Synonym Group** contains two or more synonyms.

To publish your articles to the Public Knowledge Base channel, you'll need to download the Public Knowledge app from the salesforce.com AppExchange at www.appexchange.com. Creating a Public Knowledge Base requires Force.com Sites and Force.com pages.

Articles are the content on which your internal product expertise and externally sourced conversations are housed for future reference.

Creating articles

To try your hand at creating an article, do the following:

1. **On the Article Management tab, click New.**

   The New Article box appears.

2. **Choose an article type, enter the article title, and click OK.**

   The article type determines the page layout of the type of article you'll be writing.

3. **Edit the article's fields as appropriate.**

4. **If categories have already been set up in the Categories area, choose the categories to associate with your article by clicking Edit next to a category group to open the Category Selection dialog box. If categories have not been set up yet, skip to Step 8.**

5. **In the Available Categories list, expand the category hierarchy to select a category.**

6. **Click Add to move a selected category to the Selected Categories list.**

   As many as eight categories are allowed there.

7. **Click OK.**

8. **In the Channels area, select where your article will be available after it's published. You can select one or more channels in which to publish your article.**

   • *Internal App:* These articles are available only to users logged in to Salesforce.

   • *Partner:* These articles are available to your partners via your Partner Community.

- *Customer:* These articles are available to your customers who log in to your Customer Community.

- *Public Knowledge Base:* These articles are available to anyone via your website.

9. **Click Save to save your changes, close the article, and go to the Article Management tab.**

10. **(Optional) Create an assignment for a user to edit or review the article.**

Publishing articles

After a draft article has been reviewed and has passed your internal quality standards for publishing, do the following to publish an article:

1. **On the Article Management tab, open the My Draft Articles or All Draft Articles view, select a check box in the list, and click Publish.**

   Alternatively, click Publish on either the detail page or the edit page of an article.

2. **Select Publish Article(s) Now.**

3. **If the article has previously been published, select the Flag as New Article(s) check box to make the new article icon display next to your article in the selected channels.**

   Users from these channels can see that this article has been modified since the last time they read it. This check box is not available when you publish an article for the first time, as the icon displays by default then.

   If the draft being published is a working copy of a currently published article, it is published as a new version of the original.

4. **Click OK.**

   Articles that you're publishing now move directly to the Published Articles view.

You can also schedule an article for publication at a later date. And, Service Cloud has you covered in case you change your mind. You can cancel a previously scheduled publication date, too, by clicking the conveniently placed Cancel Publication link for the previously scheduled article.

The Service Cloud Answers feature allows service agents to ask questions to internal and/or external groups and also see various answers from the community. Community members vote on answers they like, and the original asker can deem one response as the best answer. This is similar to how sites like www.StackOverflow.com source responses from their users, and is available in Enterprise and Performance Editions.

Helping Customers Help Themselves

You'd be surprised by how many customers would prefer to get the answers themselves (if they knew where to go), rather than call you. By creating a knowledge base of frequently discussed questions or issues, you can allow your customers to solve their own issues, decreasing call volume to your call centers. You can also improve your agents' response times so that they don't have to constantly retype repetitive solutions, and your call center managers can track topic trends to provide feedback to product and marketing teams.

Setting up Communities

When customers have a problem, they can log in to your Community and do things such as

- ✔ Log a new case
- ✔ Search the knowledge base
- ✔ Get help and training
- ✔ Interact with other customers in community forums

Before implementing Salesforce Communities, make sure that your public knowledge articles are up to snuff. That is, your knowledge articles must be populated with answers to many common customer inquiries, and the articles must be well written and appropriate for public consumption.

Salesforce Communities is an additional cost. Check with your salesforce.com account executive for details before launching it.

If you want to test Salesforce Communities, sign up for a Developer Edition trial (at www.force.com) or, if your organization has a sandbox, you can enable Communities in your sandbox.

Depending on how new your instance of Salesforce is, you may need to contact salesforce.com to enable Communities for your organization to launch it.

To determine if you already have Salesforce Communities enabled, follow these steps:

1. **From Setup, click Customize➪Communities➪Settings.**

   The Community Settings page appears.

2. **Select Enable Communities.**

   You are asked to acknowledge that enabling Communities is irreversible. If you wish to proceed, check the box to acknowledge that there's no going back.

3. **Select a subdomain name to use for your communities, then click Check Availability to make sure it's not already being used.**

   The URL defaults to a force.com web address. You get to choose the subdomain. Use something recognizable to your users, such as your company name. The domain name will be the same for all your communities, but you create a unique URL for each community during the creation process.

4. **Click Save.**

Creating a Community

Once your Salesforce Communities is enabled, it's time to create your first, well, community.

1. **From Setup, click Customize⇨Communities⇨Manage Communities.**

   The Manage Communities page appears.

2. **Click the New Community button.**

   The Create Community window appears.

3. **Add the name of the community, a brief description, and a URL.**

   The URL field will be a subdirectory that lives under the domain name that you selected earlier. This community is only visible by administrators until you share the URL with others, or publish it where others can access it. Until then, you can customize it to your desired look and feel.

4. **Choose the Create button to create the community.**

   A confirmation window appears once your community is created. You can click an Edit button to continue to fine-tune this community, or hit Close to return to the Manage Communities page.

5. **[Optional] From the Manage Communities page, click the Edit link next to a community name to continue with more customizations that we will discuss in the next section.**

 To quickly access a view of what one of your communities will look like from an end-user's perspective, click the name of the community from the Manage Communities page. Figure 16-6 shows one sample Community from the customer's perspective. The colors and tabs of the portal may be customized by you to best match your company branding. When you first get started, it will look something like what's shown in Figure 16-6.

Figure 16-6:
A customer's
view of a
Salesforce
Community.

Adding Community members

After you thoroughly test your Salesforce Community, you want to make it available to customers.

To add members to your Customer Community, take these steps:

1. **Select which community to target by going to Setup⇨Build⇨Customize⇨ Communities⇨Manage Settings.**

   The Manage Settings page appears.

2. **Click the Edit link next to the community name that you want to target.**

   A Community Settings window for that community appears.

3. **Click the Members button and select which user profiles or permission sets you want to include as members.**

   Select available profiles or permission sets from their respective left selection windows. Use the Add or Remove buttons to move your selections from the Available windows to the Select windows.

4. **[Optional] In the Flagging Content section, check the box if you want to allow members of this community to flag content.**

   This lets community members notify the community moderator to review content. This usually means the flagged content is inappropriate for your community, or at least should be reviewed.

5. **[Optional] In the Share the Community Before Publishing section, copy the URL and send it to some members whose profile you just added.**

   This lets stakeholders see what all the fuss has been about.

6. **Click Save.**

   The Community Settings window for this community reappears.

Customizing your Salesforce Community

If your business deals with several types of customers, each requiring a customized interface, you can create multiple communities for them. For example, maybe your platinum customers need Salesforce Community access to report on very specific information captured in custom fields that don't apply to your regular customer base. Or maybe you're dealing with a large set of customers testing out the newest version of your product, and you need them to provide specific feedback that isn't normally captured for your current products. Additionally, you can customize the Salesforce Community so that it fits seamlessly with the rest of your corporate website's branding.

To customize your Community, do the following:

1. **Choose Setup➪Build➪Customize➪Communities➪Manage Communities.**

2. **Click the Edit link next to the name of your Community.**

3. **Click Tabs & Pages.**

4. **Move the desired tabs from the Available Tabs into the Selected Tabs column.**

5. **Use the Up and Down buttons to change the order in which the tabs are displayed.**

6. **Click Save to save your changes.**

Changes are visible to Community users when they refresh their browsers. Take care to make updates at times when users are least likely to visit your Community.

Sharing Knowledge with your community

Collecting answers to increase your agents' efficiency is just the tip of the iceberg. Using that information to then efficiently address conversations in the cloud distinguishes your company from the rest. The extent of your customer service efforts will closely follow the pace of conversations so that your brand and its reputation stay current with all messaging. By making your knowledge base available to a customer, you can use the relevant information about a specific customer (like what products of yours they own) to automatically suggest articles relevant to that customer. Salesforce Knowledge can even suggest an article before the customer does a search!

Not only can customers find a quick answer, but they can also find out more about the products they use. The more often that customers can educate themselves, the more often that service agent interactions will start off at a more sophisticated level of dialog.

And if customers have feedback about some of the articles, they can vote on the information and see what others think about it. This closed-loop feedback provides valuable information to other customers and to the internal product folks that put that information there.

Assuming you already have Salesforce Knowledge enabled and want to associate it with Salesforce Communities, do the following to associate a Knowledge-friendly profile with a community:

1. **Choose Setup⇨Administer⇨Manage Users⇨Profiles.**

   The User Profiles page appears.

2. **Click the name of one of your profiles that's a member of a community where you want Salesforce Knowledge associated.**

3. **Click the Clone button to create a copy of this profile.**

   The Clone Profile page appears.

4. **Enter a name for your new profile and click Save.**

   Your new profile page appears.

5. **Click the Edit button to update the new profile's permissions.**

   The Profile Edit page appears, as shown in Figure 16-7.

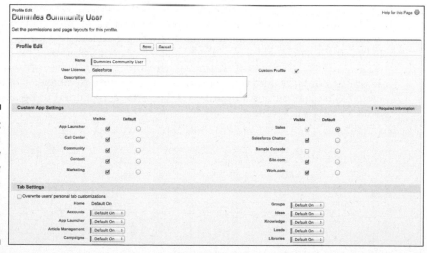

Figure 16-7: Creating a new community profile integrating Salesforce Knowledge.

6. **Verify that the tab visibility for the Article Management tab is Default On and that the check box for the Read permission for the appropriate Article Type Permissions is selected.**

7. **Click Save to finish updating your new Community Profile.**

8. **Choose Setup⇨Build⇨Customize⇨Communities⇨Manage Communities to return to the Manage Communities page.**

9. **Click the Edit link next to the name of your Community.**

   The Community detail page appears.

10. **Click the Members button.**

11. **Select the newly created profile and click Add.**

12. **When finished, click the Save button.**

Notify support agents who create articles that they must select Public Knowledge base and Customer as channel options when creating or modifying an article. If the Customer channel isn't selected, the article will not appear in the community.

Improving Agent Productivity

For those of you who operate a support center in which you handle a high volume of support issues, you probably want to make your agents' time as productive as possible. What information can you put at their fingertips to help them resolve that case that much faster? In the following sections, we review a timesaving option that may be a good fit for your team.

Using the Salesforce Agent Console

High-volume call center agents need access to a lot of information at once. Typing fewer keystrokes means that resolving a customer's issue takes less time. From a single web page, the Salesforce Agent Console allows an agent to view all his cases, handle a single case, and see all the records — including accounts, contacts, and opportunities — that relate to a case. The Salesforce Agent Console provides a multifaceted interface, designed to be a one-stop desktop for your agents.

Setting up the Agent Console

We highlight the basic steps that you need to take to get the Salesforce Agent Console up and running in the following sections. Try to walk through a scenario in which an agent handles a new case and sees it to closure from within that Agent Console. Check out the Help & Training section in Salesforce, for more details on the following summaries.

1. Create an App for your Salesforce Agent Console.

   Choose Setup➪Build➪Create➪Apps to create a new app that defines which tabs your agents will see in the console.

2. Assign Users the Service Cloud Feature License.

   Choose Setup➪Administer➪Manage Users➪Users to edit each user and select the Service Cloud User in the User License field.

3. Create a new Agent Console layout to determine what types of records your agents see in one window.

   Choose Setup➪Build➪Customize➪Agent Console➪Console Layouts➪New to build a new console layout.

Providing customer service from anywhere

Service Cloud provides two options for managing calls from your customers. The first option is already set up and seems obvious. You define some basic roles and rules for levels of support in your call center. When a person calls in, the agent searches for the contact, validates the caller against information in the Service Cloud, and captures the case in real time. Then, hopefully, the agent resolves the case in the same call.

The second option is to integrate your telephony environment with the Service Cloud to make managing customer calls easier for agents and customers.

Additionally, agents can provide customer service when they're not in an office. You can distribute your contact center across the world through the wonders of chat-based support. Service professionals constantly on the go can continue to manage multiple customers using Service Cloud mobile solutions and even look up answers to common questions from their favorite mobile device. Field technicians can view their route schedule without going into the office, and they can report issue resolutions without ever turning on a computer.

Using a call center

Service Cloud telephony integration works with more than 80 of the most popular phone systems and may include interactive voice response (IVR), automatic call distribution (ACD), and screen pops that automatically present the caller's contact record to your agents. With an open CTI integration architecture and the free Force.com Connect CTI Toolkit, available at `http://developer.force.com`, your technical resources can deliver an even more robust experience, which is especially valuable in higher-volume contact centers.

The integration can work with a bevy of on-demand telephony partners, such as Angel.com, Five9, inContact, and LiveOps, or with on-premise solutions from leading telephony providers including Avaya, Cisco, Genesys, Nortel, and more.

These providers offer prebuilt integrations from their telephony systems to salesforce.com, allowing the agent desktop to be shown right inside the salesforce.com user interface.

If your customers don't like waiting on hold, you may want to also implement Salesforce Live Agent. Live Agent lets your customer service reps hold chats with multiple visitors to your website. All the information is tracked in Salesforce in real time, and your reps will even be able to leverage your knowledge articles and other customizations.

Part VI
Measuring Overall Business Performance

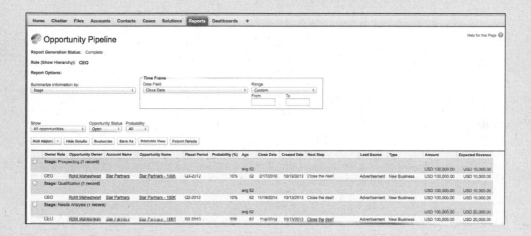

Introduce yourself to joined reports and other powerful analytic features at
www.dummies.com/extras/salesforcedotcom.

In this part . . .

- ✔ Get an overview of Salesforce's reporting feature
- ✔ Modify an existing report to make it your own and create a new report from scratch
- ✔ Use report filters to more quickly get to the data that matters to you
- ✔ Build a dashboard to graphically display a set of reports
- ✔ Organize and search for your reports and dashboards

Chapter 17

Analyzing Data with Reports

*H*ow much time do you waste every week trying to prepare reports for your manager, your team, or yourself? You have to chase down the information, get it into a useful format, and then hopefully make sense of the data. By the time you do all that, the information is probably already outdated, despite your best efforts. Have you ever felt less than confident of the details or the totals?

If this sounds like a familiar problem, you can use reports in Salesforce to generate up-to-the-moment data analysis to help you measure your business. As long as you and your teams regularly use Salesforce to manage your accounts, opportunities, and other customer-related information, you don't have to waste time wondering where to find the data and how to consolidate it. Instead, let Salesforce do that work for you.

And unlike other applications in which the business users often have to spend precious time relying on more-technical people to build their custom reports, you can do this all by yourself in minutes, with no geeky programming. With an easy-to-use reporting wizard, you can customize existing reports or build them from scratch.

This chapter includes an overview of the standard reports provided by Salesforce, building reports from scratch, and modifying existing reports to make them your own. Within a report, we take you through the different ways you can limit the report to get just the information that's necessary for creating a clearer picture of your business. Finally, be sure to check out our suggestions on how to keep your reports organized in easy-to-find folders as your universe of reports expands.

Discovering Reports

With reports, you can present your data in different formats, select a seemingly infinite number of columns, filter your data, subtotal information, use color to highlight when certain conditions are met, and embed formulas, just to name a few features. And like other pages in Salesforce, you can quickly find the details. So, for example, you can go from the Reports home page to a lead report to a lead record simply by clicking links.

Navigating the Reports home page

When you click the Reports tab, as shown in Figure 17-1, you'll see a search bar, a Folders navigation tree in the left panel of your browser, and a list of recently run reports within a particular folder in the main panel of this page. Salesforce has functionality on the Reports home page to help you more easily navigate through a large set of reports and dashboards. Salesforce comes standard with a set of predefined reports and folders that are commonly used for measuring sales, marketing, support, and other functions. For example, the Opportunity Pipeline report is an oft-used report by sales individuals and managers to help prioritize which deals to work on.

Figure 17-1:
The Reports
home page.

You can't save a custom report in a standard folder. If you're an administrator, consider creating custom folders using the New Report Folder option that's accessed from the little folder icon to the right of the Find Folders search bar in the left-side pane, as shown in Figure 17-2. Organize this according to your important functional areas that ultimately replace these standard folders.

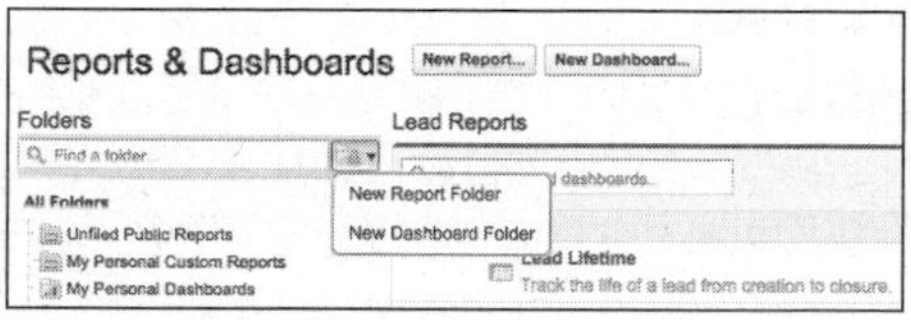

Figure 17-2:
Creating a
new report
folder.

From the Reports home page, you can do the following:

- ✔ **Find reports.** Type keywords into the Find Reports and Dashboards search bar, and while you're typing, Salesforce will return matching reports based on the report's name and description fields.

- ✔ **Search a folder.** Use the Find Folders search bar or scroll down the Folders navigation pane to quickly locate a particular folder.

- ✔ **Create a folder.** If you're an administrator, click the New Folder link as mentioned in the previous tip to create new report folders to house custom reports.

- ✔ **Select a folder.** When you click a folder from the Folders pane, the contents of that report or dashboard folder will appear in the main panel. To backtrack, click the All Reports option at the top of the Folders navigation tree in the Folders pane.

- ✔ **Filter report lists.** Use the filters on the right side of the main pane, as shown in Figure 17-3, to narrow the number of reports that you see within a particular reports folder.

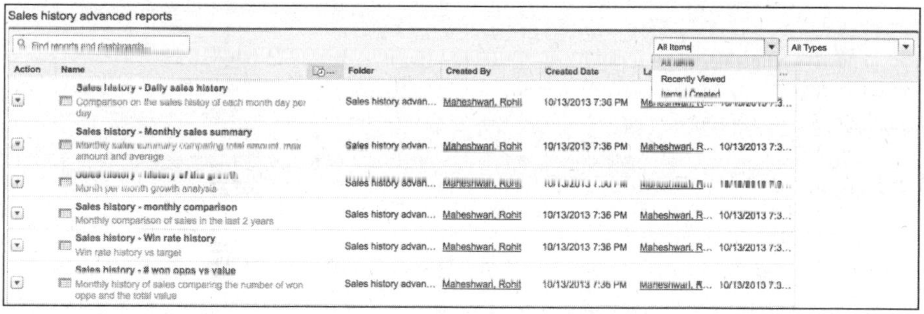

Figure 17-3:
Filtering on
Reports.

- ✔ **View recent reports.** Select the Recently Viewed option from the filter drop-down list to match the criteria of what reports you want to see. Click and hold down your mouse button over the Scheduled Items icon (that's its own column heading) to quickly select additional columns to help you more quickly find your report. You can also click and drag column headings to rearrange them or remove them.

✔ **Display the report.** Click a report title.

✔ **Edit, delete, or export data to Excel.** On standard or custom reports, click the Customize, Delete, or Export Details button. We talk more about exporting your reports in the later section "Exporting Reports to Excel."

✔ **Create a report.** Click the New Report button to start the Report Builder Wizard.

Displaying a report

When you click a report title or run a report from the wizard, a report page appears based on the criteria that was set. For example, under the Opportunity Reports folder, click the Opportunity Pipeline link. The Opportunity Pipeline report appears, as shown in Figure 17-4. This report, as we mention earlier, is one of the most-used standard reports in Salesforce.

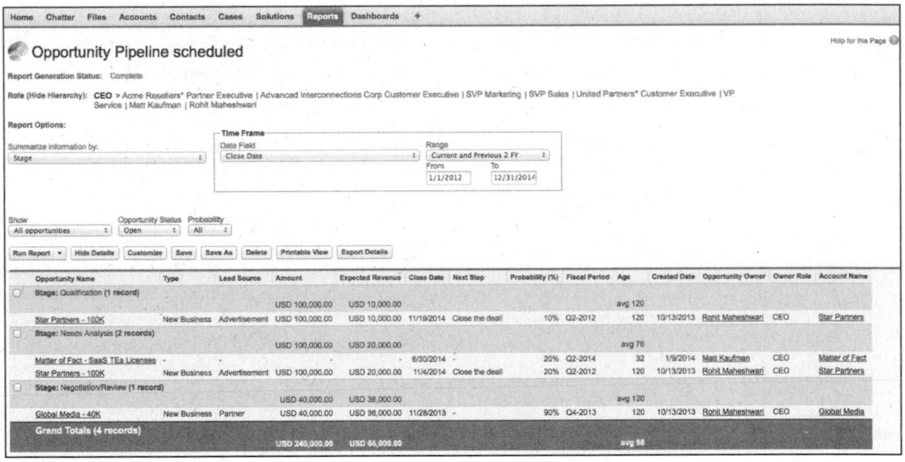

Figure 17-4: Displaying a report.

A basic report page in Salesforce is broken up into a few parts:

✔ **Org Drill Down:** You can use this area at the top of the page to quickly limit results based on role hierarchy. This helps reduce the number of redundant reports that you have to create just to see a slightly different view of the data based on a team's structure. For example, you can use the Org Drill Down to see how the Eastern region team's numbers are faring. You could drill down even further to see how a specific sales rep in the Eastern region is doing, without having to create a separate report. See Chapter 19 for steps on setting up the role hierarchy.

- ✔ **Report Options:** This section is at the top of the page, just below the Org Drill Down. You can use it to summarize, filter, and perform other operations on a report. For details on report options, see the section "Filtering on a Report," later in this chapter.

- ✔ **Additional filters:** This optional section is customized by the person building the report, and it allows additional filtering of certain fields that are picklists.

- ✔ **Generated report:** This section shows the report itself. What's visible depends on the construction of the report and what you have permission to see in Salesforce. See Chapter 19 for more details on sharing.

In the Generated Report section, you can click a column heading to quickly re-sort your report by the selected column.

Developing Reports

Salesforce comes with a huge menu of useful reports, and yet they might not be exactly what you're looking for. For example, if your company has added custom fields on the account record that are unique to your customer, a standard New Accounts report doesn't show you all the information you want to see on recent accounts.

The next time you need a custom report, don't pester the IT geeks. Instead, use Report Builder to build a new report or customize an existing one.

Building a report from scratch

You don't have to be a technical guru to create a report in Salesforce. Just make sure that you can articulate a question that you're trying to answer, and then Report Builder will guide you through the steps for creating a custom report that will help you answer the question. Anyone who can view the Reports tab can create a custom report.

To create a report from scratch, click the Reports tab and follow these steps:

1. **Click the New Report button.**

   The Create New Report page appears, as shown in Figure 17-5.

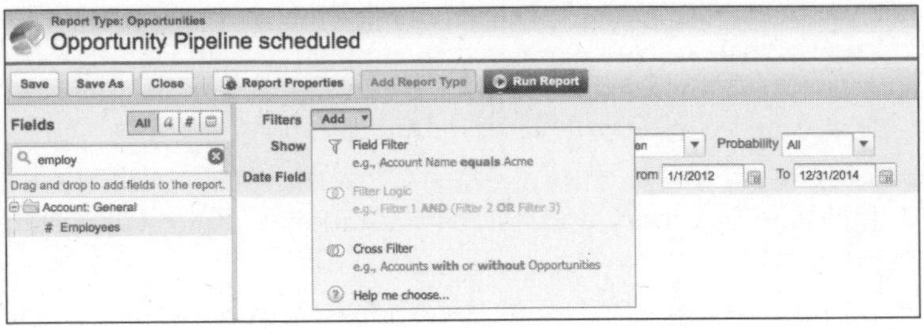

Figure 17-5:
Defining the
objects for
the report.

2. **Select the report type that you want to report on, and then click Create.**

   You do this by first selecting the basic category of object from the Select Report Type panel, which displays a list of folders representing key objects. Clicking a folder then reveals more specific report types to choose from. The standard report types will give you a visual preview of sample data and how it would look in that report template. The Create button is found at the lower-right corner of this page.

   When you click Create, the Report Builder drag-and-drop interface appears.

3. **Customize your report using the following Report Builder features:**

   • *Adjust your view and time frame.* Do you want the report to show just records that you own, ones that you and your underlings own, or all records that your role is able to see? What time range do you want the report to cover? Use the picklists in the Show and Date Field section to narrow your results.

   • *Add custom filters.* To help further narrow your result set, use the Add drop-down list along the Filters row. For example, you can create a custom filter to only show results where the opportunity amount is greater than $10,000.

   • *Drag and drop fields.* Find fields in the left sidebar that may be additional columns that you want to have in your report. Simply click and drag that field name over to the Preview section of the Report Builder and then place that new column among your other headers.

   • *Add a chart.* Look for an optional Add Chart button in the Preview pane to add a graphical summary of your results. Use the Chart Editor to choose a chart type, determine what data to represent, and decide how you want that data to be visually presented.

4. **When you're done creating your report, click the Save button.**

   The report saves, and a sample preview appears in the Report Builder Preview pane.

You can get pretty advanced with filtering options. As long as you can explain to yourself in plain English what criteria you are looking for, you should be able to build a report for it using options under the Filter⇨Add drop-down list, as shown in Figure 17-6. For example, if you define strategic accounts as companies that did *either* more than $1 billion in annual revenue *or* had more than 500 employees plus $500 million in annual revenue, you can generate this report. To do this, add your field filters from the Filters⇨Add picklist and then choose the Filter Logic option. A field will appear where you can order each filter you have and associate it using AND or OR logic.

Customizing existing reports

A fast and easy way to generate reports is to customize an existing report and save it as a new one. For example, if you like the standard Pipeline Report but you want to modify the columns, you can simply work from the existing report.

To customize an existing report, go to the Reports tab and follow these steps:

1. **Find a folder that contains a report that you want to customize. After clicking that folder, click a link for that report in the main Reports pane.**

   The report appears.

2. **Click the Customize button.**

   Using the Customize button, the Report Builder page appears. You can then drag and drop interface fields into columns for that report (as discussed in the previous section). A preview of the report appears while you are customizing it.

3. **Continue customizing your report until you're satisfied, and then click the Run Report button.**

   The report appears modified based on your settings from the wizard.

4. **When you're done, click Save or Save As.**

   The Save button replaces the prior custom report. The Save As button saves a new one. In either case, a page appears to save the report.

5. **Complete the fields and click Save.**

   The Reports home page appears, with a link to your new report.

Creating custom report types

The Report Wizard is pretty darn thorough. At the same time, your company's quant jocks may want to perform even more advanced reporting than what's offered in the standard Report Wizard. Or you may want to simplify the number of fields that your report users see when they go through the wizard. Professional, Enterprise, and Performance Edition administrators can create custom report types (CRTs) to address both of these needs.

For more advanced reporting capabilities, in techno-speak, CRTs let you change the joins on the table. So if you have a Projects object and want to report on all accounts with projects and project team members, you can create a CRT and determine which fields show up in your Select Columns to Total step. For more information on setting up CRTs, go to the Help & Training section within Salesforce and search for "Create a Custom Report Type."

Filtering on a Report

Over time, you'll develop core reports that have the columns that you want in a format that makes sense to you. One of the huge benefits of reporting in Salesforce is that you can use existing reports on the fly and apply report options to limit or reorder the report results.

All those options and more are possible in seconds without having to use the Customize button. In the following sections, we show you how to filter your reports with tools and enhanced drill-down and break-out options.

Using the Report Options section

When you open a report, it appears with a variety of filters in the Report Options section at the top of the page, as seen in Figure 17-6. By using the filters in the Report Options section, you can look at your data from multiple angles. The available standard filters depend on the type of report that you selected.

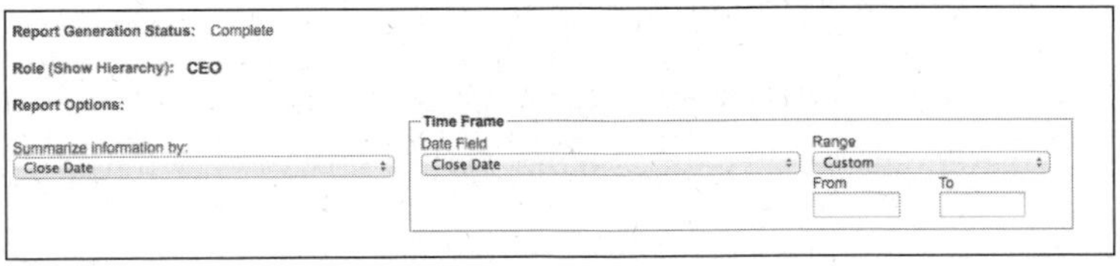

Figure 17-6: Identifying your report options.

Report Generation Status: Complete

Role (Show Hierarchy): CEO

Report Options:

Summarize information by:
Close Date

Time Frame
Date Field
Close Date

Range
Custom

From   To

To try out the standard filters in the Report Options section by using the Opportunity Pipeline report as an example, first go to the Reports home page and click the Opportunity Pipeline link. The report appears. From the report, you can do the following with the filters in the Report Options section:

- **Summarize your report by a field.** From the Summarize Information By drop-down list, select a field that determines how your information is summarized. For example, if you want to look at your opportunities by rep, select Opportunity Owner.

- **Choose a time frame.** From the Time Frame area, first select a date field, and then in the drop-down list to the right, select a standard range or create one of your own. For example, if you want to look at all opportunities created from 2014 to the present, you'd first select Created Date, and then define the interval.

- **Choose a scope.** From the Show drop-down list, select the scope of records.

- **Look at open or closed records.** Use the Opportunity Status drop-down list if you want open and/or closed records.

- **Limit results.** Use the Probability drop-down list if you want to limit the results by probability.

At any particular time, click the Run Report button to apply your selected filters. The report reappears based on the filters you defined.

If you ultimately want to save the report, click the Save or Save As button, and then save the report as usual. (See the section "Building a report from scratch," earlier in this chapter, for details on saving.)

Hiding and showing details

To see a collapsed or expanded view of your report data, click the Hide/Show Details button in the Report Options section. For example, from the Reports home page, click the Sales by Account report under Sales Reports. When the report appears, click the Hide Details button. The report reappears in a collapsed view, and the Hide Details button morphs into the Show Details button. Now click the Show Details button, and the report expands again. By using Hide Details, you can easily view headings, subtotals, and totals, especially for matrix reports.

Filtering with the drill-down menu

Reports in Salesforce have a drill-down function that you can use to select rows within a report and instantly break them down by a different field. For example, if you're reviewing an Opportunity by Rep report, you might want to select a specific rep and then sort the rep's opportunities by stage. With enhanced drill-down and break-out options, you can do this in just a few quick clicks.

To use the drill-down and break-out options (using Sales by Rep as the example), follow these steps:

1. **From the Reports home page, click the Sales by Rep link under the Sales Reports folder.**

   The report appears.

2. **In the left column of the report, select check boxes for records you want to view.**

   If you don't see check boxes and you know you've closed opportunities in Salesforce, select an interval in the Report Options section to see all your historical opportunities and click Run Report to view more records.

3. **At the bottom of the page, select a field from the Check Rows to Filter, Then Drill Down By drop-down list to summarize the information, if desired, and then click the Drill Down button.**

   The report reappears based on your selections. For example, if you chose the Close Month option from the Drill Down By drop-down list, your selected opportunities would be sorted by close month.

4. **If you want to use the report in the future, click Save As, and then follow the normal directions for saving reports.**

   See the section "Building a report from scratch," earlier in this chapter, for saving details.

Clearing filters

If you have reports with advanced filters, you can easily view and clear the filters to expand the results. For example, if you created and saved the test report in the preceding section, you might want to clear the filter on the selected rep(s) to see all closed opportunities by close month for all reps. The advanced filters, if any, appear just below the Generated Report header on a report page.

To clear a filter, follow these steps:

1. **Click the link for a report to which you applied filters.**

   The report appears, and your criteria filters are listed under the Filtered By header directly below the Generated Report header, as shown in Figure 17-7.

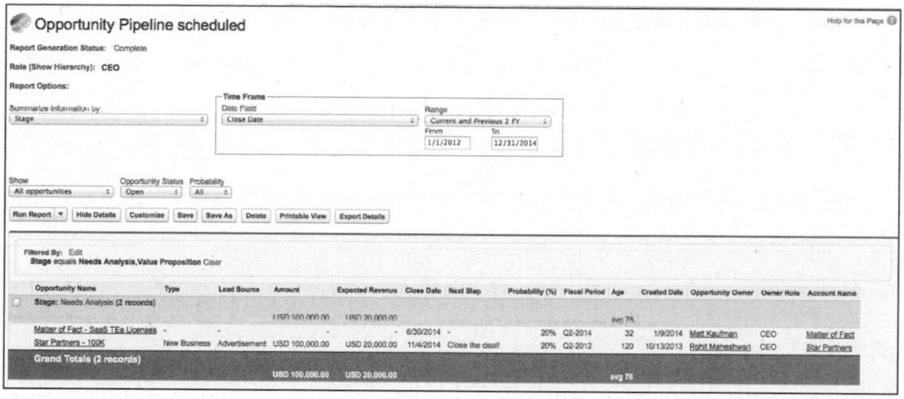

Figure 17-7:
Clearing
criteria
filters in a
drill-down
report.

2. **Right below the Filtered By header, click the Clear link to remove a filter.**

   The report reappears, displaying a potentially wider universe of data.

3. **Be sure to click the Save or Save As button if you want to save this report.**

You can quickly modify advanced filters by clicking the Edit link next to the Filtered By header. The Report Builder page appears.

Exporting Reports to Excel

Ideally, you want to run your reports right out of the application, getting rid of that mad scramble of collecting data before your next big meeting. However, sometimes you'll want to generate a report and then export it to Excel. Maybe you need to run some complex spreadsheet calculations, or you need to plug numbers into an existing macro template. No problem. You can do that with the click of a button.

To export a report, click the Reports tab and follow these steps:

1. **Click the Name for the report you want to export.**

   The report appears. For some reports, you can skip this step by selecting the Export option in the Action drop-down menu next to the report name.

2. **Click the Export Details button.**

   A page appears to define your settings for exporting the file.

3. **Complete the fields and click the Export button.**

   A window appears, prompting you to open or save the file.

4. **Follow the steps, as desired.**

   When the file opens, the report data appears in Excel.

5. **Click Done to return to your Salesforce report.**

   The report page reappears.

 Some companies get nervous about certain users having the ability to export company data. If this is a concern, and you have the Enterprise or Performance Edition, you can take one precaution by using custom profiles to eliminate the ability of some users to export to Excel. See Chapter 20 for more details on creating custom profiles.

Organizing Your Reports

A word to the wise: Reports start multiplying like rabbits as you become addicted to reporting in Salesforce. Do yourself a favor: Organize them from day one and lay out a process for maintaining and deleting reports.

Creating new folders

Nothing is worse than seeing a gazillion reports under the Unfiled Public Reports folder. You start wasting a ridiculous amount of time just identifying which one is the report you want. If you have permission to manage public folders, avoid the headache by creating new report folders.

To create a new report folder, click the Reports tab and follow these steps:

1. **Click the New Folder link to the right of the Find Folders search bar.**

   A New Report Folder page appears.

2. **Type a name for the folder in the Report Folder Label field.**

   For example, if you want a folder for operational reports, you might name it Sales Ops Reports.

3. **Use the Public Folder Access drop-down list to determine read versus read/write privileges to the folder.**

   For example, if you select Read/Write, a user with access to the folder could save over the original report.

4. **Use the two list boxes and the Add/Remove buttons to select reports in the Unfiled Public Reports folder and move them to the new folder.**

5. **Use the radio buttons to select who should have access to the folder.**

   As with other Salesforce folder tools, your choices amount to all, none, and selective.

6. **If you chose the Selective option in Step 5, use the two list boxes and Add/Remove buttons to highlight groups or roles and move them to the Shared To list box.**

7. **When you're done, click Save.**

   The Reports home page reappears, and your folder is added to the Folder menu.

Maintaining your report library

Actually, what's worse than a gazillion reports under Unfiled Public Reports is a universe of reports, some of which are valuable, others of which are useless. Creating public report folders is a good first step, but you might want to apply some of these additional hints on a periodic basis:

- ✔ **Accurately name your reports.** You and your users can't know what's behind a report link unless you name it clearly and precisely.

- ✔ **Consider using report numbers within your report names.** For instance, use standard file-naming conventions like 1.1 North America Pipeline. By doing this, managers can refer to report numbers so that everyone's looking at the same report.

- ✔ **Delete unnecessary reports.** If multiple people in your company have permission to manage public reports, you might want to survey them before accidentally deleting a report. Unnecessary or redundant reports just make it harder for everyone to find what he or she wants. And in case you mistakenly delete a report (you'll find out soon enough), you have up to 30 days to rescue it from the Recycle Bin.

- ✔ **Update existing reports as needs arise.** For example, if you created an Opportunity Product Report and used an advanced filter such as Product Family Equals Software, make sure that you manually update the report if the product family name changes. Otherwise, your reports will be off.

- ✔ **Use clear report questions.** For example, you might use the Report Question field to summarize certain filters to your report.

Advancing Beyond the Basics

As Salesforce has matured over the years and more users rely on it to house the bulk of its customer-touching information, users' reporting needs have also matured. Salesforce has done a great job making potentially very complicated database queries still accessible to the business user. Here we talk briefly about some of the more advanced functionality, in case you are feeling stuck about how to get information in your reports in a certain way. Most likely, you have a way to get you what you want but you might need to dig a little deeper into Salesforce.

Building custom summary formulas

Salesforce provides prebuilt functionality that calculates the sum, average, highest value, and lowest value of certain fields that you select for your reports. However, you may need additional summary information based on calculations unique to your business. For example, your business may want to see win-rate percentages or coverage ratios in your reports. Salesforce allows the addition of custom formula calculations for your reports (and dashboards). This means that you can take summary information from other fields and lump them together to come up with a new calculation and corresponding result. It doesn't matter whether you know old math or new math, Salesforce can derive these values for you using Excel-like commands.

To create a new custom summary formula, follow these steps:

1. **Click a link for an existing report.**

   The report appears.

2. **Click the Customize button.**

   The Report Builder appears.

3. **In the Fields column in the left pane of the Report Builder, find the Formulas folder and click into that to drill down. Select the Add Formula option, as shown in Figure 17-8, and drag it into the preview pane as its own column.**

   The Custom Summary Formula Wizard page pops up.

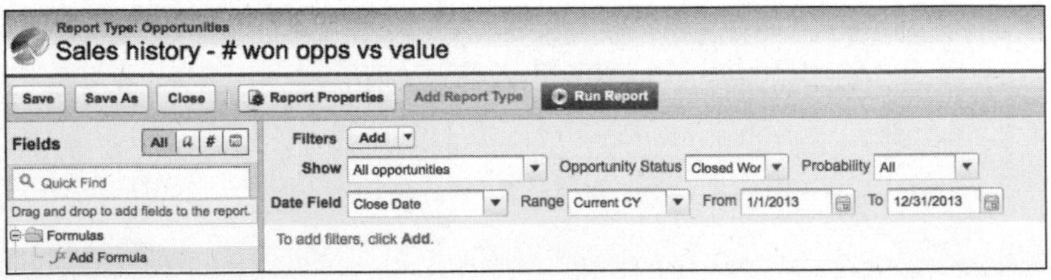

Figure 17-8:
Adding a custom formula.

4. Complete the fields, as required:

- *Enter a column name* as it will appear on the report in the Label field.

  Optionally, type a description. Ideally, this field helps explain the math formula in layman's terms.

- *Select the type of format* that you want your results to be in from the Format drop-down list. For example, if you want to calculate the revenue per item of all your products in the pipeline this year, you'll want your result to be Currency.

- *Select the number of decimal places to display* for your selected data type from the Decimal Places drop-down list.

- *Choose where you want the summary calculations to be displayed in the report.* Reference the visual guide to assist you in determining if you want the output to appear at all summary levels or just specific ones.

5. Build your formula in the Formula section, as shown in Figure 17-9:

- *a. Select one of the fields listed in the Summary Fields drop-down list, and then choose the kind of summary type to use in your formula.*

  This field's value, and how it will be summarized, are automatically added into your formula. In our example, we select Amount and Average.

- *b. Click the appropriate operator icons from the drop-down list with the same name.*

  In our example, we select the / (Divide) option.

- *c. Repeat these steps, as needed, to build your formula.*

  If you need to know what functions to use for a particular operation, use the Functions picklist. Salesforce will also return some help text to give you an idea of how those functions should be formatted.

6. Click Check Syntax to check your formula.

Syntax that contains errors is automatically highlighted.

7. Click OK when finished.

The pop-up window closes, and you're back at the Report Wizard. You should see the new column showing sample data in the Preview section.

The custom summary formula isn't saved until you save the report. Clicking Done just includes it in this step of the Report Wizard. Make sure that you save the report.

8. Click Run Report to see the new column showing real data.

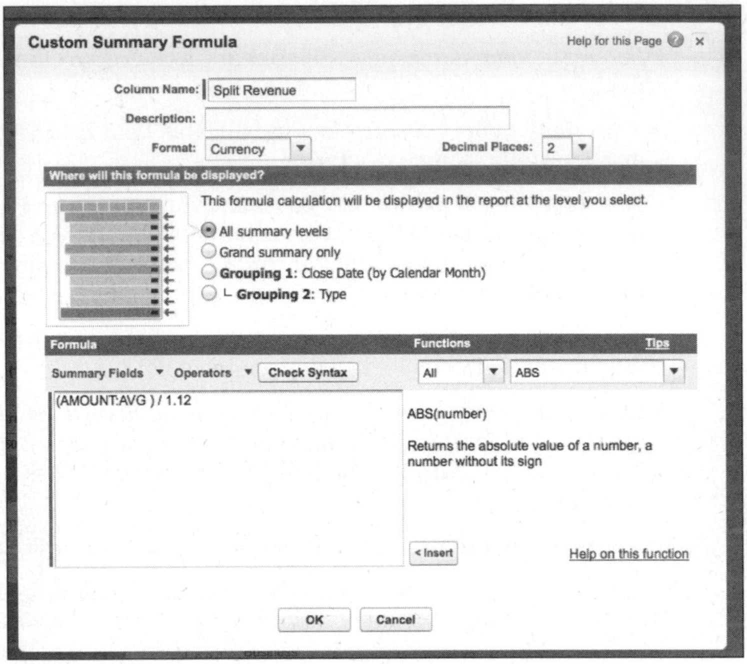

Figure 17-9:
Building
your custom
formula for
your report.

Understanding additional reporting options

You can do a lot more fun things with reports. Even many long-term users of Salesforce reports may not fully know about these additional analytics capabilities. Here is a brief summary to get data detectives more excited about it:

- **Conditional highlighting:** You can apply conditional highlighting to summarize matrix reports and help you easily highlight values that might deserve more of your attention. You can use this with custom summary formulas to highlight high or low percentages, averages, and ratios. You see a lot of syllables in this feature, but conditional highlighting translates into setting thresholds for certain key numerical values and color-coding them to show whether a threshold has been surpassed. In an Opportunity Pipeline by Rep report, you can quickly get an understanding of how people are doing when each rep's total won opportunities are highlighted in red, green, or yellow.

- **Bucketing fields:** Bucketing a field lets you select a column in a report, define ranges for data in that field, and group them into "buckets" with names that you get to define. For example, the currency captured in an

Amount field could be updated into three categories: small, medium, and large. You can define what currency ranges fall under the small bucket, what range falls under the medium bucket, and so on. You can identify columns in reports that are bucket fields by the little bucket icon to the left of the column name. To see an example of how a bucket field is created, refer to Figure 17-10.

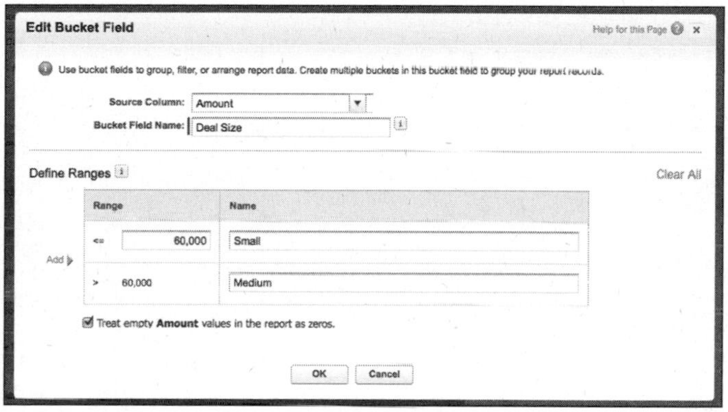

Figure 17-10:
Building
bucket field
ranges.

✔ **Joined reports:** This is a powerful tool that allows you to create one report that consists of report "blocks" that are each separate reports that may or may not be reporting off the same objects. So, if you were trying to run a report that showed both your closed won opportunities as well as the opportunity win rate, you could join two reports. One block would show the total of all your closed won opportunities for a time range, while a second block could be based off of all opportunities so that you can calculate that win ratio.

✔ **Scheduled report runs:** If you have the fun job of providing the powers that be with the same type of report every Monday morning, or at the end of every month, you can automate the running and e-mailing of a report after you've customized it and made it just right for everyone.

For more in-depth information on each of these advanced analytics capabilities, click the Help & Training link in Salesforce and search using the appropriate keywords (conditional highlighting, bucketed fields, and joined reports) in the search bar.

Chapter 18

Seeing the Big Picture with Dashboards

. . . .

In This Chapter

▶ Planning your dashboard strategy

▶ Creating dashboards

▶ Adding and editing components

▶ Organizing dashboards

. . . .

Dashboards are visual representations of custom reports that you create in Salesforce. For example, you can see data in a chart, a graph, or a gauge. You can use dashboards to illustrate key performance indicators (KPIs) and other metrics important to your business. A *metric* is simply something you want to measure (for example, sales by rep, leads by source, opportunities by partner, cases by agent, and so on).

What does this mean for you? If you're a sales or service rep, you can track your daily progress against attainment of goals. If you're a manager, you can easily see how reps stack up against each other and where you need to get involved to hit your numbers. And if you're on the executive team, you have dashboards with actionable charts and graphs for strategic decision making to improve the business.

In this chapter, we share tips on planning your metric reporting strategy, and then we show you how to create dashboards. We walk you through updating dashboard properties and components. You also discover how to organize dashboards and their related reports so that you know you're looking at the right information.

Figuring Out Dashboards

Dashboards are pages in Salesforce comprising tables and charts designed to help you understand important aspects of your business, such as opportunities per territory and leads by source. Dashboards are critical to being able to assess the health of your business and spot trends early. The following sections show you some basic concepts so that you can consider your strategies before you start unleashing them on your organization.

Breaking down basic elements

You can build a dashboard with as many as 20 individual charts, tables, metrics, gauges, or custom components; each item is a *dashboard component.* Similar to building charts with the Report Wizard (see Chapter 17), components are based on reports that you create. In fact, you can click a component on a dashboard to make the underlying report appear. Here's a quick summary of the components that are available to you:

- ✔ **Horizontal bar or vertical column charts** are great when you want to depict a simple measurement with an *x* axis and a *y* axis. For example, use bar charts if you want to create a component that displays pipeline by stage. See Figure 18-1 for an example.

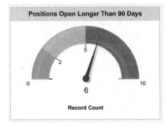

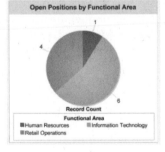
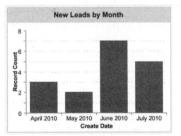

Figure 18-1:
A gauge, pie chart, and vertical bar chart.

- ✔ **Horizontal bar or vertical column grouped charts** work well when you want to compare groups of bars with each other. For example, use grouped bar charts if you want to create a chart that displays pipeline by stage broken out for each month.

- **Horizontal bar or vertical column stacked charts** work well when you want grouping within a bar. For example, use stacked column charts if you want to create a chart that shows cases by status and then by type (such as problems versus feature requests).

- **Horizontal bar or vertical column stacked-to-100% charts** are excellent when you're more interested in percentages than amounts. If you're comparing new versus existing business, stacked-to-100% charts can help you understand what percentage of each stage was new business versus existing business.

- **Pie charts** work just like the standard bar charts, but the data is shown as a pie with the percentage and amount for each wedge; see Figure 18-1.

- **Donut charts** work just like pie charts but also show the total for the whole chart. (Goes great with coffee and morning meetings.)

- **Funnel charts** add an additional visual element to the mix by changing the height of each grouping based on its proportion. For example, use a funnel chart if you want to easily see how much each stage in your pipeline is worth.

- **Line charts** are helpful if you're trying to express trends, particularly when time is part of the measurement. For example, use a line chart if you want to analyze the number of newly created opportunities by month for your entire company.

- **Grouped line charts** add a layer of complexity. For example, a line group chart could help you express the number of newly created opportunities by month broken out by region or unit.

- **Cumulative line charts** allow you to track the progress of a single metric over time. For example, a line cumulative chart could help you see the number of closed cases by day over the course of an entire month.

- **Grouped cumulative line charts** allow you to track progress over multiple metrics over time. For example, a line grouped cumulative chart could help you see the number of closed cases grouped by agent per day over the course of an entire month.

- **Tables** create simple but powerful four-column tables. For example, use tables if you want your dashboard to show the top ten forecasted deals in the quarter in descending value.

  You can create tables in dashboards but not in the charting tool of the Report Wizard.

- **Metrics** insert the grand total of a report at the end of a dashboard label that you customize. Metrics are compelling when you want to tell a story that might require a bit more explanation. Metrics tend to work well in concert with other components. For example, if you use a pie chart to summarize opportunity by stage, you could add a metric to summarize total pipeline.

- ✔ **Gauges** are useful when you have a specific measurable objective and you want to track your progress — see Figure 18-1. A gauge applies the grand total of a report as a point on a scale that you define. For example, use a gauge if you want to measure actual quarterly new bookings against a quota that you define.

- ✔ **Scatter charts** aid in showing correlation between one to two groupings of data. For example you can look at all closed-won opportunities last quarter, and group those by account owner. On your x-axis you can measure the total amount of those closed-won deals (still grouped by the opportunity owner), and your y-axis can show the annual revenue for each account (which is a standard field on that account record). Do your sales people tend to close a higher value of deals when the customer itself generates more revenue? Let your scatter chart tell you.

- ✔ **Visualforce Pages** allow you to create your own custom dashboard components (or download other people's). Even if you're just interested in a snazzier graphic element, go to www.appexchange.com and click the Components category to see what others have created.

If you're an administrator or a user with permission to manage dashboards, you can create, edit, and organize them. And even if you don't have such permissions, you can still view them by clicking the Dashboards tab on the home page.

Planning useful dashboards

We always say that the best way to build a system is to envision what you want to ultimately measure. Do you want to know who your top sales reps are? Would you like to understand what your best accounts are buying from you and how much? Do you wonder how long it takes to close a case? This method of starting with the business questions you want to answer applies to your building of reports and is true of dashboards. If you're an administrator or part of the team responsible for deploying Salesforce, consider these tips as you develop your dashboards:

- ✔ **Focus on your end users.** Meet with sales, marketing, and support management and have them define their KPIs for their teams and business. Knowing this helps you customize Salesforce and construct useful dashboards.

- ✔ **Create a common set of components to reflect a universal way to look at business health.** This is especially true if your company has multiple sales teams. For example, after you determine the key sales metrics for your company's overall dashboard, you can replicate the dashboard and then customize other dashboards for each sales team. By doing this, everyone in the company is speaking a common language.

Building Dashboards

To build a dashboard, you need to create your custom reports first. You also need to create public folders for your dashboard reports if you want dashboards to be viewable for other users. See Chapter 17 for all the details on creating custom reports and organizing them in folders.

Only system administrators and users with permission to manage dashboards can add, edit, and delete dashboards. See Chapter 19 for details on how to grant permissions.

In the following sections, we show you how to install a pre-built dashboard and then how to clone a dashboard. Then, we cover the steps to build a dashboard from scratch.

Installing sample dashboards and reports

One of the best ways to get your feet wet with dashboards is to install sample dashboards from the AppExchange. Salesforce not only creates the dashboard for you but also builds the underlying sample reports to generate the components.

To install sample dashboards, follow these steps:

1. **In your web browser go to** www.appexchange.com.

   The AppExchange home page appears.

2. **Type** Dashboards **in the Search bar at the top and click the Magnifying Glass button.**

   A page full of AppExchange apps appears. The apps with the Salesforce or Salesforce Labs logos are made and provided for free by Salesforce.

3. **Click an app's listing to see more information about it.**

   The App Overview page appears with a description and images. If you find a set of dashboards that you'd like to download and install, check out Chapter 21 for more information on installing apps from the AppExchange.

   If you're having trouble accessing dashboards, you might not have the proper permissions. In this circumstance, consult with your administrator.

Cloning a dashboard

To save time or repurpose useful features, you can generate a dashboard by cloning an existing one and then modifying it. For example, if you envision creating multiple dashboards for different sales units with common components, you can use this shortcut and then modify the associated reports.

When you clone a dashboard, you don't clone another set of identical reports. Instead, the newly cloned dashboard *references* the same custom reports that the original dashboard references. If you want the new dashboard to refer to different reports, see the "Editing a component" section, later in this chapter.

To clone a dashboard, follow these steps:

1. **Click the Dashboards tab.**

   The last dashboard that you viewed appears.

2. **Type the name of a dashboard in the Find a dashboard. . . search bar to search for a dashboard, or browse and select an option from the Find a dashboard. . . drop-down list to select a dashboard that you want to clone.**

   In this example, choose the sample dashboard entitled Company Performance Dashboard.

   The dashboard appears.

3. **Click the Clone button.**

   The Dashboard Builder page appears, as shown in Figure 18-2.

Figure 18-2:
The Dashboard Builder page.

4. **Update any of the dashboard components as you see fit.**

5. **Click Save to leave the Dashboard Builder.**

   The Save Dashboard dialog box appears.

6. **Change your new dashboard's settings, paying close attention to the following:**

   - *Title:* Change the title of the dashboard.

   - *Dashboard Unique Name:* This field is automatically populated for you with your title, but any spaces are replaced by underscores. The Dashboard Unique Name is used by Salesforce to distinguish dashboards from a database perspective.

   - *Save To:* Select the folder in which to store this dashboard from this drop-down list.

   - *Running User:* The *running user* is the user whose security settings will apply to the dashboard. So, any user who can view the dashboard will see what that running user sees.

7. **Click Save to view your new dashboard.**

Developing a dashboard from scratch

In the preceding sections, you have the opportunity to test the waters and even generate some sample custom reports. In this section, you find out how to develop a dashboard from scratch.

To create a new dashboard, follow these steps:

1. **Click the Reports tab.**

   The Reports & Dashboards home page appears.

   You need to build your custom reports before you can develop a dashing new dashboard.

2. **Build your custom reports and save them to a public folder.**

   See Chapter 17 to find out how to build custom reports.

   Dashboards that you want others to see can't use reports in your My Personal Reports folder. For purposes of this running example, find and click the Sales Reports folder (located in the left sidebar of the Reports & Dashboards folder navigation tree on the Reports & Dashboards home page) and click the following reports that show up in the main page:

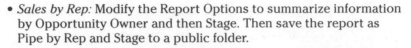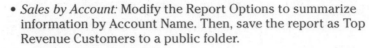

    • *Sales by Rep:* Modify the Report Options to summarize information by Opportunity Owner and then Stage. Then save the report as Pipe by Rep and Stage to a public folder.

    • *Sales by Account:* Modify the Report Options to summarize information by Account Name. Then, save the report as Top Revenue Customers to a public folder.

You must be an administrator or a user with permission to manage public reports if you want to add report folders.

3. **Click back on the Reports tab.**

The Reports & Dashboards home page appears.

4. **Click the New Dashboard button.**

The Dashboard Builder page appears.

5. **Drag the horizontal bar chart component from the Components tab on the left to one of the three available dashboard columns on the right.**

A New Dashboard Component appears in Edit mode.

6. **Complete the fields, entering a header, footer, and/or title.**

For this running example, name the header **PIPELINE METRICS** and enter the title **Pipe by Rep and Stage**. You could also add a footer at the stage, but don't bother for this example.

7. **Click the Data Sources tab on the left.**

A list of reports grouped by folder appears.

8. **Find the Pipe by Rep and Stage report you saved in Step 2 by expanding the folder you saved it in.**

You can use the plus and minus signs to expand and collapse the report folders.

9. **Drag the report onto your dashboard component.**

A preview of your dashboard component appears.

10. **Click Save.**

The Save Dashboard dialog box appears.

11. **Enter a title and select a folder to save to. Click the Save and Run Dashboard button to run the dashboard.**

Your new dashboard appears with your dashboard component.

Updating Dashboards

Over time, you might have to make changes to your dashboards, whether for cosmetic reasons or to make substantive updates. We can come up with a dozen common edits, but the good news is that updating is easy.

Editing dashboard properties

If you need to change the basic settings of a dashboard — such as the title, folder, or running user — you need to edit the dashboard properties. To edit the properties, follow these steps:

1. **Click the Dashboards tab.**

   A dashboard appears.

2. **Select a desired dashboard from the Find a dashboard. . . . . . search bar that also doubles as a drop-down list.**

   The dashboard you are trying to locate appears.

   You can also just start typing a portion of the name of one of your dashboards to be presented with a list of matching dashboards.

3. **Click the Edit button at the top of the dashboard page.**

   The Dashboard Builder appears.

4. **Click the Dashboard Properties button.**

   The Dashboard Properties dialog box appears.

5. **Modify the settings, as needed, and then click OK.**

   When you click OK, the Dashboard Builder reappears, and your setting changes are applied.

Editing a component

You might want to add or change — *edit* — an existing component. To edit a component, follow these steps:

1. **Go to a dashboard and click the Edit button.**

   The Dashboard Builder appears.

2. **Click the Wrench icon above a component that you want to modify.**

For example, you might want to change the chart type or display units.

The Component Editor dialog box appears, as shown in Figure 18-3.

3. **Modify the component data to adjust settings:**

- *For bar, column, or line charts:* From the Group By drop-down list, click on a chart type to select the way multiple groups of values are displayed.

- *For unit of measurement:* Use the Display Units drop-down list.

- *Component type:* Click a chart image to select a component type. See the earlier section "Breaking down basic elements" for details on the components. In the example, select the vertical bar chart option. The steps will differ, depending on which component type you select.

Figure 18-3:
Modifying component data.

4. **Click the Formatting tab to change the type and formatting of your dashboard component to best display your data:**

- *Table and chart components:* Use the Sort Rows By drop-down list to select the order of sorting. For example, if you want to rank the reps from biggest to smallest pipeline, choose Row Value Descending. You can also sort the row labels if you want to rank the reps by their names.

- *Maximum values displayed:* (Optional) If you want, enter a number under Maximum Values Displayed.

- *Bar, column, scatter, or line charts:* Select an option from the Axis Range drop-down list. If you select Manual, the next two fields (Chart Axis Range Minimum and Chart Axis Range Maximum) become available for input.

- *Legend position:* Select an option from the Legend Position drop-down list to display your graph's legend to the right of the chart, below it, or to not show it at all.

- *Chart labeling:* Adjust the chart labeling by selecting the Show Values and the Show Details on Hover check boxes.

- *Tables, metrics, and gauges:* Set up to two breakpoint values to separate different range colors from each other. Select Range Colors to represent a range of data, separated by the breakpoint values. (See Chapter 17 for more information on conditional highlighting.)

- *Gauges:* Set your Minimum and Maximum Values to represent the lowest and highest values on the gauge.

5. **Click OK.**

   The Dashboard Builder reappears with the changes you applied to the component.

6. **Click Save.**

   Your changes are saved, and your dashboard reappears.

Modifying the layout

If you need to modify the dashboard layout, you can also perform this while in the Dashboard Builder (refer to Figure 18-3).

Go to a dashboard, click the Edit button, and alter the layout. You can

- ✔ **Modify a column size:** Select Narrow, Medium, or Wide from the drop-down list at the top of each dashboard component. All the components in the column change in size based on your setting.

- ✔ **Add a component:** Drag a component or data source to a column and follow the steps in the section "Developing a dashboard from scratch," earlier in this chapter.

- ✔ **Delete a component:** Click the X button located at the upper-right corner of a component. A pop-up window appears to confirm the deletion. When you click OK, the pop-up closes and the dashboard reappears, minus the deleted component.

✔ **Add a column:** If you have fewer than three columns in your dashboard, you can click the plus button at the upper right or left of a column to insert a new column on that side, respectively.

✔ **Delete a column:** Click the X button located at the top of a column. A pop-up window appears to confirm the deletion. When you click OK, the pop-up closes and the dashboard reappears, minus the deleted column.

✔ **Rearrange components:** Drag and drop components in your dashboard to arrange them exactly as you see fit.

When you're satisfied with your changes, click the Done button. The dashboard then reappears with your modifications.

You can add up to 20 components per Dashboard, but best practice is to keep your dashboards simple and easy to read. Your most important components should comprise the top row. The top row's components for a dashboard are displayed on the home pages of users who have chosen that dashboard as the one to view.

Refreshing the dashboard

Before you make decisions based on your dashboard, you'll want to make sure that it is based on the latest data. Click any dashboard from your dashboard list. In the upper-right corner of the dashboard is a timestamp starting with As Of. You can use this to find out the last time your dashboard data was updated.

When you want to manually update your dashboard data, simply click the Refresh button at the top of the dashboard page. The components reappear one by one, and when the refresh is completed, a new timestamp appears.

Enterprise and Performance Edition customers can schedule their dashboards to be automatically refreshed on a daily, weekly, or monthly basis. Just use the drop-down list next to the Refresh button.

To schedule a dashboard to automatically refresh, follow these steps:

1. **Click the Dashboards tab.**

   A dashboard appears.

2. **Click the down arrow on the Refresh button.**

3. **Click the Schedule Refresh option.**

   The Schedule Dashboard Refresh screen appears, as shown in Figure 18-4.

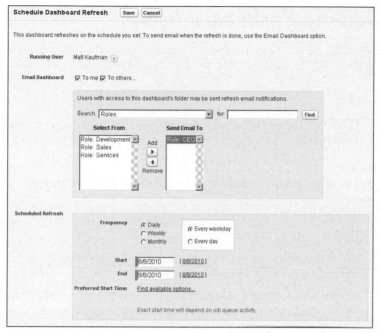

Figure 18-4:
Schedule
a time to
refresh your
dashboard.

4. **(Optional) Select the To Me and/or the To Others check boxes to e-mail a copy of the dashboard when it's refreshed.**

If you have regularly scheduled meetings, you can automatically e-mail your dashboard to the meeting attendees prior to the meeting to give them a sneak peak of what will be discussed.

5. **Select the frequency that you want your dashboard to be refreshed.**

Each frequency option has additional options that allow you to specify exactly when the dashboard will be refreshed.

6. **Select a start and end date for the frequency that you want your dashboard to be refreshed.**

7. **Select a refresh time from the Preferred Start Time drop-down list.**

The dashboard reappears.

Organizing Your Dashboards

If you have permissions to manage dashboards, manage public reports, and view all data, you can organize your company's dashboards in folders and define the proper security access for users. By organizing dashboards, you can make sure that the right people are focusing on the right metrics to manage their business.

Viewing dashboard lists

Unlike most other tabs in Salesforce, clicking the Dashboard tab doesn't take you to its home page. Instead, the last dashboard that you viewed appears.

To access your viewable dashboards, follow these steps:

1. **Click the Go to Dashboard List link at the upper-left corner of any dashboard.**

   A dashboard folder list page appears.

2. **Use the Folder drop-down list to select a desired folder.**

   The Reports & Dashboards home page appears. The page for the selected folder appears in the main window with a list of available dashboards in the folder.

   From this list page, users with the permissions mentioned in the preceding section can perform a variety of functions that include

   - *Re-sort:* Click a column header to re-sort a dashboard list. (See Chapter 2 for more details on navigating list pages.)

   - *View:* Click a title name to view a dashboard.

   - *Modify:* Click the downward-pointing triangle in the Action column of the row that matches the dashboard you want to edit. A drop-down list appears. The Edit link appears in the drop-down list for your selection.

   - *Delete:* Click the downward-pointing triangle in the Action column of the row that matches the dashboard you want to delete. A drop-down list appears. The Delete link appears in the drop-down list for your selection. Select the Del link to delete the dashboard.

   - *Build:* Click the New Dashboard that appears to the right of the Reports & Dashboards heading, or the folder icon to the right of the Find a folder. . . search bar.

Building dashboard folders

From the Reports tab, which takes you to the Reports & Dashboards home page, you can also create and edit folders. Editing a folder is easy when you understand how to create one.

To create a folder, follow these steps:

1. **On the Reports page, click the Folder icon to the right of the Find a folder. . . search bar and select the New Dashboard Folder option in the Folder drop-down list.**

   A New Dashboard Folder page appears.

2. **Type an intuitive name for the folder in the Dashboard Folder field.**

   For example, if you want a folder for only senior management, you might name it Executive Dashboards.

3. **Use the Public Folder Access field to determine read versus read/write privileges to the folder.**

4. **Use the radio buttons to select who should have access to the folder.**

   Your choices amount to All, None, and Selective.

5. **If you chose Selective in Step 4 (the third radio button), highlight Groups or Roles in the Available for Sharing list box and add them to the Shared To list box.**

6. **Click Save.**

   The folder list page reappears, and now you can add dashboards or move existing dashboards to the new folder, which we explain in the section "Editing dashboard properties," earlier in this chapter.

 When naming folders, dashboards, and dashboard reports, consider using a standard numbering convention. For example, you could name the senior management folder 1.0 Executive Dashboards. Then the executive sales subordinate dashboard might be 1.1 and the executive marketing dashboard 1.2. By using a standard numbering methodology, you can more efficiently create, clone, and organize dashboards and dashboard reports.

Part VII

Designing the Solution with Force.com

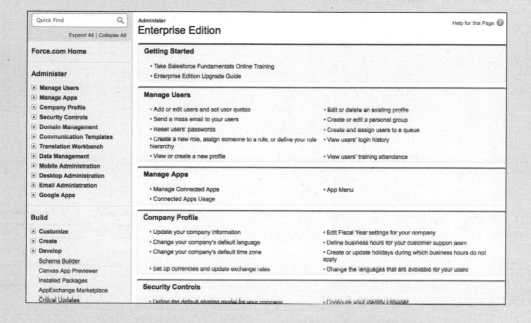

In this part . . .

- ✔ Secure Salesforce with Roles, Profiles and Sharing
- ✔ Add custom fields to tailor Salesforce to meet your business
- ✔ Learn how to play safely in a Sandbox
- ✔ Explore the infinite possibilities of the AppExchange

Chapter 19

Fine-Tuning the Configuration

*I*n earlier chapters, you discover how to add custom fields, define picklists, and create standard templates so that Salesforce looks like it was made exactly for your business. If you're starting to think about additional ways to tweak the system so that each user sees only pertinent information, you've come to the right chapter.

For administrators or members of your customer relationship management (CRM) project team with the right privileges, Salesforce allows you to easily configure your system so that users can access and share information according to your goals. Regardless of which Salesforce edition your company has chosen, you have a variety of ways to control access and sharing of data, from system-wide sharing rules to assigning profiles. And, if you have Enterprise or Performance Edition, you have industrial-strength flexibility, even to the point of field-level security.

In this chapter, we show you all the steps you can take (or should consider) for configuring Salesforce, including modifying your configuration, creating the role hierarchy, assigning profiles, determining field-level security, creating users, setting up your sharing rules, and managing groups. We also show you other methods for controlling security, which include password policies, session settings, audit trails, and delegating administrative privileges.

Figuring Out Configuration

All the things that you can change can be conveniently accessed from the Setup menu of Salesforce. If you have administrative permissions, log in to Salesforce and follow these steps:

1. **Choose the Setup link from the upper-right corner of your Salesforce window.**

   The Force.com home page appears displaying three columns, as shown in Figure 19-1, containing

   - A Quick Find search bar on the left, to help system administrators quickly locate sections or settings

   - A collapsible and expandable navigation menu below the Quick Find search bar

   - A middle section with a Getting Started area, a list of recent administrator-related items you were last looking at, Quick Links to common administrator tasks, and a Community section that provides resources in case you have additional Salesforce questions that this wonderful book hasn't been able to cover

   - Additional technical resources on the right, as well as information on content, events, and AppExchange apps that salesforce.com wants to feature

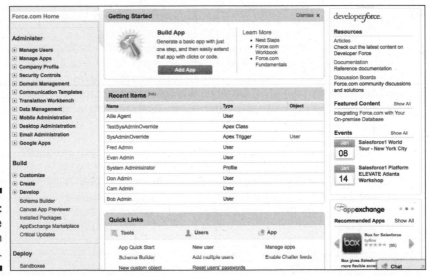

Figure 19-1: Visiting the Force.com home page.

2. **In the left sidebar, click the arrow buttons to expand some of the first folders under the Administer section: Manage Users, Company Profile, and Security Controls.**

   These are your basic options and the first things that you should use when configuring Salesforce.

3. **The section heading can also be clicked on to reveal additional subsections below each of the folders, as shown in Figure 19-2.**

   The Administer page appears too, with the page title that includes the edition (or version) of Salesforce that you're using.

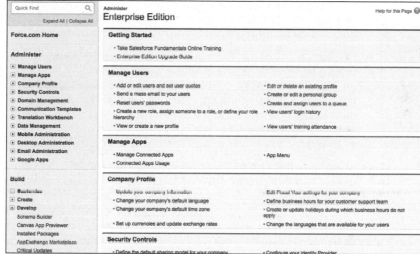

Figure 19-2: Summarizing the Administer section.

Breaking down basic elements

Before jumping into the guts of system configuration, take a minute to review five basic configuration elements:

- ✔ **Users:** These are the specific people who use your Salesforce system.

- ✔ **Sharing model:** Defines the baseline, general access that users have to each other's data. Also known as organization-wide defaults, org-wide defaults, or simply, OWD. If you already know that certain groups should not be seeing other groups' information, you want to start with the most restrictive sharing model and use things like the role hierarchy and sharing rules to open access to information. It's easier to provide more access than it is to selectively restrict it.

- ✔ **Roles and role hierarchy:** Define who reports to whom in your organization, for the purposes of running reports. Roles determine who is able to see and report on records owned by others. Think of roles as a way to provide "vertical access" to data (that is, up and down a hierarchy). People higher up in the hierarchy are able to report on those below them in the hierarchy. For example, if you're a manager of a team of sales reps, you will have a role above your team and be able to see all the account, contact, and opportunity data owned by your team. Individual sales reps, however, might not be able to see opportunity information owned by their peers. This does not always have to mimic your company's org chart exactly, however. Another example is that a sales operations analyst may not have any direct reports, but must run reports on the entire sales team. This person could share a role with the head of sales, only because of her reporting needs. Each user should have an assigned role within your defined role hierarchy.

- ✔ **Profiles:** Control a user's capability to access different fields within a record in Salesforce. For example, service reps will find some fields on an account record more relevant than other fields that may be very important to a marketing operations analyst. To make the service reps' view of the account record more pertinent and less confusing, you could hide certain irrelevant fields from their view. You must assign a profile to each user.

- ✔ **Sharing rules:** Opens up access to data for specific users or groups of users. Think of this as opening lateral or horizontal access to your data, by giving certain peer groups or individuals this exception.

You use these five elements as the primary levers to deliver the proper level of access and control for your company in Salesforce.

Planning configuration to achieve success

Put the major stakeholders of your Salesforce solution in a room and ask them one question: "How do you envision people sharing information in Salesforce?" More often than not, you'll get blank stares.

Discuss sharing issues with your CRM project team after you hear about their current CRM processes. Current business processes, explained without any Salesforce jargon from the team, can often help you formulate an opinion based on what you believe would be best for your company. Take into consideration the culture, size, and type of sales organization at your company. Use this opinion to guide the specific nature of your questions.

Now, you *should* ask that question, but we suggest following it up with scenarios. Here are a few ideas to get you started:

✔ Should a sales development rep be able see what the CEO sees?

✔ Should a sales rep be able to view data from other reps? Should one sales rep be allowed to edit another's lead record?

✔ Do certain groups need wider access than others? For example, does a call center team that supports all customers need more or less access than a team of sales reps? What about a professional services team member who both helps during the sales cycle as well as the implementation, and any postlaunch questions for up to a certain number of days?

✔ Do you have marketing operations or sales operations staff? How will they be interacting with Salesforce? Should they be able to see everything that VPs of their organizations see, especially because they'll probably be doing all the leg work for them?

✔ Does a manager require different permissions than a rep?

✔ Do multiple people commonly work on the same account or opportunity?

✔ Do you have any concerns with a fully open or completely private sharing model?

Use these types of questions and their answers to guide your configuration.

Verifying Your Company Profile

In the Company Profile section, you can modify many basic settings for your organization that include default time zone, language, and currency. If you're the administrator, you can also use this section to monitor and anticipate your future needs relative to purchased licenses.

This is an easy but important step. If you're an administrator beginning your implementation, get this done before you even think of adding a new user.

To update your company information, click the Setup link in the upper-right corner of Salesforce and follow these steps:

1. **Choose Administer⇨Company Profile⇨Company Information.**

   The Company Information page appears. You can also find a lot of information here about the number and type of licenses that you've purchased. This comes in handy as you amass more licenses and have users that need different extra-cost features, or aren't using Salesforce as often as you are.

2. **Click the Edit button.**

   The Edit Organization Profile page appears. Review all the fields. Pay closest attention to verifying the accuracy of the three or four required fields in the Locale Settings section:

   - *Default Locale:* From this drop-down list, select your company's primary geographic locale. *Note:* This setting affects the format of date and time fields (for example, 06/30/2014 versus 30/06/2014) as well as calendar display (week starts Monday versus Sunday).

   - *Default Language:* Set language from this drop-down list.

   - *Default Time Zone:* Verify that your time zone is correctly set from this drop-down list.

   - *Currency Locale:* If you use a single currency, choose the proper location from this drop-down list. This sets the corporate currency. (You won't see this field if you set up multiple currencies.)

   Users can still modify their individual locale settings in the future.

3. **Click Save.**

   The Company Information page reappears with any changes you made.

Defining Your Sharing Model

As an administrator or member of your CRM project team, one of your biggest decisions in Salesforce is how users will share information. A *sharing model* controls the level of access that users have across an organization's information, not just up and down the chain. You can use the sharing model with the role hierarchy, public groups, personal groups, and the default access for each role to get pretty specific about what you want people to view or change. You use the organization-wide sharing model and, if necessary, public groups and expanded sharing rules in Salesforce to configure your sharing model.

For smaller, younger organizations, start with an open, collaborative sharing model, as opposed to a secretive sharing model in which no one knows what anyone else is doing. (A secretive sharing model sounds like any oxymoron, right? Well, it can be because if you don't carefully think about ramifications, you could be back to where you started with giant heaps of information.) If collaboration is one of your goals, a more-restrictive sharing model can have a greater potential negative impact on end-user adoption. You can always change the sharing model in the future if people scream loudly enough. But nine times out of ten, the value of collaboration overcomes the initial concerns with users viewing other users' data.

Setting organization-wide defaults

The organization-wide defaults (OWDs) set the default sharing access that users have to each other's data. Sharing access determines how data created by users in a certain role or public group is viewed by users within another role or public group. For example, you many want your Sales Operations team to see the dollar value of won opportunities so that they can calculate commissions, but you probably don't want them editing the amount of that opportunity. If any role or public group possesses data that at least one other role or group shouldn't see, your sharing model must be private; all other levels of openness must be granted as an exception via groups (more on that later).

No matter which defaults you set to the sharing model, users will still have access to all data owned by or shared with users below them in the role hierarchy.

To configure the organization-wide defaults, click the Setup link and follow these steps:

1. **Choose Administer⇨Security Controls⇨Sharing Settings.**

   The Sharing Settings page appears, showing org-wide defaults for several objects, as well as specific sharing rules for those objects.

2. **Click the Edit button in the Organization Wide Defaults list.**

   The Organization Sharing Edit page appears.

3. **Select the desired settings.**

   Click some picklists to see the different options. The options are typically Private, Public Read Only, and Public Read/Write. For example, if you want the most restrictive model, choose the following as your defaults: Private for the major records and Hide Details for Calendar. Some standard objects, like the Lead and Case objects, have extra special powers and have an additional option, Public Read/Write/Transfer. This assumes that someone working heavily in leads or cases will often need to transfer a lead or case record that isn't owned by him to someone else.

   Remember what we said about role hierarchy providing "vertical access" to data? A Private sharing setting on an object still assumes that people with a role above yours in the role hierarchy can see and report on those records. Salesforce always, by default, respects the hierarchy structure — sharing settings determine only how peers and those outside your typical chain of command see your data. For more complex sharing scenarios, you can have the option to deselect the ability to grant access to records based on role hierarchy, but, you may want to consult with Salesforce support or a Salesforce Partner before making such a complex change.

4. **Click Save.**

   The Sharing Settings page reappears with your settings listed under the Organization Wide Defaults list.

Creating groups

You can create public and personal groups in Salesforce to extend greater sharing privileges through the use of sharing rules. Groups comprise users, roles, or even other groups. So, if your organization-wide default is geared toward a private sharing model, use groups and sharing rules to create exceptions.

Public groups work in combination with sharing rules to expand sharing access to information beyond the organization-wide defaults. You can access public groups from the Manage Users heading on the sidebar on the Administer page.

To create a public group, click the Setup link in the upper-right corner and follow these steps:

1. **Choose Administer➪Manage Users➪Public Groups.**

   The Public Groups page appears.

2. **Click the New button.**

   A Group Membership page appears.

3. **Enter a name for the group in the Group Name field, as shown in Figure 19-3.**

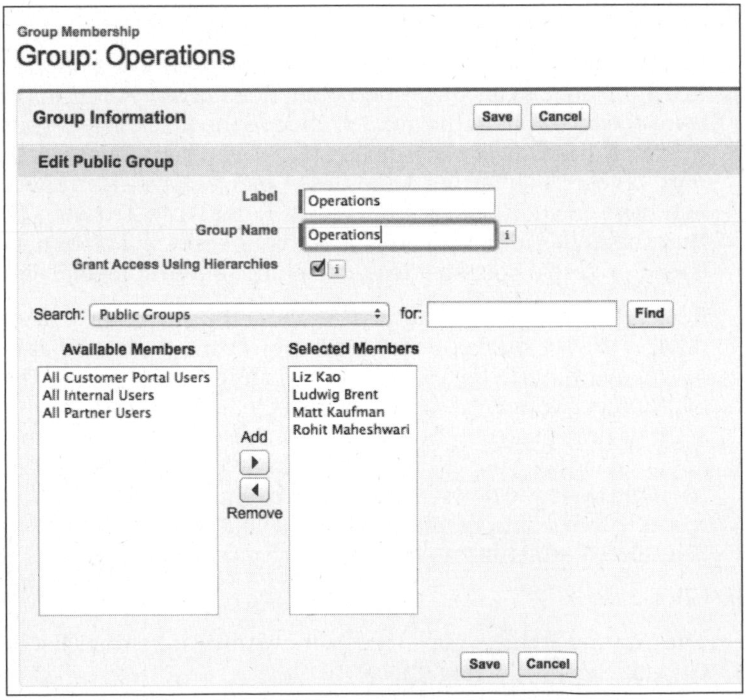

Figure 19-3:
Creating a new public group.

Group Membership
Group: Operations

Group Information   Save   Cancel

Edit Public Group

Label | Operations
Group Name | Operations [i]
Grant Access Using Hierarchies ☑ [i]

Search: Public Groups   for: Find

Available Members   Selected Members
All Customer Portal Users   Liz Kao
All Internal Users   Ludwig Brent
All Partner Users   Matt Kaufman
                                 Rohit Maheshwari
                    Add
                     ▶
                     ◀
                    Remove

                                 Save   Cancel

4. **Highlight users, roles, roles and their subordinates, or other groups in the Available Members list box and click the right arrow to add them to the Selected Members list box.**

5. **Click Save.**

   The Public Groups page reappears with groups that you added.

Granting greater access with sharing rules

By using public groups, roles, or roles and subordinates, you can create sharing rules to extend access above and beyond the organization-wide defaults. For example, if your default sharing model is read-only but you want a group of call center agents to have edit privileges on account records, you could do this with a custom sharing rule.

To add a sharing rule and apply it to your data, click the Setup link and follow these steps:

1. **Click the Sharing Settings link under the Administer⇨Security Controls heading on the sidebar.**

   The Sharing Settings page appears.

2. **Scroll down and click the New button next to any of the standard or custom object Sharing Rules lists, as shown in Figure 19-4.**

   All lists operate much the same but relate to different records. A Sharing Rule page appears for your selected record.

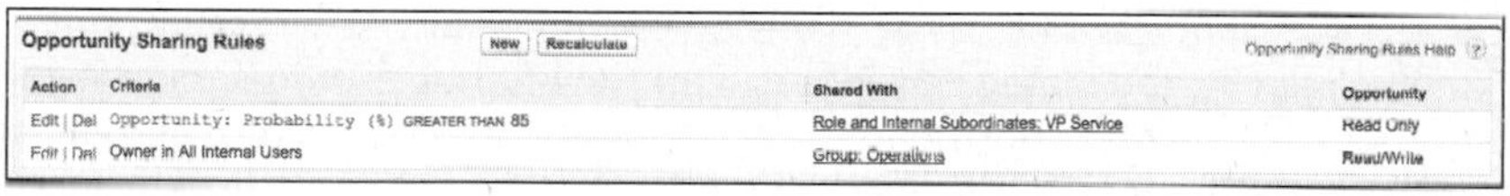

Figure 19-4: Adding a new sharing rule.

3. **Use the drop-down lists to define the data you want to share and the related roles or groups that you want to share that data with, as shown in Figure 19-5.**

   For example, you might create a public group for your call center team and then grant the team read-write privileges to data owned by members of the Entire Organization group.

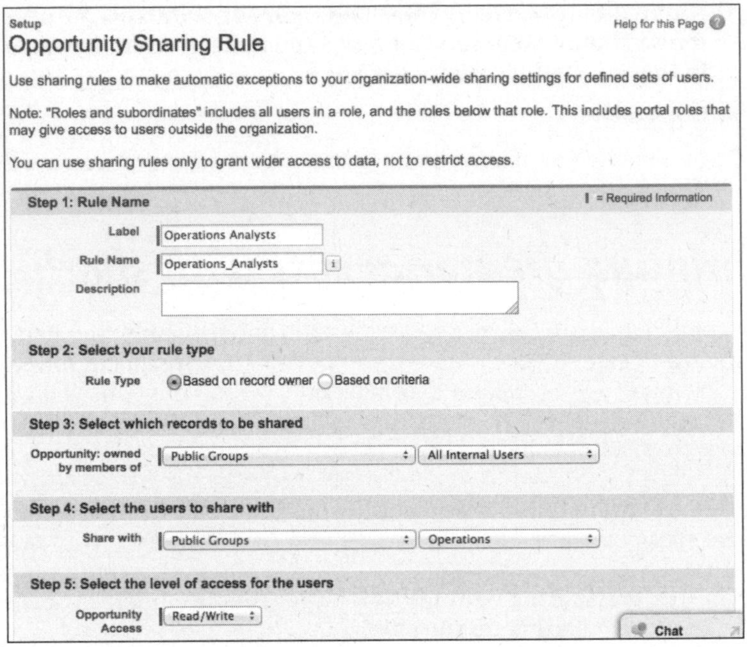

Setup
Opportunity Sharing Rule
Help for this Page

Use sharing rules to make automatic exceptions to your organization-wide sharing settings for defined sets of users.

Note: "Roles and subordinates" includes all users in a role, and the roles below that role. This includes portal roles that may give access to users outside the organization.

You can use sharing rules only to grant wider access to data, not to restrict access.

Step 1: Rule Name   I = Required Information

Label | Operations Analysts |

Rule Name | Operations_Analysts | i

Description | [   ] |

Step 2: Select your rule type

Rule Type   ◉ Based on record owner ○ Based on criteria

Step 3: Select which records to be shared

Opportunity: owned | Public Groups ▾ | All Internal Users ▾
by members of

Step 4: Select the users to share with

Share with | Public Groups ▾ | Operations ▾

Step 5: Select the level of access for the users

Opportunity | Read/Write ▾ |
Access   💬 Chat

Figure 19-5:
Showing a
sharing rule.

4. **Click Save.**

> The Sharing Settings page reappears with your new rule listed under the appropriate related list.

When you add a new sharing rule, Salesforce automatically reevaluates the sharing rules to apply the changes to all your records. If your modifications are substantial, you'll be warned with a dialog box that the operation could take significant time, and Salesforce will e-mail you when complete. When you click OK, the dialog box closes, and the Sharing Settings page reappears. Use the Recalculate button in the appropriate related list to manually apply the changes when you've made modifications to groups, roles, or territories.

Defining the Role Hierarchy

Think of a *role hierarchy* as the Salesforce system's data-access trickle-down org chart: If you're assigned to the role at the top of the chart, you have full access to your own data, and that privilege trickles down to the data of everyone below you in the hierarchy — and life is good.

When you're constructing your hierarchy, don't confuse your actual company org chart with the role hierarchy. Role hierarchy is all about access to data to perform your duties in Salesforce and how you want to organize certain sales-related reports. As such, hierarchies often have fewer layers than a typical org chart. For example, if your executive team will be users, you might simply create a role called Executive Team, assuming that many of those users will have similar trickle-down viewing and editing privileges.

You can use the role hierarchy in Salesforce as a primary method to control a user's visibility and access to other users' data. After you assign a role to a user, that user has owner-like access to all records owned by or shared with subordinate users in the hierarchy. For example, if you set up a hierarchy with a Sales Rep role subordinate to a Sales Manager role, users assigned to Sales Manager would have read and write access to records owned by or shared with users in the Sales Rep role.

To set up your company's role hierarchy, click the Setup link in the upper-right corner and follow these steps:

1. **Choose Administer⇨Manage Users⇨Roles.**

   The Understanding Roles page appears, and you see a sample hierarchy, as shown in Figure 19-6.

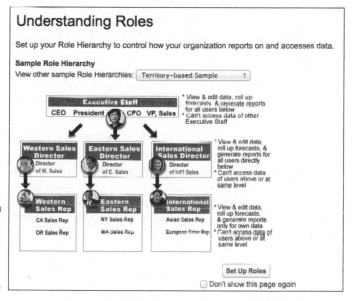

Figure 19-6:
Seeing a sample role hierarchy.

2. **(Optional) To select a different sample hierarchy, make a selection from the View Other Sample Role Hierarchies drop-down list.**

3. **Click the Set Up Roles button.**

   The Creating the Role Hierarchy page appears.

4. **(Optional) To select a different view of the hierarchy, make a selection from the drop-down list on the right side of the page.**

Salesforce provides three standard views for displaying the role hierarchy: tree, list, and sorted list. For this example, we're opting for the default, Tree view.

5. In Tree view, click the Add Role button.

A Role Edit page appears for the new role.

6. Complete the fields.

The fields are pretty obvious, but here are some tips:

- *This Role Reports To:* Use this lookup field to define the role's place in the hierarchy. Because the lookup field is based on roles you already created, add roles by starting at the top of your hierarchy and then working your way down, as shown in Figure 19-7.

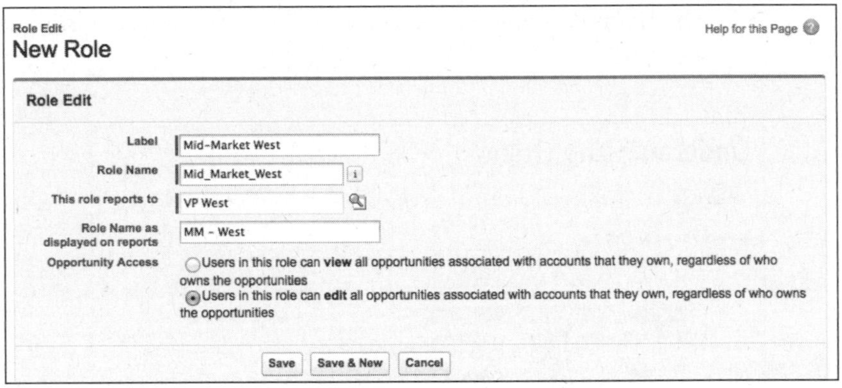

Figure 19-7:
Creating a new role in the hierarchy.

Role Edit
New Role   Help for this Page

Role Edit

Label: Mid–Market West
Role Name: Mid_Market_West
This role reports to: VP West
Role Name as displayed on reports: MM – West
Opportunity Access:
○ Users in this role can **view** all opportunities associated with accounts that they own, regardless of who owns the opportunities
● Users in this role can **edit** all opportunities associated with accounts that they own, regardless of who owns the opportunities

Save   Save & New   Cancel

- *Contact, Opportunity, and Case Access:* Select these options that fit your company's objectives. (You may not see these fields if you have a very public sharing model — more on that in the following section.) You can provide an account owner with read-write access to related opportunities or cases that she doesn't own, has view-only access, or has no access to. This flexibility comes in handy in heavily regulated industries, in which you might have to prevent an account executive from knowing about certain deals or issues going on with her account.

7. Click the Save button or the Save & New button.

- *Save:* The Role: *Role Name* page appears, displaying the detail information you just entered and listing any users in this role. From the users in the *Role Name* Role detail list, you may also assign existing users to this role or create new users with this role. (Check out the section "Adding Users to Salesforce," later in this chapter.)

- *Save & New:* A New Role page appears, and you can continue building the hierarchy. Repeat Steps 3–6 until your hierarchy is done.

Setting Up Profiles

In Enterprise and Performance Editions of Salesforce, you can use profiles to control a user's permission to view and perform many functions. Roles and sharing rules determine which objects a person sees, and a profile determines what details a person sees on that object. Depending on which edition you're using, you can use profiles to

- ✔ Define which page layouts a user will see
- ✔ Control field-level access
- ✔ Determine the apps viewed by a user
- ✔ Alter the tabs displayed to users
- ✔ Make record types available to certain users
- ✔ Secure certain login settings

Reviewing the standard profiles

Most editions of Salesforce come with five or six standard profiles, which can't be altered except for the tab settings. Many large organizations can stick to these standard profiles and address the majority of their company's requirements related to user permissions. If you have Group or Professional Edition, you can't actually view the settings on the standard profiles.

If you have Enterprise or Performance Edition, choose Setup➪Administer➪ Manage Users➪Profiles to see your profiles. Otherwise, here's a brief explanation of the more common standard profiles for Salesforce license types and how they're typically applied:

- ✔ **System Administrators** have full permissions and access across all Salesforce functions that don't require a separate license. You'd typically grant this level of control only to users administering the system or who play a critical part in configuring and customizing Salesforce.

- ✔ **Standard Users** can create and edit most record types, run reports, and view but not modify many areas of the administration setup. If you can't create custom profiles, you'd probably choose to assign sales reps to the standard user profile.

- ✔ **Solution Managers** have all the rights of standard users and can review and publish solutions.

- ✔ **Marketing Users** have all the rights of standard users and can perform a variety of marketing-related functions, including importing leads and managing public documents and e-mail templates. If your Salesforce edition has campaigns, marketing users can also administer campaigns.

✔ **Contract Managers** can add, edit, approve, and activate contracts. They can also delete nonactivated contracts.

✔ **Read Only** is just what its name implies. Users assigned to this profile can view data and export reports, but can't edit anything.

Profiles never conflict with your organization's sharing model or role hierarchy. For example, a Standard User profile allows a user to create, edit, or delete leads, but if your sharing model is read-only for leads, the Standard User won't be able to delete leads owned by others.

Over the years, salesforce.com has expanded the types of licenses you can buy, to better accommodate your organization's users and how often and what they need to access in Salesforce. To get the latest comprehensive list with definitions, click the Help & Training link from within any Salesforce page and type **license types** into the search bar.

Creating custom profiles

If you have Enterprise or Performance Edition, you can build custom profiles that provide you greater flexibility than the standard permissions granted to users and the layouts that they see. For example, you may want to create a custom profile for your Finance team so that only users with that profile can edit check boxes on the opportunity that track whether certain signed forms have been submitted when you close a deal. See Chapter 20 for details on creating custom layouts, business processes, and record types.

To create a custom profile, you can start from scratch, but we suggest cloning and modifying an existing profile by following these steps:

1. **Choose Setup➪Administer➪Manage Users➪Profiles.**

   The User Profiles page appears. You can see which profiles are standard or custom ones.

2. **Click the Standard User link in the Profile Name list.**

   The Profile: Standard User page appears. In practice, you can clone from any of the profiles, but by starting from the Standard User profile, you can simply add or remove permissions.

3. **Click the Clone button.**

   The Clone Profile page appears.

4. **Type a title in the Profile Name field and then click Save.**

   The Profile page for your new profile appears.

5. **Click the Edit button to modify the permissions, as shown in Figure 19-8.**

   The Profile Edit page appears.

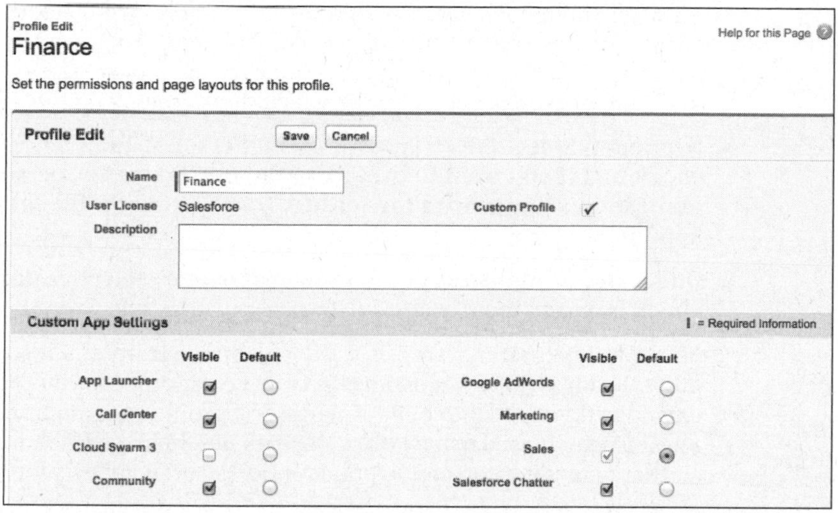

Figure 19-8:
Previewing
a Profile Edit
page.

Profile Edit
Finance   Help for this Page

Set the permissions and page layouts for this profile.

Profile Edit	Save	Cancel

Name	Finance	
User License	Salesforce	Custom Profile ✓
Description		

Custom App Settings   I = Required Information

	Visible	Default		Visible	Default
App Launcher	☑	○	Google AdWords	☑	○
Call Center	☑	○	Marketing	☑	○
Cloud Swarm 3	☐	○	Sales	☑	⦿
Community	☑	○	Salesforce Chatter	☑	○

Salesforce packs a plethora of possible permissions into a profile page.
Some of those permissions aren't obvious; others are dependent on
your selecting other permissions. If you have questions as you're working through the Profile Edit page, click the Help for This Page link in
the upper-right corner of the page to go directly to the relevant Help
documentation. If you place your cursor over the *i* icons, located next to
certain Administrative Permissions on the Profile Edit page, rollover text
appears with tips on other required settings.

6. **Under the Custom App Setting section, determine which standard and
   custom apps are visible for a profile and which one is the default.**

   This determines the content of the AppExchange app drop-down list.

7. **Under the Tab Settings section, use the drop-down lists to determine
   the tab settings for your new profile.**

   Choose from the three possible options:

   - *Default On:* You want a tab to be displayed.

   - *Default Off:* You want a tab not to appear while still allowing a
     user assigned to the profile the choice to turn the tab back on.
     For example, if you created a profile for sales reps and you want
     to hide the Contracts tab but give the rep the option to display it,
     select Default Off on the Contracts field.

   - *Tab Hidden:* You want the tab to be hidden without an option for
     the user to turn the tab back on. For example, if your company
     isn't going to use cases, you might decide to hide the tab.

Making a tab hidden in a user's profile doesn't prevent the user from accessing those records (in reports, for example). To prevent a user from accessing a particular type of record altogether, remove the Read permission on that type of data from the Object Permissions sections of the page.

8. **(Optional) Select the Overwrite Users' Personal Tab Customizations check box if you want to overwrite the user's current personal customization settings with the settings for the new profile that you're applying.**

9. **Under the Administrative Permissions header, select or deselect check boxes to modify administrative permissions from the profile.**

   Most of these settings are designed for administrators, but some of these might be important, depending on your goals for a custom profile. For example, if you want to build a manager's profile, you might retain permissions such as Manage Public Reports and Manage Public List Views so that managers can create public reports and list views for their teams.

10. **Under the General User Permissions header, select or deselect check boxes to modify common user permissions from the profile.**

    For example, if you don't want sales reps to be able to export customer data to a file, you could create a custom profile for reps and remove the Export Reports setting.

11. **Under the Standard Object and Custom Object Permissions headers, select or deselect check boxes to modify standard or custom object permissions from the profile.**

    For example, if you don't want support reps to be able to modify opportunities, you could create a custom profile for support reps and select only the Read check box in the row for opportunities.

12. **Click Save.**

    The Profile page reappears for your new profile. Your new profile will now appear the next time you follow the instructions in Step 1.

13. **Click the View Users button if you want to assign users to the profile.**

    A Custom: *Custom Profile Name* list page appears in which you can view, add, or reset passwords for users in the profile. See the following section to add users to Salesforce.

Adding Users to Salesforce

When salesforce.com supplies user licenses for your organization, administrators can add users into Salesforce. (See the "Setting Up Profiles" section, earlier in this chapter, for the scoop on viewing and modifying your company profile.) You don't have to create the roles and profiles before you add users, but we recommend doing so because Role and Profile are required fields when you're creating a user record.

To add users, click the Setup link and follow these steps:

1. **Click the Users link under the Administer➪Manage Users heading on the sidebar.**

   A users list page appears.

2. **(Optional) Use the View drop-down list if you want to select from standard or custom list views of your users.**

   Salesforce presets your views with three standard options: All Users, Active Users, and Admin Users.

3. **Click the New User button to add users one at a time.**

   A New User page appears in Edit mode.

   To enter a list of users (instead of one at a time) that need to be created, click the Add Multiple Users button instead.

4. **Complete the fields, paying close attention to selecting appropriate Role and Profile values.**

   Select the Generate New Password and Notify User Immediately check box at the bottom of the New User page if you want the user to immediately receive an e-mail with her username and temporary password. If you're in the midst of an implementation, we recommend deselecting this check box and doling out passwords when you're good and ready.

5. **Click Save.**

   The User detail page appears.

Using Other Security Controls

Beyond the major configuration settings (such as roles, profiles, and sharing model), as an administrator, you have other settings for managing the use and security of your data in Salesforce. You can find these features by choosing Setup➪Administer➪Security Controls.

In the following sections, we discuss how to manage field-level access and delegate a subset of administration to others.

Setting field-level security

If you have Enterprise or Performance Edition, you have three primary ways to control access and editing on specific fields: profiles (which we discuss earlier in this chapter), page layouts (Chapter 20 covers these), and field-level settings (stay right here for the details). With field-level security, you can further restrict users' access to fields by setting whether those fields are visible, editable, or read-only.

To view and administer field-level security, click the Setup link and follow these steps:

1. **Choose Administer⇨Security Controls⇨Field Accessibility.**

   The Field Accessibility page appears, listing all objects.

2. **Click the link for the type of record for which you want to view and manage field-level security.**

   A Field Accessibility page for the selected record type appears, as shown in Figure 19-9. For example, click the Account link if you want to review the security settings on account fields.

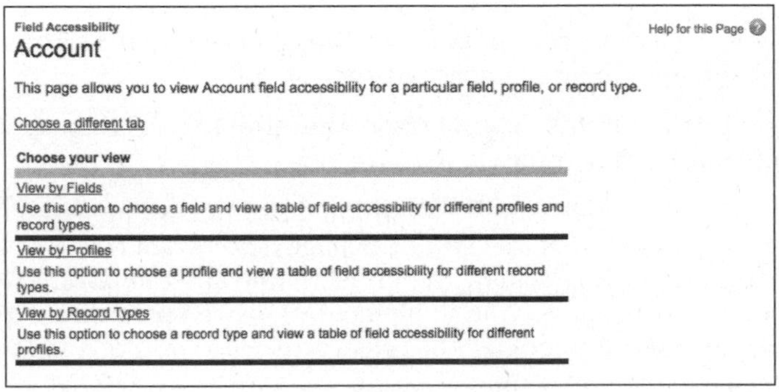

Figure 19-9:
Preparing
to view field
accessibility.

3. **Under the Choose Your View header, click the View by Fields link.**

   The Field Accessibility page for the record type reappears with a Field drop-down list. If you want to see a different view of this information — in which you get to see one profile and the security levels for all the fields for the selected data type — click the View by Profiles link.

4. **Select a field from the Field drop-down list.**

   The page reappears with a table displaying your company's profiles and the profiles' accessibility to the selected field.

5. **In the Field Accessibility table, click a link in a cell to edit the profile's field access for a specific record type.**

   An Access Settings page for the selected profile and selected field appears, as shown in Figure 19-10.

6. **Select the check boxes to modify the field-level settings, and then click Save.**

   The Field Accessibility page for the selected record type reappears.

Access Settings for Account Field
Help for this Page ?
Employees

The **Employees** field is currently **Editable** for the **Standard User** profile when viewing the **Master** record type.

Save   Cancel

Field-Level Security:

Profile	Field	Visible	Read-Only
Standard User	Employees	☑	☐

Page Layout:

⦿ Remove or change editability of the **Employees** field on the **Account Layout** page layout.
◯ Choose a different page layout for the **Standard User** profile for the **Master** record type.

Use the checkboxes below to change the page layout settings for the **Employees** field on the **Account Layout** page layout.

Page Layout	Field	Visible	Read-Only	Required
Account Layout	Employees	☑	☐	☐

Changes to the **Account Layout** page layout will apply to all record type / profile combinations that are assigned to this page layout. The table below shows which record type / profile combinations are currently assigned to the page layout.

	Record Types			
Profiles	Master	Advanced	Partner	Simple
*Customer Portal User - Solutions	✓	✓	✓	✓
Chatter Only User	✓	✓	✓	✓
Cirrus Computers (OLD) Profile	✓	✓	✓	✓

Figure 19-10:
Modifying field-level access on a profile.

If you modify a field-level security setting for a profile by deselecting the Visible check box, this means that the record related to that field is still searchable. The field will never be viewable to a person with that profile, and thus that person won't be able to create reports or search using it, but he can use reports created by others that leverage that field. So if an account, ABC Corp., had its Employees field filled out with the number 1001, but that field was not visible to Watson who has the Standard User profile, Watson could still run a report created by Holmes, who, with a different profile, was able to customize a report looking for all accounts where the Employees field was greater than 1000. In that report, ABC Corp. would be listed and Watson would see ABC Corp., but he would not see the Employees field in the output. Watson would also not be able to customize a report using the Employees field because he can't see it to modify a query.

If you need to provide someone with similar access to records as an existing user, with the exception of visibility to a few fields, we (and salesforce.com!) recommend that you do this via field-level security on a new custom profile, versus removing the field from the page layout. It might not be visible on a page, but that field is still visible elsewhere in Salesforce — like when creating and running reports and list views. Even if you're not strict about a group of people not seeing a field, field-level security can help reduce end users seeing an overwhelming number of fields that they have to wade through when creating reports.

Delegating administration

As an administrator for your growing world of Salesforce users within your company, you hold the key to who accesses your Salesforce instance. You shouldn't try to cut corners by making everyone system administrators just because you're annoyed each time they bug you to add a new user, or because they get impatient about your asking "why?" to their requests. Salesforce allows you to delegate some administrative duties to nonadministrators. Delegated administrators can help you create and edit users in roles you specify, reset passwords for those users, assign users to certain profiles, and manage custom objects. For example, if your marketing department is growing quickly, you may want to allow a manager in the Marketing Manager role to create and edit users in the Marketing Manager role and all subordinate roles.

To delegate administration, you must first define the groups of users to whom you want to delegate these new privileges. Then you have to specify what you want those newly delegated administrators to do. To define delegated administrators, follow these steps:

1. **Choose Setup➪Administer➪Security Controls➪Delegated Administration.**

   The Manage Delegated Groups page appears.

2. **Click New.**

   The Edit Delegated Group page for the new delegated group appears.

3. **Enter the Delegated Group Name.**

   In our example, we selected Sales Operations.

4. **Click Save.**

   The Delegated Group page for your new group appears.

5. **Click the Add button in the Delegated Administrators related list to specify which users will belong in this group.**

   The Delegated Administrators page appears.

6. **Use the Lookup icons to find and add users to this group.**

7. **Click Save.**

   The Delegated Group page for your group reappears.

8. **To specify which roles and subordinate roles a delegated administrator can manage, click the Add button in the User Administration related list.**

   The Roles and Subordinates page appears.

9. **Use the Lookup icons to find and add roles that your delegated group may manage.**

10. **Click Save.**

    The Delegated Group page for your group reappears.

11. **Click Add in the Assignable Profiles related list to specify which profiles these delegated administrators may assign to users.**

    The Assignable Profiles page appears.

12. **Use the Lookup icons to find and add profiles that your delegated group may assign.**

13. **Click Save.**

    The Delegated Group page for your group reappears.

14. **Click Add in the Custom Object Administration related list to specify which custom objects and related tabs a delegated administrator may manage.**

    The Custom Object Administration page appears.

15. **Use the Lookup icons to find and add custom objects that your delegated group may assign.**

16. **Click Save.**

    The Delegated Group page for your group reappears.

Customizing the Look and Feel

If your business wants to take advantage of some optional and advanced customizations that improve your efficiency, keep reading!

Drag and drop, hovers, and other tweaks

To update your organization's look and feel, the User Interface page allows you to turn on some timesaving functions that will greatly increase your organization's productivity.

Here's a quick summary of just some of the features available to you:

- ✔ **Enable Collapsible Sections** lets users minimize or maximize page sections on a record, which is especially helpful if you have many departments all with their specific fields on one record. By collapsing certain sections that aren't relevant to you, you can scroll to your section that much faster. Look for the little triangle icons to the left of a page section — they look like the ones to the left of the Force.com Home navigation folders.

- ✔ **Enable Hover Details** displays an interactive overlay with details about a record when you leave your mouse hovering over a lookup link to that record.

✔ **Enable Related List Hover Links** adds shortcuts to related lists to the top of each record so that you never have to scroll to see your related lists. In Figure 19-11, you see an example of the Contacts related list hover link, above the Business Account Detail information.

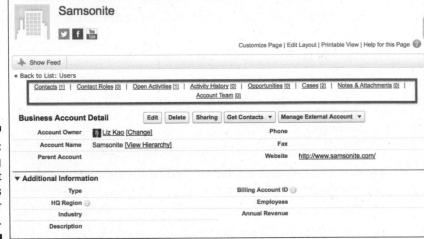

Figure 19-11:
Adding related list hover links to your records.

✔ **Enable Inline Editing** allows you to edit a field on a record just by double-clicking it. You don't have to click the Edit button and wait for the page to reload anymore.

✔ **Enable Enhanced Lists** turns your existing Custom Views into a spreadsheet-like page on which you can mass-edit values across multiple records.

✔ **Enable Home Page Hover Links for Events** allows you to see more information about an event on your Salesforce calendar just by hovering your mouse over it.

✔ **Enable Drag-and-Drop Editing on Calendar Views** allows you to rearrange events on your Salesforce calendar simply by dragging the event from one time to another.

✔ **Enable Hover Links for My Tasks List** allows you to see more information about a task in your Salesforce task list just by hovering your mouse over it.

All these tweaks and more can be made from the User Interface page as follows:

1. **Choose Setup⇨Build⇨Customize⇨User Interface.**

   The User Interface settings page appears, as shown in Figure 19-12.

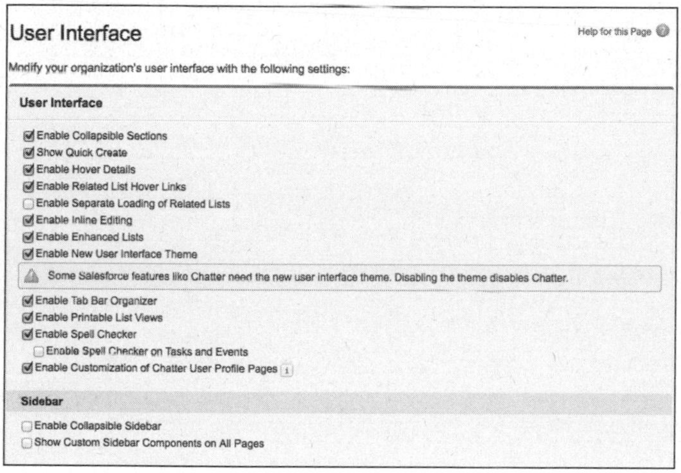

User Interface

Modify your organization's user interface with the following settings:

User Interface

☑ Enable Collapsible Sections
☑ Show Quick Create
☑ Enable Hover Details
☑ Enable Related List Hover Links
☐ Enable Separate Loading of Related Lists
☑ Enable Inline Editing
☑ Enable Enhanced Lists
☑ Enable New User Interface Theme

⚠ Some Salesforce features like Chatter need the new user interface theme. Disabling the theme disables Chatter.

☑ Enable Tab Bar Organizer
☑ Enable Printable List Views
☑ Enable Spell Checker
   ☐ Enable Spell Checker on Tasks and Events
☑ Enable Customization of Chatter User Profile Pages ⓘ

Sidebar

☐ Enable Collapsible Sidebar
☐ Show Custom Sidebar Components on All Pages

Figure 19-12: Tweaking user interface settings.

2. **Select one or more of the user interface setting check boxes.**

3. **Click Save.**

Chapter 20

Customizing Salesforce with Force.com

*I*f you're just beginning your implementation, Salesforce comes preconfigured with a number of common fields in simple layouts for each of the tabs. You could buy your licenses, log in, and without any customization, start using it to track your customers. So why is it that as the top cloud-based CRM provider, no two instances of Salesforce are likely to be identical?

The answer is a key ingredient to your success: The more Salesforce is customized to your business, the more likely your company will use it effectively and productively . . . as long as you lay a strong foundation (using this book will help)!

If you're an administrator or a user with permission to customize Salesforce, you have a universe of tools to design Salesforce to fit the way you do business. And you don't need to be a technical wizard to make these changes. With common sense, patience, and a little help from this book, you can customize Salesforce on your own in a way that will allow Salesforce to scale as your business matures.

REMEMBER

You may hear the phrase *Force.com* used when talking about Salesforce's customization capabilities. That is the umbrella term used to describe everything under the Setup link, where all the many Salesforce customization features are located. It's described as the foundational platform that makes Salesforce and its many custom applications possible.

We could write another book if we tried to address each feature. In this chapter, we show you how to perform all the core customization options, including creating fields, building in your standard processes, adding web links, and rearranging layouts. Then, for companies that have Enterprise or Performance Edition and possess complex needs, we show you how to develop custom page layouts, multiple business processes, and record types that link to custom profiles.

Discovering Customization

All your customization tools are conveniently accessible from the Customize menu located under the Build heading of Setup in Salesforce. Navigating the Customize menu is simple when you understand some basics. If you have administrative permissions, log in to Salesforce and do this now:

1. **Choose Setup⇨Build⇨Customize.**

   The Customize page of Setup appears, and the sidebar expands to display headings for the various objects that can be customized; see Figure 20-1. Under the Customize heading on the sidebar, you see a few select headings for other areas of Salesforce (such as Call Center and Self-Service), which can also be customized.

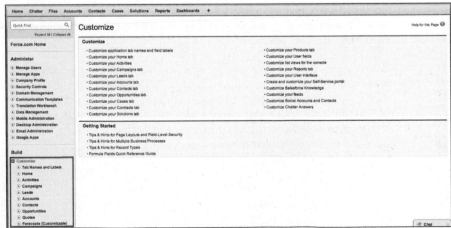

Figure 20-1: Expanding the customization sidebar.

2. **Click the arrow buttons or headings that correspond to the major tabs, such as Accounts, Contacts, and Leads.**

   The sidebar expands with the different customization features available under each heading. These are all the things you can do when customizing a standard tab. Notice that although certain headings have more features, most of the headings have links to common customization features, such as Fields, Page Layouts, Search Layouts, Buttons and Links, and in certain editions, Record Types and Processes.

3. **Click the Fields link under a tab-related heading (like Accounts) on the sidebar.**

   A Fields page appears based on the selected tab heading. This easy and consistent navigation will help you through the customization.

If you hadn't noticed, the tab names listed under the Customize header aren't in alphabetical order. The list used to be much shorter back in Salesforce's infancy. Over time, more features and tabs (also known as *objects*) were created. For new users like yourself, you don't have to keep scrolling to find where a certain object header is listed. Just use the Quick Find search bar in the upper left of the left sidebar (see Figure 20-2). When you type in a tab name or feature setting name, links containing those words will appear.

Breaking down basic elements

When diving into customization, keep these five basic concepts in mind:

- **Records** are the high-level data elements (such as accounts, contacts, and opportunities) that are stored in the Salesforce database. Each tab corresponds to a type of record. Records consist of fields. If you think of the Salesforce database as a filing cabinet holding all your company's information, a record is like a type of form that you house in your filing cabinet.

- **Page Layouts** allow you to control how a page is displayed to users. Different users (like those in Marketing and Sales) may need to see some common fields on a Contact record, while also focusing on other fields relevant to just their departments. Different page layouts help different teams see fields that are most relevant to them, which helps with adoption and increased usage of your CRM system.

- **Search Layouts** is the feature that allows you to control how search results are displayed to users. Search layouts correspond to the organization of columns that are displayed on a Search Results page, lookup dialog page, or record home page in Salesforce.

 ✔ **Processes** is an option for some objects, allowing you to build various sales, marketing, and service processes in Salesforce that you want your reps to follow.

 ✔ **Record Types** allow you to offer certain business processes and subsets of drop-down lists to users based on their profiles. Not to be confused with a type of record (such as an account or contact), a record type, when used with page layouts and profiles, can make only some of the drop-down list values available to users within a profile. For example, an enterprise sales rep with a longer sales cycle may need to track more opportunity stages of his sales cycle, compared to a general business rep whose high-volume transactions only require tracking of a few opportunity stages.

Figure 20-2: Using the Quick Find search bar to find account-related settings.

Customizing for relevance

Prior to customizing Salesforce, your CRM project team should conduct a series of business process reviews with functional representatives or stakeholders of the teams that will be using Salesforce. In those meetings, not only should you map out current and desired processes, but you should also ask sets of leading questions that will impact the design of fields, records, layouts, and more. Key questions should include

- ✔ How do you define your customer?
- ✔ What information do you want to collect on a contact?
- ✔ Who do you expect to fill out this information? Is that realistic?
- ✔ How do you know that you have a qualified lead?
- ✔ What do you want to know about an opportunity?

Use the answers to construct a list of standard and custom fields per record that you believe should be in Salesforce. That spreadsheet should include columns for field name, field type, field values, justification, and so on, and you should review it with your project team prior to customization.

When customizing, keep it simple at the beginning. Don't add or keep a field unless you ultimately believe that you or someone else will use it. You can always build additional fields in the future, especially if you build momentum based on early user adoption success.

 When you create custom fields, fill in the Help and Description fields for them, too. This is often overlooked, and results in future generations of employees often scratching their heads as to a field's usefulness. Custom fields get created over time, names sound familiar (but may be obvious in their differences when you create them), and this tacit knowledge rarely gets passed on. Consider the Help text as your future self, training the next new sales rep, marketing manager, service agent, and so on. Use the Description field to give a little more background to which group requested this field and to what they were trying to report with this data.

Building and Editing Fields

When it comes to customizing Salesforce fields, two words describe the experience: It's easy. The hard part is confirming why you want it, who will be realistically filling out the information that you want to capture, and whether this will be easily reportable when hundreds or thousands of records have this data. The more relevant you make the record fields to your actual business, the better the user adoption batting average and the higher the likelihood of hitting a home run.

Adding fields

All editions of Salesforce allow you to add fields, but some versions allow you to add significantly more fields than others. For example, if you have Group Edition, you can add 100 custom fields per record; with Enterprise Edition, you can create up to 500 per record.

To add a field, click the Setup link in the upper-right corner of Salesforce and follow these steps:

1. **Click any tab-related heading under the Customize heading on the sidebar.**

   The options under the selected heading appear.

2. **Click the Fields link under the heading.**

   The Fields page for the tab appears, displaying a list of standard fields at the top and a list of custom fields and relationships at the bottom.

3. **Click New in the Custom Fields & Relationships related list.**

   Step 1 of the New Custom Field Wizard appears. Data types with descriptions of each of them appear in a list, as shown in Figure 20-3.

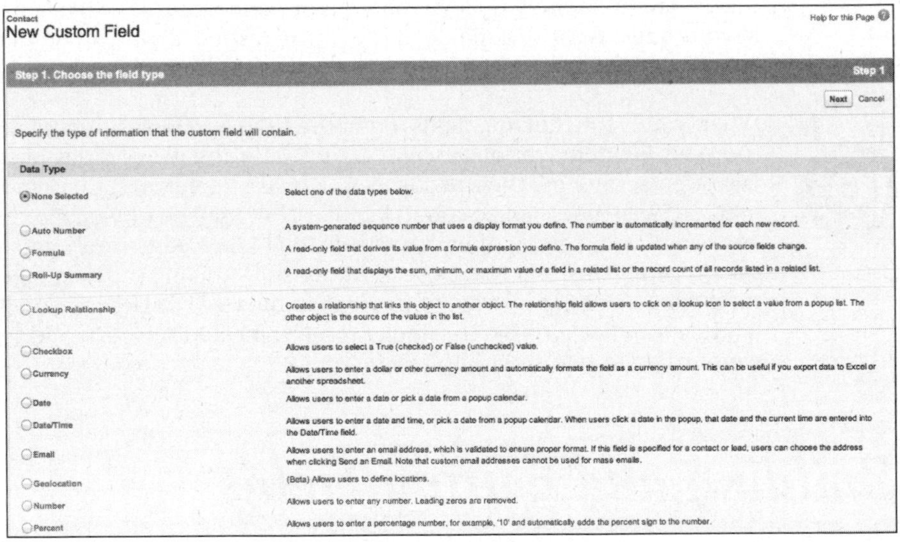

Figure 20-3: Choosing a new contact custom field's data type.

4. **Select a radio button matching the type of field that you want to create and then click Next.**

   Step 2 of the wizard appears, asking you to enter details about the field you want to create. These two fields are required:

   - A *field label* is what's displayed on page layouts, in reports, and to end users' eyes, for example, "Reimbursement Date."

   - A *field name* may be the exact same as a field label but must use an underline (_) as a substitute for a space character. Field names are used as an internal reference by Salesforce and are key for integration, for example, "Reimbursement_Date."

5. **Enter the details and click Next.**

   Step 3 of the wizard appears. The details page varies based on the field type you selected. For example, the settings for a Text Area field are different than for a Currency field.

   If your company's edition is not Enterprise or Performance Edition, click Save and you're done. Optionally, click Save & New to immediately save this custom field and begin creating another one.

6. **For Enterprise or Performance Edition, use the check boxes to select the field-level security access and edit rights per profile and then click Next.**

   Step 4 of the wizard appears.

7. **For Enterprise or Performance Edition, use the check boxes to select the page layouts that should include this field and then click Save.**

   The Fields page for the selected record reappears.

Viewing and updating fields

On an ongoing basis, situations come up in which you might need to update the properties of a field. For example, management changes or adds statuses, nomenclature changes so that field labels need to change, and so on.

To view and update your fields, choose Setup➪Build➪Customize. Then click the Fields link under a tab heading under the Customize heading on the sidebar. The Fields page for the selected tab appears, displaying lists of standard and custom fields. From this page, you can do the following:

- **Update a field:** Click the Edit link to the left of whichever field you want to modify.

- **Change the field type on a field:** Click the Edit link for that field, and then click the Change Field Type button at the top of the Edit page. Step 1 of the wizard appears, and you can follow the steps in the preceding section, starting with Step 4.

If data already exists in a field and you want to change its data type, you risk losing that data. Also, not all data types can be converted into a different data type. For more details, go to the Help & Training link in the upper-right corner of any Salesforce page and search for "changing custom field types" in the search bar.

✔ **View the field and its properties:** Click a link in the Field Label column.

✔ **Delete a custom field:** Click the Del link to the left of the field, next to the Edit link.

✔ **Add values to a drop-down list:** Click the Field Name link in the Label column, and then click the New button in the Picklist Values related list, as shown in Figure 20-4.

Figure 20-4:
Adding a
new picklist
value to a
drop-down
list.

✔ **Replace values in a drop-down list:** Click the Replace link next to a field. A Find and Replace Picklist page appears. Make sure to add the new value before trying to replace.

The Replace feature is really helpful when you have existing records with old values that need to be switched to new values. Take the Lead Status field, for example: You could use the Replace feature to update leads formerly marked as Unresponsive and replace them all instantly with a new value called Nurture.

✔ **Reorder values in a drop-down list:** Click the field name link in the Label column, and then click the Reorder button in the Picklist Values list.

Replicating your key standard processes

On certain standard records in Salesforce, you use a standard drop-down list to map your business processes.

You'll probably want to put some careful thought into handling each type of record. To define your standard business processes, do the following:

1. **Expand the Customize menu until you see the Fields links for various records (under the Activities heading, refer to the Task Fields link).**

2. **Click a Fields link under one of the records mentioned in Step 1.**

   The Fields page appears with Standard Fields and Custom Fields & Relationships related lists.

3. **Depending on the record you chose, look in the Standard Fields related list and then click the Status or Stage link to modify the corresponding processes.**

   In each circumstance, a field page appears with a Picklist Values related list, listing all the values within the process.

4. **In the Picklist Values related list, adjust your process, as necessary.**

   See the preceding section for details on updating picklist fields.

Understanding custom formula fields

After you get the hang of adding custom fields, explore some additional cool things you can do with them.

Custom formula fields are a custom field type that automatically calculate their values based on the content of other values or fields. For example, if you charge your customers a shipping and handling fee based on the total quantity of a product listed in an opportunity, create a custom formula field called S&H that multiplies your total quantity amount with a predefined value.

To create a custom formula field, first define the task at hand. What is it you want to calculate? Then follow up to Step 3 of the numbered list in the section "Adding fields," earlier in this chapter, and choose to add a Formula field. Then continue with these steps:

1. **At Step 2 of the New Custom Field Wizard, provide a field label and field name.**

2. **Use the radio buttons to select the format that your returned value will take and then click Next.**

   Depending on your selection, Salesforce may ask you how many decimal places you want your returned value to display.

3. **Type your formula in Step 3 (as shown in Figure 20-5).**

   Salesforce displays two subtabs — Simple Formula and Advanced Formula — to help you with creating your formula, and adding your formula for Salesforce to process:

   - *Simple Formula:* Reveals a subset of merge fields to add to your formula, along with standard math operators

   - *Advanced Formula:* Reveals all possible merge fields for your record, provides more operators, and shows you a set of Excel-like function categories that you can use to plug into your formula

   To use either, simply move your mouse over the tab that you want to use and click it. The body of that tab appears.

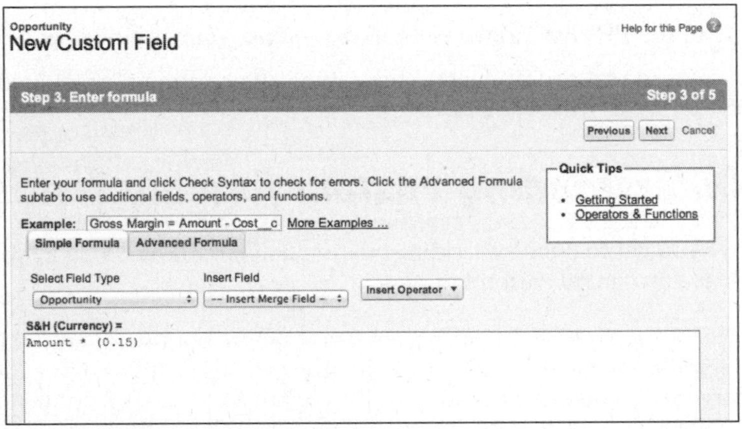

Figure 20-5:
Creating
a custom
formula.

4. **Click Check Syntax when complete to make sure that your formula is up to snuff. Click Next.**

   If you get an error message, go back and check your formula. Salesforce's error messages will tell you if it can't find the fields you're referencing, if you used an incorrect parameter, and so on.

5. **In Step 4, confirm field-level security for your new field and then click Next.**

   Because it derives its content automatically, the field will be a read-only field. You just have to confirm who can see it.

6. **In Step 5, confirm which page layout you want to add this new field to. Click Save when finished.**

   The Fields page for the record reappears.

You don't have to be a math or Excel whiz to benefit from custom formula fields, although those skills sure can help you master it faster. If you're like the rest of us and would rather not even figure out the tip on your dinner tab, make sure that you go to the Help & Training section from the upper right of any page in Salesforce and search for "examples of advanced formula fields" for a ton of suggestions on how your organization can benefit from prebuilt formulas grouped by specific topics.

Using Custom Buttons and Links

Many sales, marketing, and support teams rely on websites and secure cloud-based applications to perform their jobs. For example, your company might use a research website for market intelligence. By building powerful custom links that connect to important websites, users can use Salesforce more efficiently without having to manually open another browser window.

The Salesforce Force.com platform allows you to create custom buttons to represent your links or to perform actions that would usually take several mouse clicks to complete, such as escalating a case.

To build a custom button or link, click the Setup link in the upper-right corner and then follow these steps:

1. **Click any record heading under the Customize heading on the sidebar.**

   The selected heading expands.

2. **Click the Buttons & Links link under the record heading.**

   The Buttons, Links, and Actions page for the selected record appears

3. **Click the New Button or Link button in the Buttons, Links, and Actions list.**

   The New Button or Link page appears in Edit mode. Complete the fields as explained, telling Salesforce whether you're creating a button or a link, and what action should occur when you click it. If you're creating a button, you can decide whether it goes on the detail page or within a list. You see links to examples, just to make sure.

4. **Click Save when finished.**

   The Custom Button or Link page reappears.

This book doesn't go into any technical detail about Visualforce. Here's what you should know about Visualforce: If your company has specific business processes not addressed by Salesforce, you can use Visualforce to build your own application in Salesforce. Visualforce combines HTML with browser-based styling similar to CSS, so you'll need to recruit some techie geeks if this sounds foreign. Think, though, how much time your company could save if, for example, your reps could click a custom link on an opportunity page and immediately populate an order form in Salesforce. You could do that. For additional information on Visualforce, go to `http://developer.force.com`.

To display your custom buttons or links to users, you must add the new buttons or links to the appropriate page layout. See the section "Modifying a page layout," later in this chapter.

Customizing Page and Search Layouts

Wouldn't it be great if you could take the fields on a record and rearrange them like jigsaw puzzle pieces on a page until they fit just right? Sounds too good to be true, but with Salesforce, you can do just that and more.

Use page layouts to modify the position of fields, custom links, and related lists on Record detail pages and Edit pages. While you're modifying a page layout, you can also edit field properties to determine which fields should be required or read-only.

And with Enterprise and Performance Editions, you can create multiple page layouts and assign them to profiles, record types, or a combination of both. By doing this, you can ensure that different users are viewing just the right information to do their jobs.

Modifying a page layout

If you have permission to customize Salesforce, you can modify page layouts at any time. We typically recommend that you create some or the majority of your proposed custom fields first before rearranging them on the layout.

To edit a page layout, click the Setup link in the upper-right corner of any Salesforce page and follow these steps:

1. **Click any tab heading under the Customize heading on the sidebar.**

   The selected heading expands with links to customization options.

2. **Click the Page Layouts link under the tab heading.**

   The Page Layout page for the selected tab appears.

3. **Click the Edit link next to a page layout that you want to modify.**

   A Page Layout editor appears, with the editor at the top and a sample layout below it (see Figure 20-6).

4. **Choose from the following options to edit the layout using the nifty drag-and-drop user interface:**

   • *Arrange fields, buttons, custom links, related lists, and more:* By default, you see fields that go into the detail section for that record. Select other options to edit from the left sidebar of the layout editor. If you have a lot of fields to wade through, use the Quick Find search bar in the layout editor to quickly locate a field. If it's grayed out, it means that its already on the layout — clicking it will take you to it. If the field isn't grayed out, you can then click and drag it from the main body of the layout editor to desired locations on the sample layout.

   • *Rearrange existing fields:* Hover over them in the sample layout to highlight them, and then click and drag them to the updated destination on the layout. A dark bar shows you where the field will "land" after you drop it.

   • *Modify field properties:* Hover over a field on the sample layout, and then click the wrench icon to the right of the field. In the pop-up window that appears, use the check boxes to modify Read Only and Required settings and then click OK.

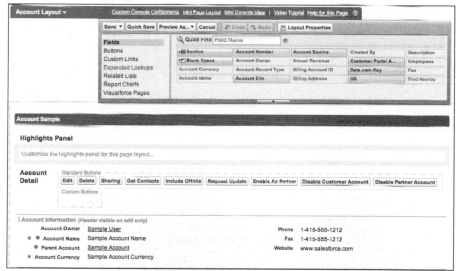

Figure 20-6:
Viewing the Page Layout editor.

- *Organize the record with sections:* Hover over a section header and click its wrench icon. Alternatively, click the + Section button in the main body of the layout editor and drag it to where you want it to appear in the sample layout. In the pop-up window that appears, type a name for the section, use the drop-down lists to adjust basic settings (such as columns), and then click OK.

  For example, on an account page layout, you might want to build a section named Strategic Account Planning to organize fields for account planning. When you click OK, the window closes.

5. **To preview the layout, click the Preview As button in the layout editor.**

   Select which user perspective you want to view. A window appears with sample data displayed in the layout as it's currently modified. In the preview window that opens, review the layout and click Close.

6. **When you're satisfied with your layout changes, click Save in the layout editor.**

   The Page Layout page for your selected record reappears.

Assigning layouts to profiles

After you create custom page layouts, you can assign your layouts to profiles. By doing this, users will view detail pages based on their profile and associated page layout.

To assign layouts to profiles, click the Setup link in the upper-right corner of any Salesforce page and follow these steps:

1. **Click any tab heading under the Customize heading on the sidebar.**

   The selected heading expands with a menu of options.

2. **Click the Page Layouts link under the tab heading.**

   The Page Layouts page for the selected tab appears.

3. **Click the Page Layout Assignment button at the top of the Page Layouts list.**

   A Page Layout Assignment page appears with a list of current assignments.

4. **Click the Edit Assignment button.**

   The page reappears in Edit mode.

5. **In the Page Layout column, highlight one or multiple cells by clicking the links.**

   Ctrl-click or Shift-click to select multiple cells.

6. **From the Page Layout to Use drop-down list, choose the page layout that you want to assign to the selected profiles.**

7. **When you're done, click Save.**

   The Page Layout Assignment page reappears, displaying your changes.

Changing search layouts

If you've ever seen some search results and wished that they showed a few more column headers, you're in for a treat. Search layouts allow you to determine which standard or custom fields appear as headers in multiple types of search features for your organization:

- ✔ Search results from the sidebar or advanced search
- ✔ Lookup dialog boxes that pop up a window when you click the Lookup magnifying glass next to a field
- ✔ Lookup phone dialog boxes that pop up a window when you click the magnifying glass icon on a SoftPhone dial pad, which then allows you to make calls from your computer
- ✔ Recent Records lists that appear on a tab's home page
- ✔ Search results filter fields for narrowing down searches

Additionally, you can choose to show or hide standard and custom buttons in a list view page.

To change a search layout, follow these steps:

1. **Click any tab heading under the Customize heading on the sidebar.**

   The selected heading expands with a menu of options.

2. **Click the Search Layouts link under the tab heading.**

   The Search Layouts Page for the selected tab appears.

3. **Click the Edit link next to any of the search features you'd like to change.**

   The Edit Search Layout page for the chosen search feature appears.

4. **Move fields from the Available Fields column to the Selected Fields column using the Add and Remove arrows, as needed. Select or clear any standard or custom buttons that you'd like to have on your list view.**

5. **Click Save when finished.**

   The Search Layouts page for the selected tab reappears.

Managing Multiple Business Processes

Configuring multiple business processes is particularly helpful if you have several groups of users who use a common tab (such as Leads) but whose processes are different. (And maybe the group leaders don't want to compromise.) For example, if your company has two sales teams that follow different sales methodologies, you can use multiple business processes and keep everyone happy. Multiple business process features are available only in Enterprise and Performance Editions and pertain only to lead, opportunity, case, and solution records.

To set up multiple business processes, click the Setup link in the upper-right corner of any Salesforce page and follow these steps:

1. **Click the Lead, Opportunity, Case, or Solution heading under the Customize heading on the sidebar.**

   The selected tab headings expand.

2. **Click the Fields link under one of the selected tab headings.**

   The Fields page for the selected tab appears, displaying a list of standard fields at the top and a list of custom fields at the bottom.

3. **Under the Standard Fields list, click the Edit link next to the Status or Stage field to modify the drop-down list.**

   For example, on the Opportunities Fields page, click the Edit link next to the Stage field.

   A Picklist Edit page appears for the selected field.

4. **Review the existing values and then click the New button to add additional values.**

   An Add Picklist Values page appears.

5. **Add one or more values and then click Save.**

   The Picklist Edit page reappears.

6. **Review the list to verify that you have a complete master list of statuses or stages to support all business processes for that record.**

7. **(Optional) Click the Reorder button to change the order of the values. Click Save.**

   The Picklist Edit page appears in Edit mode, where you can reorder the list by using the arrow buttons to change the order of the drop-down list. When you click Save, the Picklist Edit page reappears.

8. **On the sidebar, click the Processes link under the selected record heading.**

   For example, under the Opportunities heading, click the Sales Processes link.

   The Processes page for the selected record appears.

9. **Click the New button to create a new process.**

   A Process Edit page appears.

10. **Choose the Existing Process, name the new process, and then click Save.**

    A Process page appears, and you can select the values for your new business process.

    If you select Master as the Existing Process, you can choose from the master list generated from the Status or Stage field of the record.

11. **Highlight values and use the arrow buttons to modify your Selected Values list.**

    For example, if your company has a sales team that handles boat orders, you could create a simple sales process, as shown in Figure 20-7.

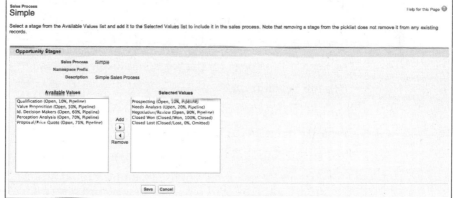

Figure 20-7: Creating a simple sales process.

12. **Choose a default value from the drop-down list; when you're done, click Save.**

    The Default Value drop-down list appears for lead, case, and solution processes but not for sales processes. The Processes page for your selected record reappears.

Managing Record Types

If you're using Enterprise or Performance Edition, you can use record types to make subsets of drop-down lists and those custom business processes that you just read about, which are available to specific sets of users. For example, if you have two sales teams — say, one that sells into healthcare services and another that sells into retail verticals — both teams might share common picklist fields on an account record but with very different values. With record types, you can customize accounts so that the same Industry field displays retail sectors for one group and healthcare services verticals for the other. When you provide record types to your users, the big benefit is that you make common drop-down lists easier to fill out and more relevant.

You can build record types to support all the major records in Salesforce, including leads, accounts, opportunities, and so on. Before users can take advantage of the record type feature, though, you need to first create the record types and then assign them to profiles. The good news is that with the Salesforce Record Type Wizard, you can perform both actions in a series of guided steps.

Before creating your record types, check that you first added all values to a master picklist field (drop-down list). (See the section "Viewing and updating fields," earlier in this chapter, for details on editing drop-down lists.)

To create a record type, click the Setup link in the upper-right corner of any Salesforce page and follow these steps:

1. **Click any tab heading under the Customize heading on the sidebar.**

   The selected tab heading expands.

2. **Click the Record Types link under the tab heading.**

   The Record Type page for the selected tab appears.

3. **Click the New button.**

   Step 1 of the New Record Type Wizard appears, as shown in Figure 20-8.

4. **Complete the fields at the top of the page.**

   Most are obvious, but here are three important pointers:

   - *Existing Record Type:* Choose from this drop-down list to clone from another record type. The new record type will inherit all the drop-down list values from the existing record type. You can then modify it later.

   If you choose not to clone, the record type automatically includes the master drop-down list values for both custom and standard fields. That's okay; you can edit the drop-down lists later.

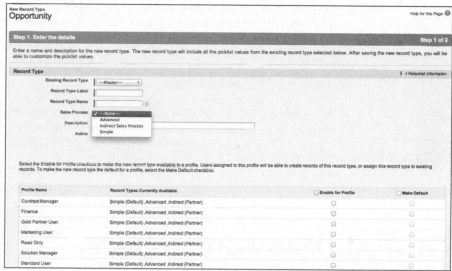

Figure 20-8:
Creating a new record type.

- *Business process:* On a lead, opportunity, case, or solution record type, select the business process from the drop-down list. See the preceding section for details.

- *Active:* Select this check box if you want to make the record type active.

5. **Select the check boxes in the table to make the new record type available to different profiles.**

   If you ever need to modify the assignment of record types to profiles, you can do this from the Record Type Settings section of a profile page. Simply scroll down the profile page until you see the Record Type Settings section, click the Edit link next to a record type, and follow the easy steps on the page that appears. (See Chapter 19 for details on updating profile settings.)

6. **When you're done, click Next.**

   Step 2 of the wizard appears.

7. **Use the drop-down lists to select the page layout that different profiles will see for records of this record type.**

   You can apply one layout to all profiles or assign different layouts to different profiles.

8. **When you're done, click Save.**

   The new Record Type page appears with a section called Picklists Available for Editing, which list the drop-down lists on the record type.

9. **Click the Edit link next to a picklist to modify the values.**

   A Record Type Edit page appears.

10. **Highlight values in the Available Values or Selected Values list box and use the arrow buttons to build the Selected Values list as you want it.**

11. **Select a value from the Default drop-down list, if necessary, and then click Save.**

    The Record Type page reappears.

If a user will need to make use of multiple record types, remember to add the Record Type field manually to a page layout. For example, if a sales rep sells both generators and engines (and opportunity record types exist for both), providing the Record Type field on a layout allows the rep to switch a generator opportunity to an engine opportunity, if needed. See the section "Customizing Page and Search Layouts," earlier in this chapter, for details.

Creating Dependent Picklists

If you find your picklist values building up and affecting the user's experience, you should consider using *dependent picklists* to show values in one list based on what's selected in another list. For example, you could create a custom picklist field called Reason for your opportunity record and offer two sets of reasons, depending on whether the opportunity was won or lost.

Creating these lists is a two-step process:

1. Your two fields must first exist.

   Think about which fields will dictate the drop-down list for what other fields. The field that determines another field's values is the *controlling field* and can be a standard or custom picklist, or a check box. The field that's dependent on the controlling field to determine its displayed values is the *dependent field*. We cover this step in the "Adding fields" section, earlier in this chapter.

2. Tell Salesforce about these two fields and their roles in this relationship.

   That's what we cover in this section.

To define field dependencies, follow these steps:

1. **Expand the Customize menu until you see the Fields links under the appropriate tab (under the Activities heading, refer to Activity Custom Fields).**

   The Fields page appears.

2. **Click Field Dependencies in the Custom Fields & Relationships related list.**

   The Field Dependencies page for your record appears.

3. **Click New.**

   The New Field Dependency page appears in Edit mode.

4. **Select your controlling and dependent fields. Click Continue to determine what gets filtered.**

   A field can be dependent to just one controlling field. However, that dependent field may also act as a controlling field to daisy-chain together several dependencies.

5. **At the Edit Field Dependency page, select which dependent list items are visible for which controlling field values, and then click Include Values.**

   If your controlling field has several items in its drop-down list, you might have to click the Next link to see additional columns. You can also select multiple values at once by Shift-clicking to select a range of adjacent cells or Ctrl-clicking to select cells that aren't adjacent.

6. **(Optional) Click the Preview button to see a pop-up window demo your dependent picklist.**

7. **Click Save.**

   The Field Dependencies page returns with your new dependent picklist listed.

Record types allow certain people to see the same subset of picklist values every time. Dependent picklists allow a user to see different subsets of picklist values based on what they choose in the controlling field.

Managing Workflow & Approvals

How many times have you lost or delayed business because someone forgot to do something in your sales process? With the workflow feature in Salesforce, you can create a rule and associate it to e-mails, tasks, and alerts that can be assigned to different users. You can also update the value of a field on a record if a certain rule occurs. Enterprise and Performance Edition users can use workflow to automate certain standard processes to make sure that important balls don't get dropped. For example, if your sales reps create opportunities that sometimes require special pricing paperwork, you can use a workflow rule to automatically send e-mail alerts and tasks to finance and sales managers, and you can set these alerts and tasks to go out a set number of hours later.

Before creating a workflow process, take a moment to understand some basic workflow concepts:

✔ **Workflow rules** are the criteria you set that, when triggered, tell Salesforce to assign tasks or send e-mails.

✔ **Workflow field updates** specify what field is updated on an object when a workflow rule is triggered.

✔ **Workflow tasks** are the tasks that a workflow rule assigns to users when triggered.

✔ **Workflow alerts** are the e-mail templates that a workflow rule sends to specific recipients. (Before creating a workflow alert, make sure that you've created the e-mail template that you'll be sending.)

✔ **Workflow tasks and alerts** may be reused for different workflow rules.

To create a workflow process, first make sure that you can fill in the blanks in this sentence: *When X happens, I want A, B, and C to happen.* Your X is your workflow rule, and the A, B, and C actions are the field updates, tasks, and e-mail alerts. Choose Setup➪Build➪Create➪Workflow & Approvals to begin.

Creating workflow rules

To create a workflow rule, follow these steps:

1. **Click the Workflow Rules link under the Workflow & Approvals heading on the sidebar.**

   If this is your first time, the Understanding Workflow page appears.

2. **Click Continue after reading the overview.**

   The All Workflow Rules page appears.

3. **Click the New Rule button to create a new rule.**

   Step 1 of the Workflow Rule Wizard appears for your new rule.

4. **Select the type of object to which the workflow rule should apply.**

5. **Click Next to continue.**

   Step 2 of the Workflow Rule Wizard appears. To configure your rule, do the following steps:

   a. *Enter a Rule Name and optional description.*

   b. *Decide when the rule will be evaluated by Salesforce.* The options are only when a new record is created, when the record is created or it's been edited and didn't previously meet the triggering criteria (listed as anytime the field is edited to subsequently meet criteria), or every time the record is created or edited.

   c. *Use the rule criteria to determine what conditions must be met to trigger the rule.* Use the Advanced Options for more complex AND/OR scenarios.

6. **Click Save & Next.**

   The Specify Workflow Actions screen appears.

7. **Identify what happens when the workflow criteria is met.**

   An action can happen immediately, or it can happen a specific number of hours or days before or after certain criteria are met. You can create new actions (see the following section for more information) or use existing ones associated with immediate or time-based workflow triggers.

Assigning workflow tasks

To create a new workflow task, first go to the workflow rule that you want to associate with this task and then follow these steps:

1. **Choose Setup⇨Build⇨Create⇨Workflow & Approvals⇨Workflow Rules and click the Rule Name of the appropriate rule.**

   The Workflow Rule page for the rule appears.

Approval processes

Approval processes are a more advanced type of workflow that notify users when an action is triggered, require the user to review and then approve or reject the action, and then set off additional actions. For example, an expense report may follow one route of approvals if it's for $250 or less and another process if it's for an amount more than $10,000. Before setting forth with activating this feature for a certain record, make sure that you think through the following questions:

✔ Do all records of this type absolutely require approval, or just certain ones?

✔ Who's allowed to submit records for approval?

✔ Should a record be automatically approved or rejected in certain circumstances?

✔ Should any actions take place on the record as it moves through the approval chain?

✔ Who should be able to edit records that are in the process of being approved?

✔ Who should approve or reject items? Can that person delegate that privilege to someone else, in his or her absence?

✔ What should happen when a record has received all necessary approvals?

✔ What should happen when a record has been rejected?

Although it may be nice to automatically shepherd an approval process through to the right people, make sure that your business process is fairly rock solid. For example, are the bottlenecks you face today in your approval process going to disappear, be reduced, or remain if the process is automated? If Philip is the busy executive who needs to approve all the expense reports but he doesn't manage his e-mail inbox well, you'll have to carefully set expectations about what efficiency gains you'll get with automated approvals.

2. **Click Edit from the Workflow Actions related list.**

   The Specify Workflow Actions step appears.

3. **In the Immediate Workflow Actions area, click the Add Workflow Action button and select New Task from the resulting drop-down list.**

4. **Configure the task as you would a regular task, but note the Due Date field.**

5. **Complete the Due Date field so that the created task has a due date that's a number of days relative to a base date you select in the drop-down list.**

6. **Click Save when finished.**

   The Workflow Task page for this task appears. Note that the Rules Using This Workflow Task related list shows the associated workflow rule.

Choose Setup⇨Build⇨Create⇨Workflow & Approvals⇨Field Updates to select what field on what object changes when a workflow rule is triggered.

Using workflow e-mail alerts

To create a new workflow e-mail alert, first go to the workflow rule that you want to associate with this task and then follow these steps:

1. **Choose Setup⇨Build⇨Create⇨Workflow & Approvals⇨Workflow Rules and click the Rule Name of the appropriate rule.**

   The Workflow Rule page for the rule appears.

2. **Click Edit from the Workflow Actions related list.**

   The Specify Workflow Actions step appears.

3. **In the Immediate Workflow Actions area, click the Add Workflow Action button and select New Email Alert from the resulting drop-down list.**

4. **Complete the fields to associate an e-mail template with a set of recipients.**

   Note that the recipients may or may not be Salesforce users. And remember that the e-mail template must have already been created.

5. **Click Save when finished.**

   The Workflow Alert page for this alert appears.

   At the Specify Workflow Actions page, you can also click the Add Workflow button to have a new field updated, or an outbound message sent when a certain event occurs.

Chapter 21

Extending Beyond CRM with the Platform

. . . .

In This Chapter

▶ Understanding the Force.com platform

▶ Creating apps on Force.com

▶ Deploying apps for your company

. . . .

*W*hat if you could modify your business applications in minutes to match the unique ways you manage your customer relationships? How much more productive could you be if you spent less time fighting your technology — and more time with your customers?

Force.com is the Salesforce platform you use to customize and create on-demand applications by simply pointing and clicking your mouse on easy-to-use web pages. In fact, with Force.com, you can not only customize your existing Salesforce applications but also now build entirely new applications to fit the way you do business. If you need a little inspiration, you can also install a preexisting solution from the AppExchange directory.

In this chapter, we demystify the Force.com platform and define some basic terms to give you a glimpse of the awesome power of creating custom apps. Then you see how to share your creation on the AppExchange (www. appexchange.com). Finally, we offer simple and critical tips for preparing your deployment game plan.

Understanding the Force.com Platform

As we mention, Force.com is the salesforce.com on-demand platform: a suite of development tools for customizing, building, integrating, and installing business applications — and you don't need to build or maintain any infrastructure yourself.

Force.com is both a collection of customization tools as well as the underlying infrastructure that powers the Salesforce app that you use. The cool part is that over time, salesforce.com engineers have exposed parts of their secret sauce so that you can use it, too, and they've also used these customization tools to build additional features onto Salesforce.

Briefly, here are some key terms to know:

✔ **Force.com:** The engine that makes Salesforce what it is today. It's the underlying technology that enables you to customize existing applications from the Setup area, create new ones (with or without any programming experience), integrate Salesforce with other company systems, and share these snippets online with others.

✔ **Apex code:** Another subset of the Force.com platform. The Salesforce procedural scripting language that allows users to write custom logic and create integrations between Salesforce and other systems. If you're technical, you now have the ability to build new objects, create triggers and classes, change the user interface to handle custom forms and interactions, use a web services API, and all that techno-speak stuff.

✔ **Visualforce:** Another powerful technical capability that Salesforce provides with which you can customize the actual front-end page design and components of your custom application. You're no longer limited to Salesforce's default colors, visual design, and tab layouts.

✔ **AppExchange:** An online directory where you can quickly browse, try, download, and install apps that can instantly run alongside your existing Salesforce applications.

Salesforce.com frequently rebrands the names of its various offerings. The preceding terms are the most recent versions as of this book's publication. The underlying functionality, look, and feel that we discuss is still the same as we describe it.

Unless you're a developer (or a glutton for punishment), you don't need to know the technical ins and outs. What you do need to know is that Force.com enables Salesforce administrators to easily customize and extend their existing on-demand applications without extensive involvement from developers. For building applications, which can take months with traditional software, you can point and click to quickly develop new applications in hours or days, completely integrated with your existing Salesforce CRM system.

To see all options available to you with building Custom apps, log in to Salesforce and follow these steps:

1. Choose Setup➪Build.

The Build page appears. This page highlights all the features and functionality available to help you customize, build, share, and integrate your CRM.

2. On the sidebar menu, notice the menu items below the Build header.

This chapter focuses on the tools listed under the Create header. We cover the Customize heading in Chapter 20. We don't discuss Develop because that's a more technical discussion, and we promised you "no code required."

Preparing Your Force.com App Strategy

Force.com places so much potential at your fingertips that just like a kid in a candy store, you may have the urge to just jump in and start building custom objects and tabs — a baptism by fire. Although that method is appetizing in theory, it's a quick way in reality to get a stomachache, especially if your business grows and more people start entering information in Salesforce. Resist that impulse until you review these simple steps for planning your strategy for on-demand applications:

1. Define and prioritize objectives.

   Your wish list doesn't need to be very involved, but it should spell out the who, what, when, why, and how.

2. Build a plan.

   With agreed-upon objectives, take your project down another level and lay out a plan to address the most pressing objectives.

3. Determine the most suitable approach.

   You have many different ways to tackle a business issue with Force.com — some better than others.

   - *Use the discussion boards* at the Salesforce Success Community web site (http://success.salesforce.com) to check existing or upcoming functionality. You may not need to build a unique solution.

   - *Browse the AppExchange* to see whether any available prebuilt applications meet your general requirements.

4. Keep it simple.

   Don't sacrifice your objectives at the expense of simplicity — although at the beginning, simple is often better.

5. Start with the end in mind.

   If a custom app seems like the right strategy, figure out what it is that you want to measure. Understand how well your solution may scale (or not).

 A great way to design your application so that it takes full advantage of relationships is to simply draw it out on a piece of paper or a whiteboard. Your design doesn't have to be fancy or complicated, but it should define the standard and custom objects you need and how they should be linked.

Creating Custom Apps with Force.com

After you sketch the basic requirements for your new application, you're ready to begin building. A good place to start is to simply create the custom app, much like a container, before you add your objects and tabs.

To see an example of custom apps that others have created, visit the AppExchange (`www.appexchange.com`) and browse apps by category. Apps created by Force.com Labs are those that came from within salesforce.com's own employees!

Choose Setup⇨Build⇨Create to get to a powerful set of customization tools that can empower your business faster than the status quo of traditional software solutions.

Setting up a custom app

Many companies want internal branding for their business applications. Before you can apply branding like this, though, you have to first add the logo to a public folder on the Documents tab. (From any page, click the Documents tab, create a new public folder that's easily identifiable, like *Logos,* and click the New Document button from within that folder.) Make sure that the image is a GIF or JPEG file smaller than 20K. Ideally, use a horizontally oriented image. If it's larger than 300 pixels × 55 pixels, Salesforce will scale the image to fit the space.

To add the custom app, choose Setup⇨Build⇨Create and then follow these steps:

1. **Click the Apps link from the sidebar.**

   The Apps page appears. You see a list of your standard Salesforce apps, plus any custom apps you created.

2. **Click the New button above the Apps list.**

   The first step of the New Custom App Wizard appears.

3. **In Step 1 of the wizard, enter a name and description for your app, and then click Next.**

   The name you type in the label field will appear on the Force.com Apps pull-down menu.

4. **In Step 2 of the wizard, assuming that you want to apply your branding, insert a logo from your Documents tab. Then click Next.**

   You have to first add the logo to a public folder on the Documents tab.

The logo will appear as the header whenever a user selects the custom app from the Force.com Apps menu. Of course, if you don't want to brand the app, you can leave the current Salesforce-provided image.

5. **In Step 3 of the wizard, select the tabs that will make up your app. Then click Next.**

   You do this step by simply clicking tabs from the Available Tabs box and using the arrow buttons to create your list of Selected Tabs.

   If you haven't created all your custom tabs yet, don't worry. As you create custom tabs, you can associate them with your custom or standard apps. (For all the details, see the section "Creating custom tabs," later in this chapter.)

6. **In Step 4 of the wizard, select the check boxes to assign the app to different user profiles.**

   You want to make sure that the right apps are available to the right people in your organization.

7. **When you're done, click Save.**

   The Apps page reappears, and your new custom app now appears in the list.

Building your custom objects

Typically, you create a custom object to house a discrete set of information that's different from what is contained in other standard objects. For example, an Opportunity object contains opportunity information. A Custom Expense object contains information about expenses that's unique from the typical purpose of other standard objects.

If you want to build a home, you have to add the basic building blocks first. The same analogy applies to custom apps and objects. For example, if you want to build a recruiting application, you might decide that you could use the Contacts object for applicants and need to build custom objects for Job Postings and Interview Feedback because they're distinct blocks of data.

To set up a new object, follow these steps:

1. **Choose Setup➪Build➪Create➪Objects.**

   The Custom Objects page appears. This page, your starting point for creating an object, is where all your custom objects are displayed.

2. **Click the New Custom Object button.**

   The New Custom Object page appears.

3. **In the Custom Object Information section, type the basic details for your object.**

   You usually just need to fill out the Label and Plural Label fields. This will then automatically populate the Object Name field. Labels are what your end users see (like "Time Off Request"). The object name is what Force.com sees (like "Time_Off_Req") in case you need to have another system (or another part of Salesforce) talk to it.

4. **Complete the Enter Record Name Label and Format fields.**

   The record name appears on page layouts, related lists, lookups, and search results. This is what you use to differentiate one record of this object from another. Depending on the type of object you're creating, you may want to switch the data type from Text to Auto Number.

   Here's how to tell when to use text versus auto numbers:

   - *Text:* The name has some intrinsic value.

   - *Auto numbers:* You're creating an object that will relate to other standard objects in a fundamental way.

     Auto Numbers are useful for sequenced business documents, such as invoices (INV-001, INV-002, INV-003, and so on), purchase orders, IT tickets, and timecards.

5. **Select the custom object's optional features.**

   With simple pointing and clicking on your part, Force.com allows you to select your custom object's features that are identical to many of the features found on standard objects, such as tracking activities, allowing reporting, or allowing notes and attachments to be added.

6. **Leave the Deployment Status as In Development so that only you can see it, instead of all the other Salesforce users within your company.**

   We recommend making sure that you can explain the business process around using the new object *before deploying it* to help guide correct adoption.

   Select the Deployed button if you're ready for your users to begin using it. If you wait to deploy the app, return to this screen by choosing Setup⇨Build⇨Create⇨Objects. Select your object from the list of custom objects, and you return to the custom object detail page.

7. **Select the Launch New Custom Tab Wizard check box and then click Save.**

   The New Custom Object Tab Wizard starts. See the section "Adding a tab to a custom object," later in this chapter, for the how-tos on building a new tab.

If you already mapped the custom objects that will be part of your app, create all the objects first before modifying them. This action is especially helpful if you're building relationships between them.

Modifying custom objects

Designing your custom object is as simple as modifying a contact record or adding to a contact record's related lists. If you need to change the basic settings, simply click the Edit button at the top of the Custom Object page for the object, and the New Custom Object Wizard reappears.

If you want to customize your new object, you can point and click through the related lists on the page.

Certain Setup features — including custom profiles, multiple page layouts, record types, workflow, and field-level security — are available only in Enterprise and Performance Editions.

Building relationships

One primary reason for building applications with Force.com is to create a single, integrated, one-stop shopping experience for your users.

The key to those linkages is building custom relationships between objects. For example, if your company wants to manage account planning in Salesforce, you want to create a relationship between the standard Account object and a custom object for the Account Plan.

To build a relationship, follow these steps:

1. **Choose Setup➪Build➪Create➪Objects.**

   The All Custom Objects page appears.

2. **Click the desired custom object under the Label column.**

   The Custom Object page appears.

3. **Click the New button in the Custom Fields & Relationships related list (see Figure 21-1).**

   The New Custom Field Wizard appears.

Figure 21-1: Create a new custom field or relationship.

Custom Fields & Relationships		New	Field Dependencies			Custom Fields & Relationships Help ?
Action	**Field Label**	**API Name**	**Data Type**	**Controlling Field**	**Modified By**	
Edit | Del	Activation Date	Activation_Date__c	Date		Matt Kaufman, 10/13/2013 7:36 PM	
Edit | Del	Expiration Date	Expiration_Date__c	Date		Matt Kaufman, 10/13/2013 7:36 PM	
Edit | Del	Item Specifications	Item_Specifications__c	Rich Text Area(32768)		Matt Kaufman, 10/13/2013 7:36 PM	
Edit | Del	Item Additional Details	Item_Additional_Details__c	Rich Text Area(32768)		Matt Kaufman, 10/13/2013 7:36 PM	
Edit | Del	Item Code	Item_Code__c	Text Area(255)		Matt Kaufman, 10/13/2013 7:36 PM	
Edit | Del	Item Detail	Item_Detail__c	Text Area(255)		Matt Kaufman, 10/13/2013 7:36 PM	
Edit | Del	Item Features	Item_Features__c	Rich Text Area(32768)		Matt Kaufman, 10/13/2013 7:36 PM	
Edit | Del	Item Image	Item_Image__c	Text Area(255)		Matt Kaufman, 10/13/2013 7:36 PM	
Edit | Del	Item Image Large	Item_Image_Large__c	Text Area(255)		Matt Kaufman, 10/13/2013 7:36 PM	
Edit | Del	Item Long Description	Item_Long_Description__c	Rich Text Area(32768)		Matt Kaufman, 10/13/2013 7:36 PM	
Edit | Del	Item Model Number	Item_Model_Number__c	Text Area(255)		Matt Kaufman, 10/13/2013 7:36 PM	
Edit | Del	Item MSRP	Item_MSRP__c	Currency(10, 2)		Matt Kaufman, 10/13/2013 7:36 PM	
Edit | Del	Item Name	Item_Name__c	Text Area(255)		Matt Kaufman, 10/13/2013 7:36 PM	
Edit | Del	Item Short Description	Item_Short_Description__c	Text Area(255)		Matt Kaufman, 10/13/2013 7:36 PM	
Edit | Del | Replace	Item Status	Item_Status__c	Picklist		Matt Kaufman, 10/13/2013 7:36 PM	

4. **In Step 1 of the New Custom Field Wizard, choose the type of relationship with another object.**

   Force.com supports two types of custom relationships: Master-Detail and Lookup. They're both one-to-many relationships.

   A Lookup relationship links one object to another. The representative custom field will have a little magnifying glass icon next to it so that you can "look up" a value from that related object to associate with another object. Master-Detail (also known as parent/child) relationships are a special type of association: The relationship is required for the detail, and the value can't be changed after the association is made. If you delete the master record, its related children are also deleted.

   The two relationships look the same in the user interface — as a lookup field with a magnifying glass on the record side and as a related list on the related object.

   But here are two big differences:

   • Master-Detail relationships cause the cascade deletion of child records to occur when the parent record is deleted. For example, if you delete an account, all related records are also deleted.

   • In a Master-Detail relationship, the detail record inherits the Owner and sharing rules of the master record. Detail objects are dependent on their masters. In Lookup relationships, however, they don't transfer sharing rules — they're completely independent.

   When you're in doubt, start with the Lookup option.

5. **Click Next to continue. In Step 2 of the wizard, select the other object that you want to relate your object to.**

   You can create as many as five Lookup relationships with a custom object.

6. **Click Next to continue. In Step 3 of the wizard, enter the label for the lookup field.**

   As a default, Force.com prefills the fields with the name of the object you selected, although you can change it.

7. **Click Next to continue. If you have Enterprise or Performance Edition, set the field-level security in Step 4 of the wizard. (If you don't, skip to Step 9 because you won't be able to set field-level security.)**

   If you chose the Master-Detail option, the security is set for you because it's locked to the profile. If you chose the Lookup option, select the appropriate check boxes to control visibility and edit rights to the field.

8. **Click Next to continue. If you have Enterprise or Performance Edition, in Step 5 of the wizard, select the page layouts in which you want to display the field.**

   Suppose that you're creating an expense application. You may want the rep's layout to be different from the manager's layout.

9. **Click Next to continue. In Step 6 of the wizard, deselect the check boxes if you don't want the custom object to appear on the related list of the selected object.**

   For example, if you're linking expenses with accounts, you may not want a long list of expenses showing up on an account record.

10. **When you're done, click Save.**

    The Custom Object page reappears, and your custom relationship is displayed in the Custom Fields & Relationships related list.

Build your relationships before loading any actual data.

Remember that between two objects, you can have only one object that allows the Master-Detail relationship, so the other object has to be a Lookup relationship.

Other ways that you can modify custom objects to fit your company's business processes include

- ✔ **Creating fields:** With Force.com, you can quickly add fields to your custom object, much like you can with a standard object, such as an account or a contact. See Chapter 20 for more information on creating custom fields.

- ✔ **Adding custom links:** Adding custom links to an object can be a powerful way to extend your solution to a business issue. You can build custom links for custom objects, too. See Chapter 20 for more information on creating custom links.

- ✔ **Changing layouts:** After or as you build fields, feel free to start rearranging the page layout for the object record. Often, that's one of the easiest ways to get a pulse on what's missing from your record. See Chapter 20 for more Information on editing page layouts.

- ✔ **Customizing related lists:** After you add your Lookup relationships and custom fields, you're ready to start customizing your related lists! Force.com allows you to modify the columns that are displayed in a related list.

Don't forget this step because without customizing this section, your users don't see much in a related list. When you add the right columns, though, the related list becomes a powerful tool for your users. By customizing the columns displayed in a related list, users can quickly see a summary of relevant information from a record's detail page. See Chapter 20 for more information on customizing related lists.

Creating custom tabs

With Force.com, you can create two types of custom tabs: custom object tabs and web tabs. They look just like the standard tabs that your users already use, and you can build the tabs in less than a minute — piece o' cake.

Adding a tab to a custom object

If you read through the section "Building your custom objects," earlier in this chapter, you've probably already built a custom tab. Sometimes, however, you build a custom object and decide later to add the tab.

Don't over-tab your application if it's not necessary. Ask yourself: "Will my users need all the object's data available from a central area?" If the answer is yes, you may need a custom tab.

To build a custom tab, follow these steps:

1. **Choose Setup➪Build➪Create➪Tabs.**

   The Custom Tabs page appears.

2. **Click New in the Custom Objects Tab related list.**

   Step 1 of the New Custom Object Tab Wizard appears.

3. **In Step 1 of the wizard, select the object from the picklist, and then use the Lookup icon to choose a tab style.**

   The tab style affects both the color of the tab and the icon associated with a custom object record under Recent Items.

4. **In Step 2 of the wizard, select the desired tab visibility for your user profiles.**

   With the radio button feature, you can control tab visibility to your profiles.

5. **In Step 3 of the wizard, select the apps to which the new custom tab will be available.**

   This step makes it simple to associate custom tabs with just the right apps for your users.

6. **When you're done, click Save.**

   The Custom Tabs page reappears with your new custom tab listed.

Building a web tab

In the normal course of a day, your users frequent other websites as part of their jobs. Here are just a few examples:

- Access an intranet
- Arrange travel plans
- Use an internal web-based application

The list goes on. Why not make it easier for users to get to your business-related sites? With Force.com, you can build web tabs that access web applications and Visualforce.

We don't go into the details of Apex code or Visualforce because they require coding, but imagine that you have a particular form to which your teams are emotionally attached (a client profile form with four columns, for example). With Visualforce and the help of an experienced developer, you can display your data in Salesforce in unique formats (and keep everyone happy). To manage these features, choose Setup⇨Build⇨Develop.

To create a simple web tab, follow these steps:

1. **Choose Setup⇨Build⇨Create⇨Tabs.**

   The Custom Tabs page appears.

2. **Click the New button in the Web Tabs related list.**

   Step 1 of the New Web Tab Wizard appears.

3. **In Step 1 of the wizard, click a button to select a layout.**

4. **In Step 2, define the content and properties.**

   In this example, we show you how to create a URL-based web tab for news labeled Company News.

5. **In Step 3 of the wizard, enter a URL and add any additional merge fields.**

   Embedding merge fields is easy after you get the hang of it. For example, this URL is the standard search results URL from Yahoo News:

   ```
   http://search.news.yahoo.com/search/news/?p=salesforce&c=
   ```

   We copied and pasted the URL in the Button or Link URL box. Then we used the merge field tool for `{!Org_Name}` and put that in place of `salesforce` in the URL.

6. **In Step 4, click the drop-down lists to control which user profiles can access the tab, and then click Save.**

Sharing Apps on AppExchange

As customers, employees, and partners began building custom applications (or *apps*), some bright person came up with an idea: Wouldn't it be great if other customers like you could simply try, download, and install these custom apps without having to build them on their own? iTunes uses the web to distribute music, so why shouldn't enterprise applications work the same way?

Enter *AppExchange,* the website owned and operated by salesforce.com where you can try, download, and quickly install apps that can extend the value of Salesforce to meet your unique needs. You can even use the AppExchange to share your custom apps.

Of course, the biggest benefit beyond how much easier your life will be is the impact on your users. The AppExchange marketplace isn't just about easy sharing — it's about your employees using integrated business apps with all your information in one place.

Customers, partners, and salesforce.com personnel can all provide AppExchange with applications. Many of them, particularly the ones published by salesforce. com employees (a.k.a. Salesforce Labs), are free to install and use. Others, such as the ones provided by partners, may have a fee associated with them.

Browsing AppExchange

Downloading music and video from the web is something we take for granted nowadays. But downloading enterprise apps? Wow, that seems like a whole 'nother animal.

Yet, when you get down to it, AppExchange is still about the exchange of a package of goods from one party to another. As with many innovations, getting the most out of a new system usually amounts to understanding some basic terms and knowing your limits before jumping in.

Here are six key things you should know before you get started:

- *Installation* is the process by which you download, install, and deploy a custom app from AppExchange.

- *Publishing* is the process by which you package a portion of your customizations and make them available, either publicly or privately, on AppExchange.

- *Managed package* is an AppExchange package created and maintained by a verified third-party vendor. Unlike unmanaged packages whose components you can modify and customize, managed package components have limited customization capabilities. This allows vendors to provide you with an upgrade path that'll leave you successful, versus stuck in the mud because you changed something that's not supported by a newer version.

- Although anyone can try out AppExchange, to install and share apps, you must have a Salesforce instance and have administrative rights to that instance. (Did we just hear a sigh of relief?)

- You can publish many types of AppExchange components, not just custom apps, on AppExchange. You can exchange custom links, dashboards, Visualforce code snippets, and more.

> ✔ Some apps are self-contained — *native* — in Salesforce. They were built
> with Force.com and don't depend on other external applications. Other
> custom apps are *composite*. Such apps may look and feel like Salesforce
> apps but connect with other services not owned by salesforce.com.
> *Caveat emptor* (let the buyer beware).

Familiarize yourself with AppExchange at www.appexchange.com, and then
try out some apps before you decide whether you want to use them.

Installing custom apps

If you want to install a custom prebuilt app, you can do it in a matter of simple
clicks. This process amounts to first downloading the package, installing the
app into your instance of Salesforce, and deploying it to all or a portion of
your users.

A *package* refers to all the components that make up the custom app. A package
may include custom tabs and objects, custom links, custom profiles,
reports, dashboards, documents, and more.

To install a custom app, follow these steps:

1. **Click the Get It Now button on the app's detail page in AppExchange
   (at www.appexchange.com).**

2. **Choose whether you wish to continue the installation of the app in
   your production or sandbox.**

   If you haven't logged in to the AppExchange yet, you will be prompted to
   enter your Salesforce username and password. Make sure you enter the
   information that reflects which org you want to install the app into.

   For larger organizations, you may have customizations that need to be
   tested with this package. A sandbox that is practically an exact copy of
   what you have in your live system is a good place to kick the tires without the potential of impacting your business if something goes wrong. If
   you don't have access to a sandbox, install the app in your production
   environment, but make sure you make it visible just to system administrators first until they've thoroughly tested the installation.

3. **Review the list that appears, which tells you what you'll be installing
   and where.**

   Salesforce makes this as transparent an installation as possible. You can
   see if this app is free or not, what the subscription model is, and where
   it is being installed.

4. **Check the box to confirm that you've read the terms and conditions. Then hit the Confirm and Install button to continue.**

5. **Enter your Salesforce login and password again for the org in which you want to install the app.**

   The Package Installation Details page appears in Salesforce.

   If you're experimenting with the AppExchange for the first time, you may want to consider using the Sandbox Edition or a free Developer Edition instance to install, customize, and test the custom app.

6. **Examine the package components, and then click Continue.**

   This page summarizes the custom app's details, including objects, fields, tabs, reports, and dashboards.

   Make sure that you examine the contents of a package thoroughly before proceeding. You may see a next page that shows you the package's API access to various objects, including details of what permissions the package will have on what objects.

7. **Select a radio button to choose the security settings and then click Next to continue.**

   This Package Installer Wizard allows you to choose either standard or custom security settings to meet your comfort level. We recommend that you choose the Select Security Settings option to start.

   After choosing the Select Security Settings option, a Customize Security page appears.

8. **Specify the level of access for each profile.**

   The access levels here determine the layout assignments, field-level security, and other fun stuff such as editing permissions for the custom objects in the package. Access levels set here don't affect those of any existing objects you have.

   Any standard profiles will have full access to custom objects in this package because permissions aren't editable for them. The only exception is the Read-Only profile, which will still maintain (duh) read-only permissions.

9. **Click Next to continue. In the last step of the wizard, click the Install button.**

   A progress page appears as installation begins. An Install Complete page appears after the installation finishes. Bet your traditional software can't create a whole new app that fast!

10. **Click OK.**

    At this point, you can choose to deploy the app immediately to users or further customize it. We suggest that you click OK to confirm the download and begin prepping some dummy data before you deploy this to users.

    The Installed Package Details page for your newly downloaded custom app appears. It shows installation details, and from here, you can click the respective buttons to view the package components or view dependencies between this app and anything else you have in your org. If you check out the upper-right corner, you'll notice that the Force.com Apps menu now contains a listing for your new app.

After you install the app, you can use Force.com to modify its tabs, objects, and other customizations, just as though you had built the custom app yourself. Even though you've installed the app, it's not available to nonadministrators until it's deployed.

Chapter 22

Migrating and Maintaining Your Data

*I*f you're a system administrator, often your greatest headache isn't configuring or customizing the system but getting your data in and maintaining it so that it's useful. Nothing hurts a rollout more than complaints from users that their data isn't in Salesforce, that information is duplicated in several records, or even worse, that the information is wrong. Your end user adoption suffers if you don't maintain your records after the rollout. If you're not diligent, you can find yourself in the same mess that drove you to Salesforce in the first place.

If data maintenance is giving you nightmares, use the data management tools in Salesforce to easily import leads, accounts, and contacts. If you have in-house expertise or engage a Salesforce partner, you can migrate other critical data (such as opportunities, cases, and activities) by using proven third-party tools. When your data is stored in Salesforce, you can rely on a variety of tools to help you manage and maintain your database.

In this chapter, we first discuss your options for data import. Then, we show you how to use Salesforce tools to manage your data (including mass-transferring, deleting, and reassigning data). Finally, we touch on advanced concepts, such as mass-transferring and mass-deleting your data. Complex data migration and updates of data between your data sources and Salesforce are beyond the scope of this book, but we make sure to point you in the right direction.

Understanding Your Options for Data Migration

Salesforce has easy-to-use wizards that step you through importing your campaign updates, leads, accounts, contacts, and custom objects. If you're a system administrator or have the right profile permissions, you can perform these tasks for your users. For other legacy data (such as opportunities, cases, and activities) that you want to have in Salesforce, you have to enter information manually or use the *Data Loader,* which is an included ETL (extract, transform, and load) tool that comes with Enterprise and Performance Editions to automatically migrate data into Salesforce. Professional and Group Edition users can enlist the help of salesforce.com professional services.

Using import wizards

Import wizards for leads, accounts, contacts, solutions, and custom objects are conveniently located under the Data Management heading in the Administration Setup section of Setup. If you're an administrator, you also see links to the import wizards in the Tools section of certain tab home pages. For example, if you want to import your company's leads, click the Leads tab, and then click the Import Leads link in the Tools section. Steps and tips for each of the import wizards are detailed in relevant chapters of this book, as follows:

- ✔ **Import leads:** Only a user with the Import Leads permission can perform this operation. See Chapter 9.

- ✔ **Import contacts and accounts:** Salesforce provides one wizard that can take you through importing contacts and/or accounts. Individual users also have the ability to import their personal contacts and accounts. See Chapters 4 and 5.

- ✔ **Import campaign leads or update contacts or leads linked to a campaign:** Salesforce provides a Campaign Member Import Wizard to update marketing statuses for leads and contacts. See Chapter 13.

Investigating the Data Loader

Data migration is a tricky matter. The *Data Loader* is a small client application that helps bulk-import or -export data in comma-separated value (`.csv`) format. You access this tool by choosing Setup➪Administer➪Data Management➪Data Loader. With this tool, you can move data into and out of any type of record in Salesforce, including opportunities and custom objects. The Data Loader supports inserting, updating, deleting, and extracting Salesforce records.

Several vendors also provide proven ETLs that enable you to migrate records to (or from) Salesforce and append those records where appropriate.

Without getting too technical, experts link data by using the Force.com API (application program interface) to enable your technical resource to access data programmatically. Force.com (`http://developer.force.com`) is the platform used to customize or integrate Salesforce to do even snazzier things than what you can do with it out of the box. And before you suffer from jargon overload, a *platform* is basically a collection of rules and commands that programmers can use to tell a program — Salesforce, in this case — to do certain things. To access the Force.com API, though, you must have Enterprise or Performance Edition.

Migrating Your Legacy Data

During the preparation phase of your implementation, you need a well-thought-out and documented plan for your data migration strategy. That plan needs to include details on objectives, resources, contingencies, and timelines based on the different steps in your plan. In the following sections, we discuss some of the steps that you should consider.

Determining your data sources

The companies we've worked with typically have some type of existing contact management tool, a variety of spreadsheets with other customer data, and often, contact information living in users' Microsoft Outlook applications (not to mention Word documents and sticky notes). As you go through your preparation, assess what and how much information needs to be in Salesforce. Here are some tips for this step:

- ✔ **Garbage in, garbage out.** When you move into a new home, you usually look through your old home's closets and decide what to haul with you and what to throw away. Moving data requires the same type of evaluation.

- ✔ **Make a list.** Catalog the different data sources, including what types of records, what range, and how many.

- ✔ **Design a storage plan.** Work with your customer relationship management (CRM) project team to determine where different information should go — and why.

- ✔ **Think about the timing and the sequence of the import.** For example, many companies create user records first, then import accounts and contacts, and finally, migrate and append opportunities.

- ✔ **Keep it simple, if possible.** The more complicated you make the migration, the greater the impact on your timeline. Assess the level of effort versus the potential value of the effort.

Preparing your data

Clean it now, or clean it later. Some project teams like to "scrub" data before importing it into Salesforce. Identifying and merging duplicates make finding the right record easier. Fixing inconsistencies in your data, such as ensuring that all State/Province fields hold two-character abbreviations, makes reports more accurate. If your legacy system doesn't make cleanup easy, you might prefer to bring all the records into Salesforce first and then use the Salesforce data management tools to clean data later. Regardless of when you do it, cleaning data is not glamorous work, but it's gotta be done.

Here are a few tips as you prepare your data:

- **Export to a simple format.** Oftentimes, it's easiest to export data to applications like Microsoft Access or Excel, with which you can delete columns, sort rows, and make global changes.

- **Strive to use standard naming conventions.** If different data sources refer to accounts by different names (for example, IBM versus International Business Machines), now is a good time to standardize naming.

- **Edit or add fields in Salesforce to support the migration.** For example, if your pipeline reports track margin per opportunity, you need to build a custom Opportunity field to support margin data. Read more about this in Chapter 20.

- **If your existing data source has unique record IDs, migrate those IDs to a custom field.** You can always delete or hide the field at a later stage. Not only can this help you verify the accuracy of your migration, but those IDs might also come in handy for integration (especially if you don't plan to shut down the other data source).

- **Map your data columns to field names in Salesforce.** For example, the Company field in Microsoft Outlook typically maps to the Account field in Salesforce. Some system administrators even rename the column headers in migration files so that they exactly match field names in Salesforce. Doing this minimizes the migration madness.

- **Conform your data to fit Salesforce standards** (or the other way around). Each field in Salesforce has certain properties that might include size limitations, decimal points, date formats, and so on.

- **Add a Data Source column to your import file and map it to a custom field in Salesforce.** By doing this, you can defend where data came from.

- **Assign the correct owners to records wherever possible.** If you don't have all records assigned, the owner defaults to whichever administrator is executing the migration.

- **Gain acceptance from stakeholders of the files you've prepared.** At least, if you offer them the chance to review, you avoid surprises.

Testing the import

Test before you execute the final migration. Often, you discover things that you missed or could improve. For example, fields can be mapped incorrectly, or you might just need to create some extra ones. Here are a couple of tips:

- ✔ **Select a small sample of significant records.** The more high-profile the records, the better — especially when reviewed by a stakeholder.

- ✔ **Review page layout.** Consider adjusting the page layouts to make validating the data import easier. Put fields in Salesforce in similar screen locations to those of your legacy systems.

Analyzing the test data results

When your test data is in Salesforce, compare it carefully with your test file to ensure accuracy and completeness. Here are a few tips on how to productively analyze the test data results:

1. **Build:** Build a custom report that allows you to look at the record data collectively.

2. **Compare:** Open a record, if necessary, and compare it against the import file. Confirm that the record's fields show what you think they should show.

3. **View:** Build a custom view from a relevant tab home page to see your imported data laid out in columns on a list page. Users could go to a report, but a view keeps them focused.

4. **Validate:** Validate the data with selected stakeholders to get their feedback and support that the test data results look correct. It's not enough that you think the test import was accurate. Your end users are the ultimate test.

5. **Tweak:** Adjust your process or make changes to the import file or Salesforce based on the results of the test import. For example, maybe you forgot to map a field, or the data didn't import correctly because of a field's properties.

Migrating your final data

After you successfully analyze the test data results, you're ready to import your file or files. (Yes, that's a simplification of what could be a complicated set of tasks, but the overall process is tried and true.)

Here are a few suggestions for this step:

- ✔ **Communicate expectations with your users.** If you're moving from one system to another, you might have a lapse in which data must be updated prior to going live.

- ✔ **Do it during downtime.** If you have significant data, consider running the migration during nonworking hours. Especially if the system is live for some groups of users already, this might avoid confusion.

- ✔ **Build yourself some cushion for error.** Don't try to execute the migration the day before sales training. Something unanticipated could happen that prevents successful completion.

Validating and augmenting your data

Similar to analyzing results of the test data (see the section "Analyzing the test data results," earlier in this chapter), when the data has been loaded, run reports to validate a cross-sampling of records to ensure accuracy and completeness. If you can, compare screens in Salesforce with those of your legacy system. Make sure that data is stored in the correct fields and that values make sense. If you see an address in a phone field, you need to clean your data or fix your field mapping. Strive for perfectly imported data — but expect less than that, too.

Prior to rolling out Salesforce, take the extra step of manually or automatically updating some records to wow users and drive more success. When giving a demonstration or training, show users these fully entered examples and let them know the potential for Salesforce.

Managing Your Salesforce Database

After you implement Salesforce, you need to make sure that you create processes for periodically updating and backing up your data. If you don't, human error can lead to frustration and heartache. Duplicate records, dead leads, records that need to be transferred when a user leaves the company — these are just a few examples of data that needs to be updated.

Most of the data maintenance tools are accessible from the Data Management heading located under the Administrative Setup heading on the sidebar of Setup. (See Chapters 4, 5, and 9 for details on de-duplicating accounts, contacts, and leads.)

Backing up your data

If you have Performance, Enterprise, or Professional Edition, Salesforce offers a weekly export service of all your data that you can use to create a backup.

To export and back up your data, follow these steps:

1. **Choose Setup⇨Administer⇨Data Management. Click the Data Export link.**

   The Weekly Export Service page appears.

2. **Click the Export Now button.**

3. **Select the appropriate export file encoding from the Export File Encoding drop-down list and select the check boxes if you want to include files and replace carriage (hard) returns with spaces.**

   If you live in the United States or Western Europe, you don't have to change the Export File Encoding selection.

4. **Specify which Salesforce objects you want to export, or just leave the default Include All Data check box selected.**

5. **When you're done, click the Data Export button.**

   The Weekly Export Service: Export Requested page appears. You'll receive an e-mail from Salesforce with a link to a page where you can retrieve zipped .csv files of all your data. You have 48 hours to download your data, after which time the data files are deleted.

6. **When you receive the e-mail entitled Your Organization Data Export Has Been Completed, click the title to open the e-mail.**

   The e-mail appears with a link to the page in which you can retrieve your data export. The file is only available for 48 hours, not indefinitely, so make sure you get the file from the link as soon as you can.

7. **Click the link and log in to Salesforce, if required.**

   The Weekly Export Service page appears, as shown in Figure 22-1.

   You can also access the Weekly Export Service page by choosing Setup⇨Application Setup⇨Data Management⇨Data Export.

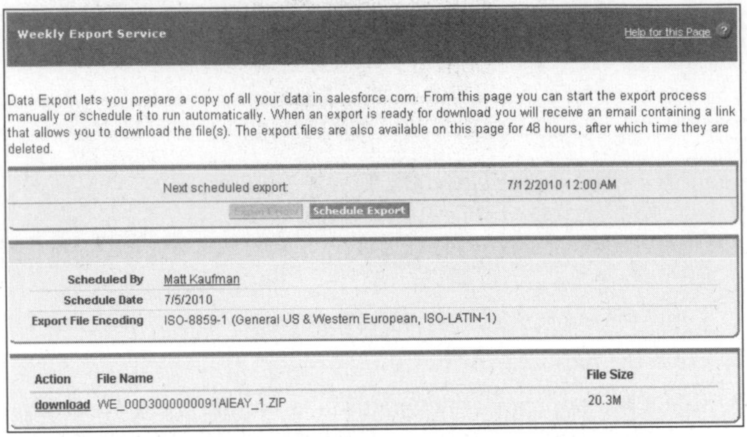

Weekly Export Service   Help for this Page ②

Data Export lets you prepare a copy of all your data in salesforce.com. From this page you can start the export process manually or schedule it to run automatically. When an export is ready for download you will receive an email containing a link that allows you to download the file(s). The export files are also available on this page for 48 hours, after which time they are deleted.

Next scheduled export: 7/12/2010 12:00 AM

Export Now   Schedule Export

Scheduled By   Matt Kaufman
Schedule Date   7/5/2010
Export File Encoding   ISO-8859-1 (General US & Western European, ISO-LATIN-1)

Action   File Name   File Size
download   WE_00D3000000091AIEAY_1.ZIP   20.3M

Figure 22-1: Downloading your data export file.

8. Click download link.

A dialog box appears, allowing you to open or save your Zip file to a location accessible from your computer.

Although not required, we recommend that you schedule a routine data export of your data by clicking the Schedule Export button on the Weekly Export Service page (see Figure 22-1). This option follows the same steps as an immediate backup, but it also allows you to select when you want your backup to automatically occur.

Mass-transferring records

A sales rep leaves. Sales territories get readjusted. You imported a file but forgot to assign records to the right owners in advance. These are just a few examples of when you might have to transfer records. Salesforce allows you to mass-transfer lead, account, and custom object records — and the processes for all three types are very similar.

When transferring leads or accounts, Salesforce automatically transfers certain linked records on the detail page.

- **For both leads and accounts:** All open activities owned by the current owner transfer to the new owner.
- **For accounts:** All notes, contacts, and open opportunities owned by the existing owner transfer to the new owner.
- **For custom object records:** No linked records are transferred.

To mass-transfer records, follow these steps:

1. **Choose Setup⇨Administer⇨Data Management⇨Mass Transfer Records.**

   A Mass Transfer Records page appears.

2. **Click the Transfer link for the appropriate type of record, depending on your needs.**

   A Mass Transfer page appears with a set of filtering options to help you search for records. You can use the filters to specify the set of data that you want to transfer, for example, all Accounts with San Francisco in the Billing City field.

3. **In the Transfer From and Transfer To fields, use the Lookup icons to find the appropriate users.**

   With leads, you can also transfer to or from queues. See Chapter 9 for details on lead queues.

4. **If you're mass-transferring accounts, select the check boxes to specify whether you want to transfer types of opportunities, cases, and teams.**

5. **Define additional criteria to filter your search by using the drop-down lists and fields provided.**

   You do this by selecting a field from the first drop-down list, selecting an operator from the second drop-down list, and then typing a value in the field. For example, if you want to transfer all of one sales rep's New York City accounts to a new rep, your criteria would be

   - *Field:* City
   - *Operator:* Equals
   - *Value:* New York

6. **When you're satisfied with your settings and filters, click the Find button.**

   The Mass Transfer page reappears with a list of results.

7. **Use the check boxes to select the records that you want to transfer.**

8. **When you're done, click the Transfer button.**

   The Mass Transfer page reappears when the transfer is complete.

Mass-deleting records

If you're the administrator, you might want or need to mass-delete records. A couple of typical examples include deleting dead leads and eliminating accounts that haven't had any activity. Salesforce allows you to mass-delete leads, accounts, contacts, activities, cases, solutions, and products — and the processes are very similar.

To mass-delete records, follow these steps:

1. **Choose Setup⇨Administer⇨Data Management⇨Mass Delete Records.**

    The Mass Delete Records page appears.

2. **Click one of the Mass Delete links, depending on the type of standard record that you want to mass-delete.**

    The Mass Delete Records page appears with a three- to five-step wizard for mass-deleting. The three-step wizard is shown in Figure 22-2. The Mass Delete Accounts page has two extra steps based on opportunities that are closed/won or that aren't owned by you. The Mass Delete Products page has one extra step to archive products with line items on opportunities.

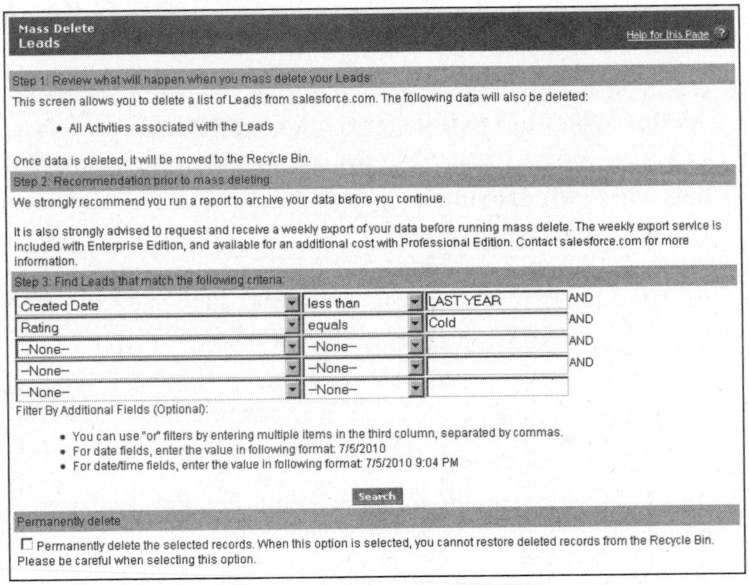

Figure 22-2: Select records for mass deletion.

3. **Review the Salesforce warnings in Step 1 of the wizard.**

4. **Back up relevant data by generating a report and exporting it to Excel as part of Step 2 of the wizard.**

    See Chapter 17 for details on building and exporting reports.

5. **Use the filters in Step 3 of the wizard to define criteria for the search.**

    You do this by selecting a field from the first drop-down list, selecting an operator from the second drop-down list, and typing a value in the field.

    You can see an example of this in the preceding section.

6. **Click the Search button.**

   The Mass Delete page reappears with a list of possible records at the bottom of the page. Do the following:

   If you're mass-deleting *accounts,* you can do two things:

   - Select the check box in Step 4 of the wizard if you want to delete accounts that have Closed/Won opportunities.

   - Select the check box to delete accounts with another owner's opportunities.

   If you're mass-deleting *products,* select the check box if you want to archive products with line items on opportunities.

   If you're mass-deleting *another object,* proceed to Step 7.

7. **Use the Action column to select records to be deleted.**

8. **When you're satisfied, click the Delete button.**

   A dialog box appears to confirm the deletion.

9. **Click OK.**

   The Mass Delete page reappears, minus the records that you deleted.

Getting Help with Complex Data Tasks

This chapter shows you some of the basic operations that you can perform to import and manage your data in Salesforce. For many companies that have complex data needs, this might be an oversimplification. If you need help with your data, here are some resources you can turn to:

- **Talk with your Customer Success Manager or account executive.** These folks can help define your needs and point you to the appropriate solution or resource.

- **Go outside.** If you're looking for outside help, contact a salesforce.com consulting partner. Your Customer Success Manager or account rep can put you in touch.

- **Check out offerings by partners on the AppExchange.** Go to www. appexchange.com and search using the phrase "Data Cleansing" in the search bar.

- **Talk to developers.** On the Developerforce site (http://developer. force.com), click the Boards tab to talk to a community of developers who have wrestled or are familiar with your data challenges. These boards are of a technical nature, but if this is what you're looking for, you might find it here.

Part VIII

The Part of Tens

In this part . . .

- ✔ Know the top five resources to get additional Salesforce help and information
- ✔ Use our top five recommended Salesforce productivity enhancers
- ✔ Understand how to implement Salesforce right the first time within your company

Chapter 23

Ten Ways to Drive More Productivity

. . . .

Salesforce.com drives much of its feature updates based on its existing road map and requests from customers just like you. A few times per year, salesforce.com comes out with a new release of its award-winning service. That's the benefit of this family of business applications, which may be referred to as "cloud-based" or "in the cloud" because the infrastructure isn't maintained by you. Unlike traditional software upgrades, these releases are immediately available to all customers and can be activated or deactivated when you are ready to make the change.

Keeping track of all the cool new updates that salesforce.com releases can get a little overwhelming. The speed with which it's able to roll out releases is often barely faster than our ability to write all about it and get it in print to you! On the flip side, perhaps you do keep track of the newest features but have been struggling with an apparent feature limitation or would like more advice on how to best implement a particular feature.

Fortunately for us, both salesforce.com and its community of users strongly believe in helping each other out to make every customer successful. Through a variety of channels, the salesforce.com community shares best practices and offers suggestions and work-arounds for even the toughest head-scratcher questions.

In this chapter, we summarize five essential resources that every user in your organization should know about. Then we cover five great productivity tools that you might have overlooked.

Finding the Top Five Resources

Salesforce.com realizes that first you need to have healthy business processes before applying any type of CRM solution to them. Combine that with providing information at its customers' fingertips, and you have several resources available to you when you want to talk about all things Salesforce. In addition to providing answers to the perennial "How do I do this?" question, salesforce. com also focuses on topics covering your business processes to address the "Why would I want to do this?" question. Here, we highlight five resources that can make a big difference in informing you and your organization about the hows and whys of Salesforce features:

- **Salesforce.com blog (`http://blogs.salesforce.com`):** Whether you're an administrator or end user, bookmark this website *now*. Here you'll find a wealth of best practices information contributed by product experts across the company. Across the top of the page, you can click on categories to focus on specific practice areas (like Sales, Customer Service, and so on).

- **Salesforce IdeaExchange (`https://success.salesforce.com/ideaSearch`):** The IdeaExchange is a forum within the Salesforce Success Community where you can post new product ideas, see what other users are requesting, and vote for the ideas most important to you. Not only do you get to see what the masses are clamoring for, but you also get to see salesforce.com employees, partners, and customers providing feedback. Then, even more satisfying, salesforce.com's product managers monitor the posts and mark which features have been delivered into new releases.

- **Salesforce.com local user groups:** One of the best ways to find out about upcoming features, hear about third-party vendor integrations, network with your peers, and provide product feedback is to join a local user group. You'll get to learn from and share tips with fellow customers in your vicinity. From the Salesforce Success Community (at `http://success.salesforce.com`), click the User Groups category at the top of the page. Look for groups based on your region or your company's industry vertical. If you don't see your city, think about starting your own group.

- **Salesforce training and certification:** One of the best ways to become an expert and have an opportunity to ask an expert about your company's particular use of Salesforce is to be trained by salesforce.com. Then you can be your company's expert and spearhead further ideas of using Salesforce to make your business processes run smoother. You find classes for every user role, and for every budget. For those of you who will be configuring and customizing Salesforce, you also find a series of certifications so that you can tell others just how special you are. Visit the salesforce.com website (`www.salesforce.com`) and look for Salesforce Training under the Services link on the home page.

- **Salesforce.com online help topics:** Finally, if you're working in Salesforce and get stuck with a question, look for a Help for This Page icon on that page — it's a question mark in a circle. Clicking that link opens a new Help & Training window that's context sensitive.

Revisiting Five Great Productivity Tools

Few companies make use of every feature when they first deploy Salesforce to their employees. It would be overwhelming to absorb, and you know that success is a function of end-user adoption. So if you're like other CRM project teams, you tend to focus on addressing the core business objectives that often include lead, account, and opportunity management.

If this sounds like you, the following list includes five tools that we'd like to remind you about. Give yourself time to set these up — you can substantially boost adoption and productivity, depending on your objectives:

- ✔ **The AppExchange (http://appexchange.salesforce.com):** "If only we could use Salesforce to do this . . . ." Does that sound familiar? Well, your business pain may be someone else's as well. Someone may have already built a solution for it. Head on over to the AppExchange to look for a custom app or component that already exists to help you. You'll find lot of popular free options, too!

- ✔ **E-mail templates:** This is a simple feature that can save your reps and marketing staff a ton of time. You no longer have to dig up an old e-mail, copy and paste it into a message, and scour the text for places where you should replace the old customer's name. E-mail templates are easy to set up and help you send out professional-looking HTML or text e-mails that are personalized to your contacts. Create a few so that your reps can begin using them on Day 1. See Chapter 8 for more information on how to use templates.

- ✔ **Online lead or case forms:** This is a classic feature in Salesforce that every customer should roll out. Capturing lead or case information via a form helps maintain consistency of your data, which will help you increase the accuracy of your reporting. Whether you roll this out in the first phase of your implementation is up to you, but it should be high on your list. See Chapter 13 for Web-to-Lead or Chapter 16 for Web-to-Case details.

- ✔ **Chatter:** If your employees are distributed (in different cities, countries, or just on different floors) but need to collaborate, consider using Salesforce Chatter. Chatter, when used to communicate relevant, short business updates in a chronological-based feed, can draw in participation from colleagues you didn't even know before. The power of Salesforce works here, as updates to records populate your Chatter feed, in addition to updates about humans, made by humans. What if you followed some top salespeople in your company, and you saw one day that they created an opportunity for a former employer of yours. You could quickly post some additional intel, or just offer yourself as resource, to help the salesperson close the deal.

- **Salesforce 1:** Smartphones and tablets are essential for busy executives and various types of people with heavy travel requirements and customer-facing jobs. salesforce.com provides free apps through Apple's App Store and the Google Play marketplace for iPhones and Android phones, respectively. These mobile-specific apps allow reps and field service employees to quickly access essential customer information from Salesforce in a way that easily fits whatever screen size you're working with. Reps stay productive while riding in their calls or visiting customer sites, and apps give them a reason to expense their latest shiny smartphone.

Chapter 24

Ten Keys to a Successful Implementation

. . . .

Several companies have rolled out customer relationship management (CRM) applications with the mistaken notion that you can buy the licenses, turn on the switch, and use the application as soon as you take it out of the box. Then, these same companies look back months later and wonder why they're not experiencing the results they envisioned.

Nine times out of ten, the root cause is poor planning. No matter what size your implementation, building a strong plan and then executing the plan will substantially improve your chance of success.

Salesforce provides you with the tools and a platform to enhance your business effectiveness and productivity. If you're involved in the rollout of Salesforce, this chapter gives you ten tips to help you do it successfully. Check out the free webinars, answers, and more on the Salesforce Community site (`http://success.salesforce.com`) for more tips on leading a successful rollout.

Identifying Your Executive Sponsor

Rolling out or replacing a CRM solution is a big deal. For some managers and reps, this initiative can cause concerns for a variety of reasons: People get set in their ways, they think it's Big Brother, they assume that it's going to take a lot of their time, and so on. Sometimes other top priorities at work begin creeping in, and the importance of the CRM implementation falls along the wayside.

Every project needs a champion to help drive the CRM initiative in your company. That person is there to rally support, break logjams, and ensure that your team has the resources to get things done. We recommend that you identify an executive sponsor on Day 1 and work with her so that she can communicate what's in it for the implementation team and set expectations for what's needed from all participants. This will go a long way in calming fears, gaining support and commitment, and nudging the team toward a decision when the team members are at an impasse.

Building Your Project Team

As you might have already figured out, CRM is less about technology and more about people, human processes, and your business. For your company to get the most out of Salesforce, you need to develop a team made up of critical stakeholders, Salesforce experts, and a cross section of end users. If you're implementing Salesforce for sales and marketing, that might mean that the team includes managers from marketing, sales operations, and IT, some respected sales reps, and hopefully a member of your executive team. This doesn't have to be a huge team, nor should members expect to be involved in this project full time. But you must have people who can speak for the business, and you must have sufficient resources to get the job done. Get every stakeholder to understand the team's objectives and to buy in from the first meeting.

Evaluating Your Processes

Conduct business process reviews as key elements to your planning process. Those meetings should include a key stakeholder (or stakeholders) who can speak for his business and to the CRM project team (for example, a channel sales session with the head of channel sales). By doing this, you gain further agreement to your plan and ensure that you're building a solution that meets existing or desired processes of managers and their teams.

Gathering Requirements

Think about why you are implementing Salesforce. Is it to increase sales, improve productivity, encourage collaboration, or all three? Because it's nearly impossible to implement anything correctly unless you know your goal, make your objectives measurable by applying specific success metrics to an objective. (A *success metric* is a numerical goal that you want to achieve, ideally within a specified time frame.) For example, it's one thing to say that you want to reduce customer service response time, and it's quite another to define that you want to reduce response time by 20 percent by the end of the year. It's important to choose the right metric to measure your company's progress.

Defining Your Scope and Prioritizing Initiatives

You can do a lot with Salesforce, but the more complex, the longer the implementation will likely take and the greater the chance you'll hit a snag. As you collect the requirements of key stakeholders, prioritize initiatives and determine what's in scope and out of scope for the initial implementation. Consider keeping the implementation limited by focusing on the major priorities. Then, you can extend your initiatives by building on prior success.

Modeling Salesforce to Your Business

After you evaluate your company's business processes and gather scope requirements from your steering committee, you next want to model Salesforce to your business. However, we realize that you're probably new to Salesforce and might have some questions as to what information should go where. For your company, what are leads, accounts, contacts, and opportunities? Make sure that you check out the various process maps on the Salesforce Success Community website (`http://success.salesforce.com`) before you start customizing Salesforce. If you still have some questions, make sure to ask your peers on the community forums or contact your Customer Success Manager for guidance.

Customizing for User Relevance

When designing records and layouts, keeping it simple isn't always appropriate. Some businesses do have complex needs. Just be aware that long, complicated records can affect end-user adoption, so don't build a field unless you think end users will use it. Focus your customization on relevancy to your users. Standardize information as often as possible, using picklists rather than free text fields, which will help with more accurate reporting. For fields that have to be text fields (such as the Opportunity Name), work out a simple standard naming convention.

As you accomplish major milestones (such as customization of different records or layouts), validate your work with a representative of your end users. By doing this, you can make sure at key points that you're building a solution that works for your internal customer.

Importing Clean Data

Identify your data sources that you want to bring over to Salesforce. Note where the information is coming from, what format it will be in, and how clean it'll be.

Armed with this information, you can discuss with your team the scope of your migration. Moving into Salesforce means that it's time for some spring cleaning. Work with your team to identify which data sources are the most valuable and whether your end users will benefit from all that information coming over. Remember that data that doesn't make it to Salesforce doesn't necessarily disappear. You can always archive it or keep it in the legacy system.

After you decide what data is going into Salesforce, you have to clean it. Scrubbing data isn't glamorous, but it has to be done. Reducing duplicates and ensuring consistency not only make Salesforce more valuable but also improve your user's adoption. If you don't have the resources to do this, check out the AppExchange (www.salesforce.com/appexchange) for partners that help with data cleansing.

Building a Comprehensive Training Plan

As early as you can in the implementation process, start building a training plan. Don't assume that users will know what to do. And don't just rely on the generic sales training offered by Salesforce; it might not be relevant enough to your customization. Blend prerequisite classes, custom sales training, and reinforcement training in your plan. The key is to make sure that enough relevant training is provided so that people effectively and correctly use the Salesforce application. Also, be sure that your end users have personal copies of *Salesforce.com For Dummies*. Just in case.

Connecting with Peers

After your teams are up and running with Salesforce, you should constantly gather feedback and track how adoption is faring. Also, get out there and meet your peers — others who have rolled out Salesforce and have advice and stories to share. Through online community discussion boards, local user group meetings, and Dreamforce (the salesforce.com annual user conference), you have several channels where you can ask questions, seek guidance, and share information that can help you take your Salesforce implementation to the next level.

Index

• *Q* •

About the Authors

Liz Kao was an enthusiastic early adopter of the software-as-a-service (Saas) model, and has been using Salesforce for more than a decade. An early employee of salesforce.com, she built Salesforce-centric solutions for both external clients and internal teams, including launching over one-third of the Salesforce Labs applications on the AppExchange. Combined with a background in sales and marketing, she blends a hands-on perspective of business needs with using Salesforce (and now, other Saas products), to build solutions that scale.

A veteran of the enterprise software industry, Liz lives in San Francisco. When she isn't busy keeping up with the latest Saas products and features, she's enjoying all the culinary delights and Internet-signal-free natural surroundings of Northern California.

Matt Kaufman was employee 273 at salesforce.com. Since 2002 he has worked with hundreds of businesses to improve their efficiency through Salesforce. He is a certified Salesforce Advanced Administrator, Sales Cloud Consultant, Service Cloud Consultant, Advanced Developer, and authorized Advanced Developer Instructor. He is the Chief Technology Officer of MK Partners (www.mkpartners.com) the leading salesforce.com implementation partner in Southern California. When he is not writing books, coding, training others to code, or speaking about code, he is thinking about it.

Publisher's Acknowledgments

Acquisitions Editor: Amy Fandrei

Senior Project Editor: Mark Enochs

Copy Editor: John Edwards

Technical Editor: Michael Wicherski

Editorial Assistant: Annie Sullivan

Sr. Editorial Assistant: Cherie Case

Project Coordinator: Rebekah Brownson

Cover Image: Main Image © iStockphoto.com/ ZarkoCvijovic; Avatar © iStockphoto.com/ iconBunny